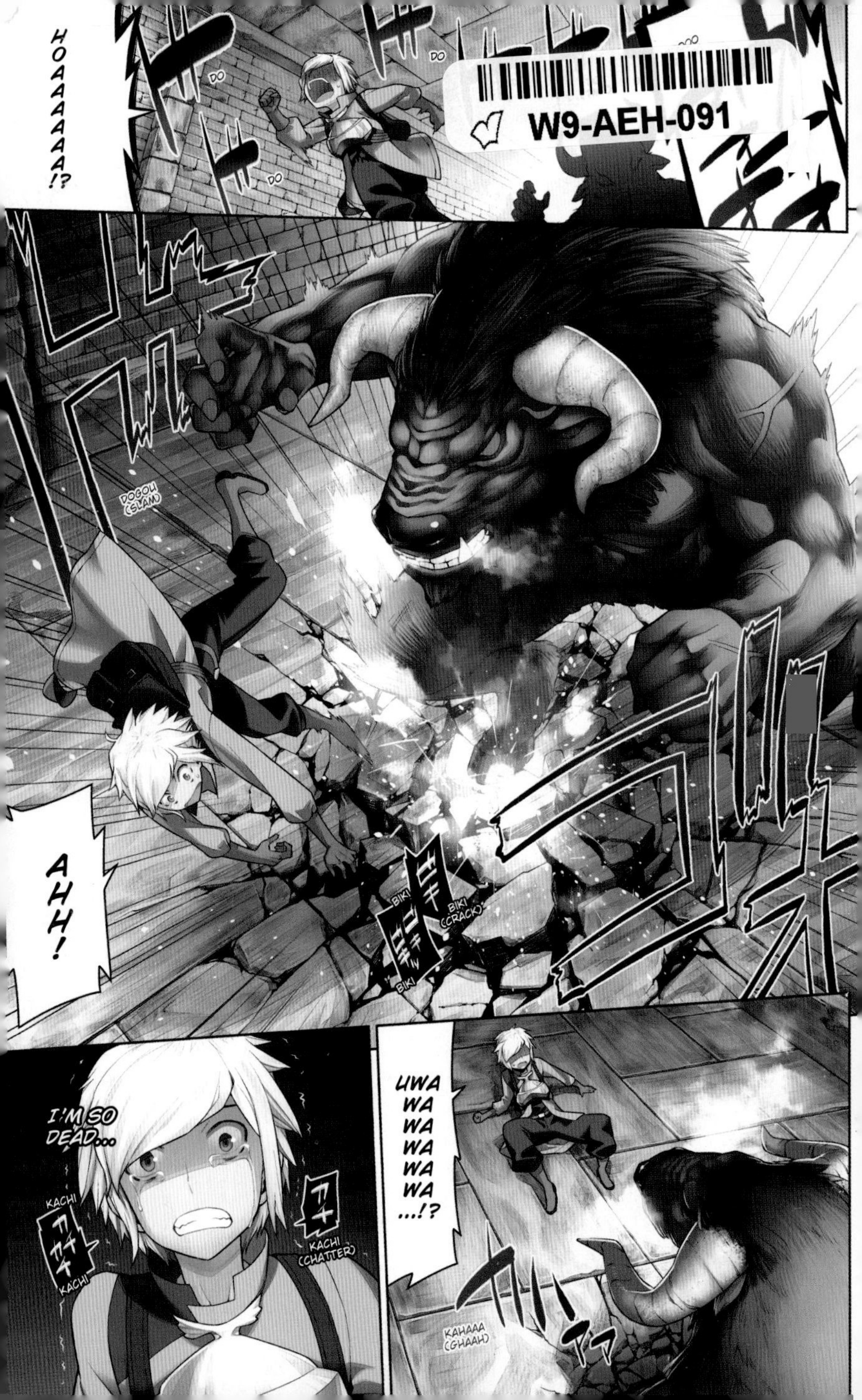
DO
DO
DO
HOAAAAAAA!?
DOGOU (SLAM)
BIKI
BIKI (CRACK)
BIKI
AHH!
UWA WA WA WA WA WA WA ...!?
KAHAAA (GHAAH)
I'M SO DEAD...
KACHI (CHATTER)
KACHI
KACHI

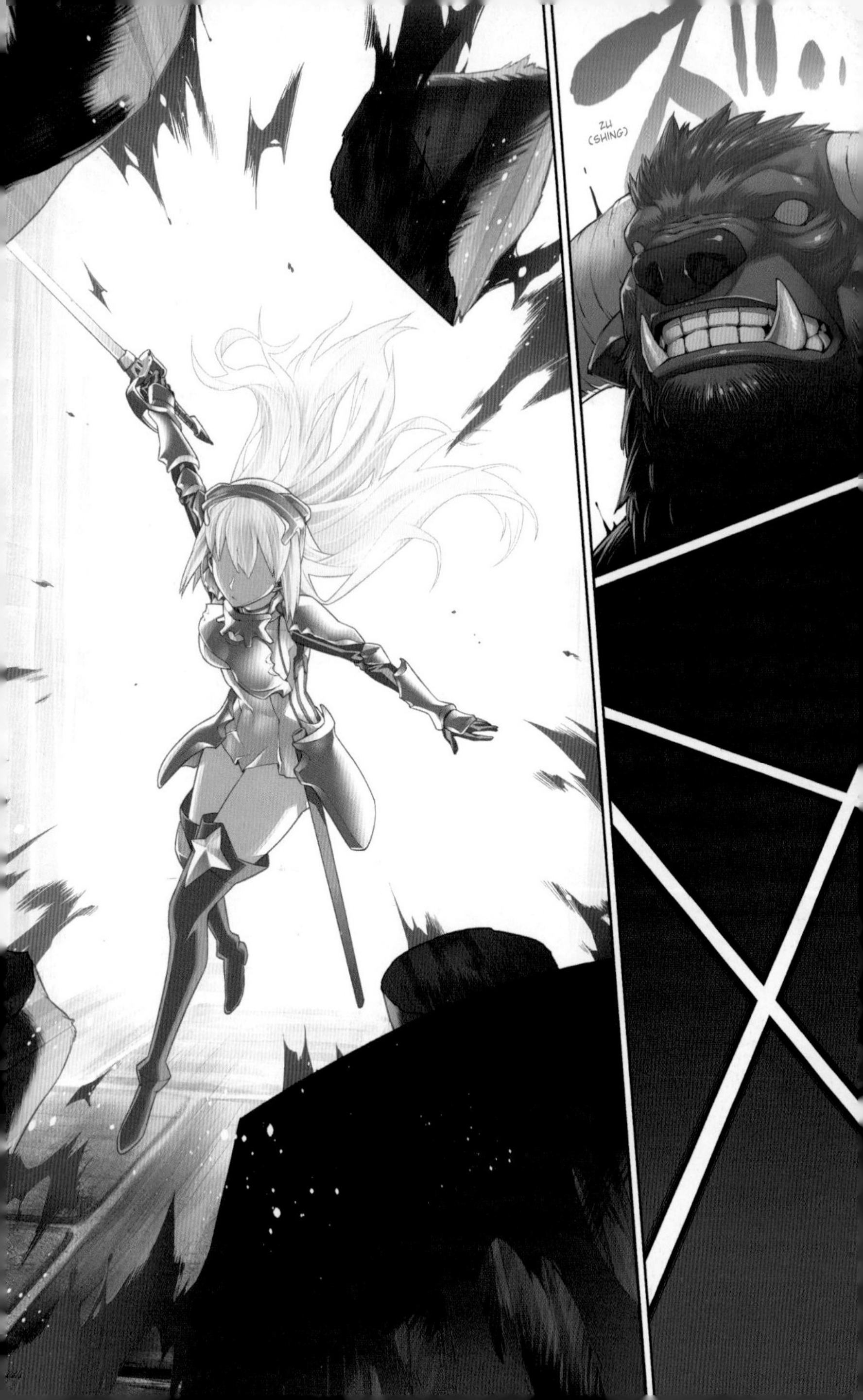
ZU
(SHING)

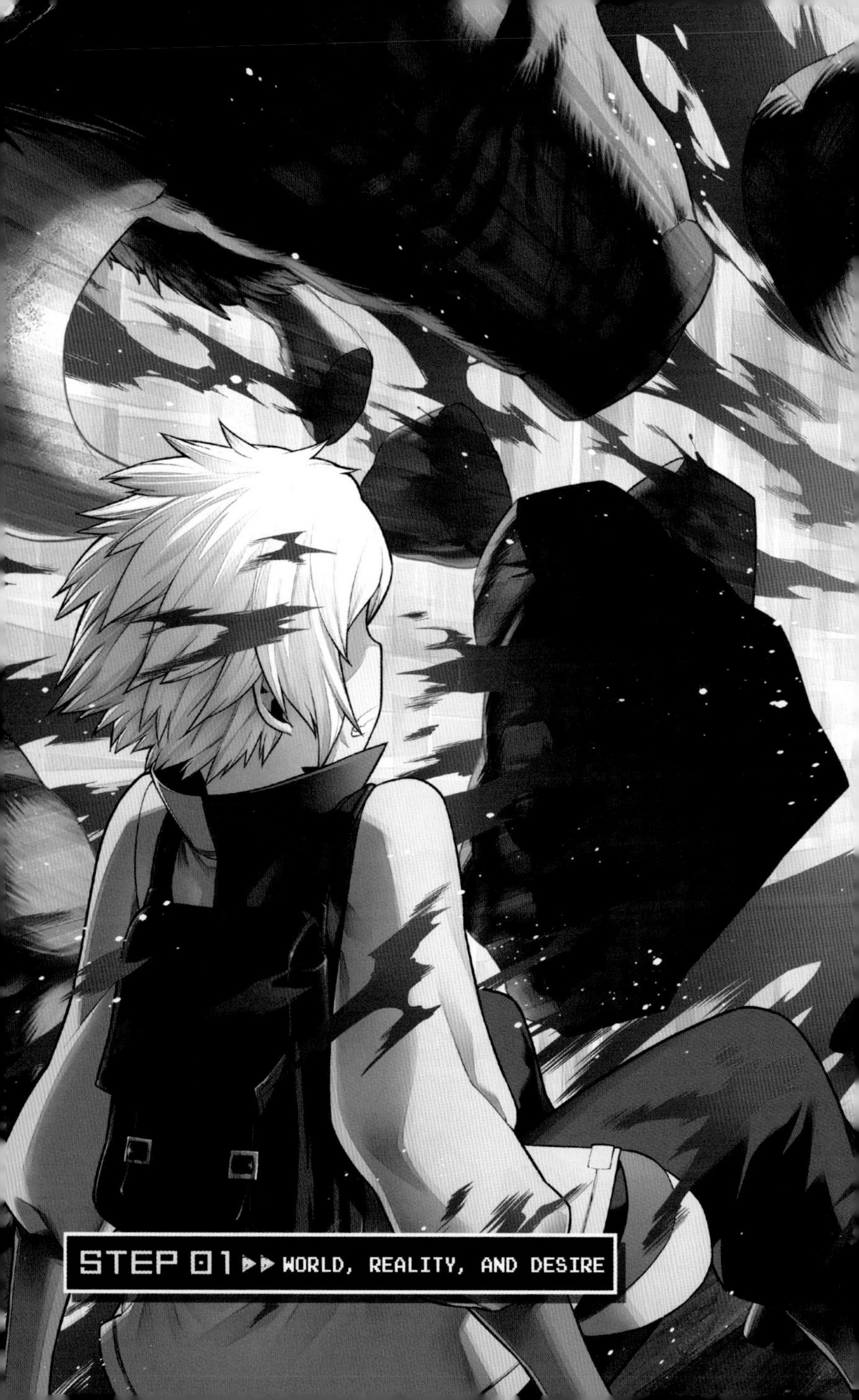
STEP 01 ▶▶ WORLD, REALITY, AND DESIRE

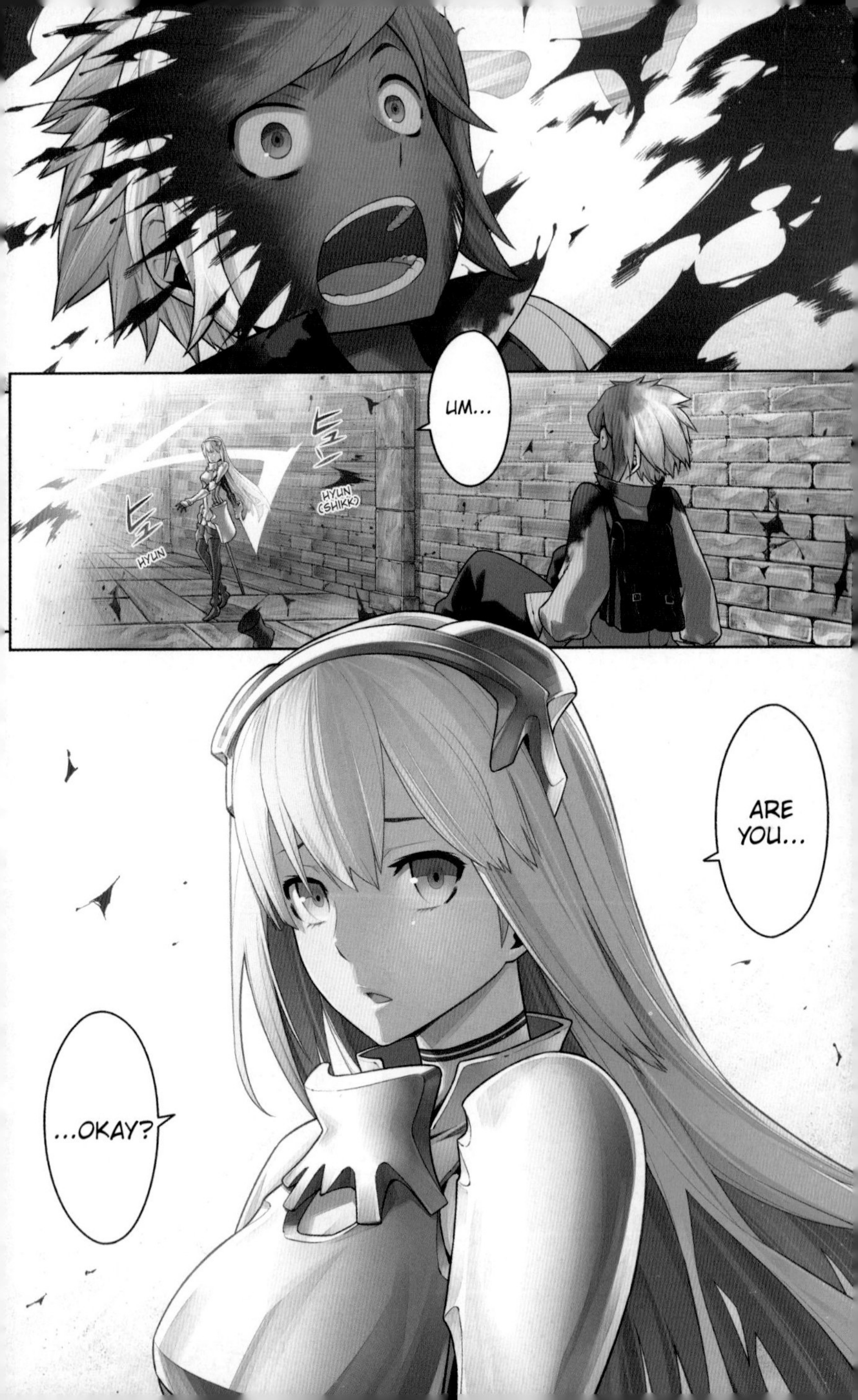
UM...
HYUN (SHIKK)
HYUN
ARE YOU...
...OKAY?

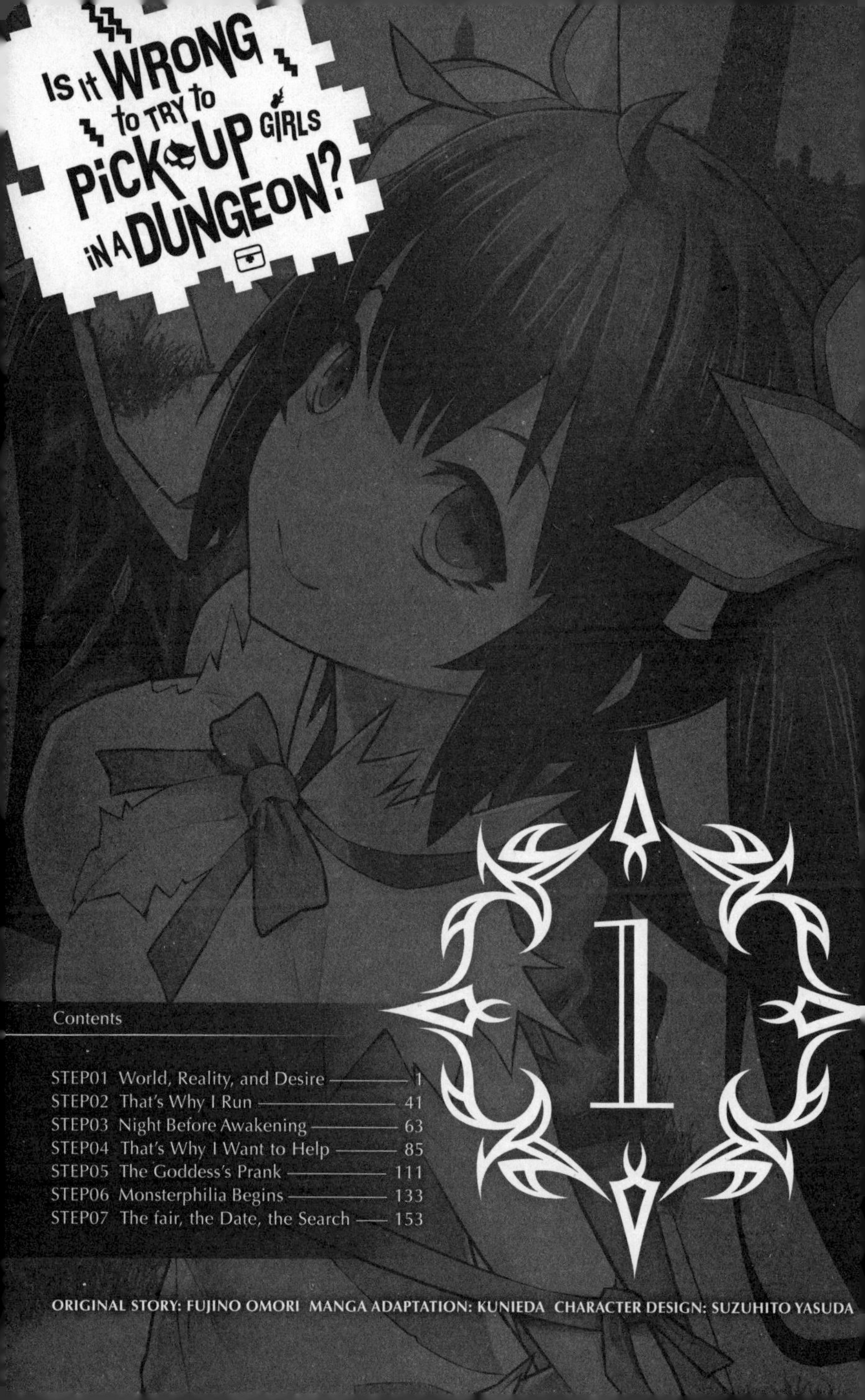

IS IT WRONG TO TRY TO PICK UP GIRLS IN A DUNGEON?

1

Contents

ORIGINAL STORY: FUJINO OMORI MANGA ADAPTATION: KUNIEDA CHARACTER DESIGN: SUZUHITO YASUDA

Is it WRONG to TRY to PICK UP GIRLS in a DUNGEON?

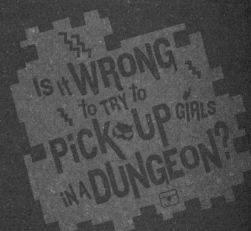

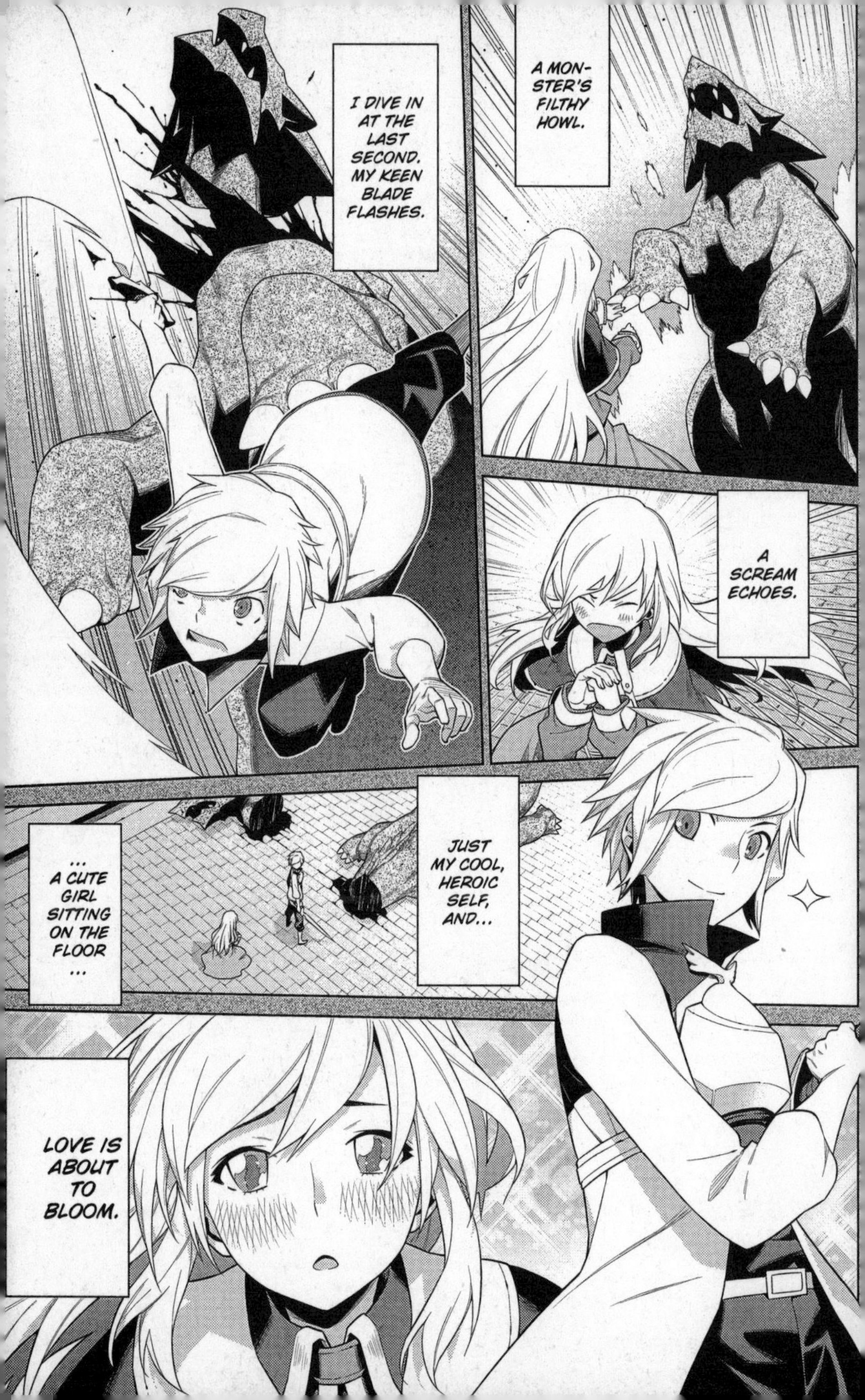
A MONSTER'S FILTHY HOWL.
A SCREAM ECHOES.
I DIVE IN AT THE LAST SECOND. MY KEEN BLADE FLASHES.
JUST MY COOL, HEROIC SELF, AND...
... A CUTE GIRL SITTING ON THE FLOOR ...
LOVE IS ABOUT TO BLOOM.

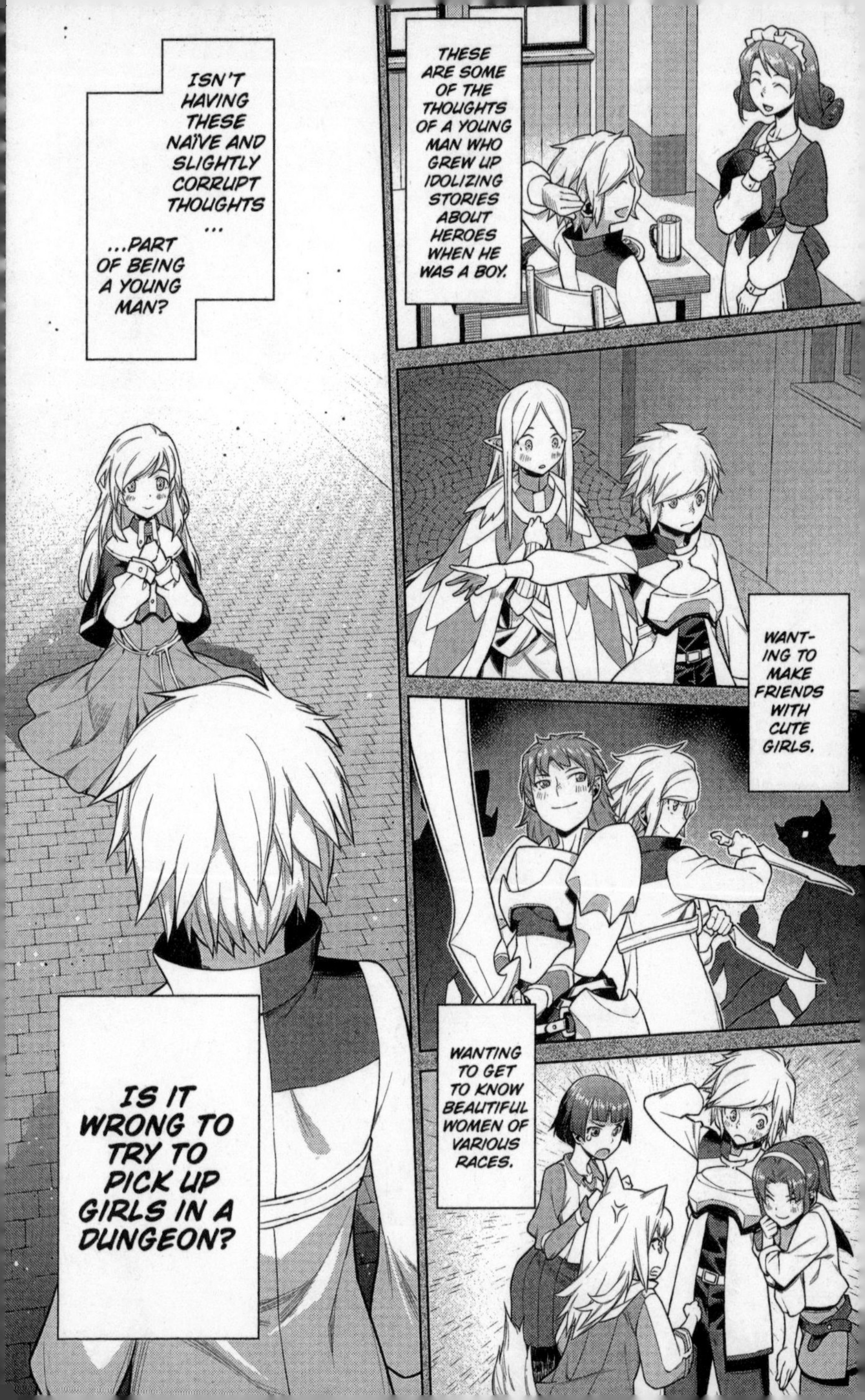
THESE ARE SOME OF THE THOUGHTS OF A YOUNG MAN WHO GREW UP IDOLIZING STORIES ABOUT HEROES WHEN HE WAS A BOY.
WANTING TO MAKE FRIENDS WITH CUTE GIRLS.
WANTING TO GET TO KNOW BEAUTIFUL WOMEN OF VARIOUS RACES.
ISN'T HAVING THESE NAÏVE AND SLIGHTLY CORRUPT THOUGHTS...
...PART OF BEING A YOUNG MAN?
IS IT WRONG TO TRY TO PICK UP GIRLS IN A DUNGEON?

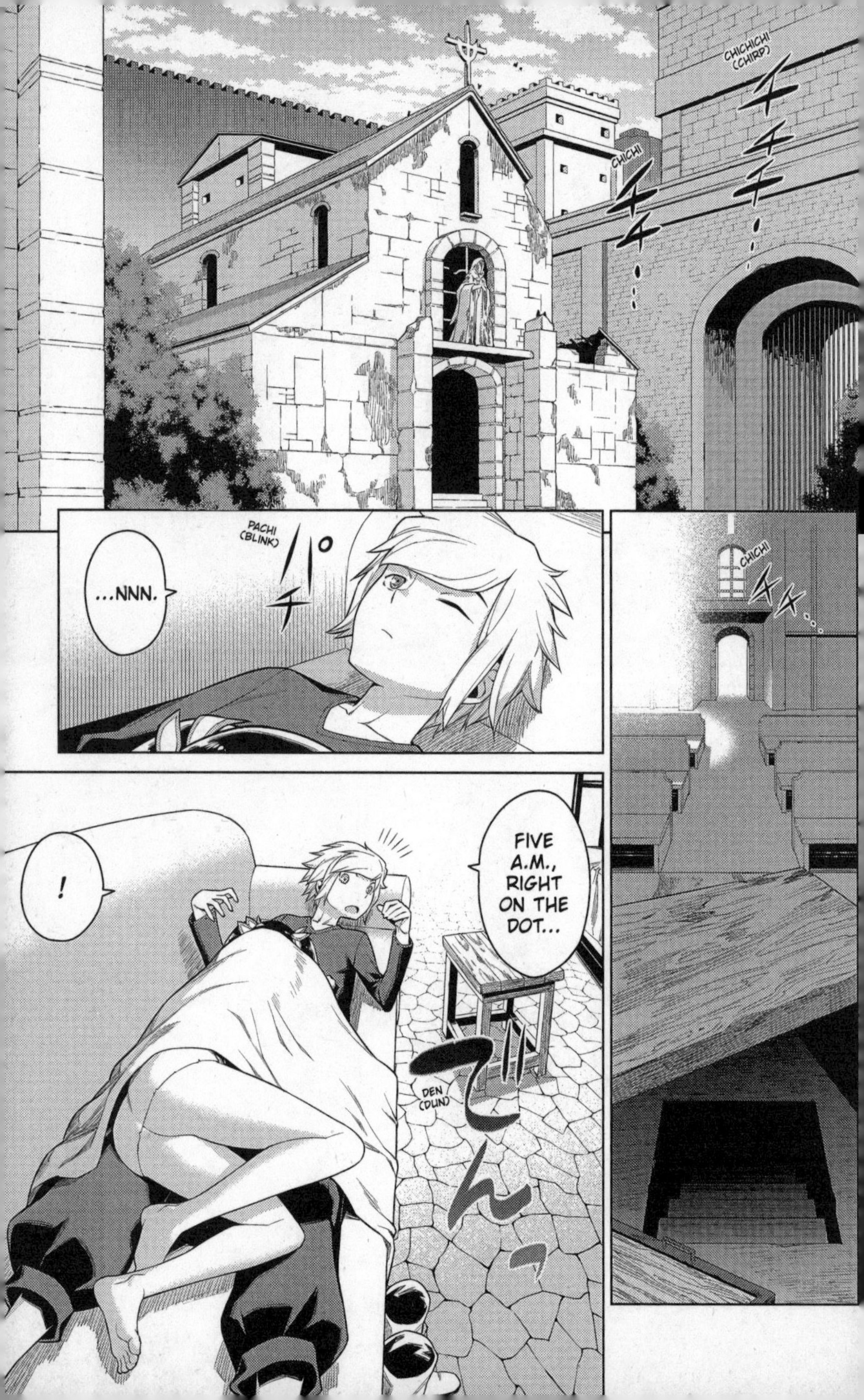
CHICHICHI (CHIRP)
CHICHI
CHICHI
PACHI (BLINK)
...NNN.
FIVE A.M., RIGHT ON THE DOT...
!
DEN (DUN)

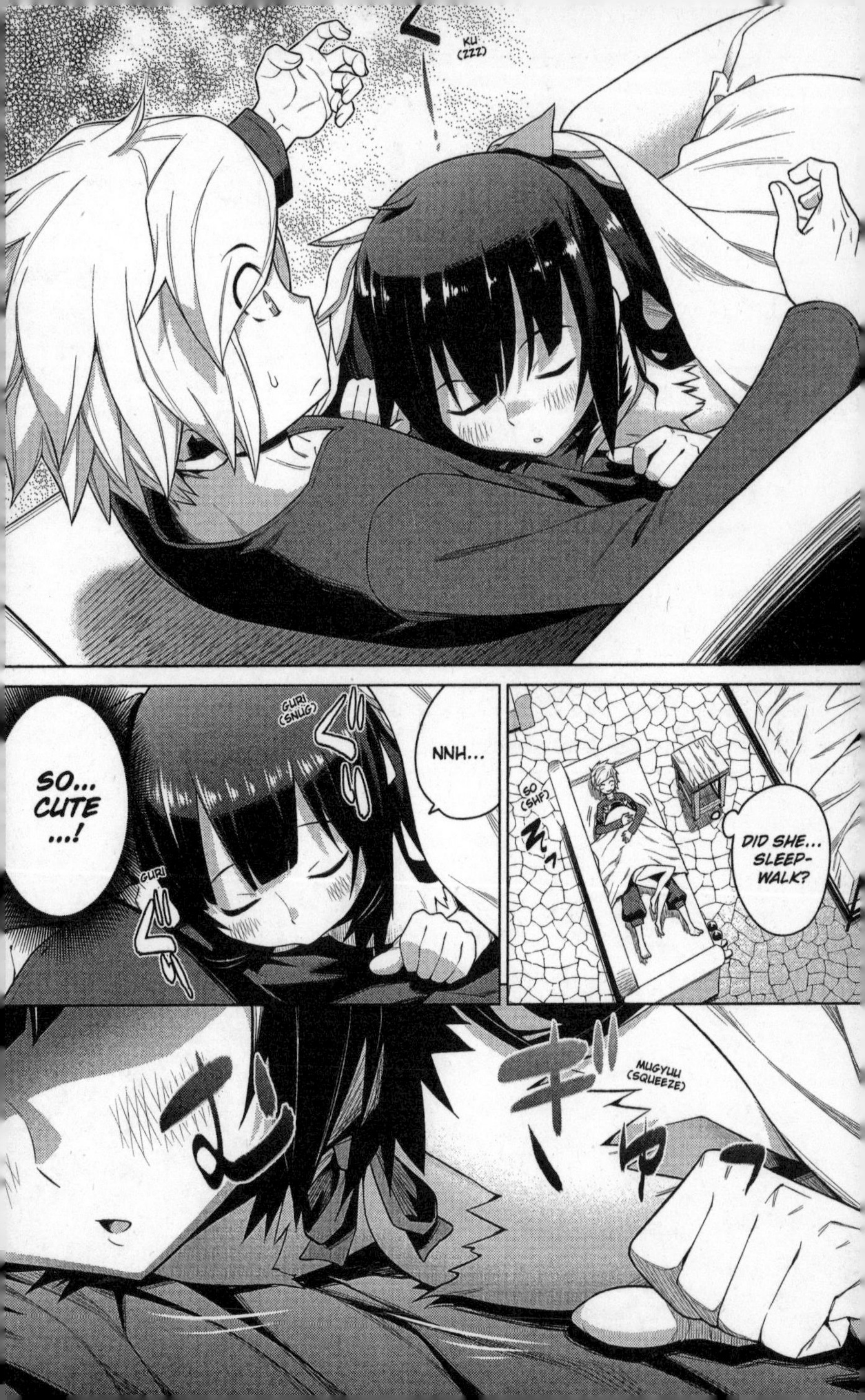
KU (ZZZ)
SO (SHF)
DID SHE... SLEEP-WALK?
NNH...
GURI (SNUG)
SO... CUTE ...!
GURI
MUGYUU (SQUEEZE)

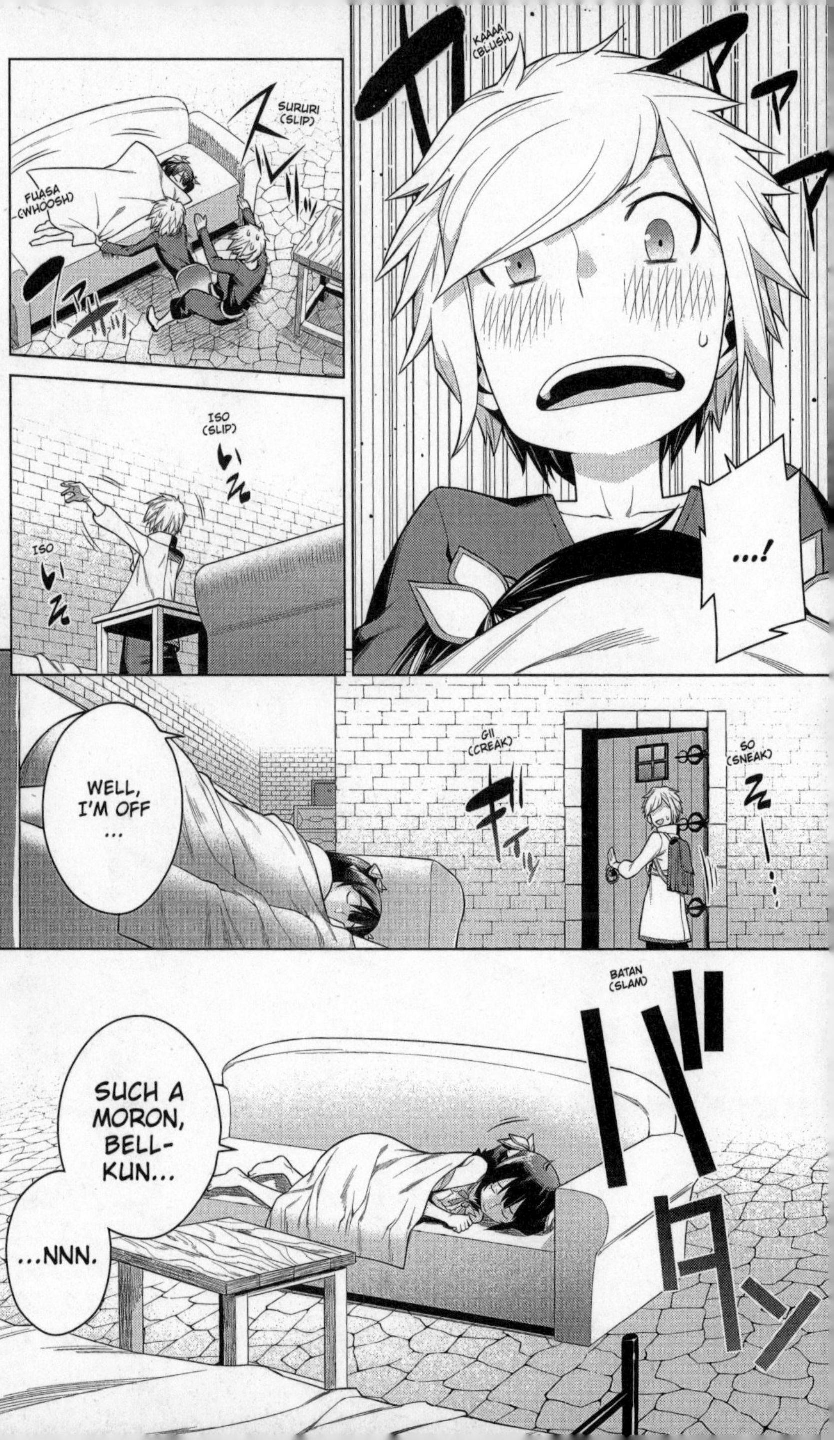
KAAAA (BLUSH)
...!
SURURI (SLIP)
FUASA (WHOOSH)
ISO (SLIP)
ISO
GII (CREAK)
SO (SNEAK)
WELL, I'M OFF ...
BATAN (SLAM)
SUCH A MORON, BELL-KUN...
...NNN.

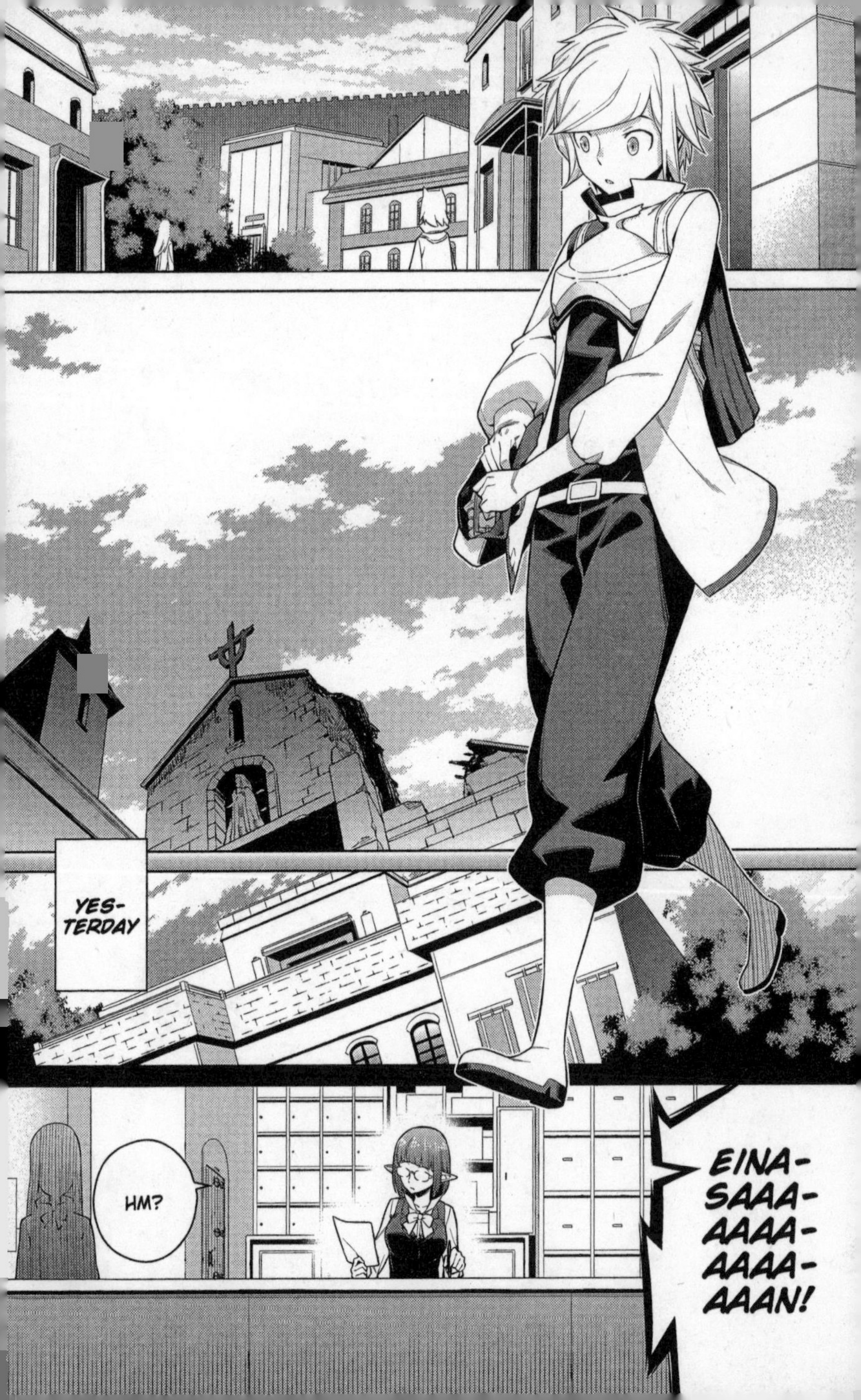
YES-TERDAY
EINA-SAAAA-AAAA-AAAA-AAAN!
HM?

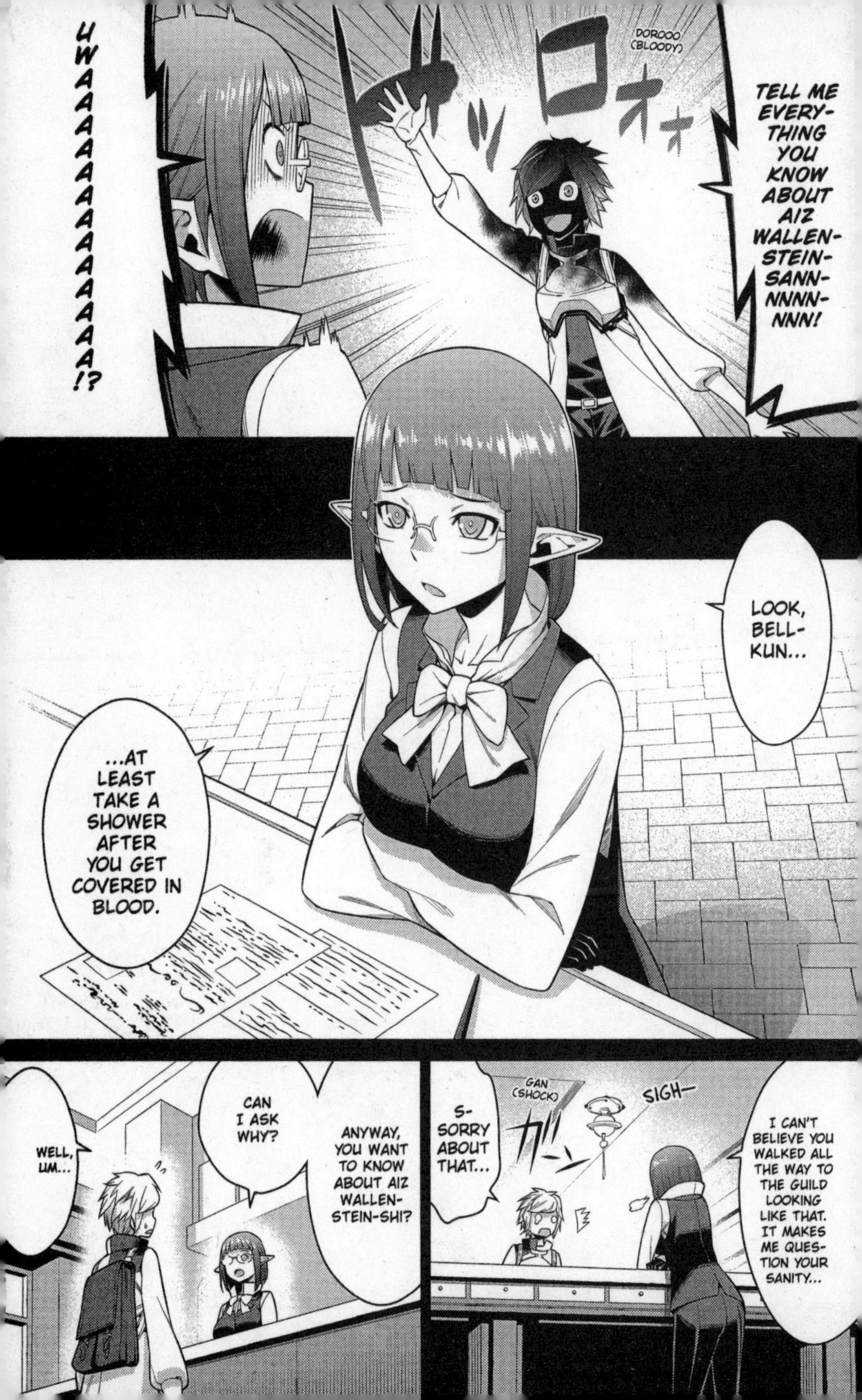

TELL ME EVERY-THING YOU KNOW ABOUT AIZ WALLEN-STEIN-SANN-NNNN-NNN!
DOROOO (BLOODY)
UWAAAAAAAAAAAAAAA!?
LOOK, BELL-KUN...
...AT LEAST TAKE A SHOWER AFTER YOU GET COVERED IN BLOOD.
I CAN'T BELIEVE YOU WALKED ALL THE WAY TO THE GUILD LOOKING LIKE THAT. IT MAKES ME QUES-TION YOUR SANITY...
SIGH—
GAN (SHOCK)
S-SORRY ABOUT THAT...
ANYWAY, YOU WANT TO KNOW ABOUT AIZ WALLEN-STEIN-SHI?
CAN I ASK WHY?
WELL, UM...

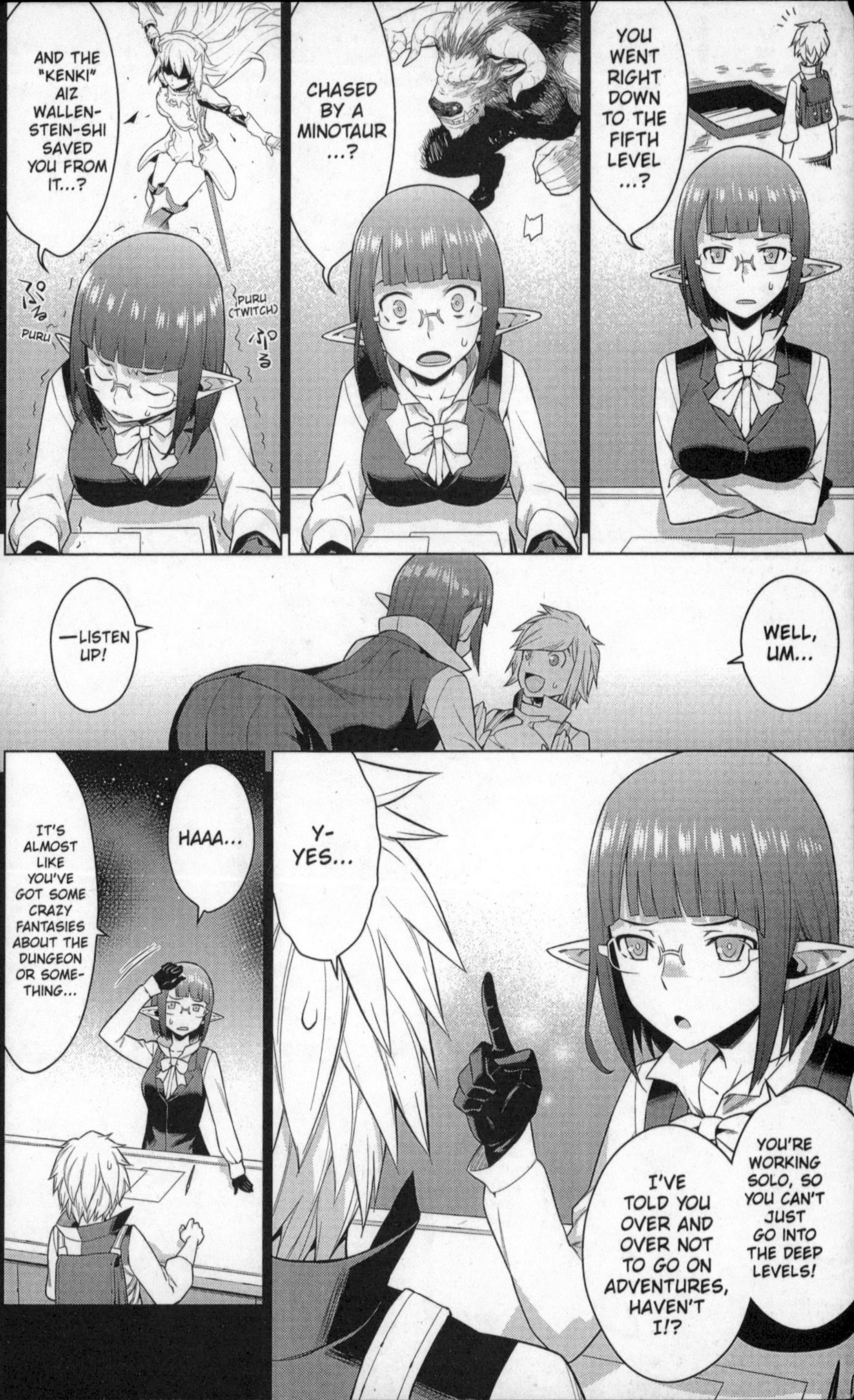
YOU WENT RIGHT DOWN TO THE FIFTH LEVEL ...?
CHASED BY A MINOTAUR ...?
AND THE "KENKI" AIZ WALLEN-STEIN-SHI SAVED YOU FROM IT...?
PURU (TWITCH)
PURU
WELL, UM...
—LISTEN UP!
I'VE TOLD YOU OVER AND OVER NOT TO GO ON ADVENTURES, HAVEN'T I!?
YOU'RE WORKING SOLO, SO YOU CAN'T JUST GO INTO THE DEEP LEVELS!
Y-YES...
HAAA...
IT'S ALMOST LIKE YOU'VE GOT SOME CRAZY FANTASIES ABOUT THE DUNGEON OR SOME-THING...

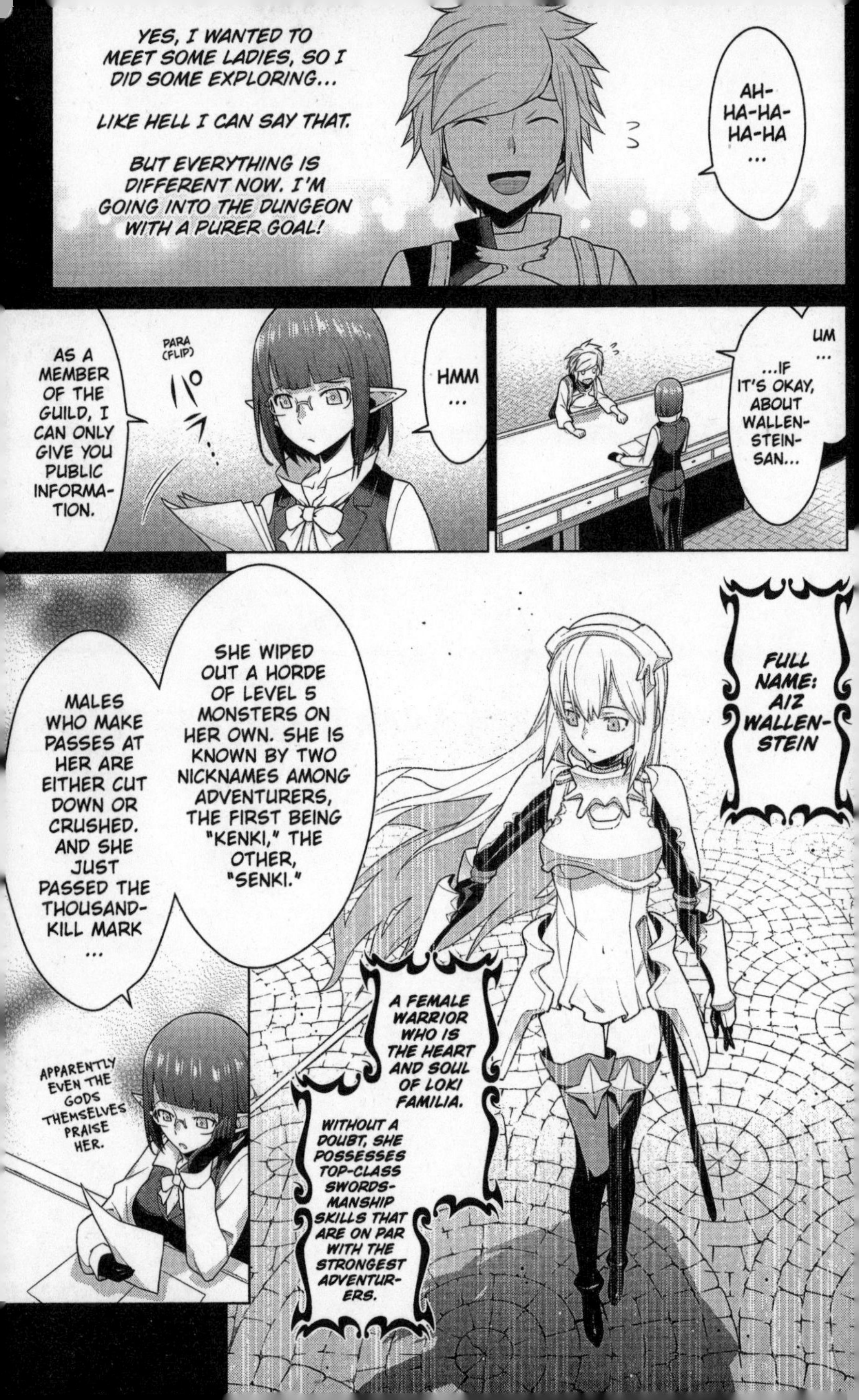
AH-HA-HA-HA-HA...
YES, I WANTED TO MEET SOME LADIES, SO I DID SOME EXPLORING...
LIKE HELL I CAN SAY THAT.
BUT EVERYTHING IS DIFFERENT NOW. I'M GOING INTO THE DUNGEON WITH A PURER GOAL!
UM...
...IF IT'S OKAY, ABOUT WALLEN-STEIN-SAN...
HMM...
PARA (FLIP)
AS A MEMBER OF THE GUILD, I CAN ONLY GIVE YOU PUBLIC INFORMA-TION.
FULL NAME: AIZ WALLEN-STEIN
SHE WIPED OUT A HORDE OF LEVEL 5 MONSTERS ON HER OWN. SHE IS KNOWN BY TWO NICKNAMES AMONG ADVENTURERS, THE FIRST BEING "KENKI," THE OTHER, "SENKI."
MALES WHO MAKE PASSES AT HER ARE EITHER CUT DOWN OR CRUSHED. AND SHE JUST PASSED THE THOUSAND-KILL MARK...
A FEMALE WARRIOR WHO IS THE HEART AND SOUL OF LOKI FAMILIA.
WITHOUT A DOUBT, SHE POSSESSES TOP-CLASS SWORDS-MANSHIP SKILLS THAT ARE ON PAR WITH THE STRONGEST ADVENTUR-ERS.
APPARENTLY EVEN THE GODS THEMSELVES PRAISE HER.

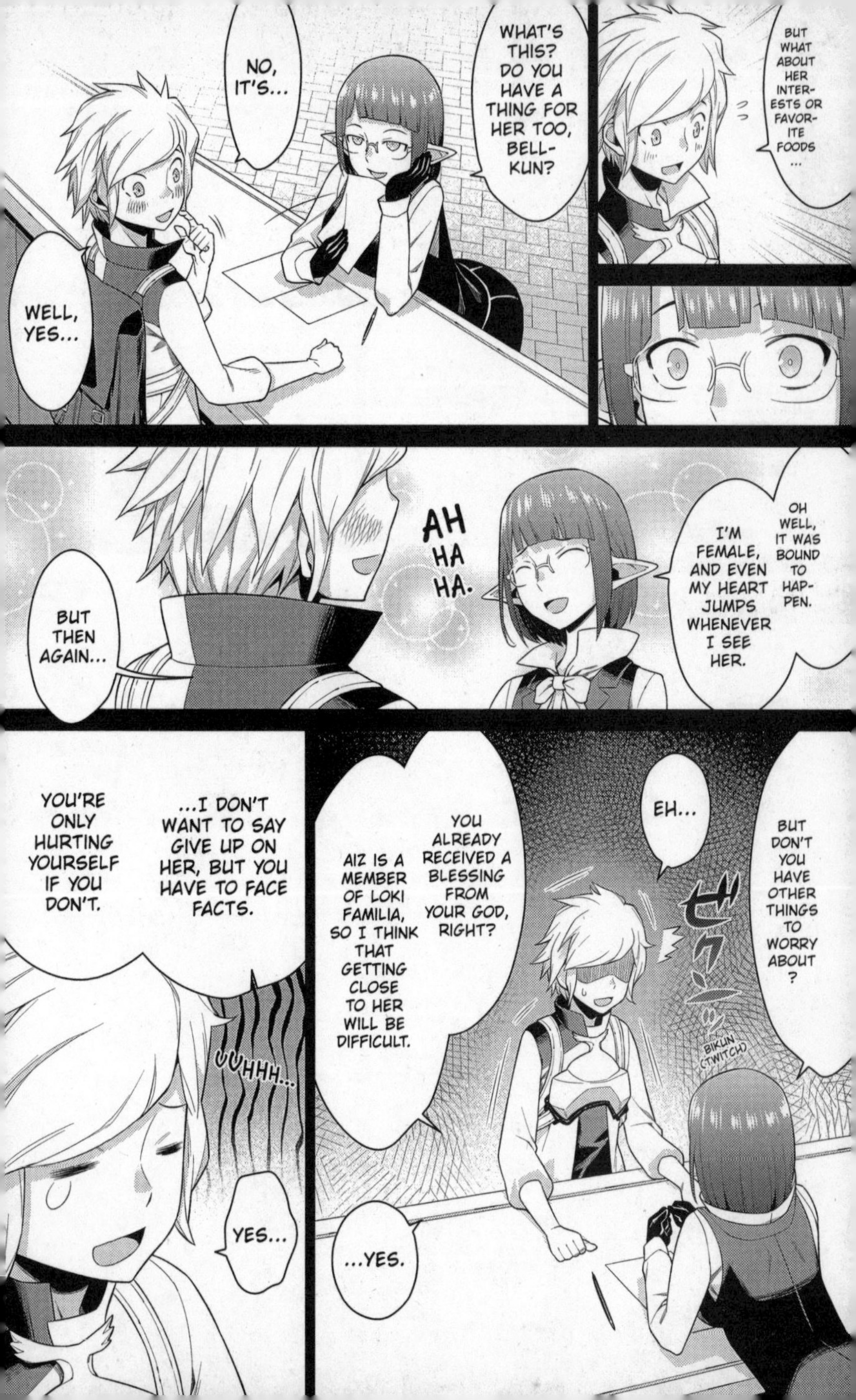

BUT WHAT ABOUT HER INTERESTS OR FAVORITE FOODS...
WHAT'S THIS? DO YOU HAVE A THING FOR HER TOO, BELL-KUN?
NO, IT'S...
WELL, YES...
OH WELL, IT WAS BOUND TO HAPPEN.
I'M FEMALE, AND EVEN MY HEART JUMPS WHENEVER I SEE HER.
AH HA HA.
BUT THEN AGAIN...
BUT DON'T YOU HAVE OTHER THINGS TO WORRY ABOUT?
EH...
BIKUN (TWITCH)
YOU ALREADY RECEIVED A BLESSING FROM YOUR GOD, RIGHT?
AIZ IS A MEMBER OF LOKI FAMILIA, SO I THINK THAT GETTING CLOSE TO HER WILL BE DIFFICULT.
...YES.
...I DON'T WANT TO SAY GIVE UP ON HER, BUT YOU HAVE TO FACE FACTS.
YOU'RE ONLY HURTING YOURSELF IF YOU DON'T.
UUHHH...
YES...

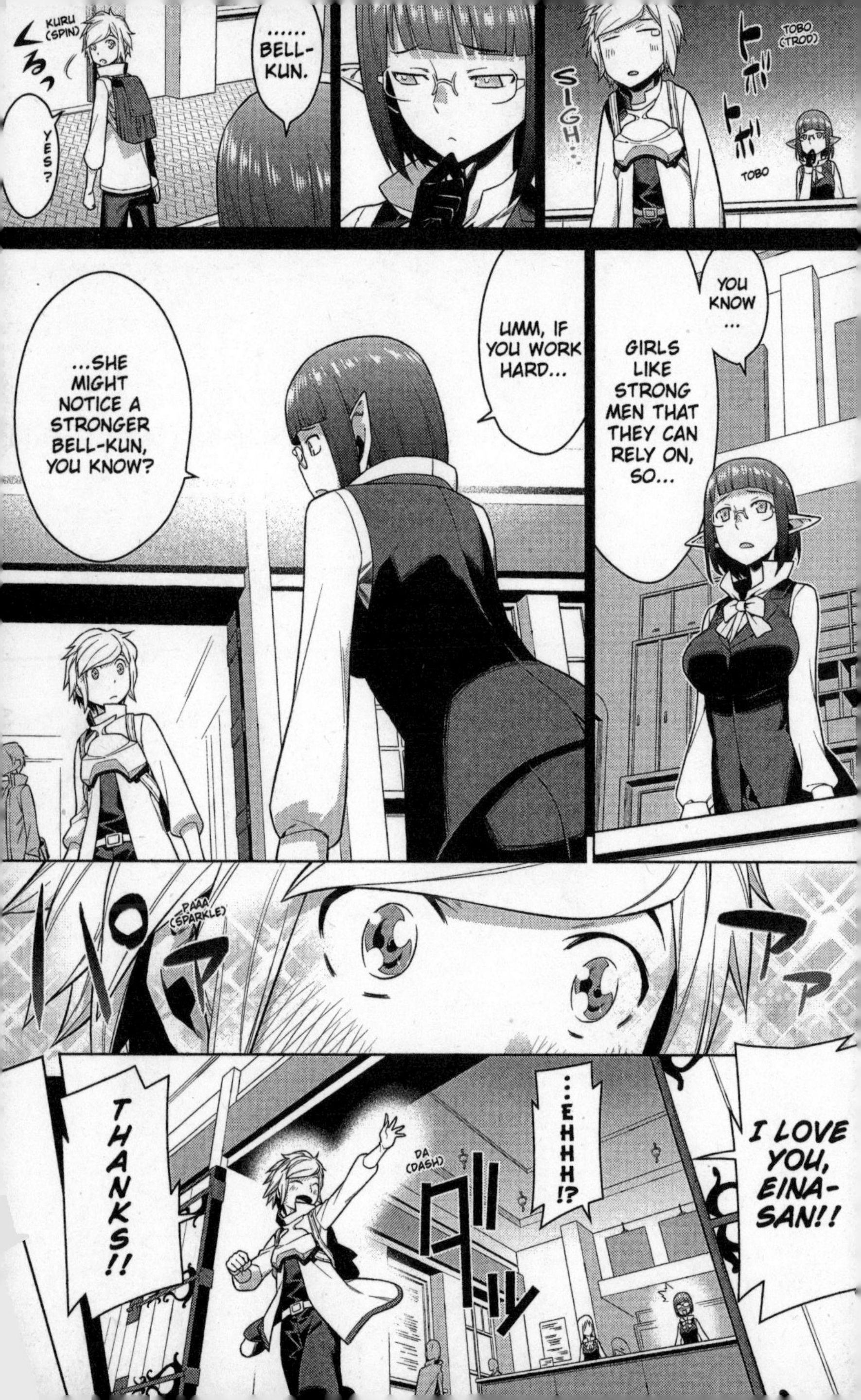
TOBO (TROD)
トボトボ
TOBO
SIGH...
......BELL-KUN.
KURU (SPIN)
くるっ
YES?
YOU KNOW...
GIRLS LIKE STRONG MEN THAT THEY CAN RELY ON, SO...
UMM, IF YOU WORK HARD...
...SHE MIGHT NOTICE A STRONGER BELL-KUN, YOU KNOW?
PAAA (SPARKLE)
I LOVE YOU, EINA-SAN!!
...EHHHH!?
DA (DASH)
ダッ
THANKS!!

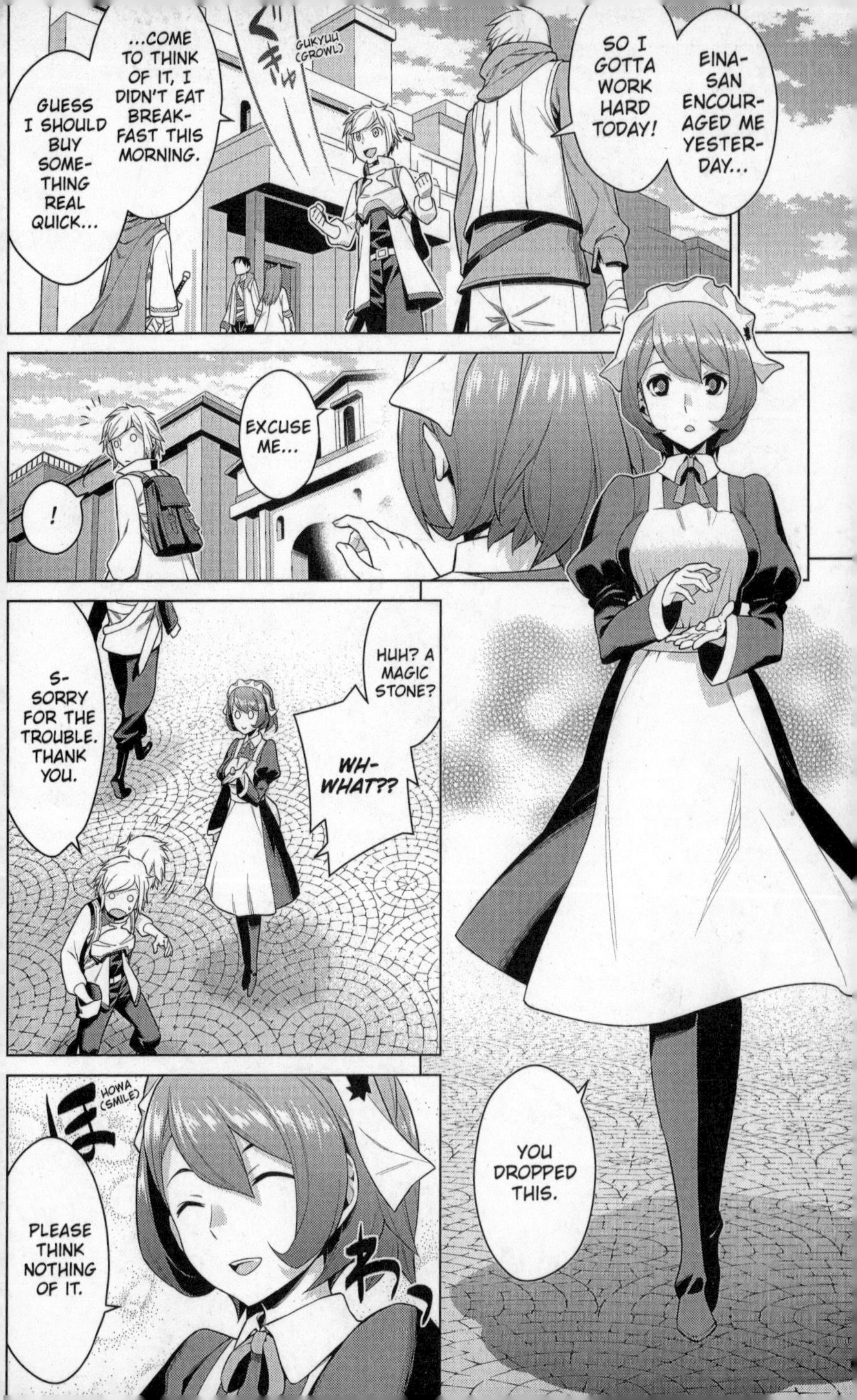
EINA-SAN ENCOURAGED ME YESTERDAY...
SO I GOTTA WORK HARD TODAY!
GUKYUU (GROWL)
...COME TO THINK OF IT, I DIDN'T EAT BREAKFAST THIS MORNING.
GUESS I SHOULD BUY SOMETHING REAL QUICK...
YOU DROPPED THIS.
EXCUSE ME...
!
HUH? A MAGIC STONE?
WH-WHAT??
S-SORRY FOR THE TROUBLE. THANK YOU.
HOWA (SMILE)
PLEASE THINK NOTHING OF IT.

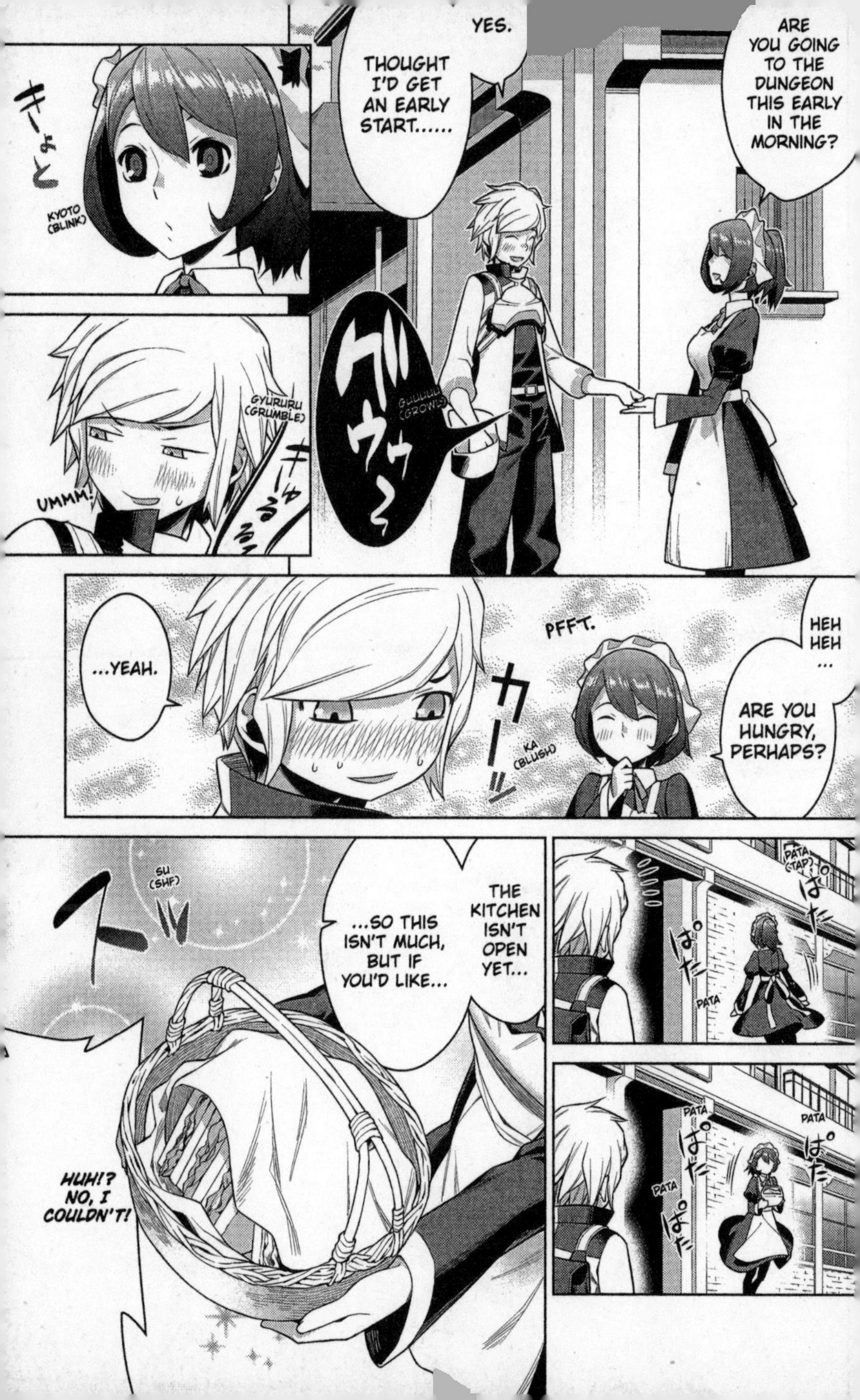

ARE YOU GOING TO THE DUNGEON THIS EARLY IN THE MORNING?
YES.
THOUGHT I'D GET AN EARLY START......
GUUUUU (GROWL)
KYOTO (BLINK)
GYURURU (GRUMBLE)
UMMM!
HEH HEH ...
ARE YOU HUNGRY, PERHAPS?
PFFT.
KA (BLUSH)
...YEAH.
PATA (TAP)
PATA
PATA
PATA
PATA
THE KITCHEN ISN'T OPEN YET...
...SO THIS ISN'T MUCH, BUT IF YOU'D LIKE...
SU (SHF)
HUH!? NO, I COULDN'T!

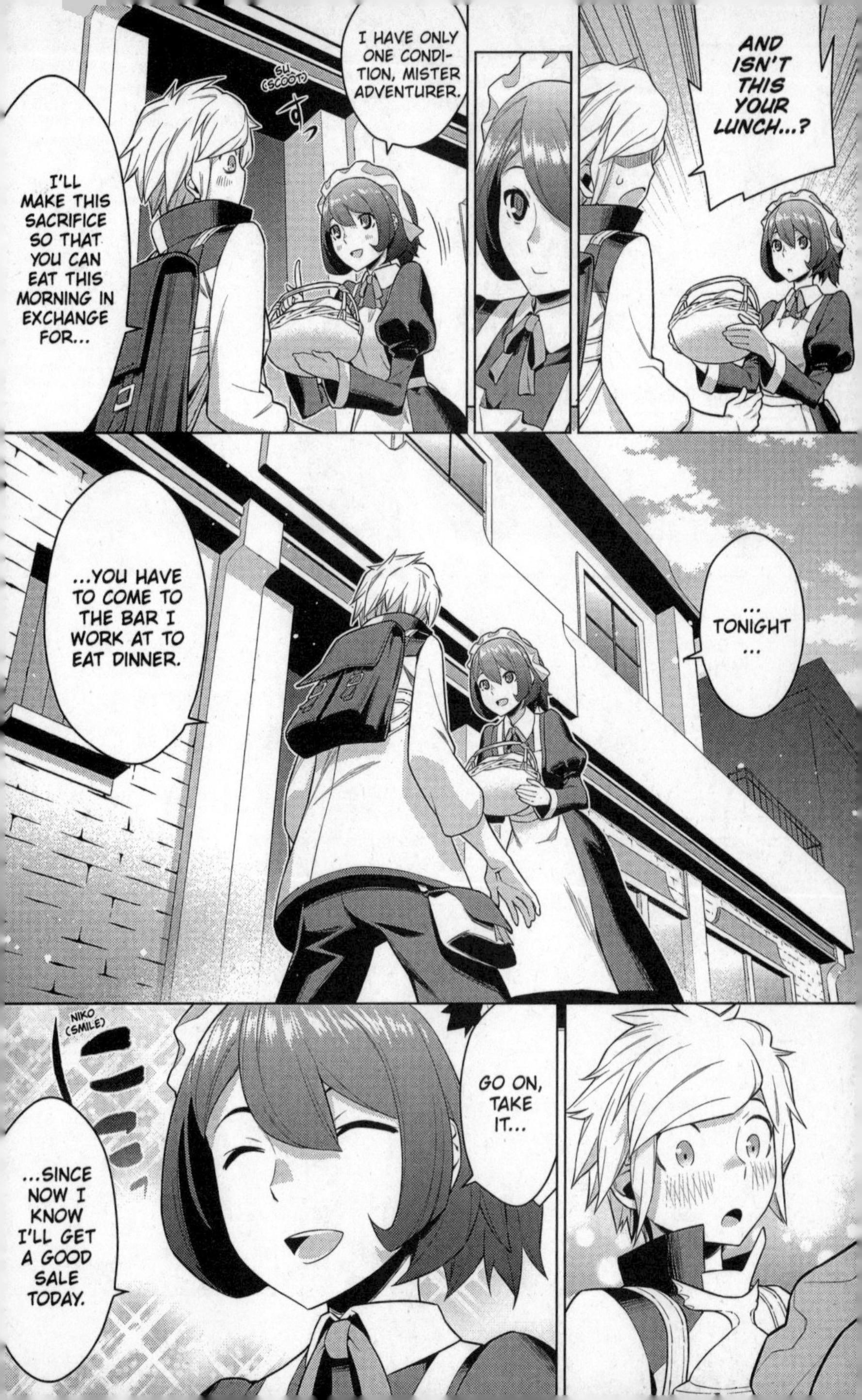
AND ISN'T THIS YOUR LUNCH...?
I HAVE ONLY ONE CONDITION, MISTER ADVENTURER.
SU (SCOOT)
I'LL MAKE THIS SACRIFICE SO THAT YOU CAN EAT THIS MORNING IN EXCHANGE FOR...
... TONIGHT ...
...YOU HAVE TO COME TO THE BAR I WORK AT TO EAT DINNER.
GO ON, TAKE IT...
NIKO (SMILE)
...SINCE NOW I KNOW I'LL GET A GOOD SALE TODAY.

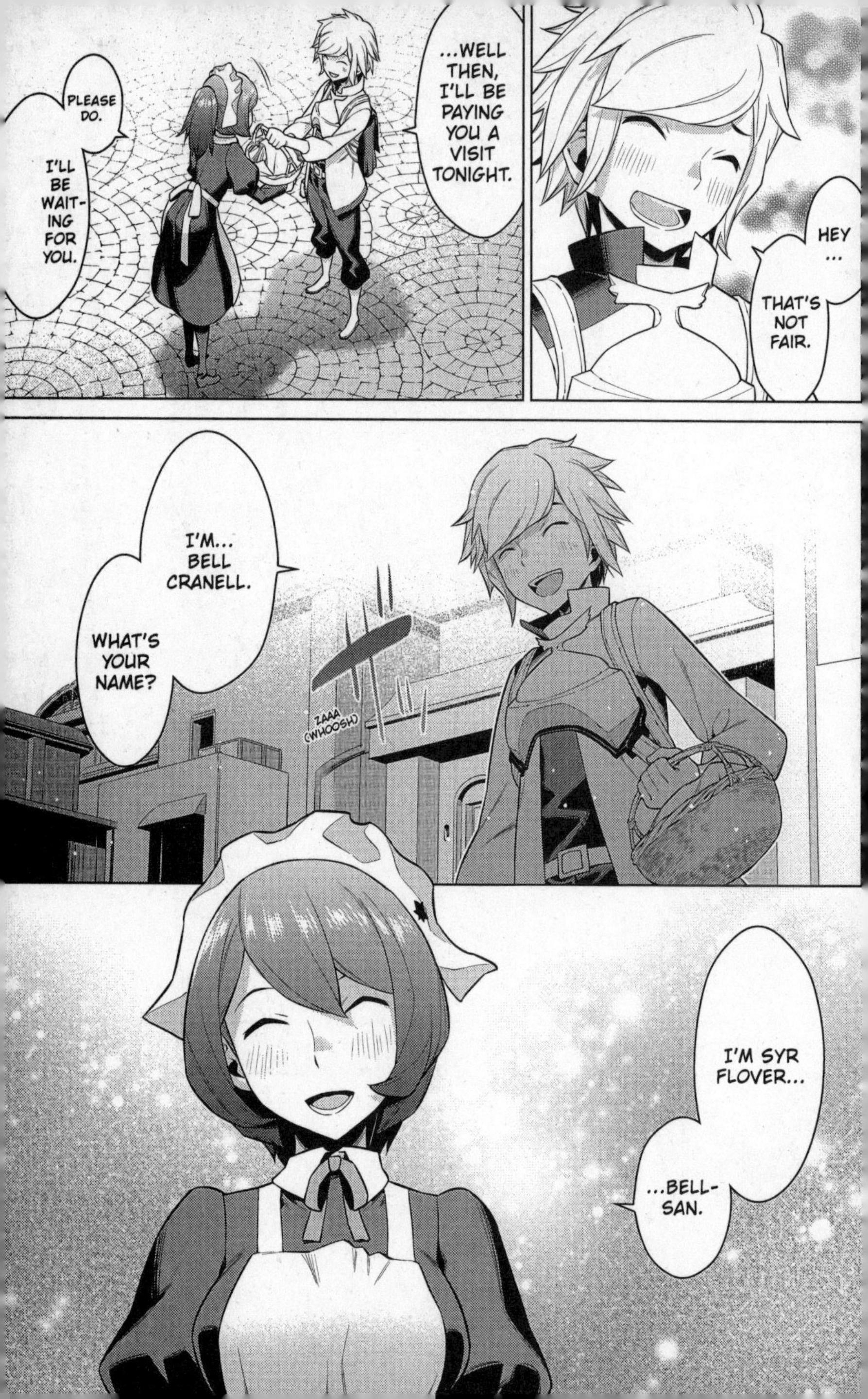
HEY ... THAT'S NOT FAIR.
...WELL THEN, I'LL BE PAYING YOU A VISIT TONIGHT.
PLEASE DO.
I'LL BE WAIT-ING FOR YOU.
I'M... BELL CRANELL.
WHAT'S YOUR NAME?
ZAAA (WHOOSH)
I'M SYR FLOVER...
...BELL-SAN.

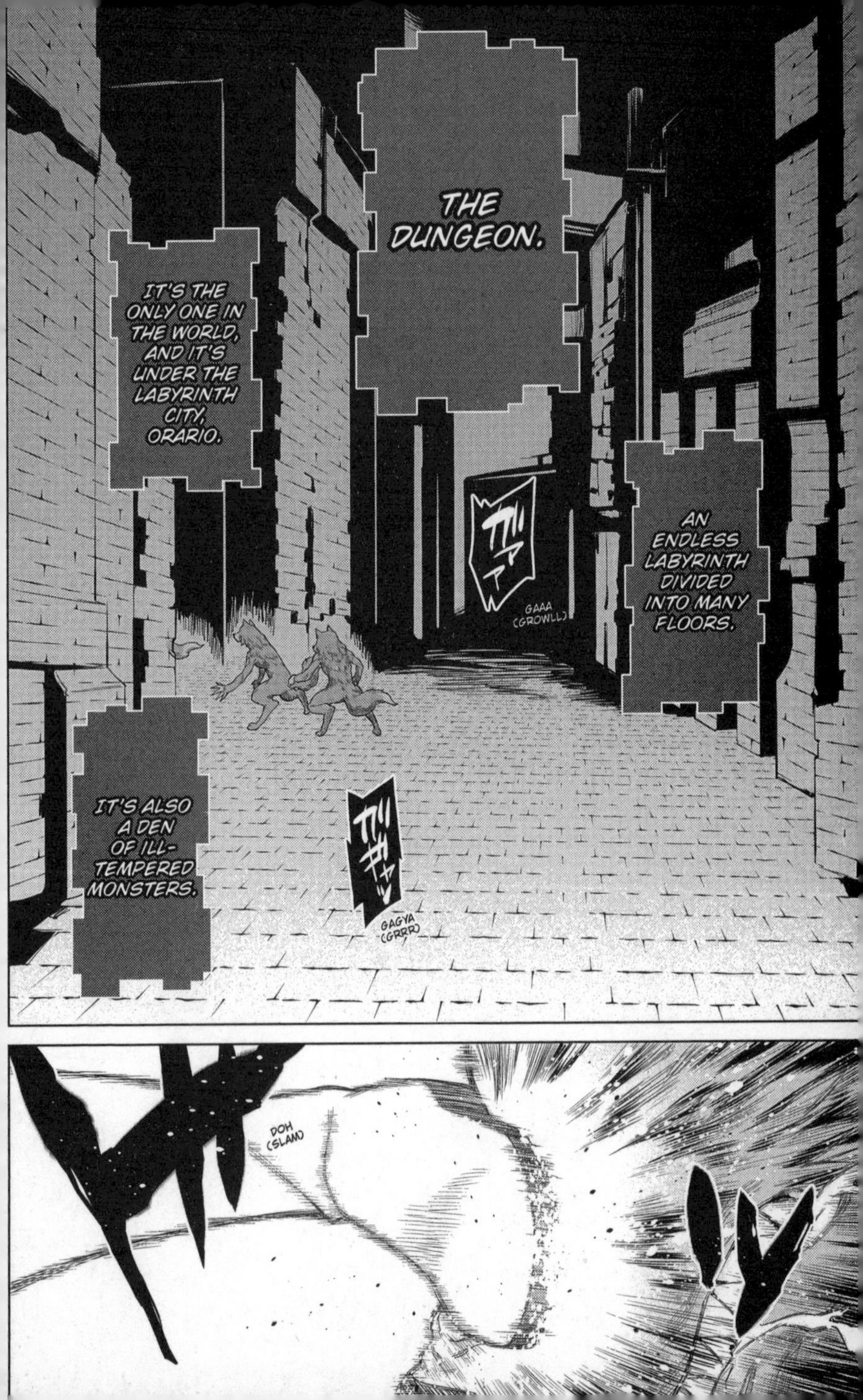
THE DUNGEON.
IT'S THE ONLY ONE IN THE WORLD, AND IT'S UNDER THE LABYRINTH CITY, ORARIO.
AN ENDLESS LABYRINTH DIVIDED INTO MANY FLOORS.
GAAA (GROWLL)
IT'S ALSO A DEN OF ILL-TEMPERED MONSTERS.
GAGYA (GRRR)
DOH (SLAM)

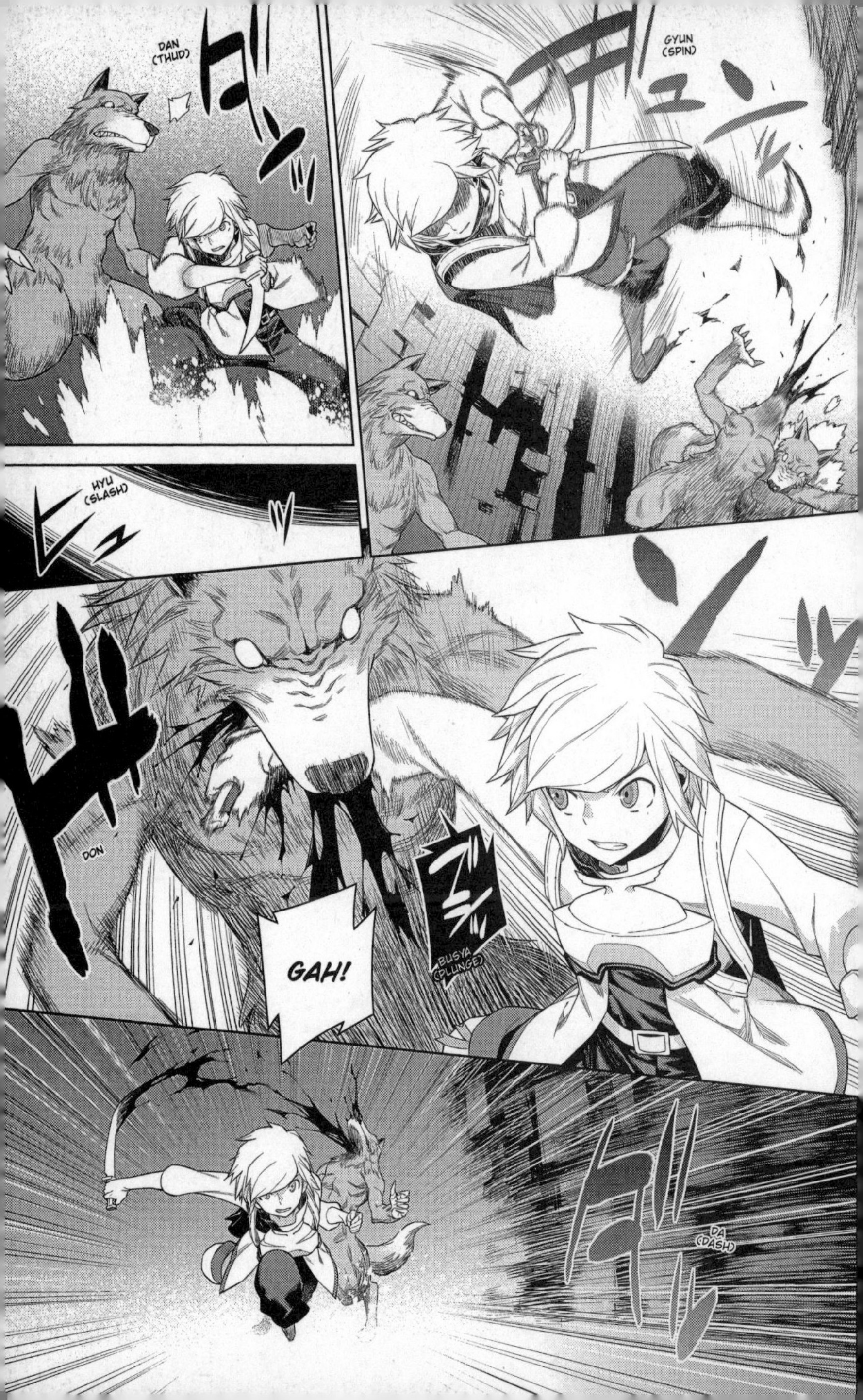
GYUN (SPIN)
DAN (THUD)
HYU (SLASH)
BUSYA (PLUNGE)
GAH!
DON
DA (DASH)

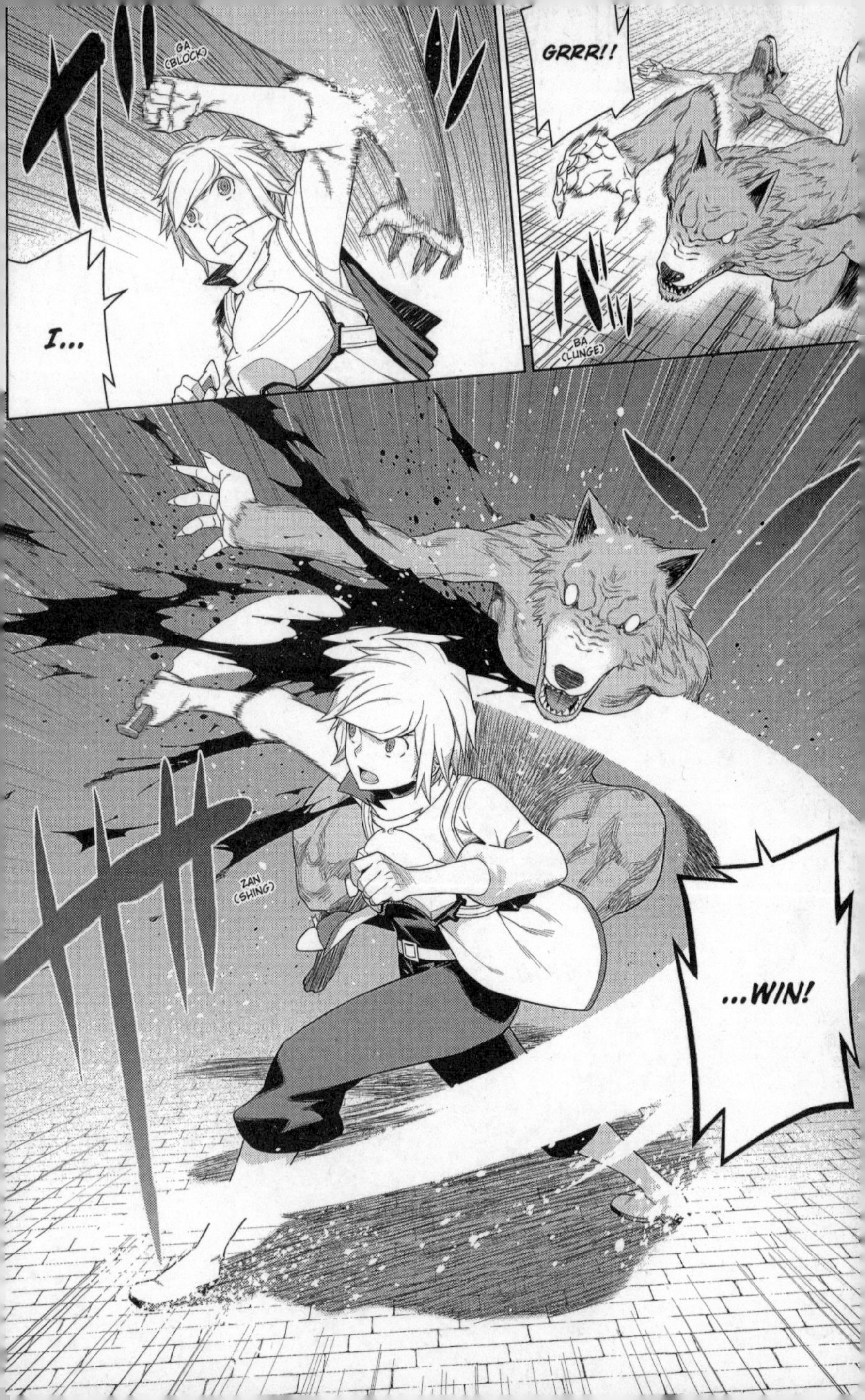
GRRR!!
BA (LUNGE)
GA (BLOCK)
I...
...WIN!
ZAN (SHING)

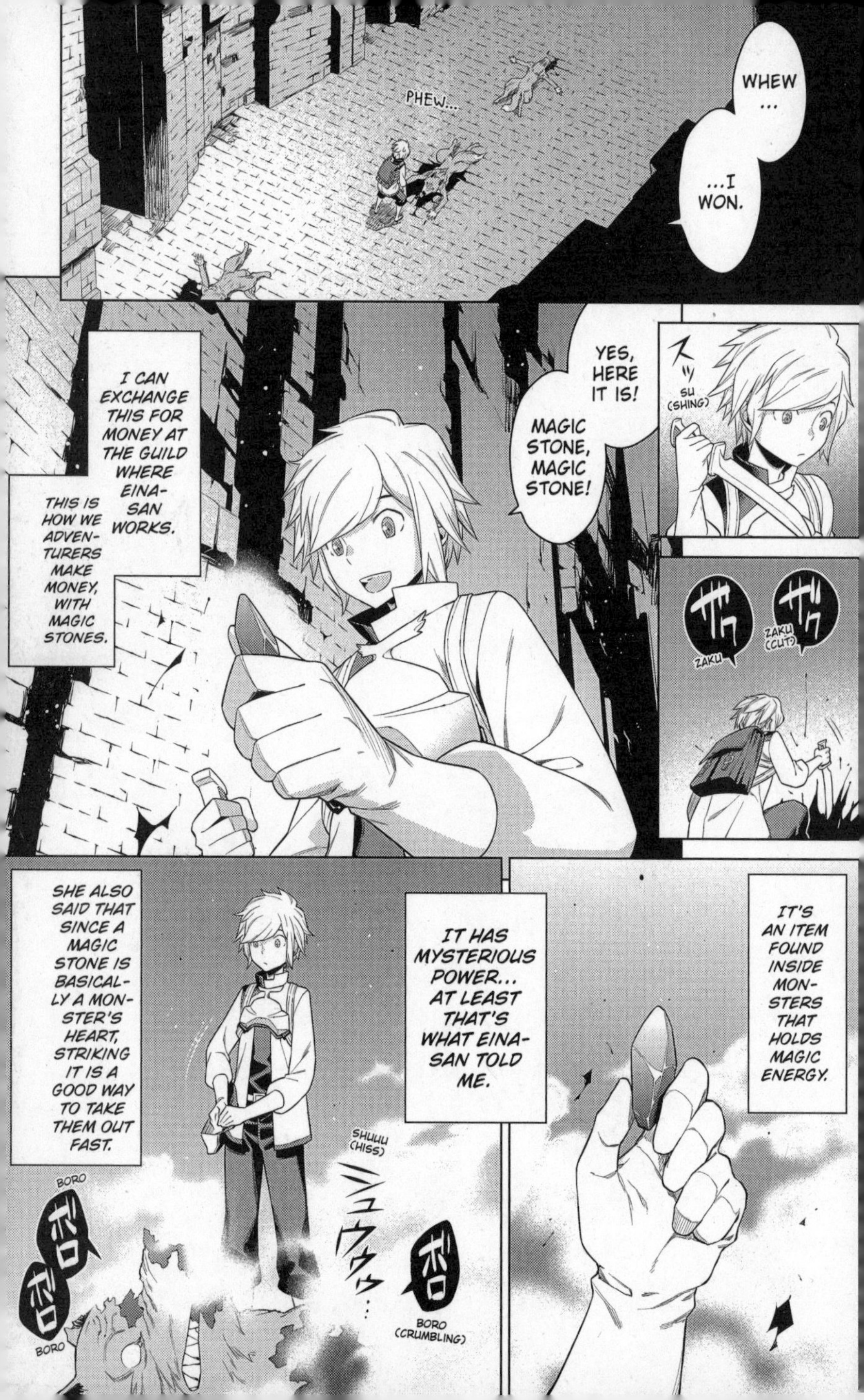
WHEW...
...I WON.
PHEW...
スッ
SU (SHING)
ザク
ZAKU (CUT)
ザク
ZAKU
YES, HERE IT IS!
MAGIC STONE, MAGIC STONE!
I CAN EXCHANGE THIS FOR MONEY AT THE GUILD WHERE EINA-SAN WORKS.
THIS IS HOW WE ADVENTURERS MAKE MONEY, WITH MAGIC STONES.
IT'S AN ITEM FOUND INSIDE MONSTERS THAT HOLDS MAGIC ENERGY.
IT HAS MYSTERIOUS POWER... AT LEAST THAT'S WHAT EINA-SAN TOLD ME.
SHE ALSO SAID THAT SINCE A MAGIC STONE IS BASICALLY A MONSTER'S HEART, STRIKING IT IS A GOOD WAY TO TAKE THEM OUT FAST.
シュウゥ...
SHUUU (HISS)
ボロ
BORO (CRUMBLING)
ボロ
BORO
ボロ
BORO

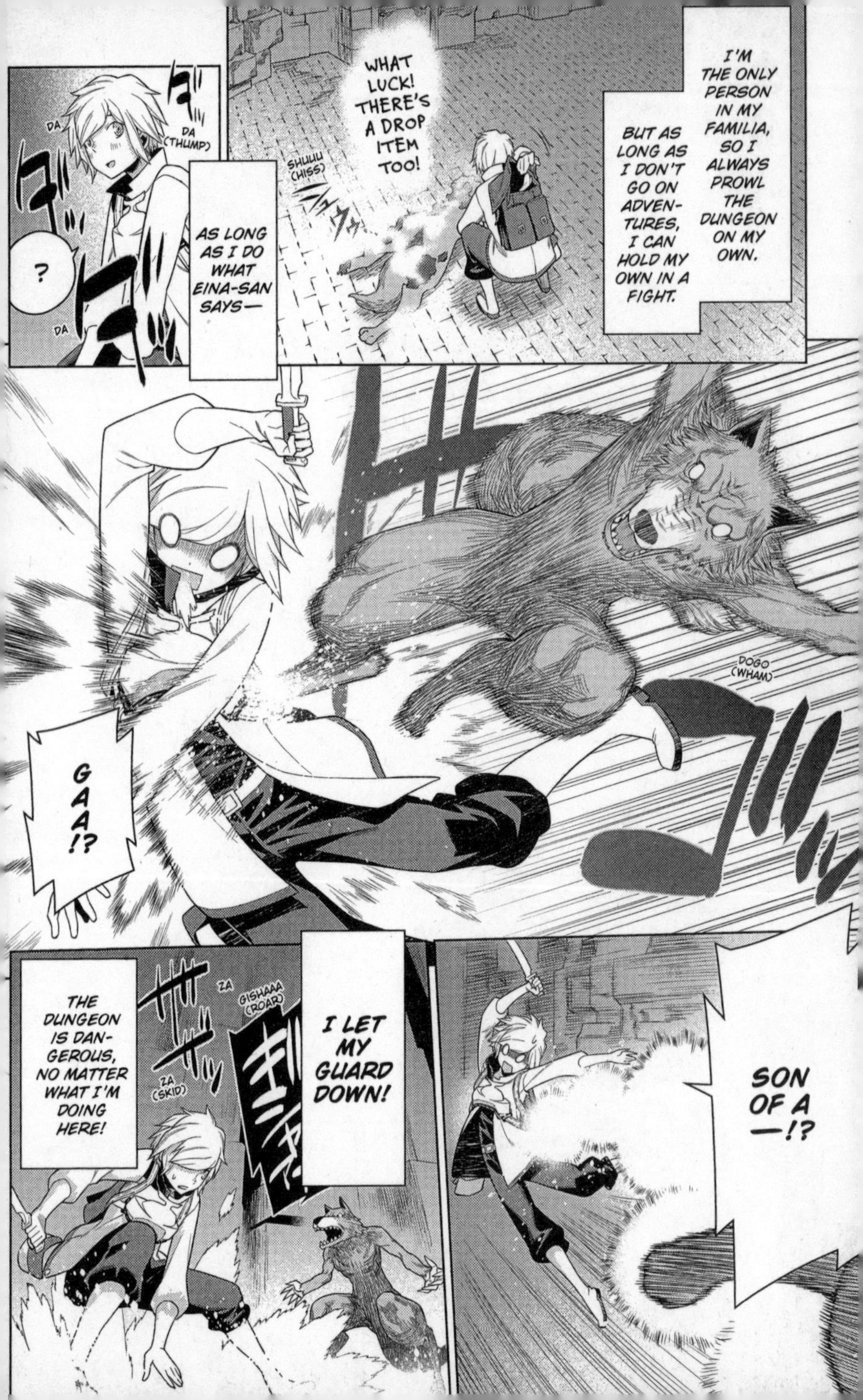
I'M THE ONLY PERSON IN MY FAMILIA, SO I ALWAYS PROWL THE DUNGEON ON MY OWN.
BUT AS LONG AS I DON'T GO ON ADVENTURES, I CAN HOLD MY OWN IN A FIGHT.
WHAT LUCK! THERE'S A DROP ITEM TOO!
SHUUU (HISS)
AS LONG AS I DO WHAT EINA-SAN SAYS—
DA (THUMP)
DA
?
DA
DOGO (WHAM)
GAA!?
SON OF A—!?
I LET MY GUARD DOWN!
GISHAAA (ROAR)
ZA
ZA (SKID)
THE DUNGEON IS DANGEROUS, NO MATTER WHAT I'M DOING HERE!

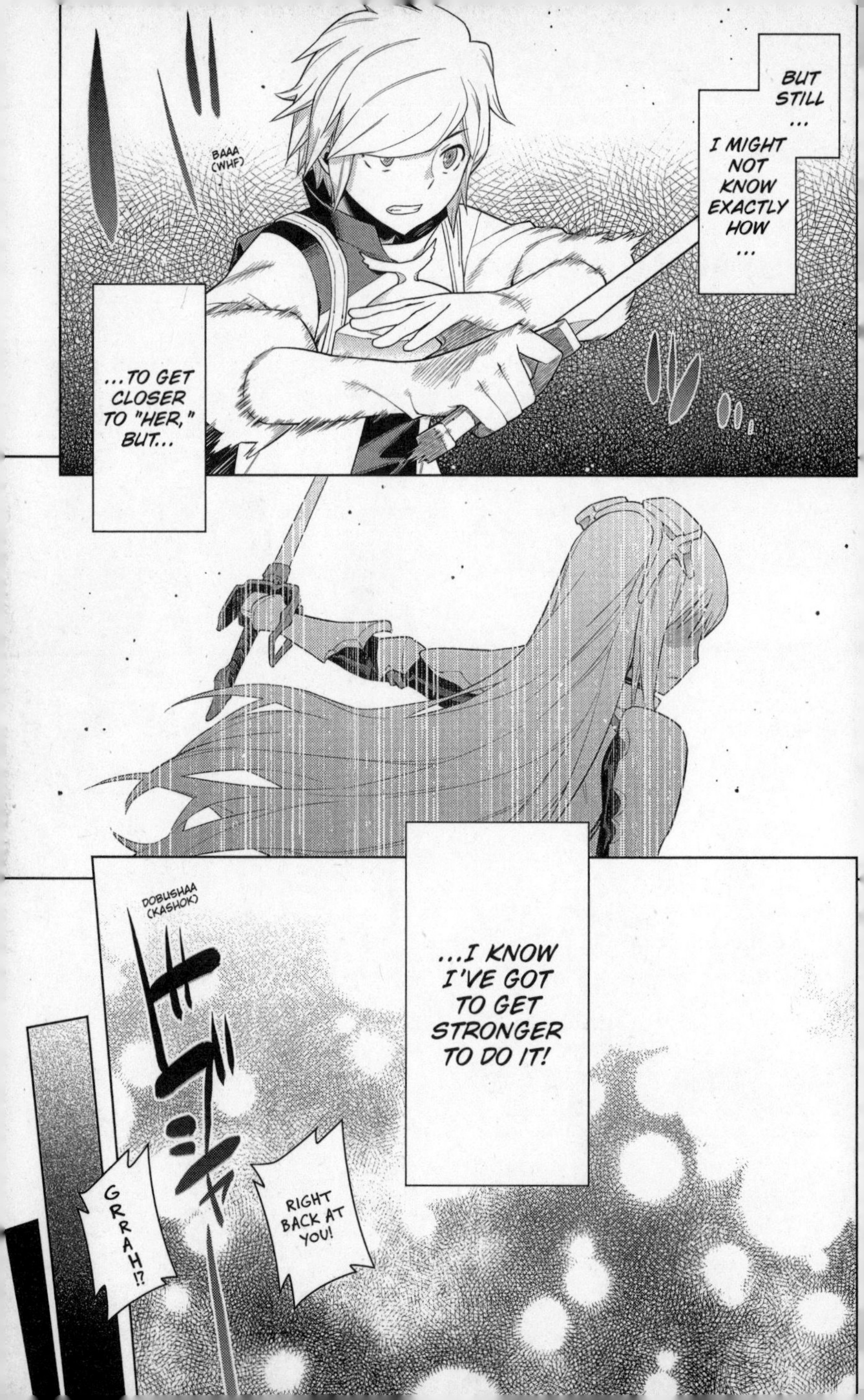
BUT STILL... I MIGHT NOT KNOW EXACTLY HOW...
BAAA (WHF)
...TO GET CLOSER TO "HER," BUT...
...I KNOW I'VE GOT TO GET STRONGER TO DO IT!
RIGHT BACK AT YOU!
DOBUSHAA (KASHOK)
GRRAH!?

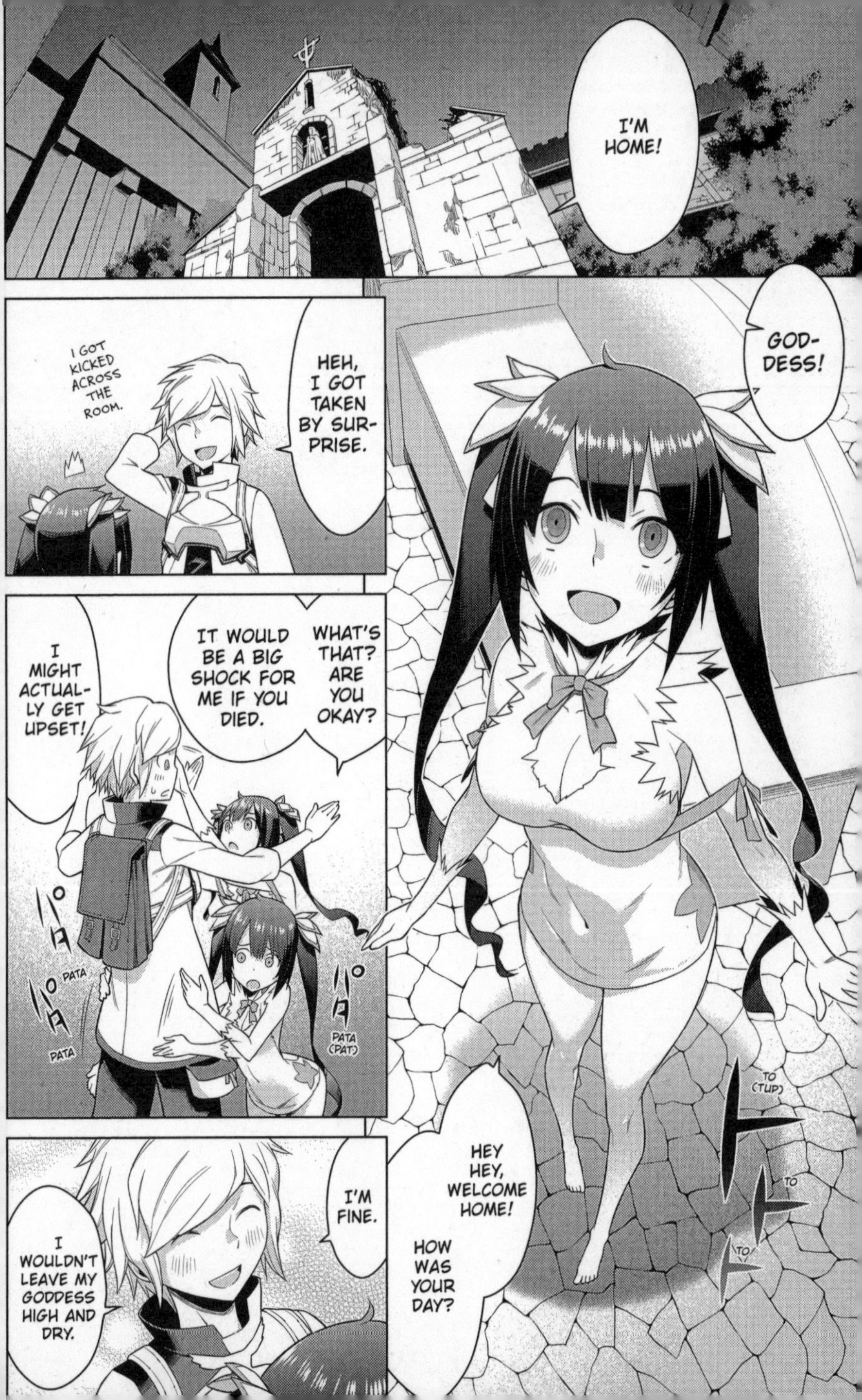
I'M HOME!
GOD-DESS!
TO (TUP)
TO
TO
HEY HEY, WELCOME HOME!
HOW WAS YOUR DAY?
HEH, I GOT TAKEN BY SUR-PRISE.
I GOT KICKED ACROSS THE ROOM.
WHAT'S THAT? ARE YOU OKAY?
IT WOULD BE A BIG SHOCK FOR ME IF YOU DIED.
I MIGHT ACTUALLY GET UPSET!
パタ
PATA (PAT)
パタ
PATA
パタ
PATA
I'M FINE.
I WOULDN'T LEAVE MY GODDESS HIGH AND DRY.

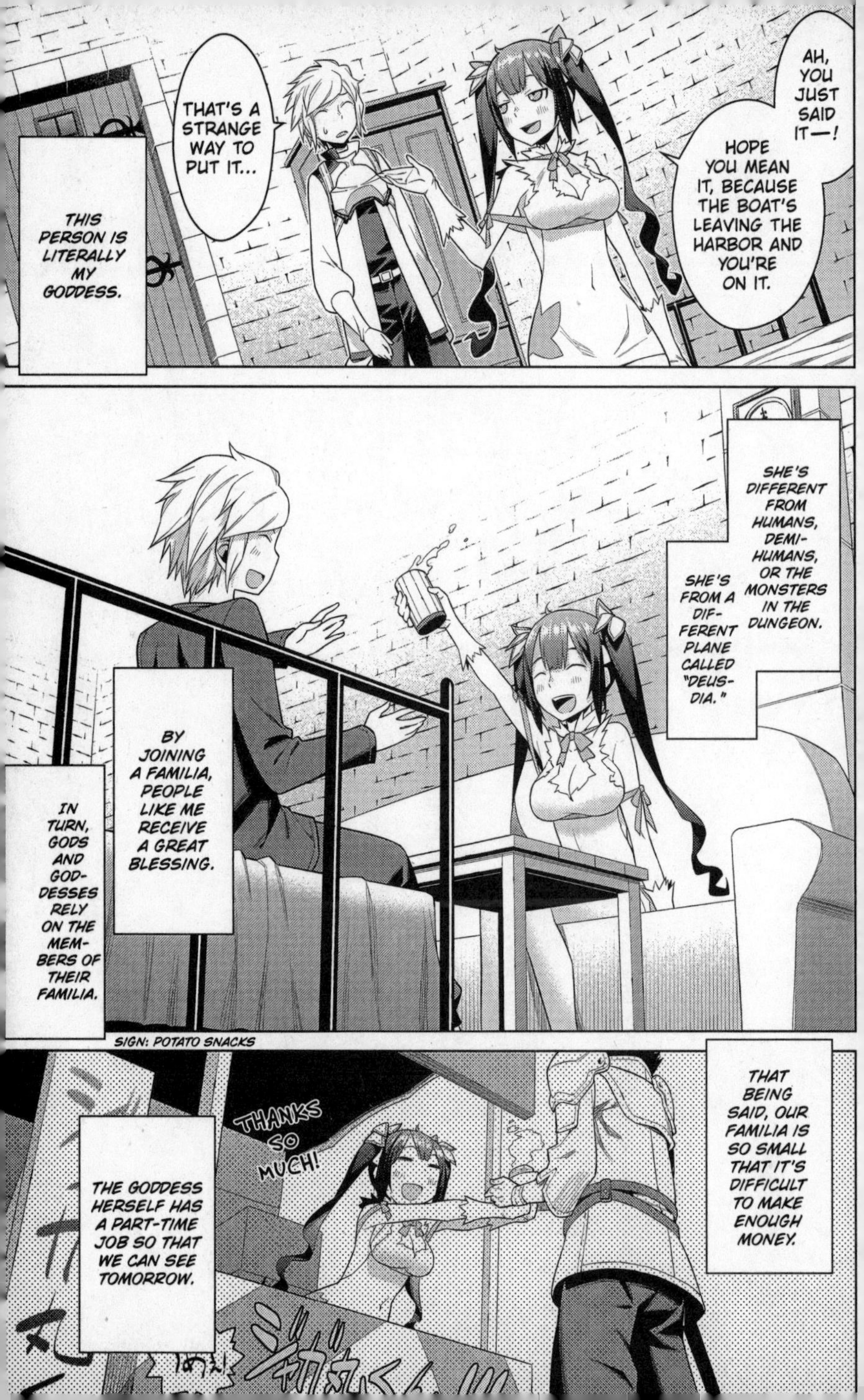
AH, YOU JUST SAID IT—!
HOPE YOU MEAN IT, BECAUSE THE BOAT'S LEAVING THE HARBOR AND YOU'RE ON IT.
THAT'S A STRANGE WAY TO PUT IT...
THIS PERSON IS LITERALLY MY GODDESS.
SHE'S DIFFERENT FROM HUMANS, DEMI-HUMANS, OR THE MONSTERS IN THE DUNGEON.
SHE'S FROM A DIFFERENT PLANE CALLED "DEUSDIA."
BY JOINING A FAMILIA, PEOPLE LIKE ME RECEIVE A GREAT BLESSING.
IN TURN, GODS AND GODDESSES RELY ON THE MEMBERS OF THEIR FAMILIA.
SIGN: POTATO SNACKS
THAT BEING SAID, OUR FAMILIA IS SO SMALL THAT IT'S DIFFICULT TO MAKE ENOUGH MONEY.
THANKS SO MUCH!
THE GODDESS HERSELF HAS A PART-TIME JOB SO THAT WE CAN SEE TOMORROW.

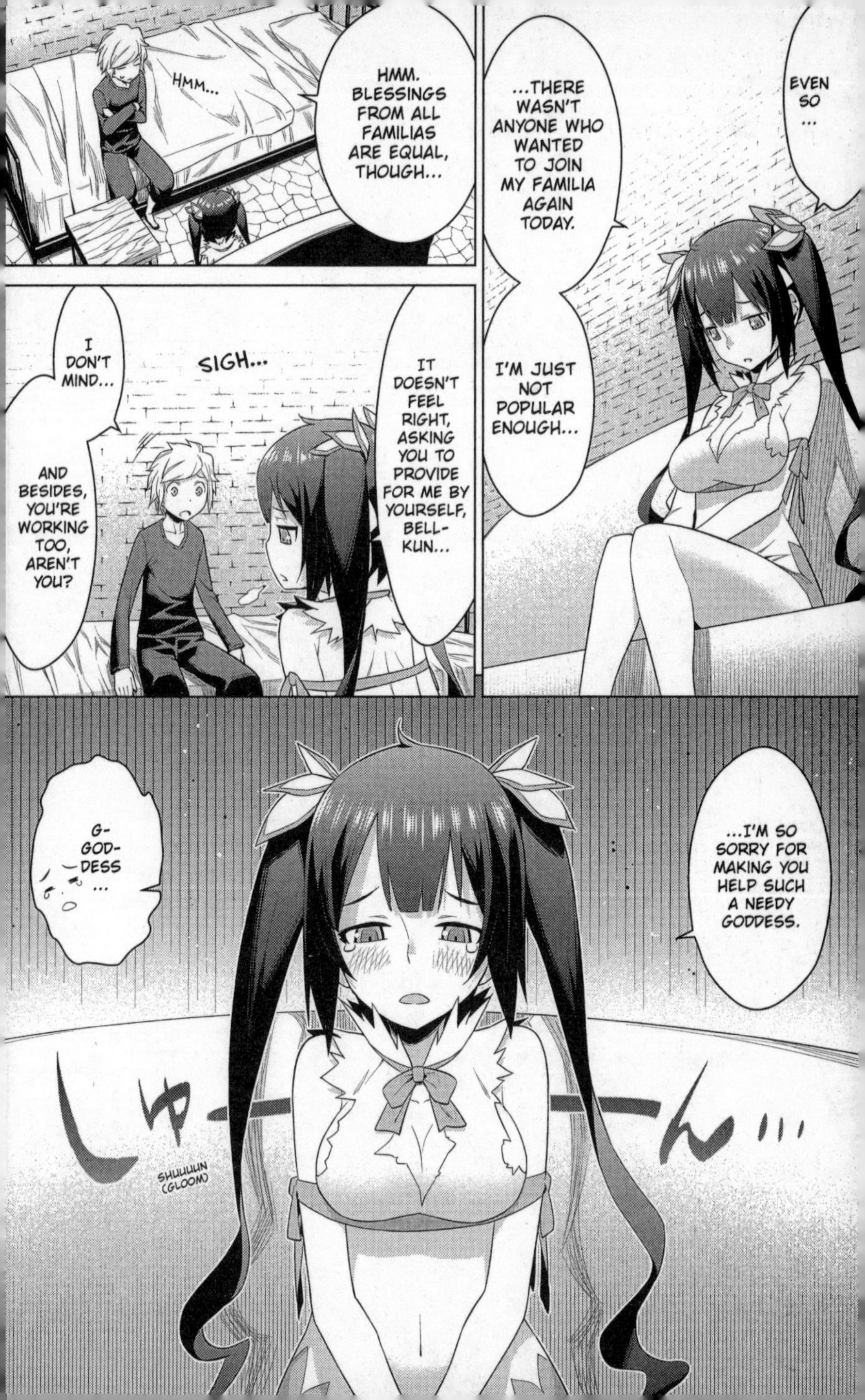
EVEN SO ...
...THERE WASN'T ANYONE WHO WANTED TO JOIN MY FAMILIA AGAIN TODAY.
I'M JUST NOT POPULAR ENOUGH...
HMM. BLESSINGS FROM ALL FAMILIAS ARE EQUAL, THOUGH...
HMM...
IT DOESN'T FEEL RIGHT, ASKING YOU TO PROVIDE FOR ME BY YOURSELF, BELL-KUN...
SIGH...
I DON'T MIND...
AND BESIDES, YOU'RE WORKING TOO, AREN'T YOU?
...I'M SO SORRY FOR MAKING YOU HELP SUCH A NEEDY GODDESS.
しゅーーん…
SHUUUUN (GLOOM)
G-GOD-DESS ...

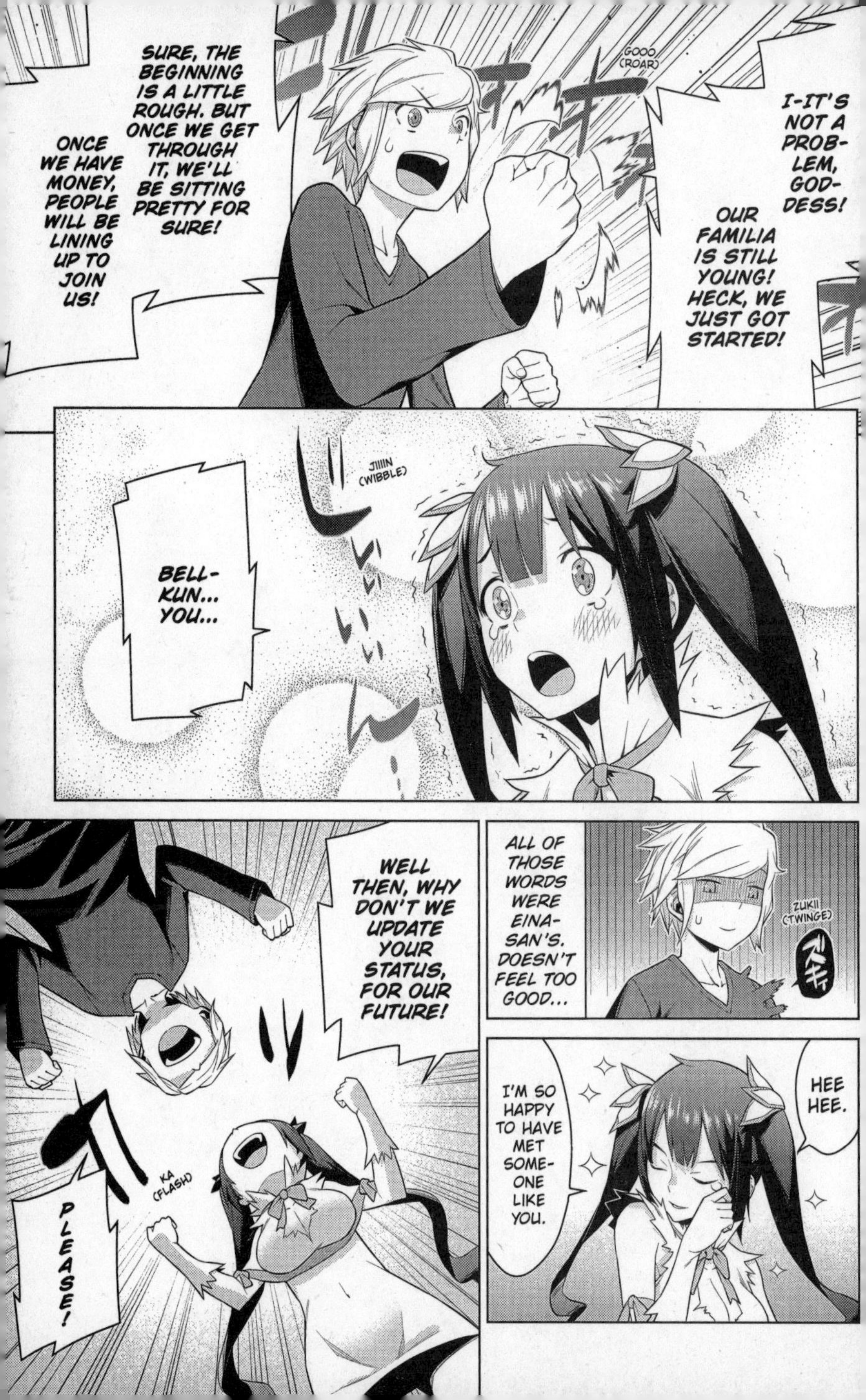
I-IT'S NOT A PROBLEM, GODDESS!
OUR FAMILIA IS STILL YOUNG! HECK, WE JUST GOT STARTED!
GOOO (ROAR)
SURE, THE BEGINNING IS A LITTLE ROUGH. BUT ONCE WE GET THROUGH IT, WE'LL BE SITTING PRETTY FOR SURE!
ONCE WE HAVE MONEY, PEOPLE WILL BE LINING UP TO JOIN US!
JIIIN (WIBBLE)
BELL-KUN... YOU...
ZUKII (TWINGE)
ALL OF THOSE WORDS WERE EINA-SAN'S. DOESN'T FEEL TOO GOOD...
HEE HEE.
I'M SO HAPPY TO HAVE MET SOMEONE LIKE YOU.
WELL THEN, WHY DON'T WE UPDATE YOUR STATUS, FOR OUR FUTURE!
KA (FLASH)
PLEASE!

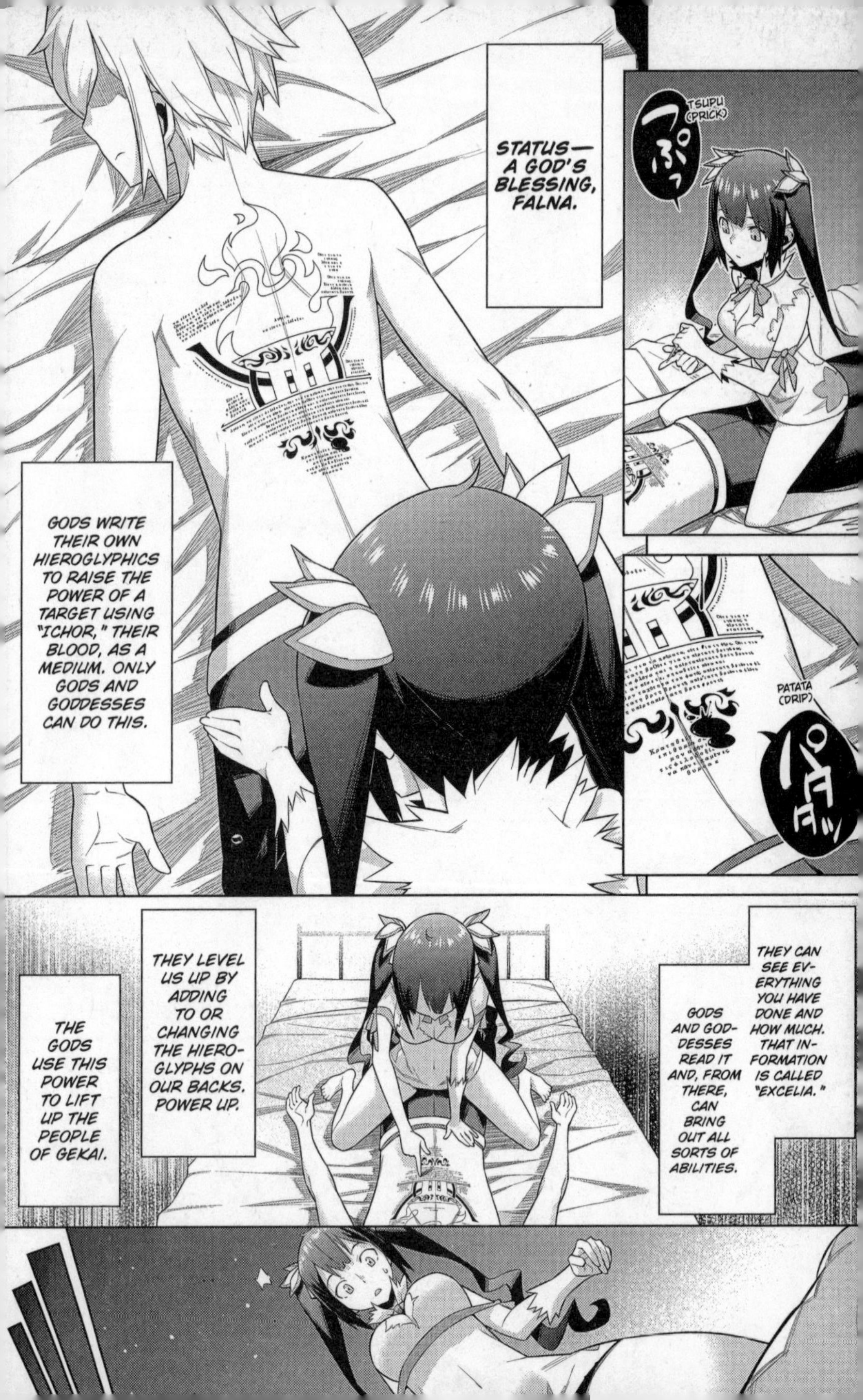

つぷっ
TSUPU (PRICK)
パタタッ
PATATA (DRIP)
STATUS— A GOD'S BLESSING, FALNA.
GODS WRITE THEIR OWN HIEROGLYPHICS TO RAISE THE POWER OF A TARGET USING "ICHOR," THEIR BLOOD, AS A MEDIUM. ONLY GODS AND GODDESSES CAN DO THIS.
THEY CAN SEE EVERYTHING YOU HAVE DONE AND HOW MUCH. THAT INFORMATION IS CALLED "EXCELIA."
GODS AND GODDESSES READ IT AND, FROM THERE, CAN BRING OUT ALL SORTS OF ABILITIES.
THEY LEVEL US UP BY ADDING TO OR CHANGING THE HIEROGLYPHS ON OUR BACKS. POWER UP.
THE GODS USE THIS POWER TO LIFT UP THE PEOPLE OF GEKAI.

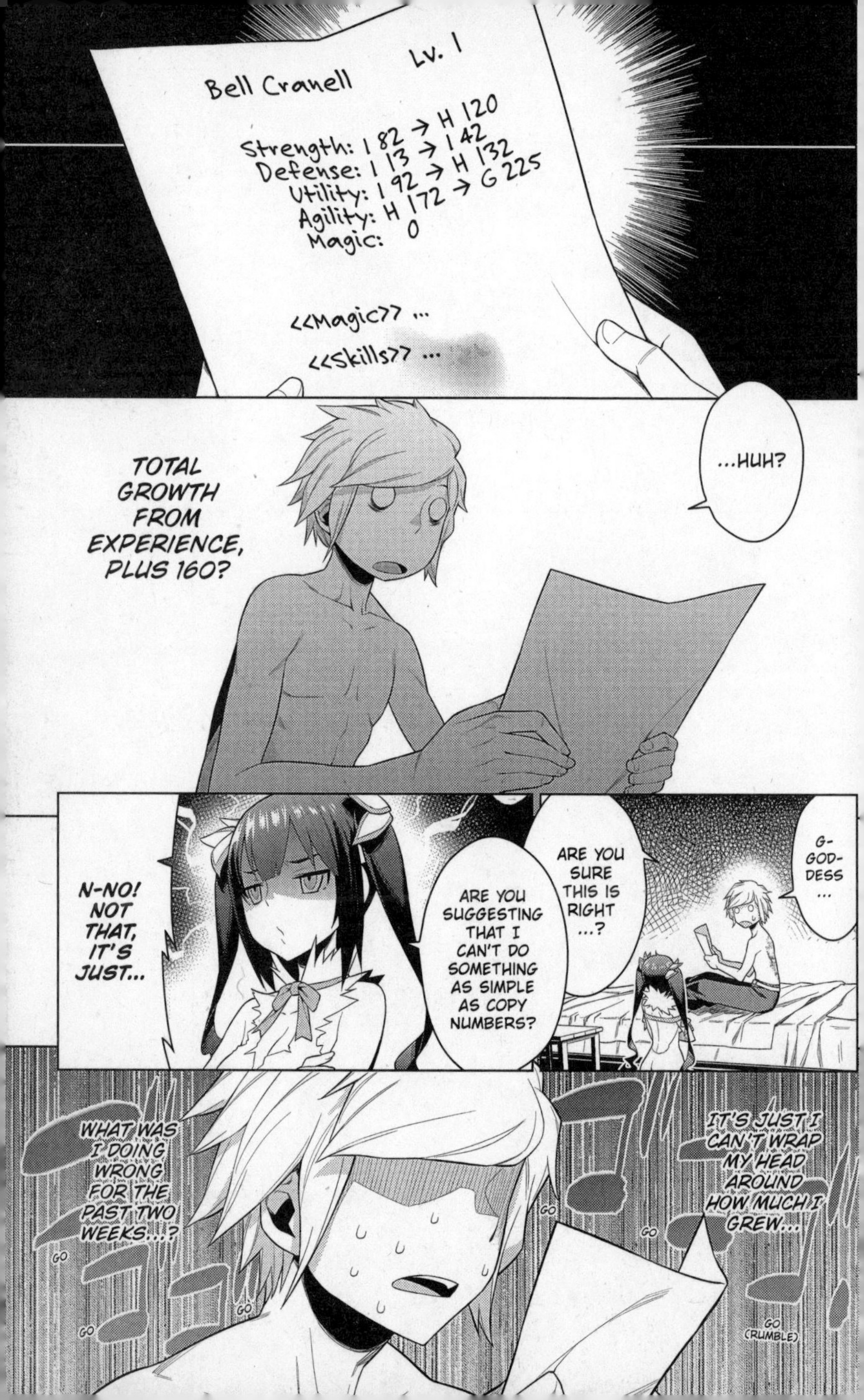

Bell Cranell Lv. 1
Strength: I 82 → H 120
Defense: I 13 → I 42
Utility: I 92 → H 132
Agility: H 172 → G 225
Magic: 0
<<Magic>> ...
<<Skills>> ...
...HUH?
TOTAL GROWTH FROM EXPERIENCE, PLUS 160?
G-GOD-DESS...
ARE YOU SURE THIS IS RIGHT...?
ARE YOU SUGGESTING THAT I CAN'T DO SOMETHING AS SIMPLE AS COPY NUMBERS?
N-NO! NOT THAT, IT'S JUST...
IT'S JUST I CAN'T WRAP MY HEAD AROUND HOW MUCH I GREW...
WHAT WAS I DOING WRONG FOR THE PAST TWO WEEKS...?
GO
GO
GO
GO
GO
GO (RUMBLE)

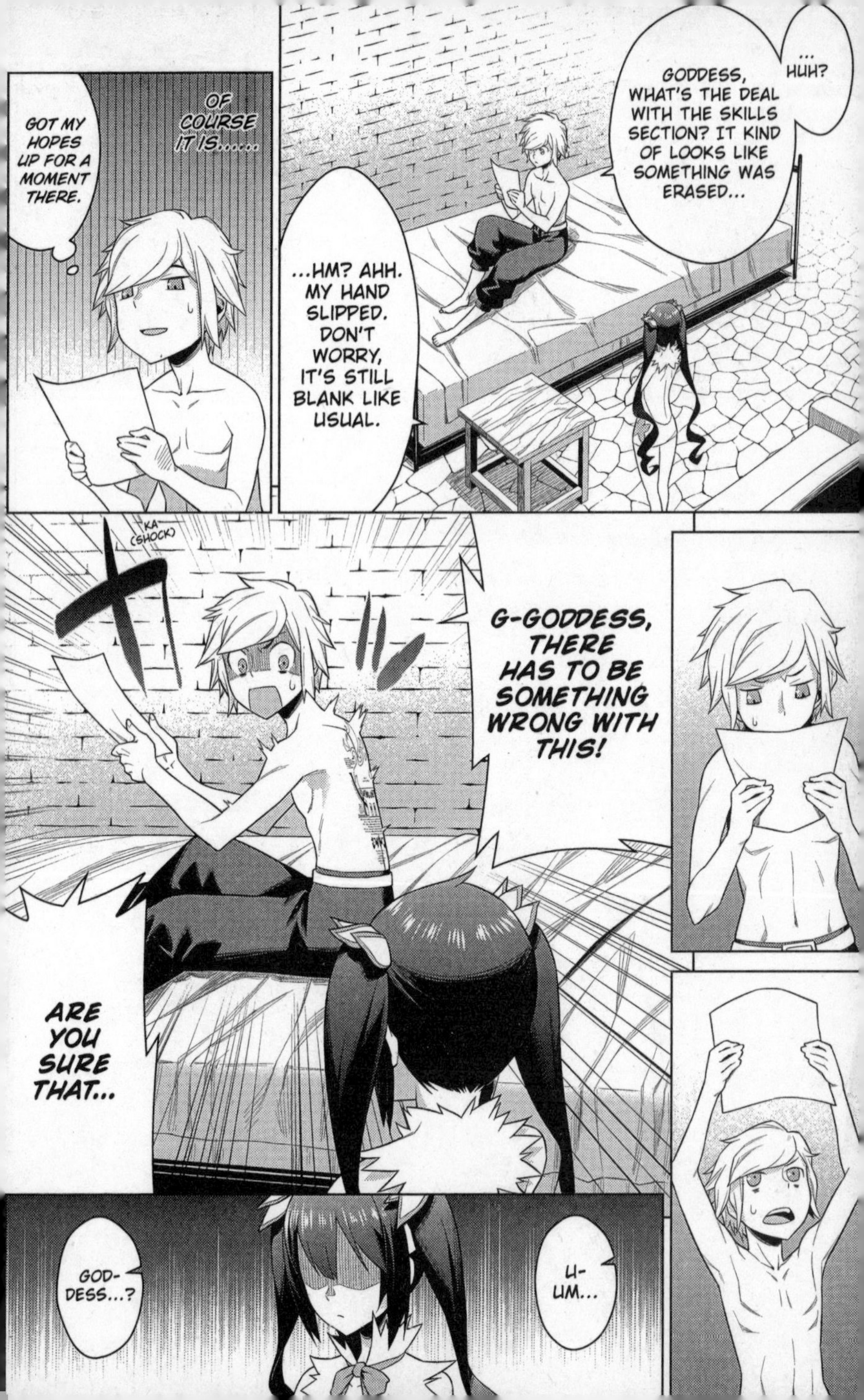
...HUH?
GODDESS, WHAT'S THE DEAL WITH THE SKILLS SECTION? IT KIND OF LOOKS LIKE SOMETHING WAS ERASED...
...HM? AHH. MY HAND SLIPPED. DON'T WORRY, IT'S STILL BLANK LIKE USUAL.
OF COURSE IT IS......
GOT MY HOPES UP FOR A MOMENT THERE.
KA (SHOCK)
G-GODDESS, THERE HAS TO BE SOMETHING WRONG WITH THIS!
ARE YOU SURE THAT...
U-UM...
GOD-DESS...?

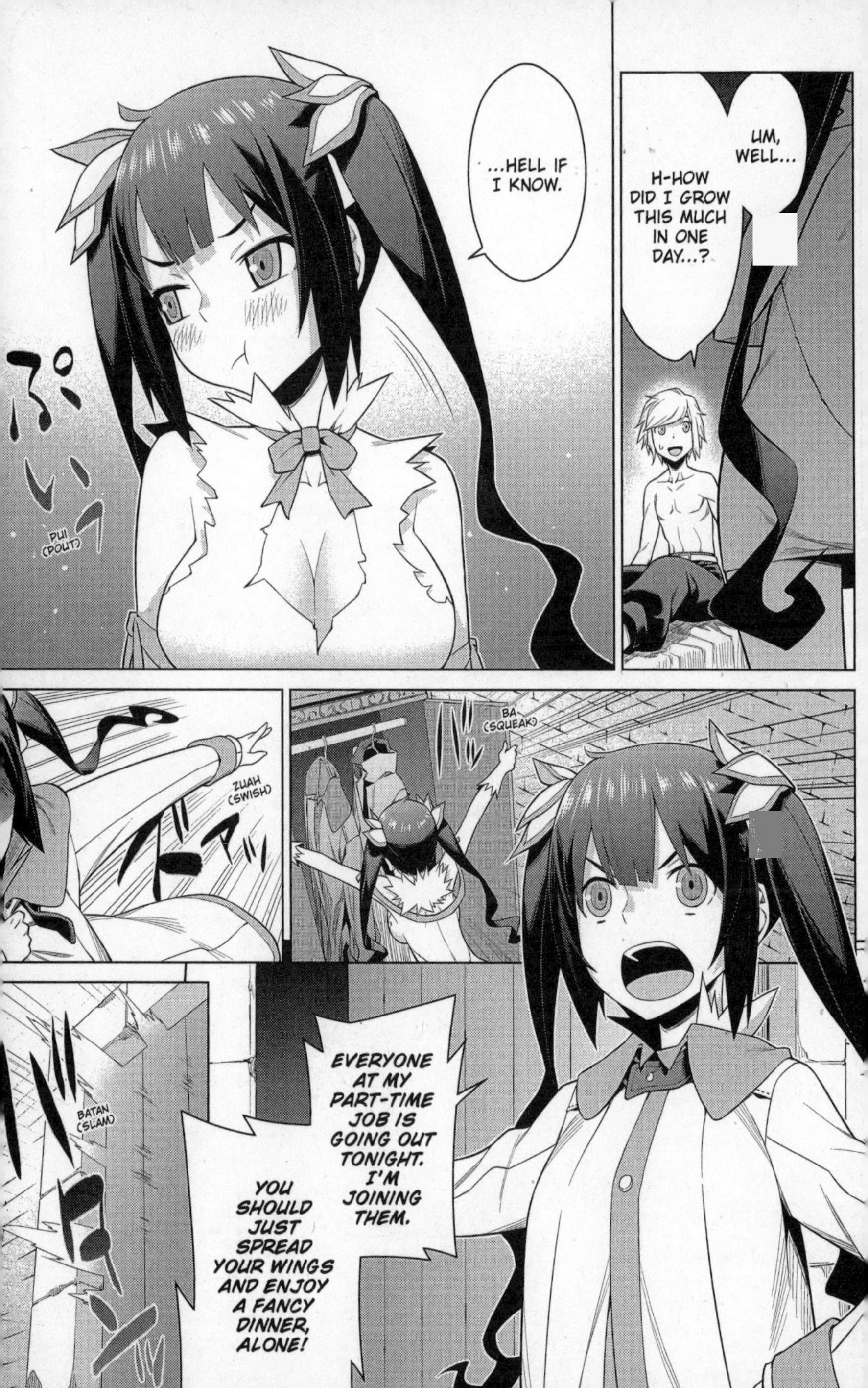
UM, WELL...
H-HOW DID I GROW THIS MUCH IN ONE DAY...?
...HELL IF I KNOW.
PUI (POUT)
BA (SQUEAK)
ZUAH (SWISH)
EVERYONE AT MY PART-TIME JOB IS GOING OUT TONIGHT. I'M JOINING THEM.
YOU SHOULD JUST SPREAD YOUR WINGS AND ENJOY A FANCY DINNER, ALONE!
BATAN (SLAM)

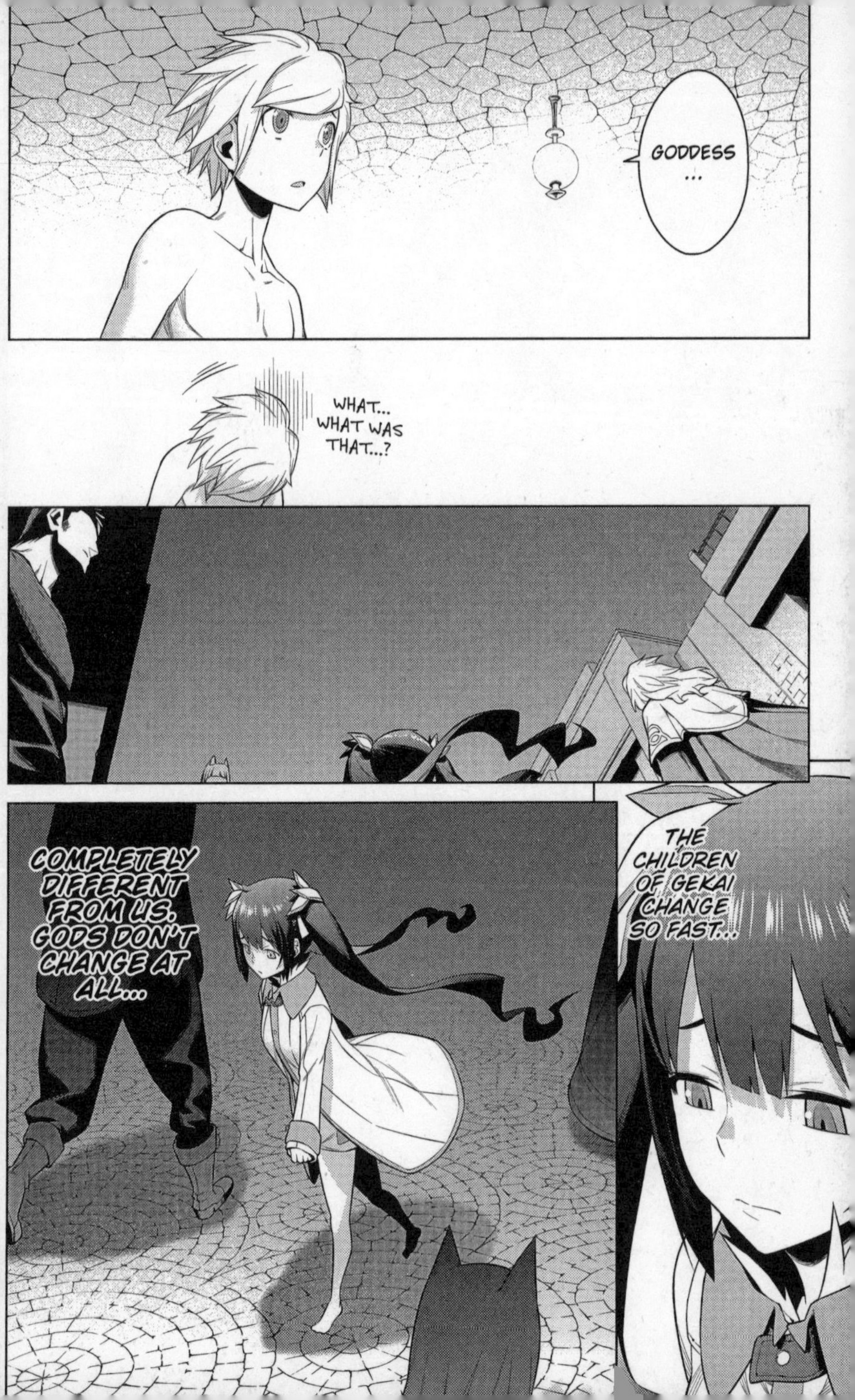
GODDESS ...
WHAT... WHAT WAS THAT...?
THE CHILDREN OF GEKAI CHANGE SO FAST...
COMPLETELY DIFFERENT FROM US. GODS DON'T CHANGE AT ALL...

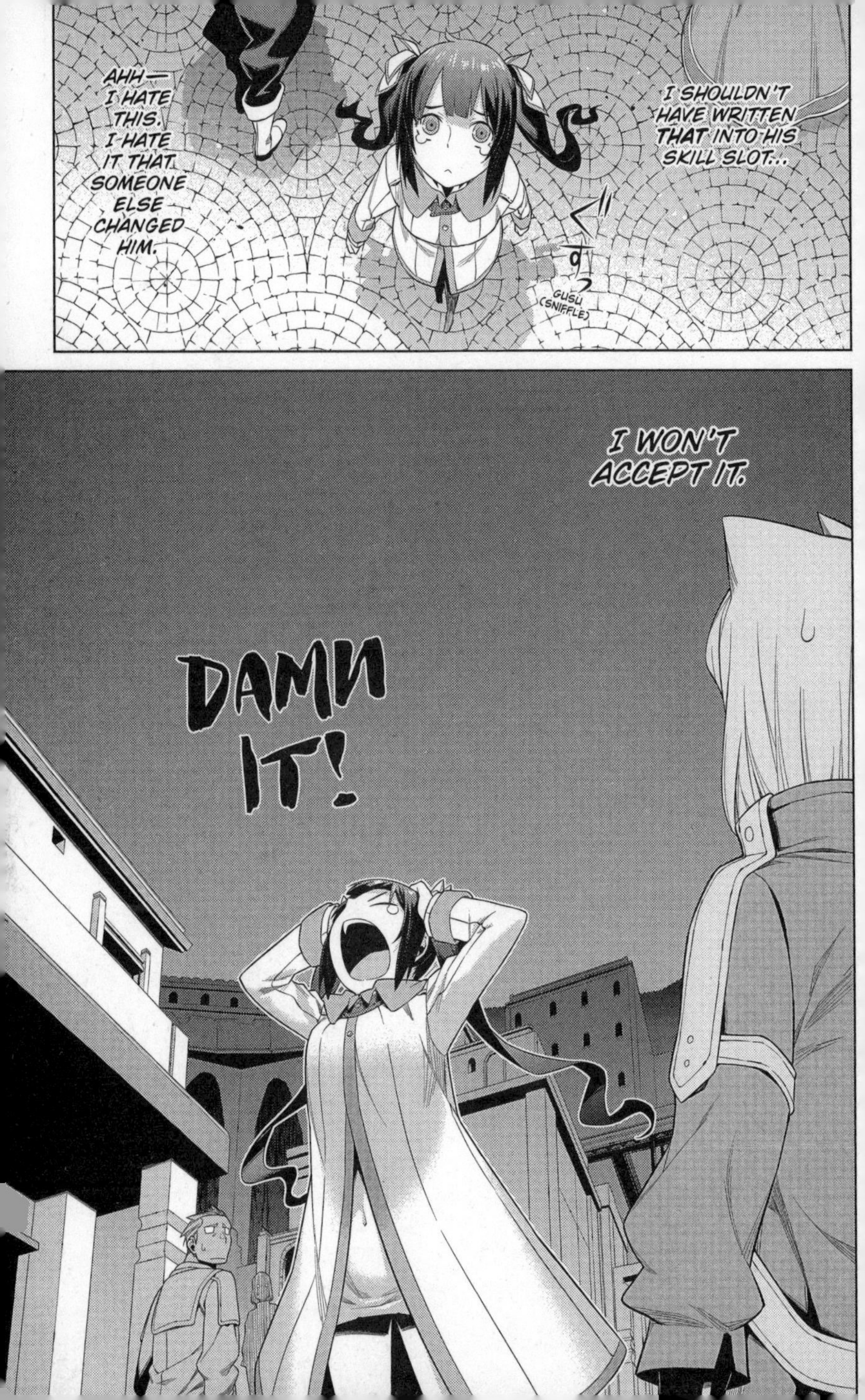
I SHOULDN'T HAVE WRITTEN THAT INTO HIS SKILL SLOT...
ぐすっ
GUSU (SNIFFLE)
AHH— I HATE THIS. I HATE IT THAT SOMEONE ELSE CHANGED HIM.
I WON'T ACCEPT IT.
DAMN IT!

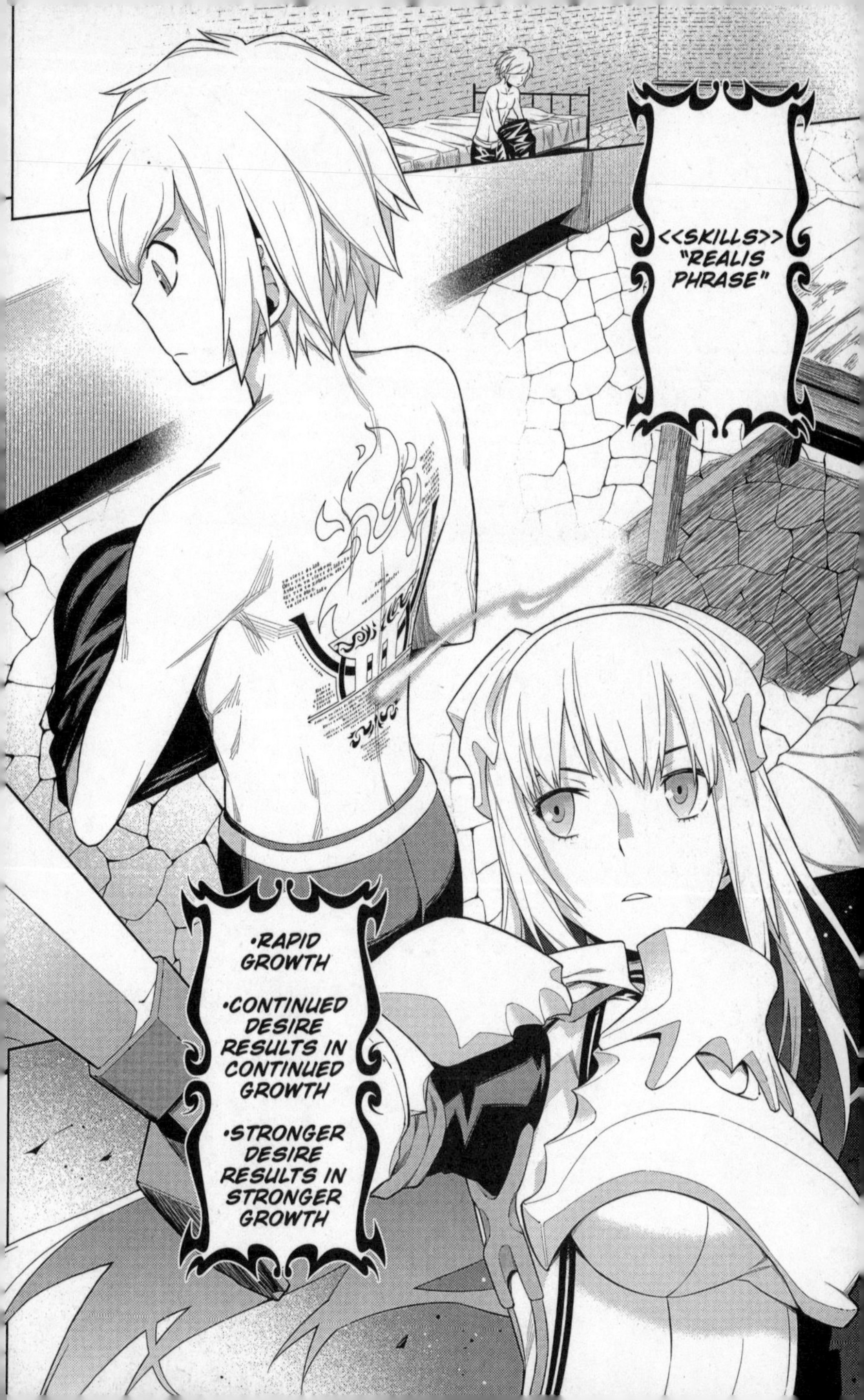

<<SKILLS>>
"REALIS PHRASE"
•RAPID GROWTH
•CONTINUED DESIRE RESULTS IN CONTINUED GROWTH
•STRONGER DESIRE RESULTS IN STRONGER GROWTH

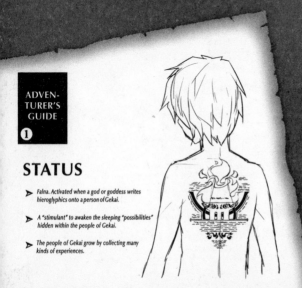

STATUS

➤ *Falna. Activated when a god or goddess writes hieroglyphics onto a person of Gekai.*

➤ *A "stimulant" to awaken the sleeping "possibilities" hidden within the people of Gekai.*

➤ *The people of Gekai grow by collecting many kinds of experiences.*

ADVEN-
TURER'S
GUIDE
2

ABILITY

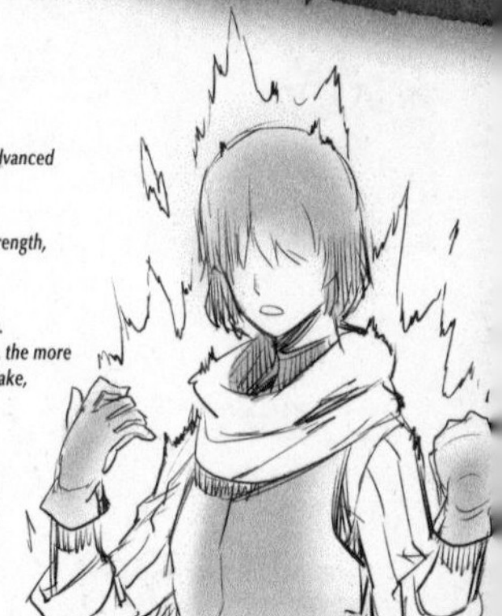

- *There are two types: "Basic Abilities" and "Advanced Abilities."*
- *"Basic Abilities" consist of five categories: Strength, Defense, Utility, Agility, and Magic.*
- *These grow by amount of experience in each. For example, the more an adventurer attacks, the more their Strength will grow. The more hits they take, the more their Defense will grow, and so on.*
- *"Advanced Abilities" activate when an adventurer levels up. They can choose what skill to learn, but their options are limited to their experience levels.*
- *They are specialized improvements focused on an adventurer's profession.*

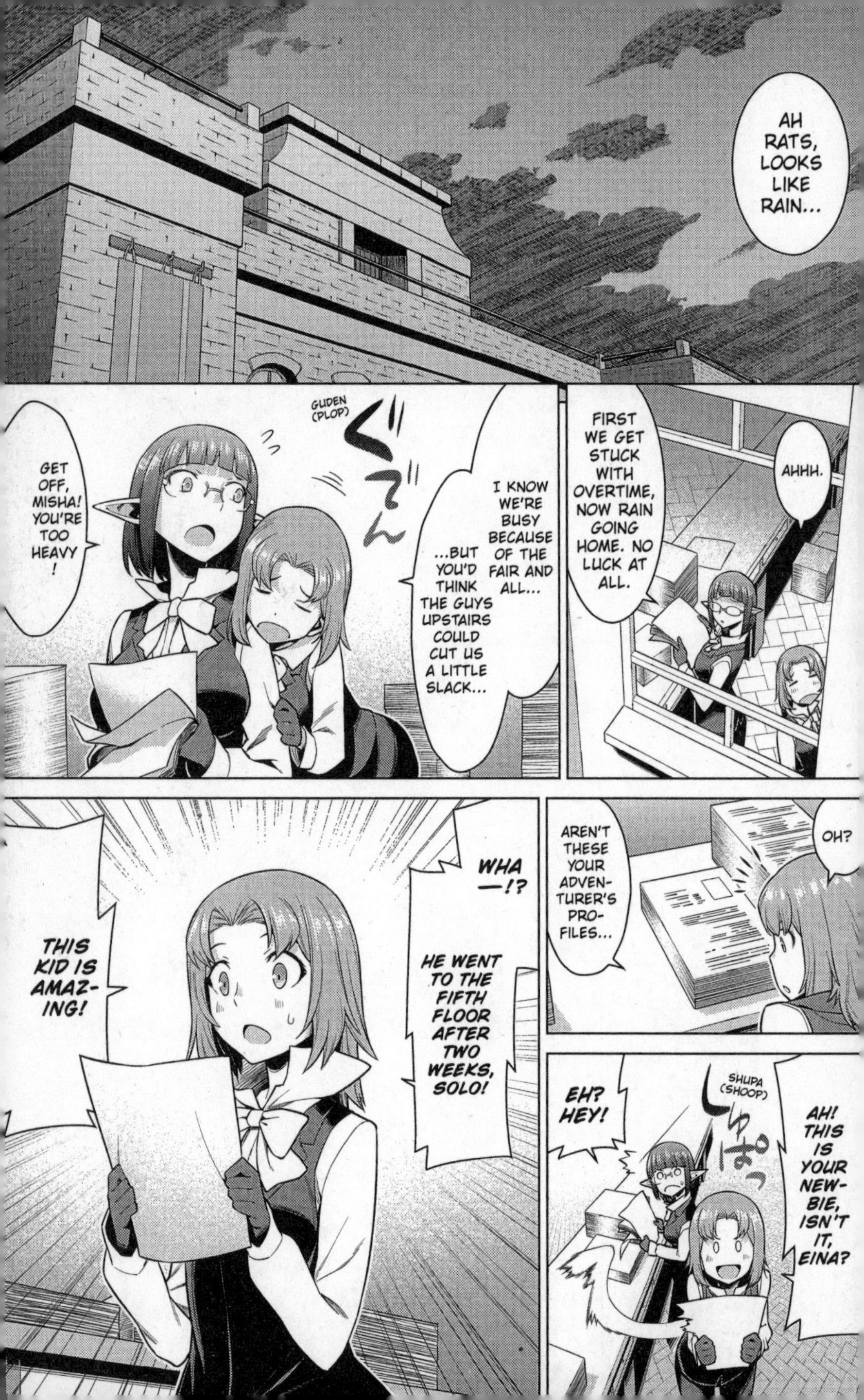
AH RATS, LOOKS LIKE RAIN...
AHHH.
FIRST WE GET STUCK WITH OVERTIME, NOW RAIN GOING HOME. NO LUCK AT ALL.
I KNOW WE'RE BUSY BECAUSE OF THE FAIR AND ALL...
...BUT YOU'D THINK THE GUYS UPSTAIRS COULD CUT US A LITTLE SLACK...
ぐでん
GUDEN (PLOP)
GET OFF, MISHA! YOU'RE TOO HEAVY!
OH?
AREN'T THESE YOUR ADVEN-TURER'S PRO-FILES...
AH! THIS IS YOUR NEW-BIE, ISN'T IT, EINA?
しゅぱっ
SHUPA (SHOOP)
EH? HEY!
WHA—!?
HE WENT TO THE FIFTH FLOOR AFTER TWO WEEKS, SOLO!
THIS KID IS AMAZ-ING!

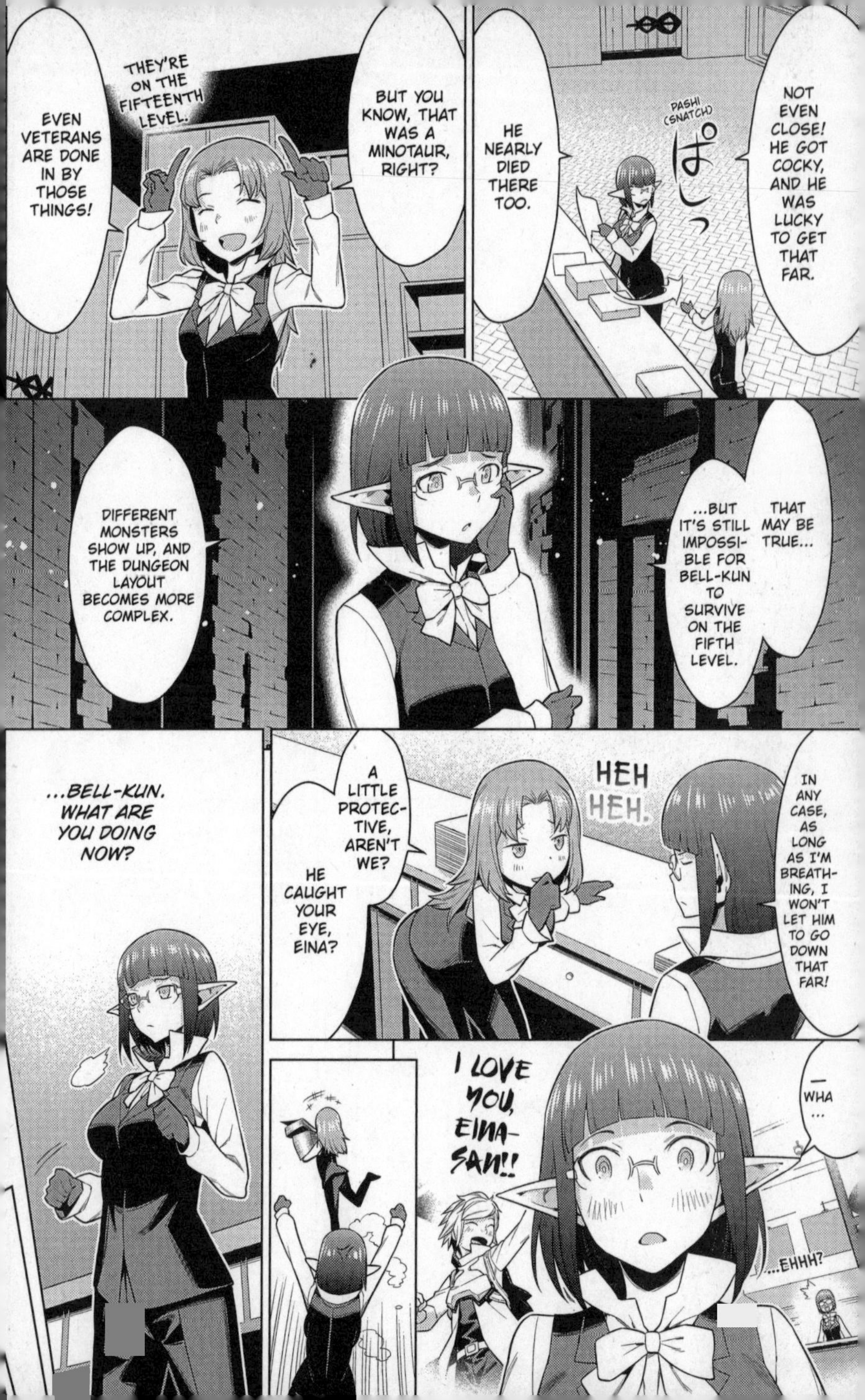
NOT EVEN CLOSE! HE GOT COCKY, AND HE WAS LUCKY TO GET THAT FAR.
PASHI (SNATCH)
ぱしっ
HE NEARLY DIED THERE TOO.
BUT YOU KNOW, THAT WAS A MINOTAUR, RIGHT?
THEY'RE ON THE FIFTEENTH LEVEL.
EVEN VETERANS ARE DONE IN BY THOSE THINGS!
THAT MAY BE TRUE...
...BUT IT'S STILL IMPOSSIBLE FOR BELL-KUN TO SURVIVE ON THE FIFTH LEVEL.
DIFFERENT MONSTERS SHOW UP, AND THE DUNGEON LAYOUT BECOMES MORE COMPLEX.
IN ANY CASE, AS LONG AS I'M BREATHING, I WON'T LET HIM TO GO DOWN THAT FAR!
HEH HEH.
A LITTLE PROTECTIVE, AREN'T WE?
HE CAUGHT YOUR EYE, EINA?
—WHA...
...EHHH?
I LOVE YOU, EINA-SAN!!
...BELL-KUN. WHAT ARE YOU DOING NOW?

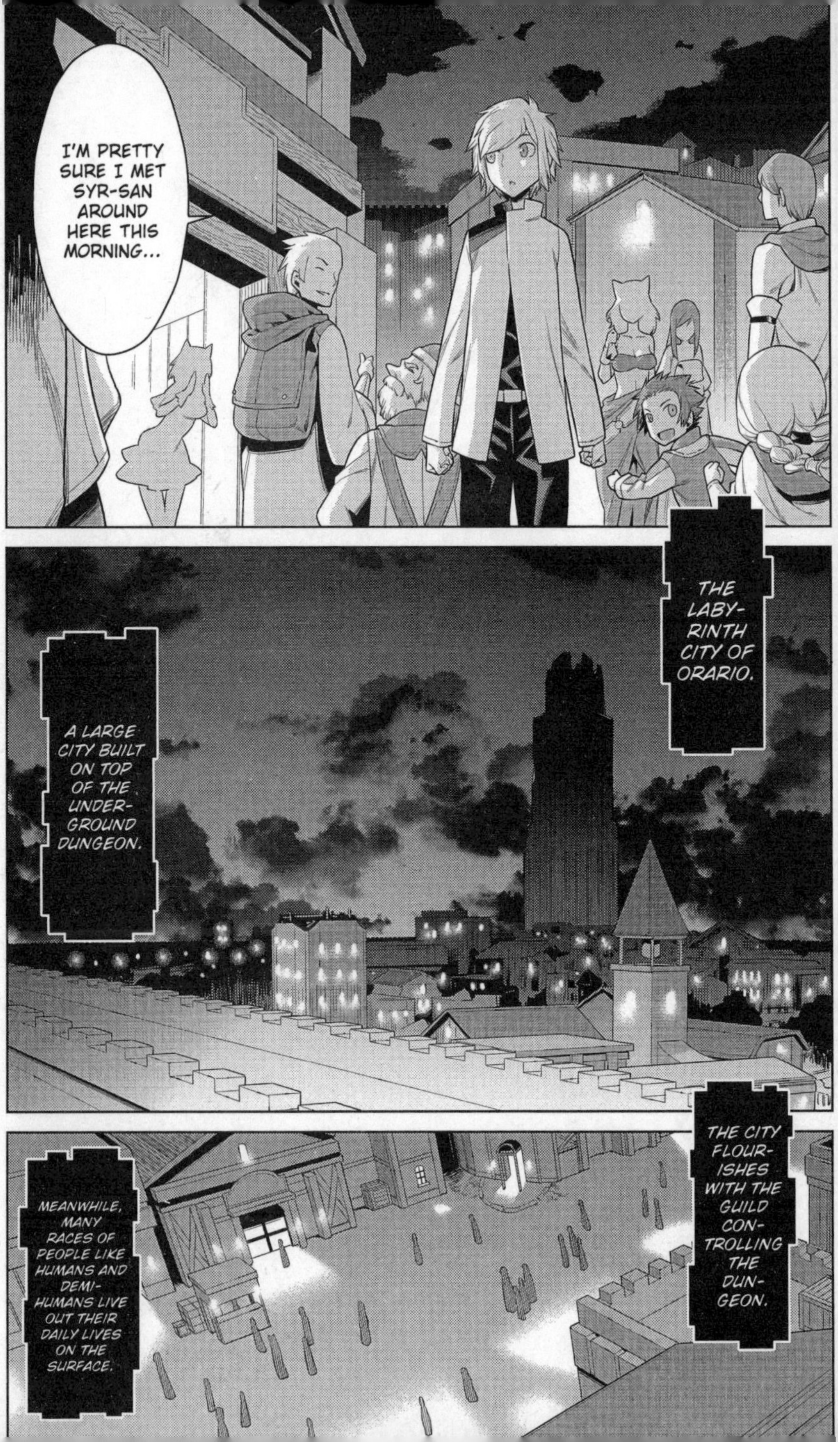
I'M PRETTY SURE I MET SYR-SAN AROUND HERE THIS MORNING...
THE LABYRINTH CITY OF ORARIO.
A LARGE CITY BUILT ON TOP OF THE UNDERGROUND DUNGEON.
THE CITY FLOURISHES WITH THE GUILD CONTROLLING THE DUNGEON.
MEANWHILE, MANY RACES OF PEOPLE LIKE HUMANS AND DEMI-HUMANS LIVE OUT THEIR DAILY LIVES ON THE SURFACE.

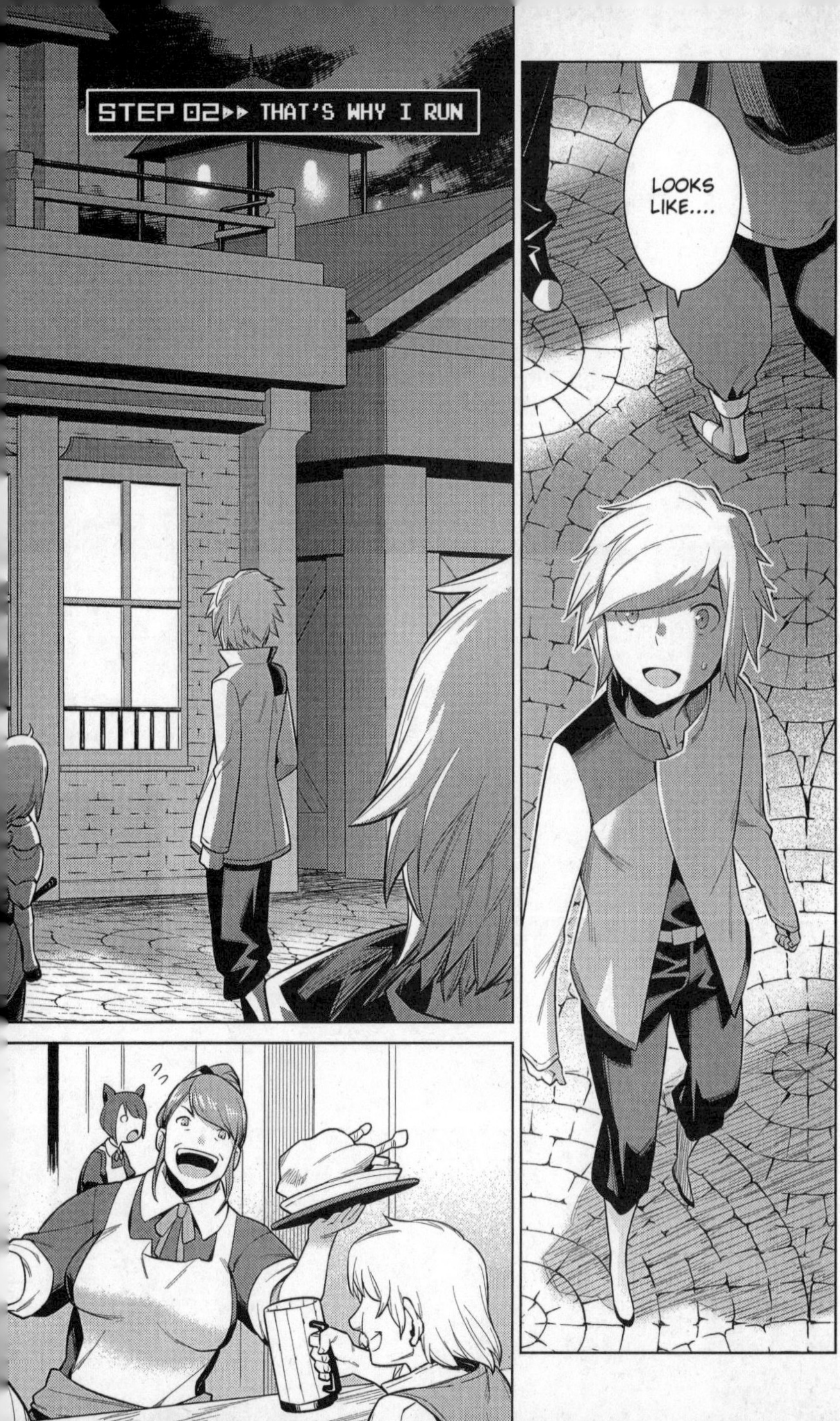
LOOKS LIKE....
STEP 02▸▸ THAT'S WHY I RUN

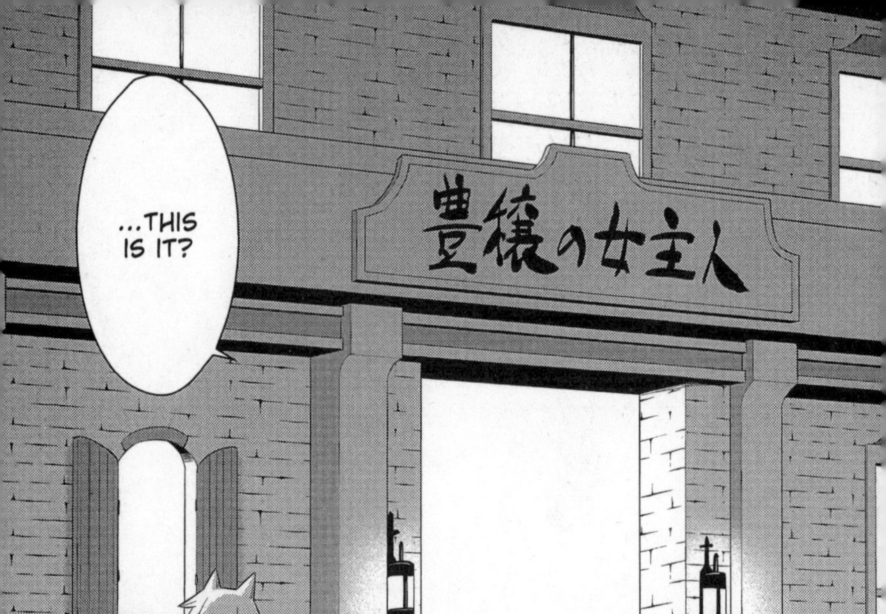
豊穣の女主人
...THIS IS IT?

SIGN: THE BENEVOLENT MISTRESS

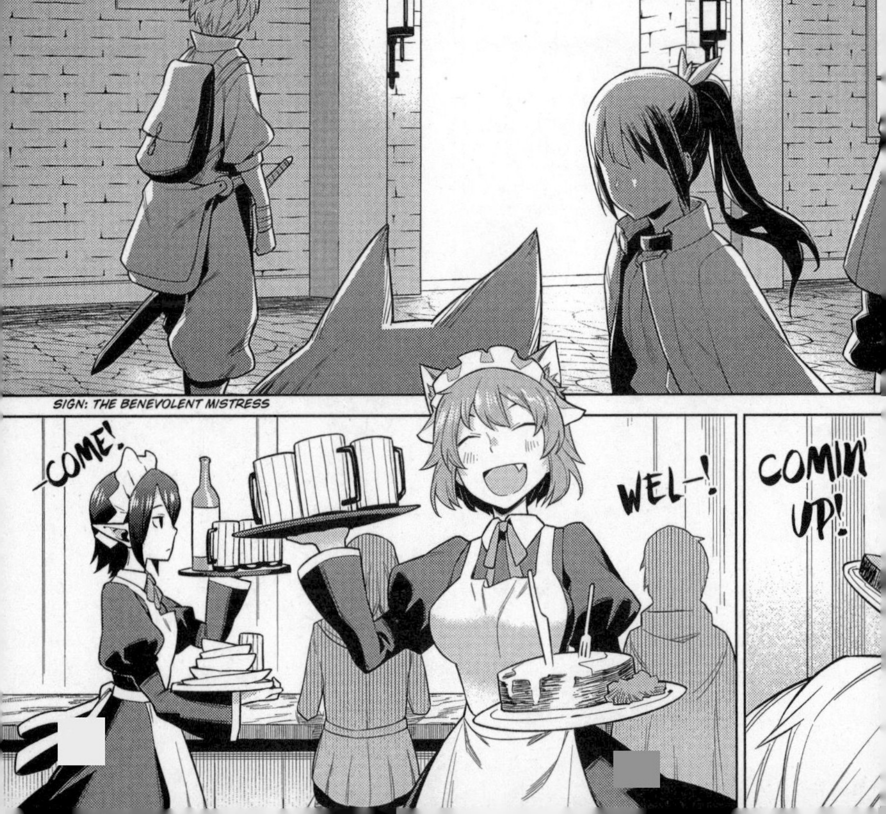
COMIN' UP!
WEL-!
-COME!

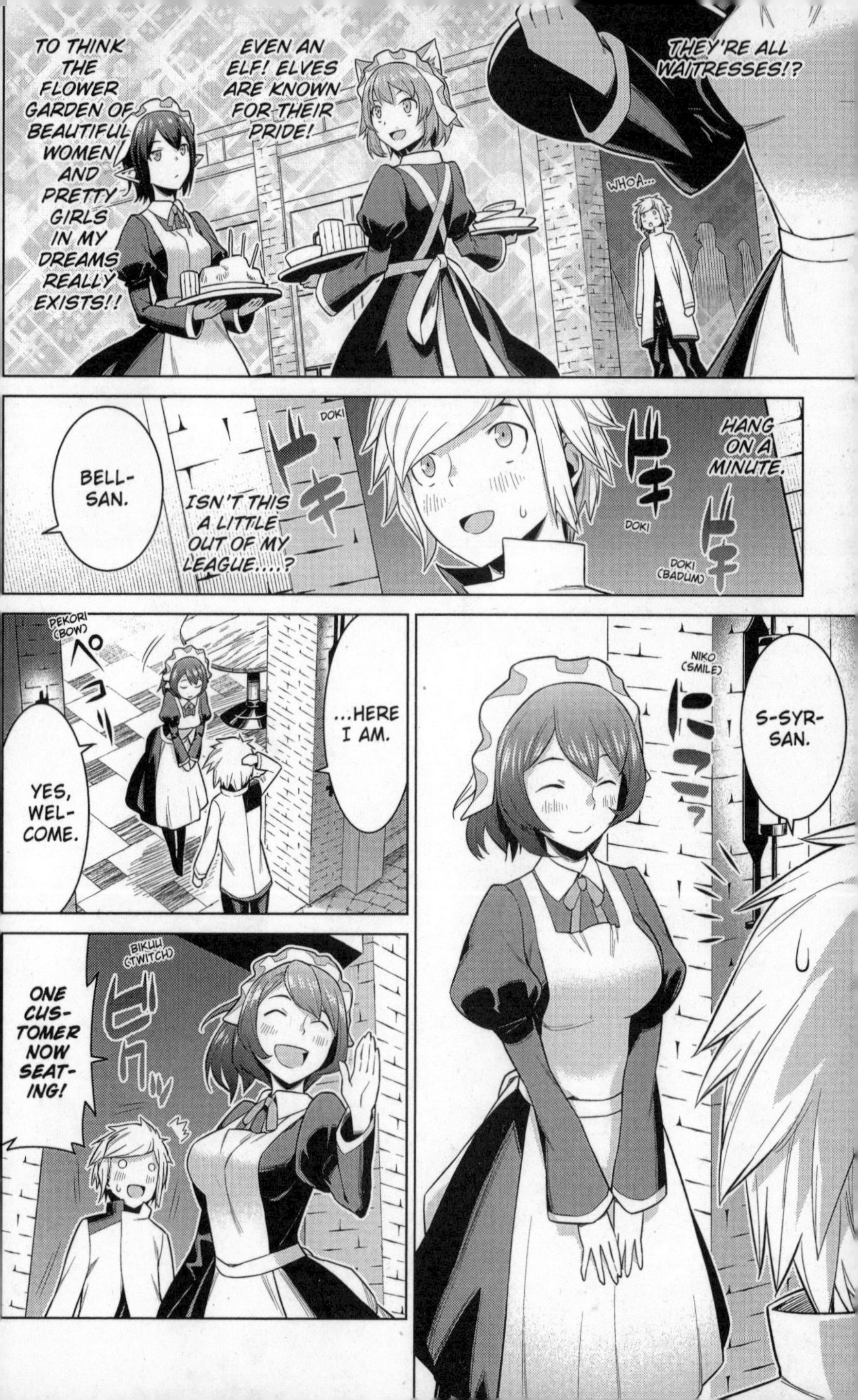
THEY'RE ALL WAITRESSES!?
WHOA...
EVEN AN ELF! ELVES ARE KNOWN FOR THEIR PRIDE!
TO THINK THE FLOWER GARDEN OF BEAUTIFUL WOMEN AND PRETTY GIRLS IN MY DREAMS REALLY EXISTS!!
HANG ON A MINUTE.
DOKI
DOKI (BADUM)
DOKI
ISN'T THIS A LITTLE OUT OF MY LEAGUE....?
BELL-SAN.
S-SYR-SAN.
NIKO (SMILE)
...HERE I AM.
PEKORI (BOW)
YES, WEL-COME.
BIKUU (TWITCH)
ONE CUS-TOMER NOW SEAT-ING!

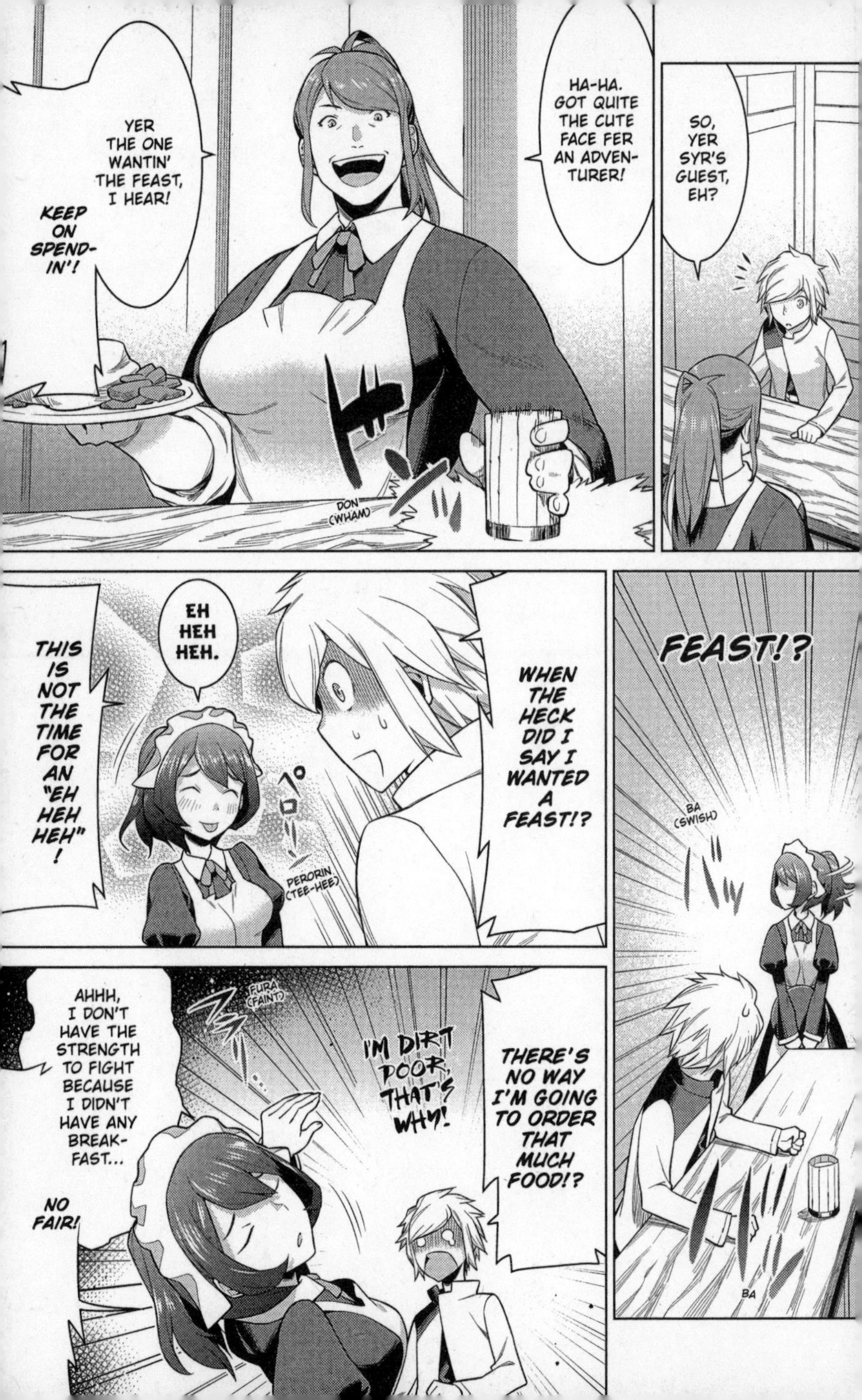

SO, YER SYR'S GUEST, EH?
HA-HA. GOT QUITE THE CUTE FACE FER AN ADVENTURER!
YER THE ONE WANTIN' THE FEAST, I HEAR!
KEEP ON SPENDIN'!
DON (WHAM)
FEAST!?
BA (SWISH)
BA
WHEN THE HECK DID I SAY I WANTED A FEAST!?
EH HEH HEH.
PERORIN (TEE-HEE)
THIS IS NOT THE TIME FOR AN "EH HEH HEH"!
THERE'S NO WAY I'M GOING TO ORDER THAT MUCH FOOD!?
I'M DIRT POOR, THAT'S WHY!
FURA (FAINT)
AHHH, I DON'T HAVE THE STRENGTH TO FIGHT BECAUSE I DIDN'T HAVE ANY BREAKFAST...
NO FAIR!

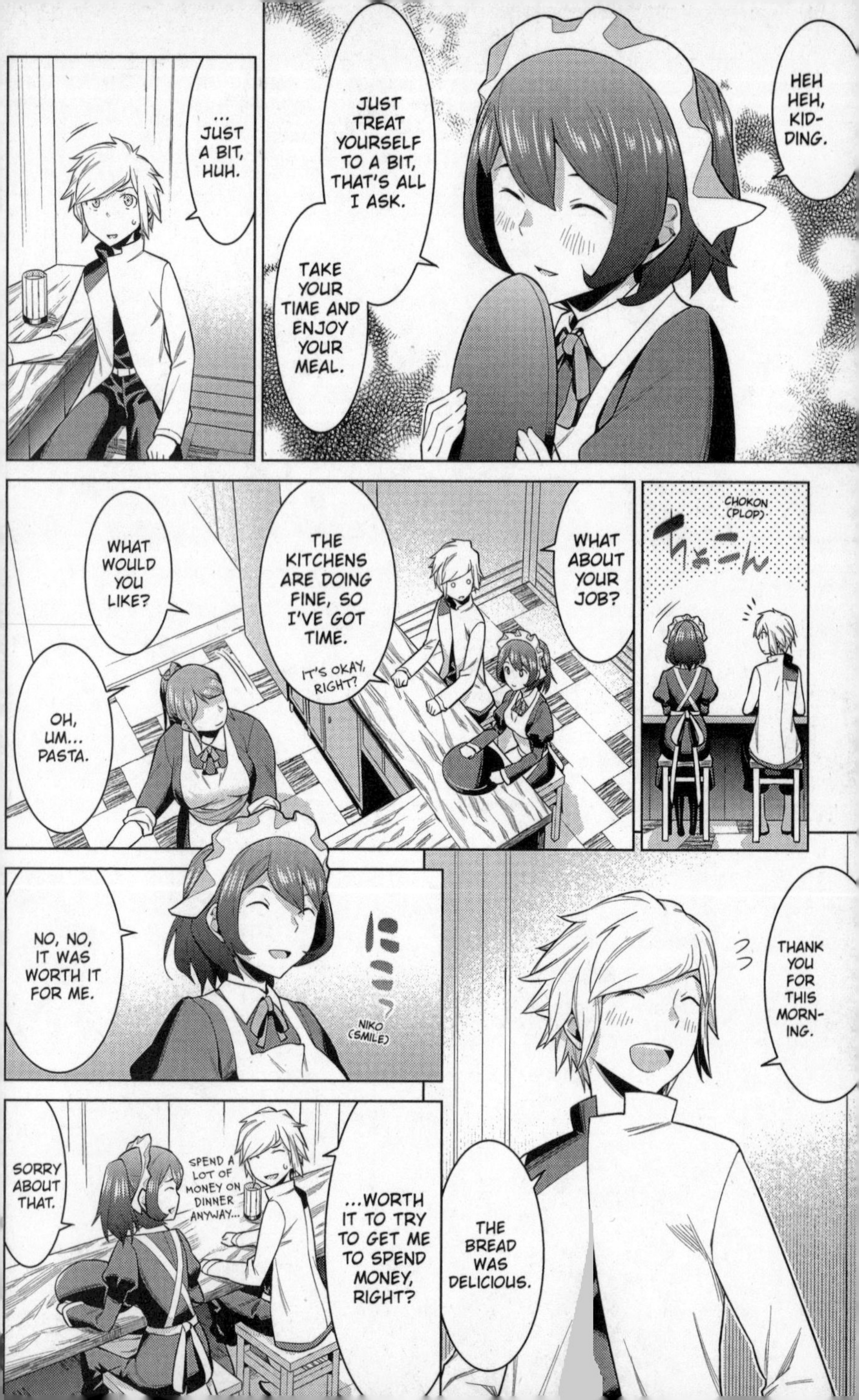

HEH HEH, KID-DING.
JUST TREAT YOURSELF TO A BIT, THAT'S ALL I ASK.
TAKE YOUR TIME AND ENJOY YOUR MEAL.
...JUST A BIT, HUH.
ちょこん
CHOKON (PLOP)
WHAT ABOUT YOUR JOB?
THE KITCHENS ARE DOING FINE, SO I'VE GOT TIME.
IT'S OKAY, RIGHT?
WHAT WOULD YOU LIKE?
OH, UM... PASTA.
THANK YOU FOR THIS MORN-ING.
THE BREAD WAS DELICIOUS.
NO, NO, IT WAS WORTH IT FOR ME.
にこっ
NIKO (SMILE)
...WORTH IT TO TRY TO GET ME TO SPEND MONEY, RIGHT?
SORRY ABOUT THAT.
SPEND A LOT OF MONEY ON DINNER ANYWAY...

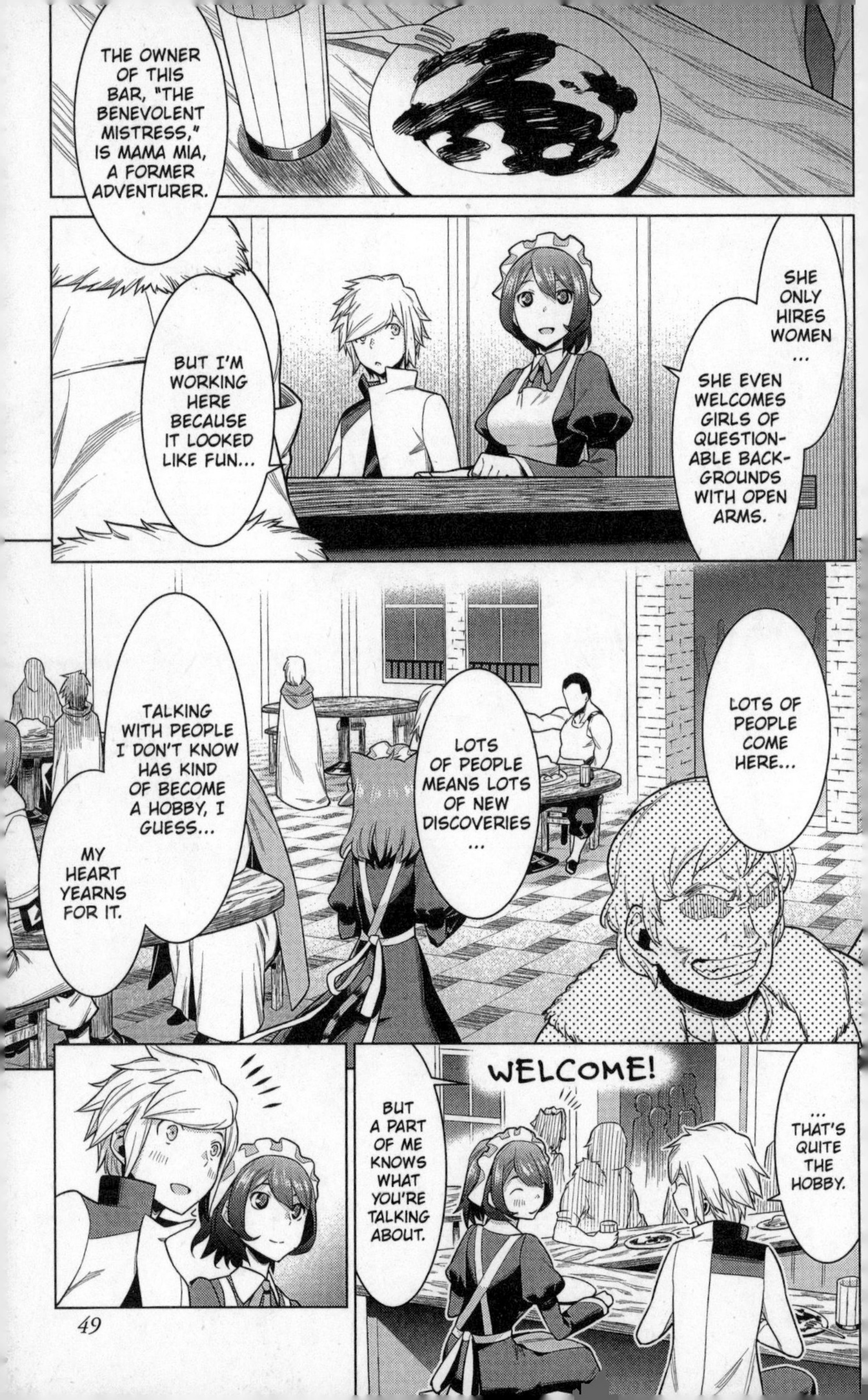
THE OWNER OF THIS BAR, "THE BENEVOLENT MISTRESS," IS MAMA MIA, A FORMER ADVENTURER.
SHE ONLY HIRES WOMEN ...
SHE EVEN WELCOMES GIRLS OF QUESTION-ABLE BACK-GROUNDS WITH OPEN ARMS.
BUT I'M WORKING HERE BECAUSE IT LOOKED LIKE FUN...
LOTS OF PEOPLE COME HERE...
LOTS OF PEOPLE MEANS LOTS OF NEW DISCOVERIES ...
TALKING WITH PEOPLE I DON'T KNOW HAS KIND OF BECOME A HOBBY, I GUESS...
MY HEART YEARNS FOR IT.
... THAT'S QUITE THE HOBBY.
WELCOME!
BUT A PART OF ME KNOWS WHAT YOU'RE TALKING ABOUT.

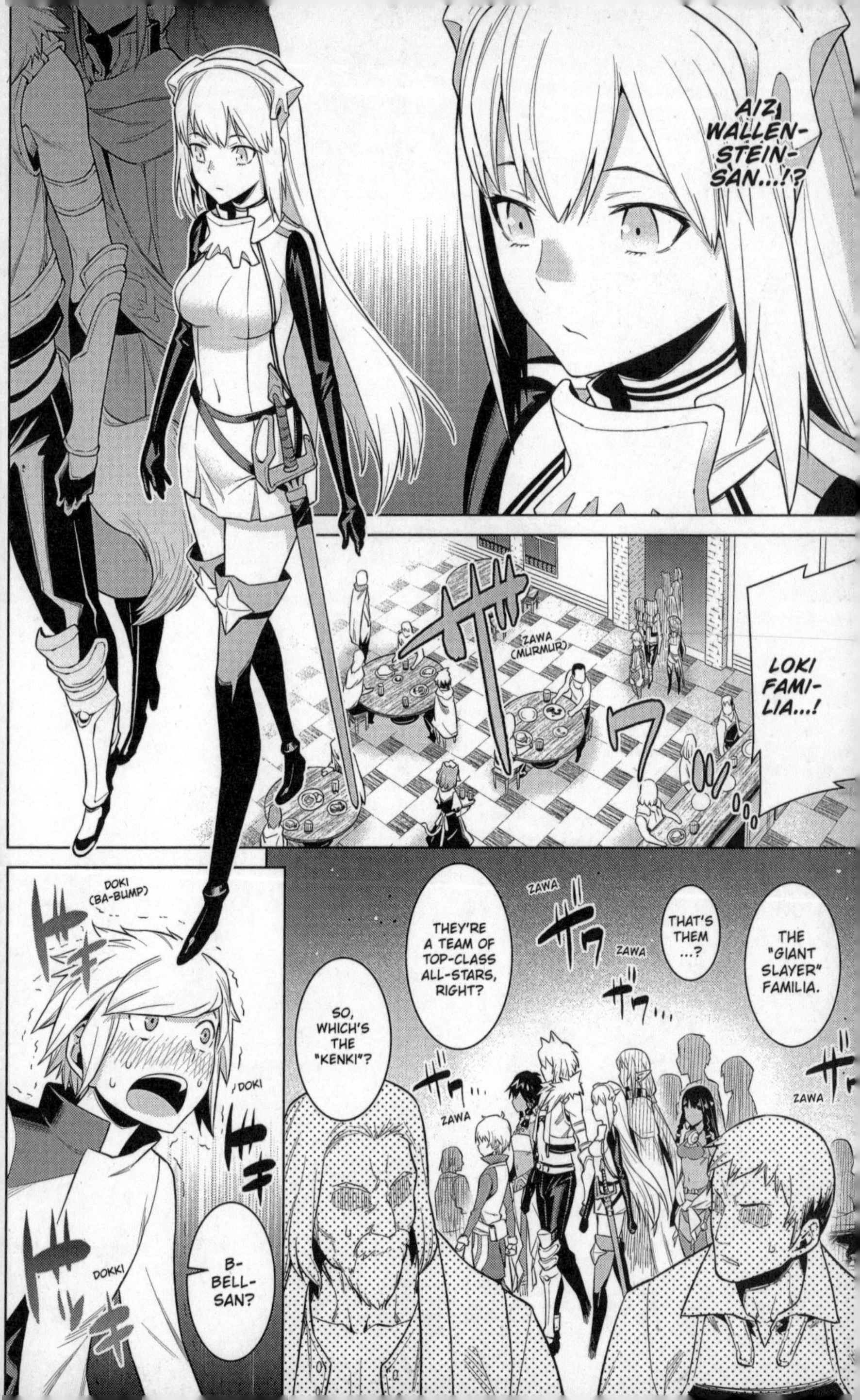
AIZ WALLEN-STEIN-SAN...!?
LOKI FAMI-LIA...!
ZAWA (MURMUR)
THE "GIANT SLAYER" FAMILIA.
THAT'S THEM ...?
ZAWA
ZAWA
THEY'RE A TEAM OF TOP-CLASS ALL-STARS, RIGHT?
SO, WHICH'S THE "KENKI"?
ZAWA
ZAWA
DOKI (BA-BUMP)
DOKI
B-BELL-SAN?
DOKKI

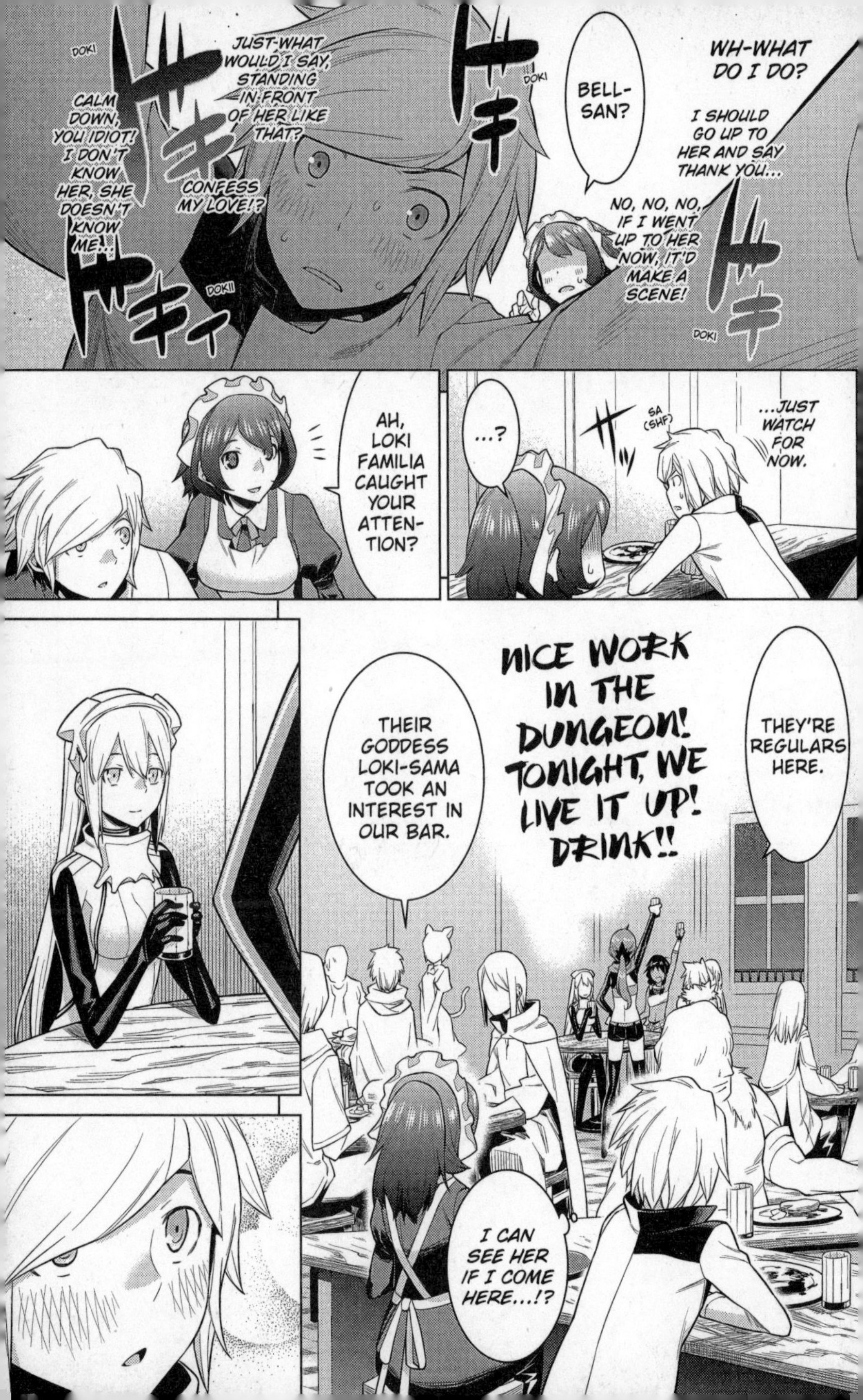
WH-WHAT DO I DO?
I SHOULD GO UP TO HER AND SAY THANK YOU...
BELL-SAN?
NO, NO, NO, IF I WENT UP TO HER NOW, IT'D MAKE A SCENE!
DOKI
DOKI
JUST-WHAT WOULD I SAY, STANDING IN FRONT OF HER LIKE THAT?
CONFESS MY LOVE!?
DOKI
CALM DOWN, YOU IDIOT! I DON'T KNOW HER, SHE DOESN'T KNOW ME...
DOKI!
...JUST WATCH FOR NOW.
SA (SHF)
...?
AH, LOKI FAMILIA CAUGHT YOUR ATTENTION?
THEY'RE REGULARS HERE.
NICE WORK IN THE DUNGEON! TONIGHT, WE LIVE IT UP! DRINK!!
THEIR GODDESS LOKI-SAMA TOOK AN INTEREST IN OUR BAR.
I CAN SEE HER IF I COME HERE...!?

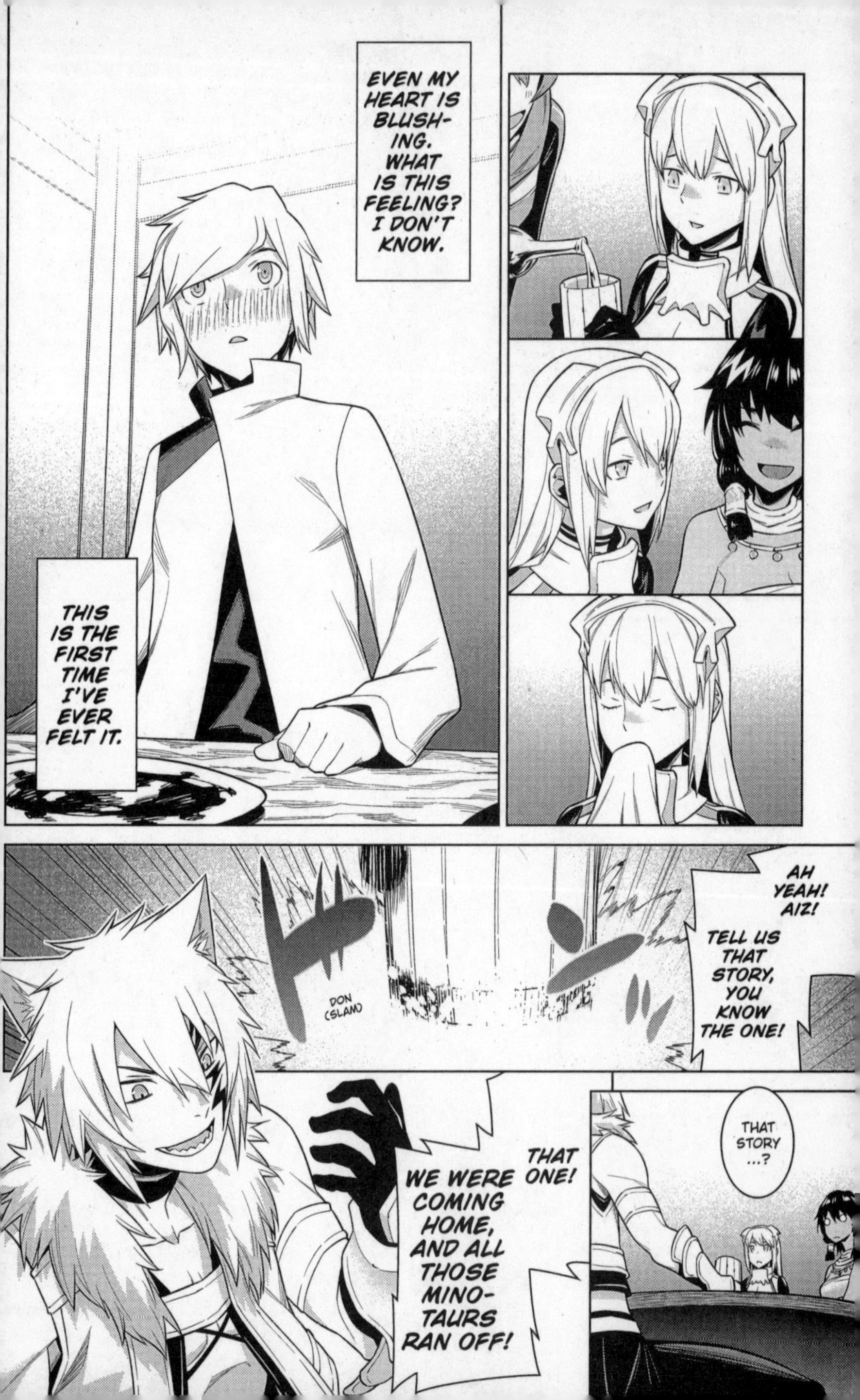
EVEN MY HEART IS BLUSHING. WHAT IS THIS FEELING? I DON'T KNOW.
THIS IS THE FIRST TIME I'VE EVER FELT IT.
AH YEAH! AIZ!
TELL US THAT STORY, YOU KNOW THE ONE!
DON (SLAM)
THAT STORY ...?
THAT ONE!
WE WERE COMING HOME, AND ALL THOSE MINOTAURS RAN OFF!

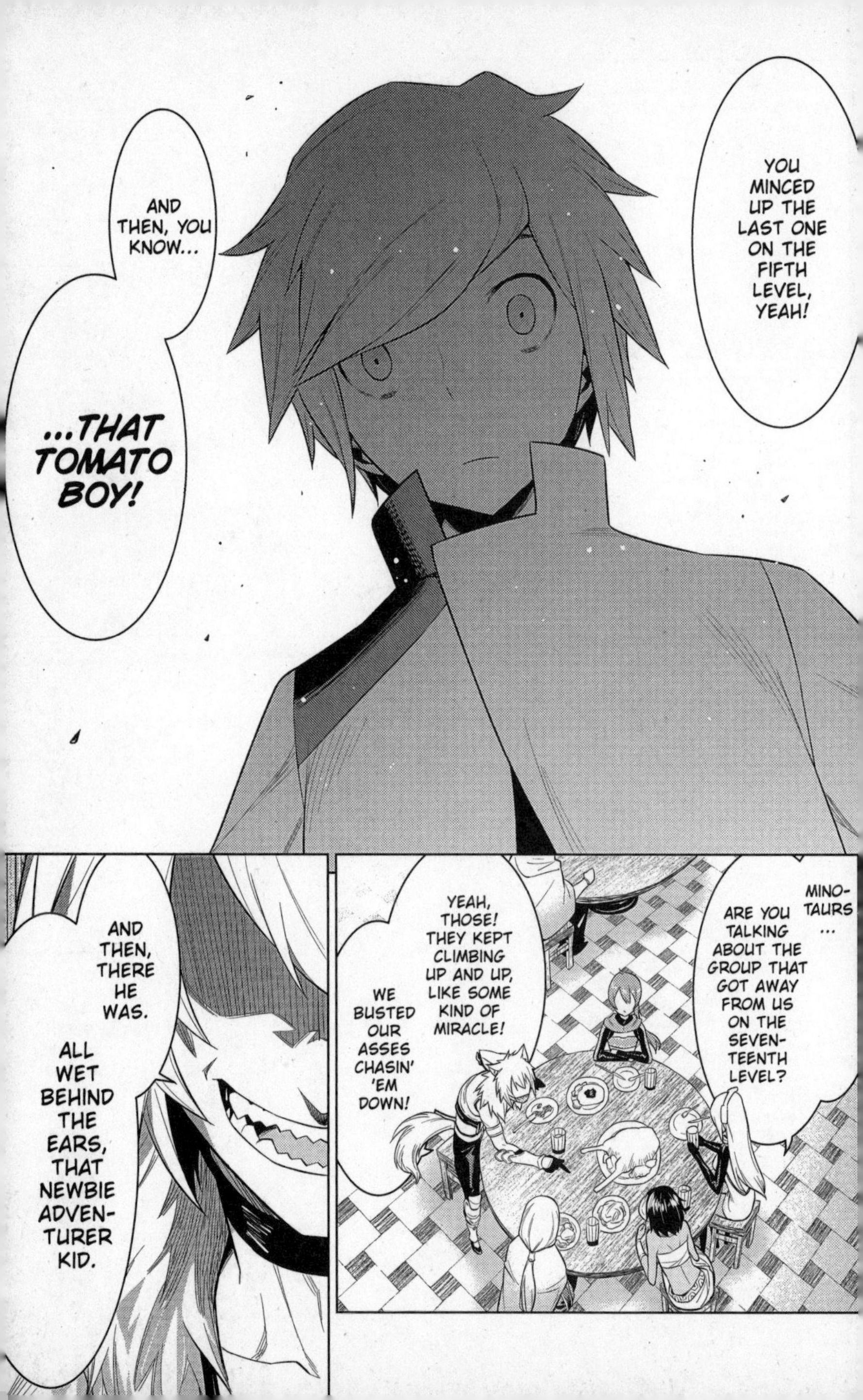
YOU MINCED UP THE LAST ONE ON THE FIFTH LEVEL, YEAH!
AND THEN, YOU KNOW...
...THAT TOMATO BOY!
MINO-TAURS...
ARE YOU TALKING ABOUT THE GROUP THAT GOT AWAY FROM US ON THE SEVEN-TEENTH LEVEL?
YEAH, THOSE! THEY KEPT CLIMBING UP AND UP, LIKE SOME KIND OF MIRACLE!
WE BUSTED OUR ASSES CHASIN' 'EM DOWN!
AND THEN, THERE HE WAS.
ALL WET BEHIND THE EARS, THAT NEWBIE ADVEN-TURER KID.

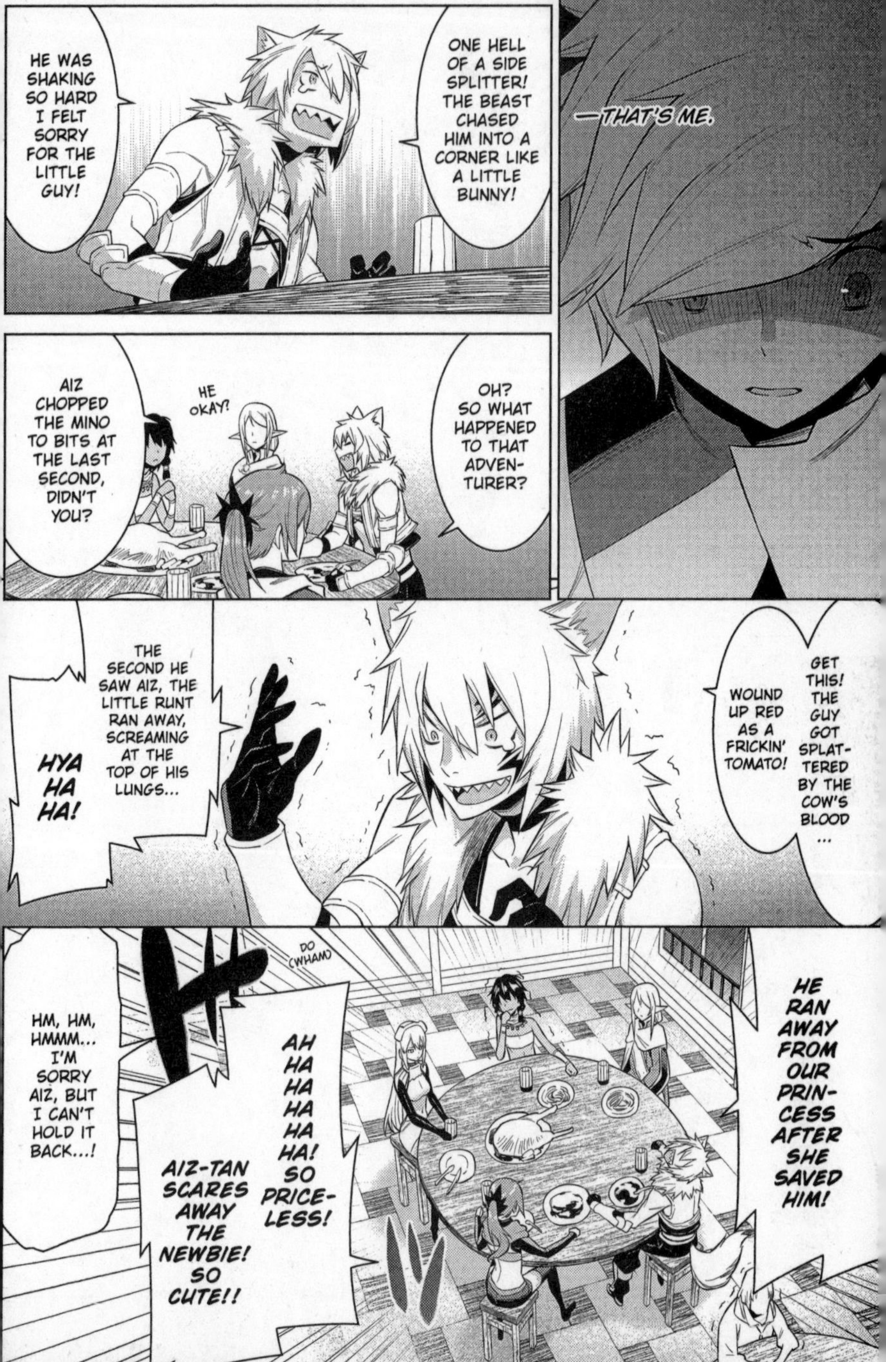
—THAT'S ME.
ONE HELL OF A SIDE SPLITTER! THE BEAST CHASED HIM INTO A CORNER LIKE A LITTLE BUNNY!
HE WAS SHAKING SO HARD I FELT SORRY FOR THE LITTLE GUY!
OH? SO WHAT HAPPENED TO THAT ADVEN-TURER?
HE OKAY?
AIZ CHOPPED THE MINO TO BITS AT THE LAST SECOND, DIDN'T YOU?
GET THIS! THE GUY GOT SPLAT-TERED BY THE COW'S BLOOD ...
WOUND UP RED AS A FRICKIN' TOMATO!
THE SECOND HE SAW AIZ, THE LITTLE RUNT RAN AWAY, SCREAMING AT THE TOP OF HIS LUNGS...
HYA HA HA!
HE RAN AWAY FROM OUR PRIN-CESS AFTER SHE SAVED HIM!
DO (WHAM)
AH HA HA HA HA HA! SO PRICE-LESS!
AIZ-TAN SCARES AWAY THE NEWBIE! SO CUTE!!
HM, HM, HMMM... I'M SORRY AIZ, BUT I CAN'T HOLD IT BACK...!

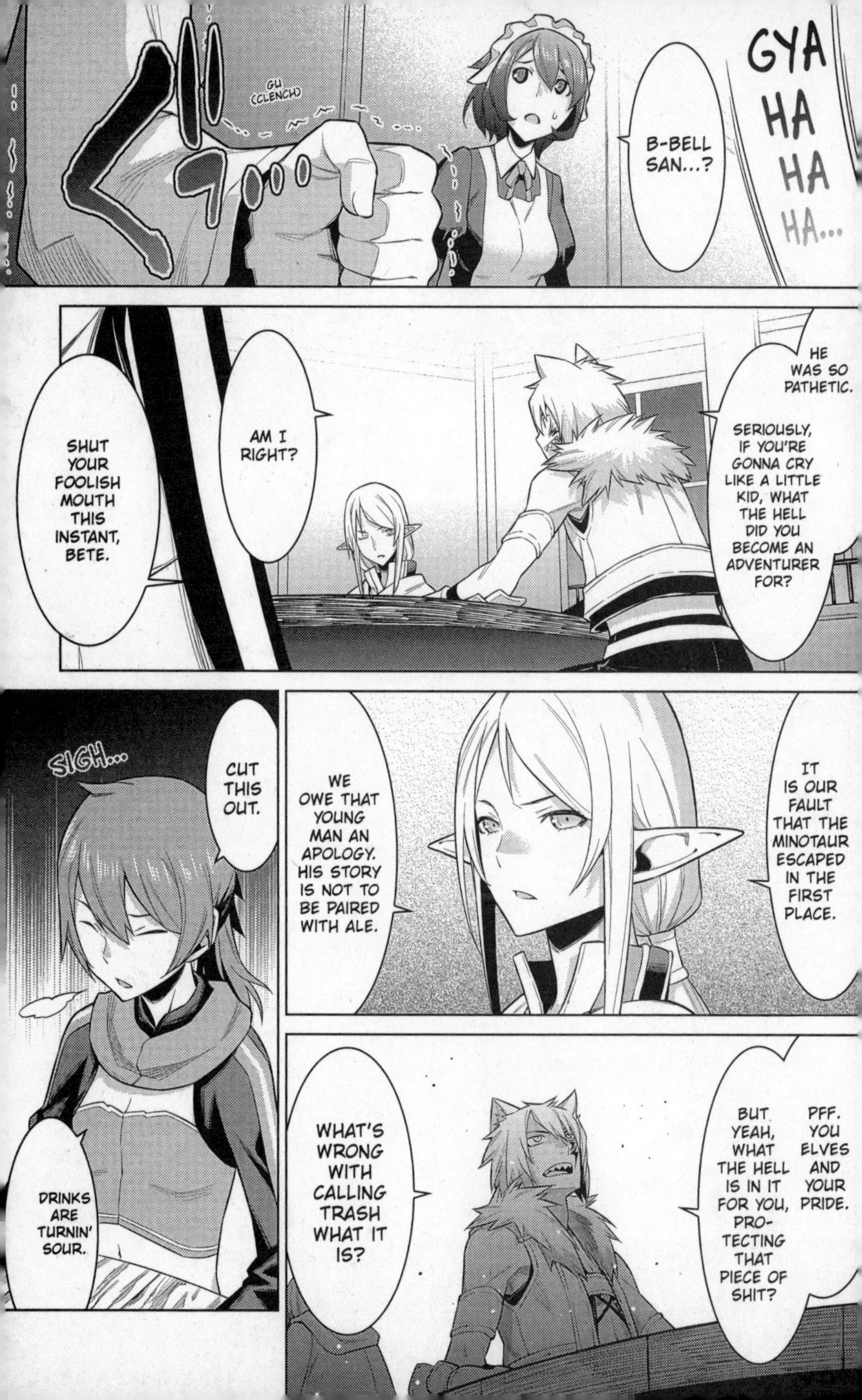
GYA HA HA HA HA...
B-BELL SAN...?
GU (CLENCH)
HE WAS SO PATHETIC.
SERIOUSLY, IF YOU'RE GONNA CRY LIKE A LITTLE KID, WHAT THE HELL DID YOU BECOME AN ADVENTURER FOR?
AM I RIGHT?
SHUT YOUR FOOLISH MOUTH THIS INSTANT, BETE.
IT IS OUR FAULT THAT THE MINOTAUR ESCAPED IN THE FIRST PLACE.
WE OWE THAT YOUNG MAN AN APOLOGY. HIS STORY IS NOT TO BE PAIRED WITH ALE.
PFF. YOU ELVES AND YOUR PRIDE.
BUT YEAH, WHAT THE HELL IS IN IT FOR YOU, PRO-TECTING THAT PIECE OF SHIT?
WHAT'S WRONG WITH CALLING TRASH WHAT IT IS?
CUT THIS OUT.
SIGH...
DRINKS ARE TURNIN' SOUR.

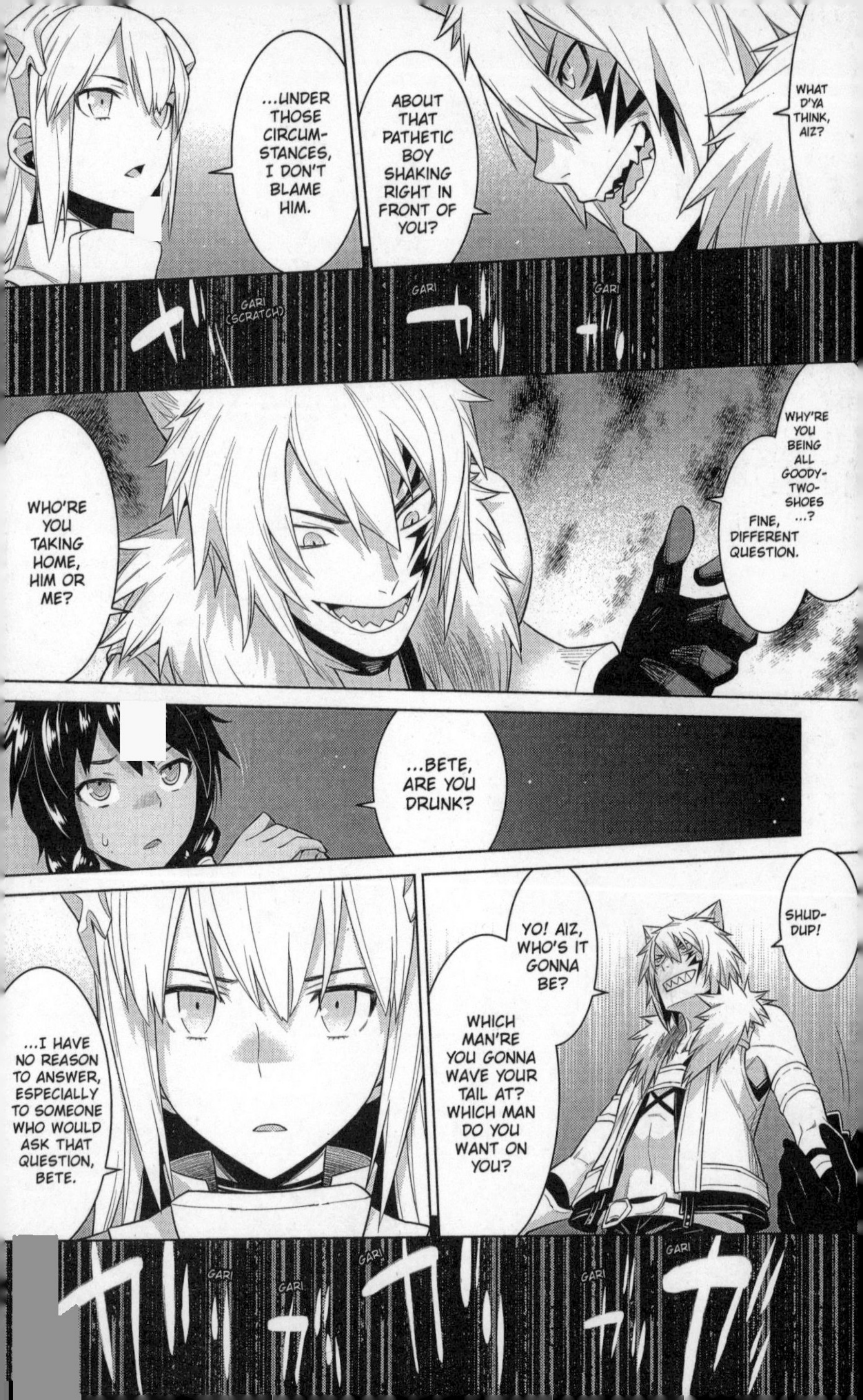
WHAT D'YA THINK, AIZ?
ABOUT THAT PATHETIC BOY SHAKING RIGHT IN FRONT OF YOU?
...UNDER THOSE CIRCUM-STANCES, I DON'T BLAME HIM.
GARI
GARI
GARI (SCRATCH)
WHY'RE YOU BEING ALL GOODY-TWO-SHOES ...?
FINE, DIFFERENT QUESTION.
WHO'RE YOU TAKING HOME, HIM OR ME?
...BETE, ARE YOU DRUNK?
SHUD-DUP!
YO! AIZ, WHO'S IT GONNA BE?
WHICH MAN'RE YOU GONNA WAVE YOUR TAIL AT? WHICH MAN DO YOU WANT ON YOU?
...I HAVE NO REASON TO ANSWER, ESPECIALLY TO SOMEONE WHO WOULD ASK THAT QUESTION, BETE.
GARI
GARI
GARI
GARI
GARI

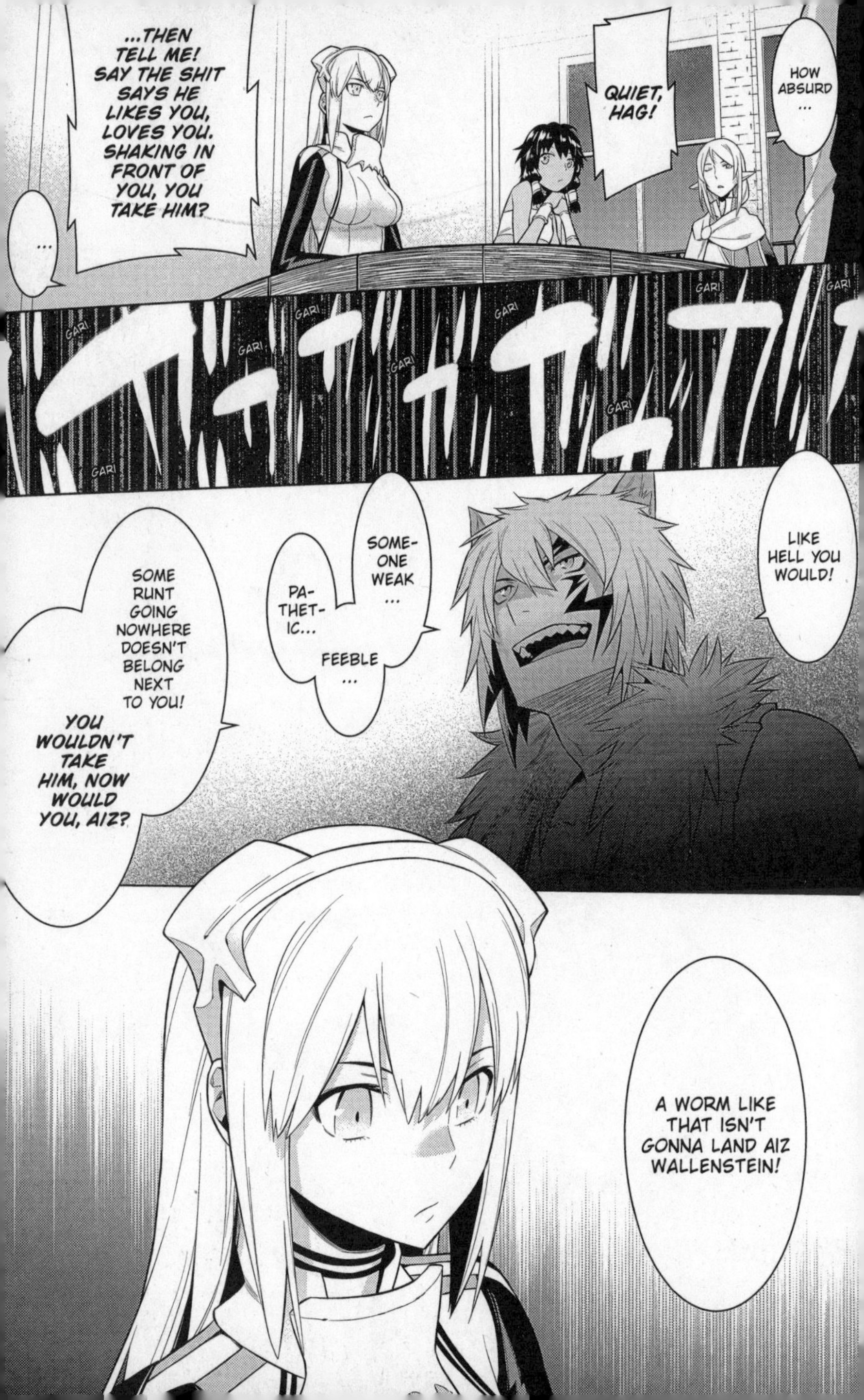
HOW ABSURD ...
QUIET, HAG!
...THEN TELL ME! SAY THE SHIT SAYS HE LIKES YOU, LOVES YOU. SHAKING IN FRONT OF YOU, YOU TAKE HIM?
...
GARI GARI GARI GARI GARI GARI GARI GARI GARI
LIKE HELL YOU WOULD!
SOME-ONE WEAK ...
PA-THET-IC...
FEEBLE ...
SOME RUNT GOING NOWHERE DOESN'T BELONG NEXT TO YOU!
YOU WOULDN'T TAKE HIM, NOW WOULD YOU, AIZ?
A WORM LIKE THAT ISN'T GONNA LAND AIZ WALLENSTEIN!

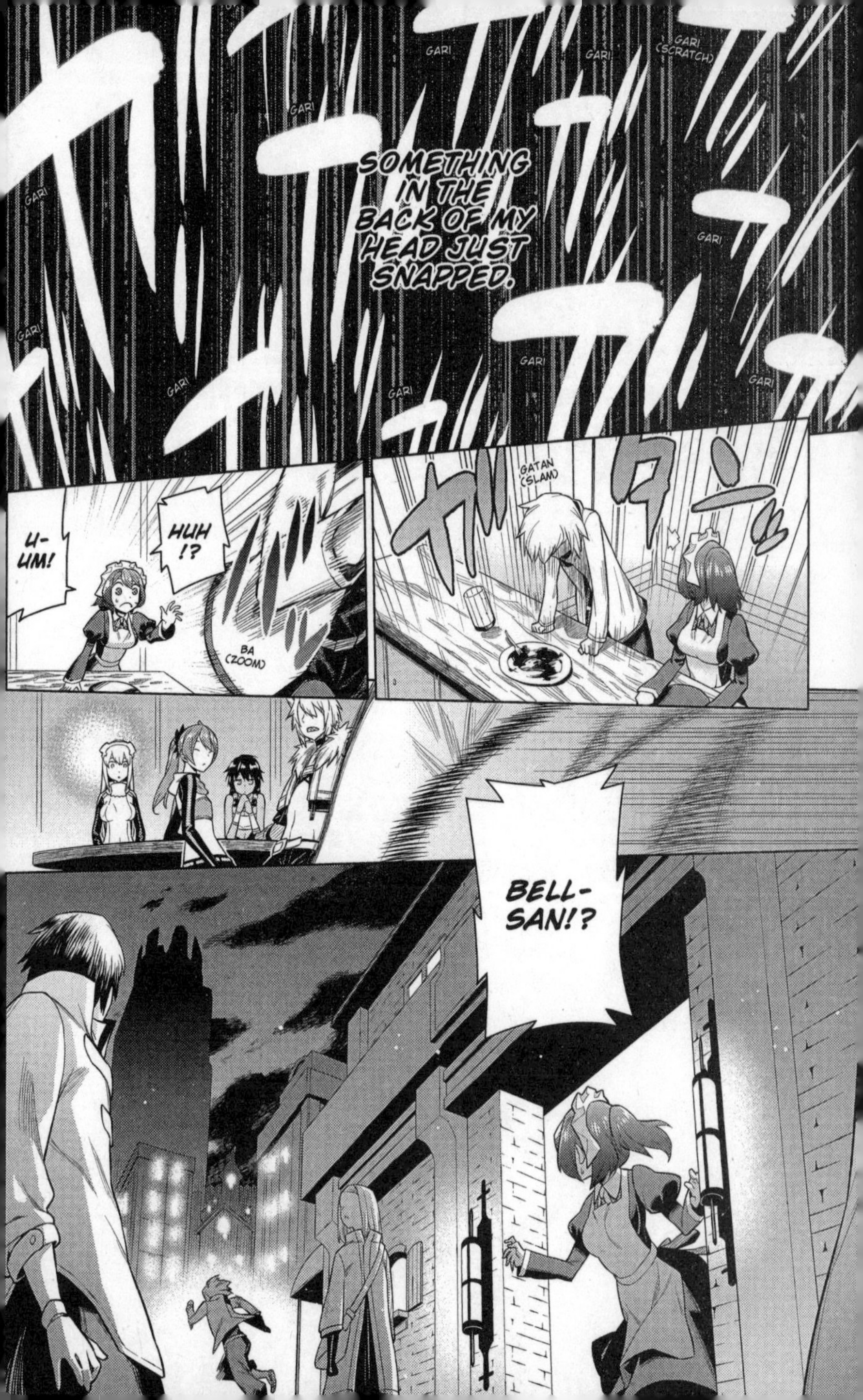
GARI (SCRATCH)
GARI
GARI
GARI
SOMETHING IN THE BACK OF MY HEAD JUST SNAPPED.
GARI
GARI
GARI
GARI
GARI
GARI
GATAN (SLAM)
HUH!?
U-UM!
BA (ZOOM)
BELL-SAN!?

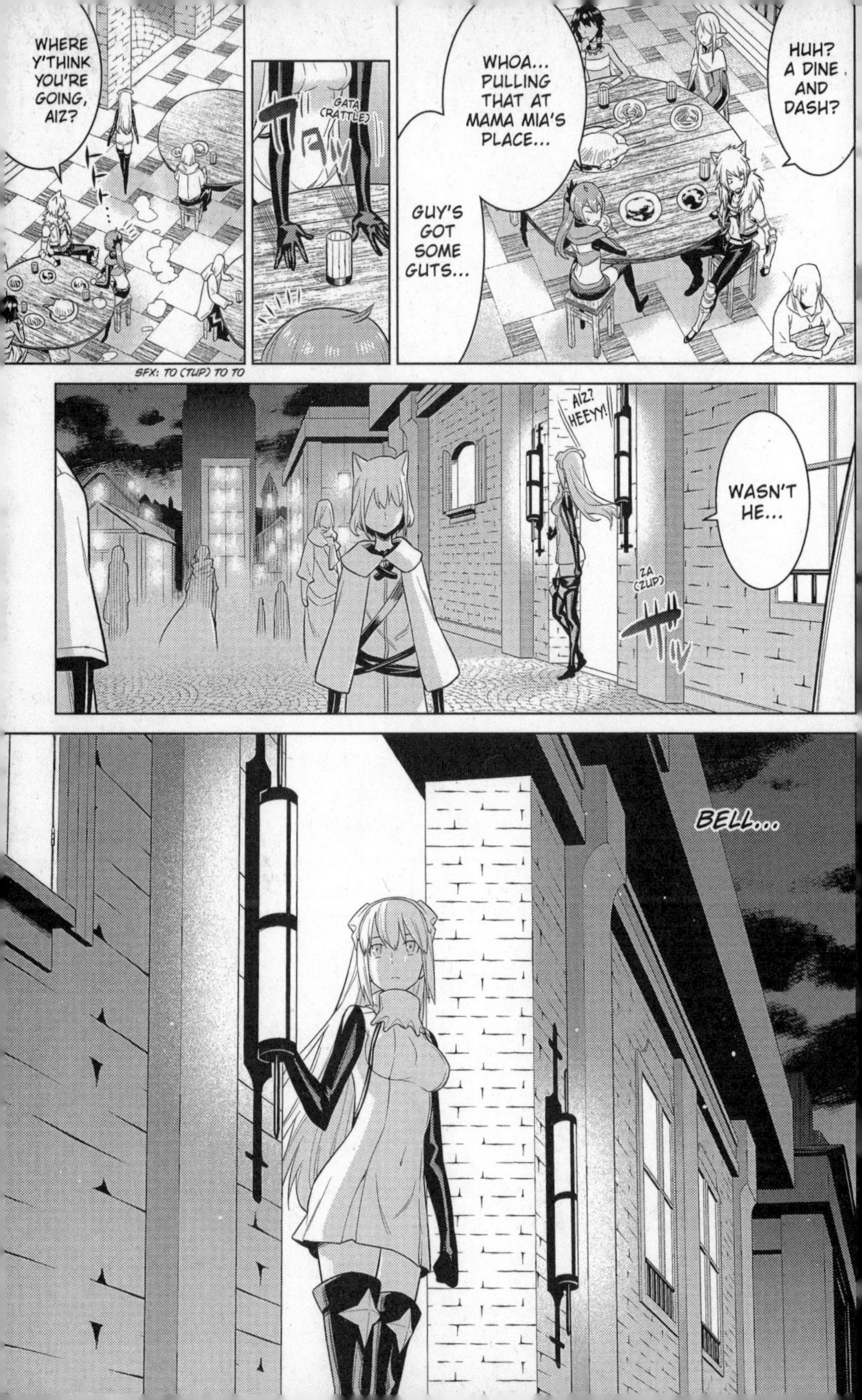
HUH? A DINE AND DASH?
WHOA... PULLING THAT AT MAMA MIA'S PLACE...
GUY'S GOT SOME GUTS...
GATA (RATTLE)
WHERE Y'THINK YOU'RE GOING, AIZ?
SFX: TO (TUP) TO TO
AIZ? HEEYY!
WASN'T HE...
ZA (ZUP)
BELL...

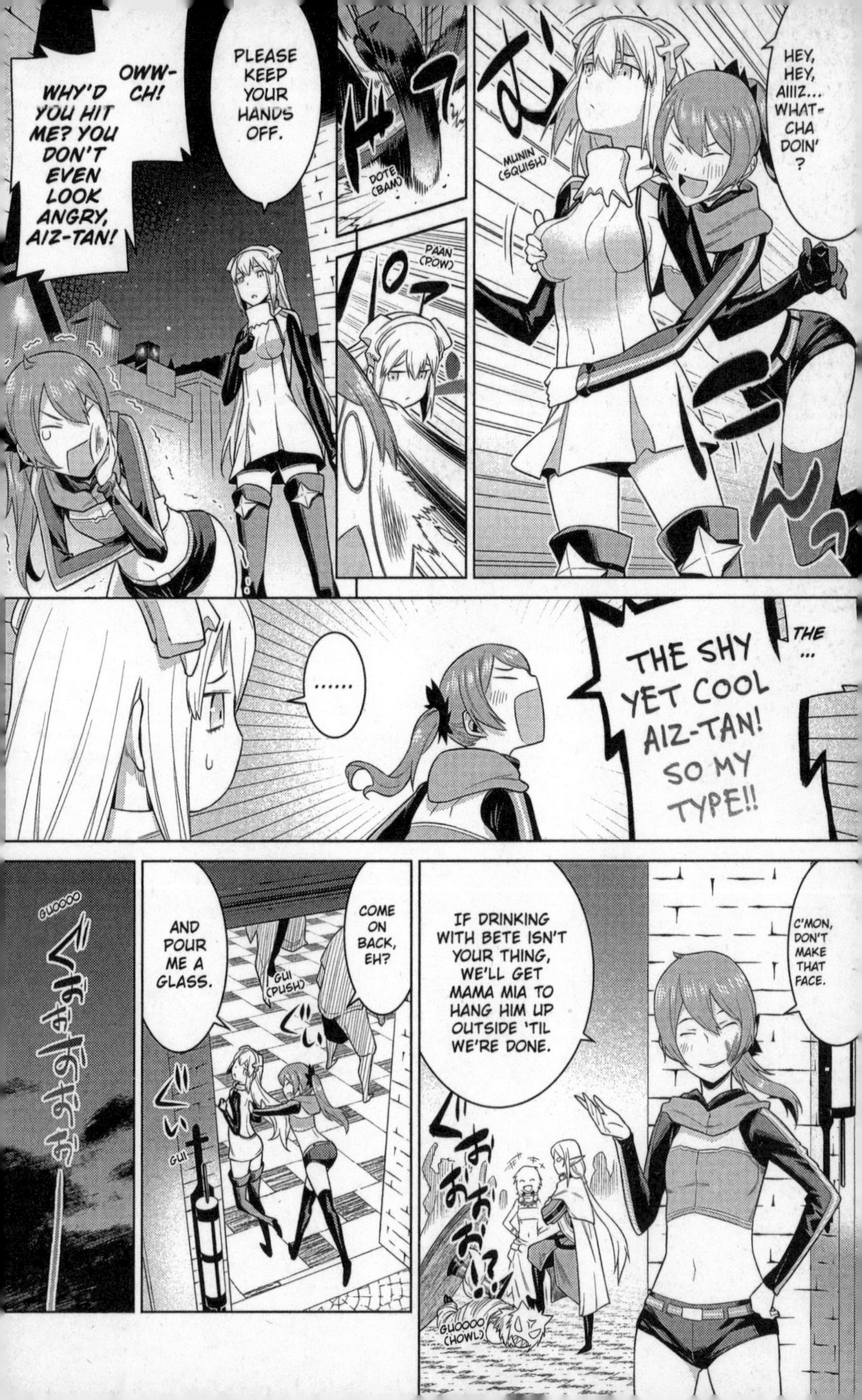
HEY, HEY, AIIIZ... WHATCHA DOIN'?
MUNIN (SQUISH)
DOTE (BAM)
PA'AN (POW)
PLEASE KEEP YOUR HANDS OFF.
OWW-CH!
WHY'D YOU HIT ME? YOU DON'T EVEN LOOK ANGRY, AIZ-TAN!
THE ...
THE SHY YET COOL AIZ-TAN! SO MY TYPE!!
......
C'MON, DON'T MAKE THAT FACE.
IF DRINKING WITH BETE ISN'T YOUR THING, WE'LL GET MAMA MIA TO HANG HIM UP OUTSIDE 'TIL WE'RE DONE.
GUOOOO (HOWL)
COME ON BACK, EH?
GUI (PUSH)
AND POUR ME A GLASS.
GUI
GUOOOO

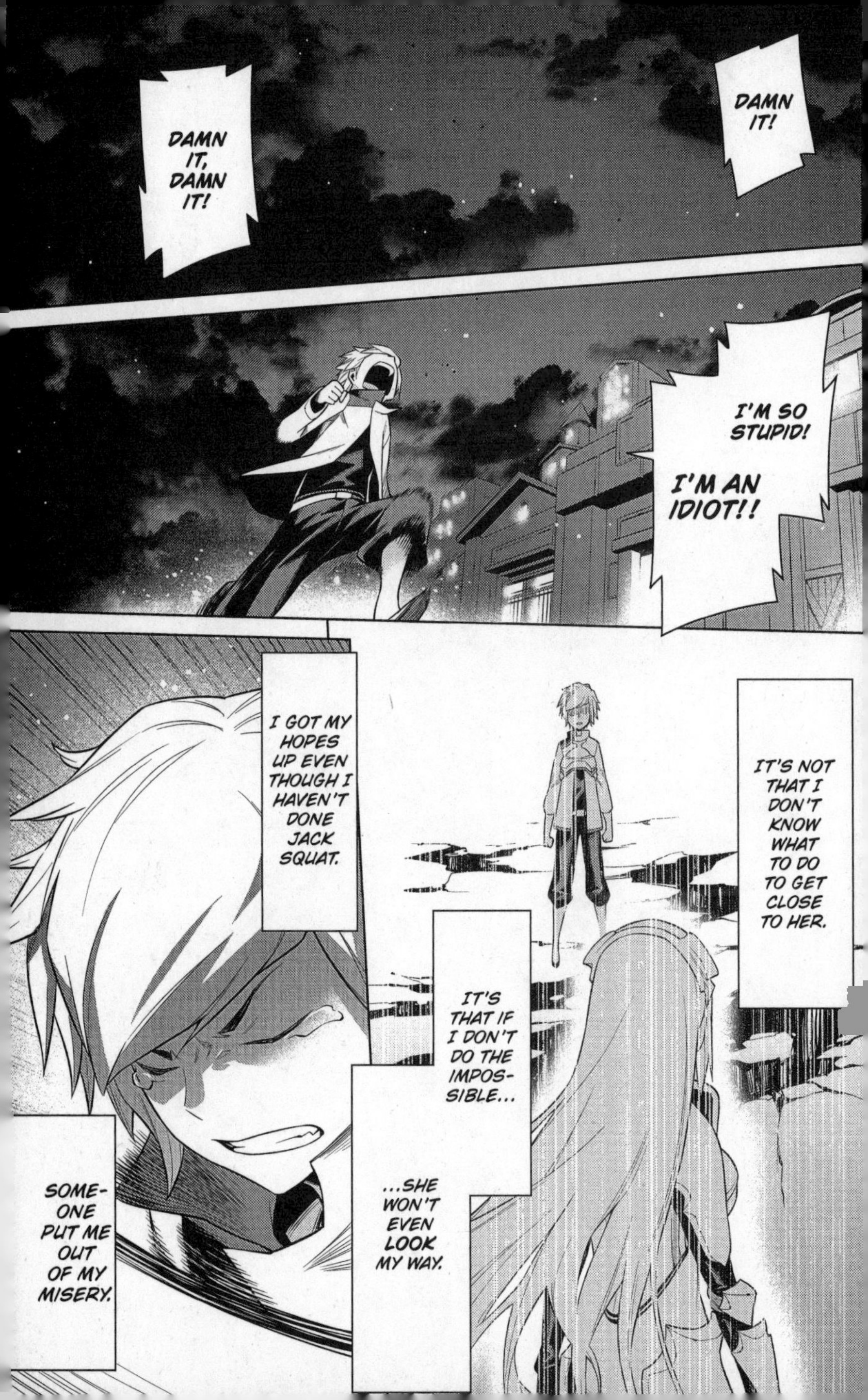
DAMN IT!
DAMN IT, DAMN IT!
I'M SO STUPID!
I'M AN IDIOT!!
IT'S NOT THAT I DON'T KNOW WHAT TO DO TO GET CLOSE TO HER.
IT'S THAT IF I DON'T DO THE IMPOS-SIBLE...
...SHE WON'T EVEN LOOK MY WAY.
I GOT MY HOPES UP EVEN THOUGH I HAVEN'T DONE JACK SQUAT.
SOME-ONE PUT ME OUT OF MY MISERY.

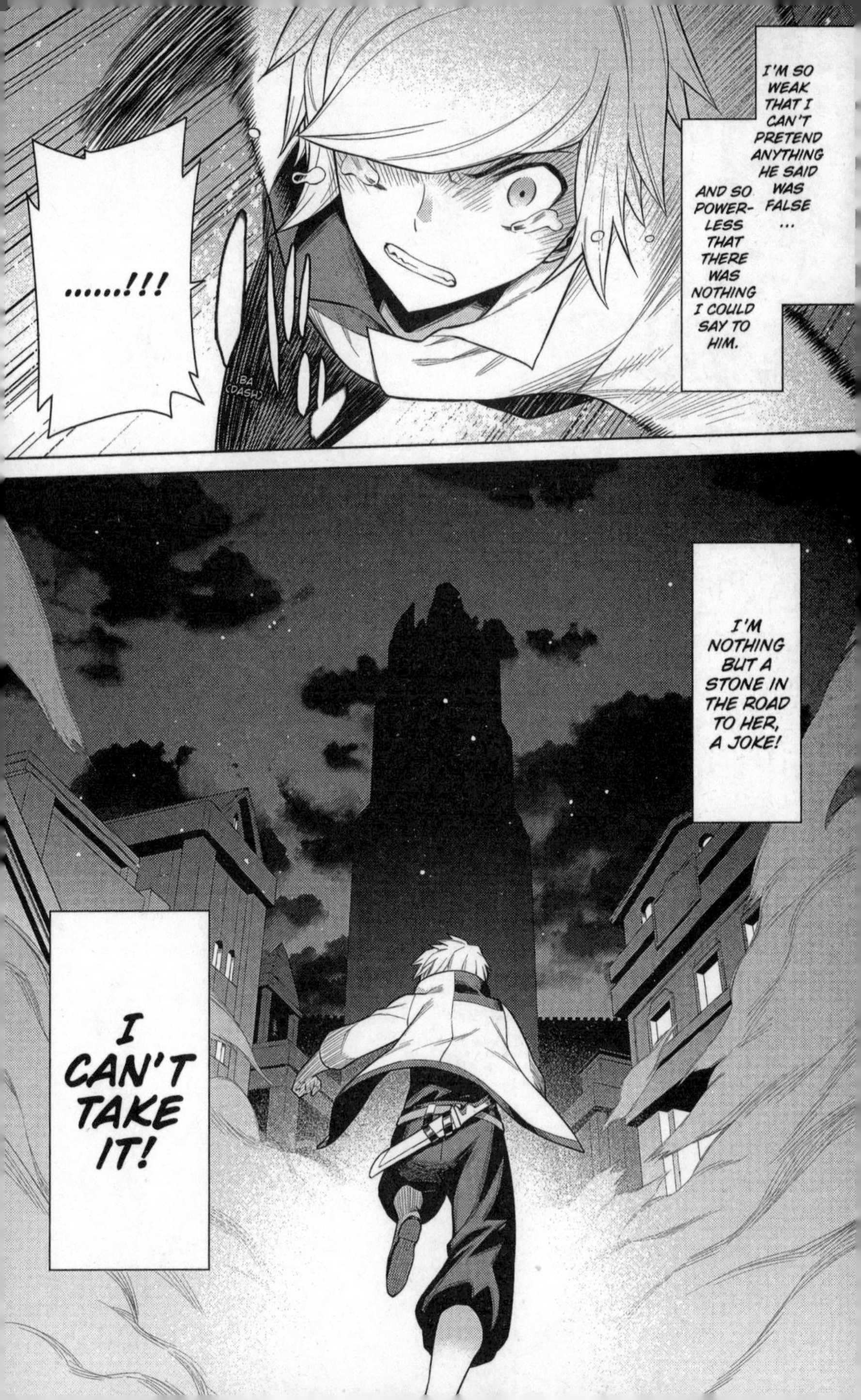
I'M SO WEAK THAT I CAN'T PRETEND ANYTHING HE SAID WAS FALSE ...
AND SO POWER-LESS THAT THERE WAS NOTHING I COULD SAY TO HIM.
......!!!
BA (DASH)
I'M NOTHING BUT A STONE IN THE ROAD TO HER, A JOKE!
I CAN'T TAKE IT!

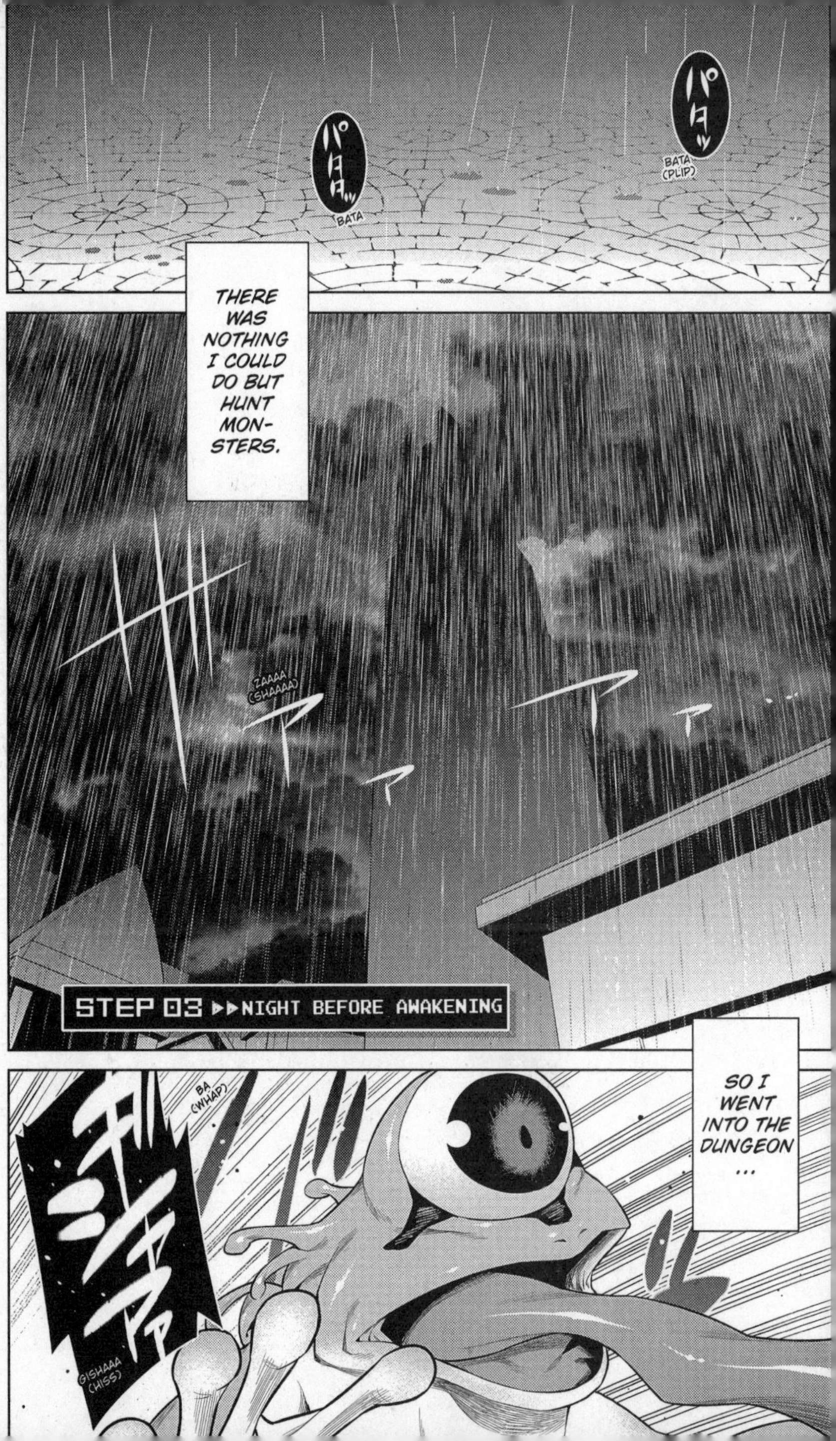
BATA (PLIP)
BATA
THERE WAS NOTHING I COULD DO BUT HUNT MON-STERS.
ZAAAA (SHAAAA)
STEP 03 ▶▶NIGHT BEFORE AWAKENING
SO I WENT INTO THE DUNGEON ...
BA (WHAP)
GISHAAA (HISS)

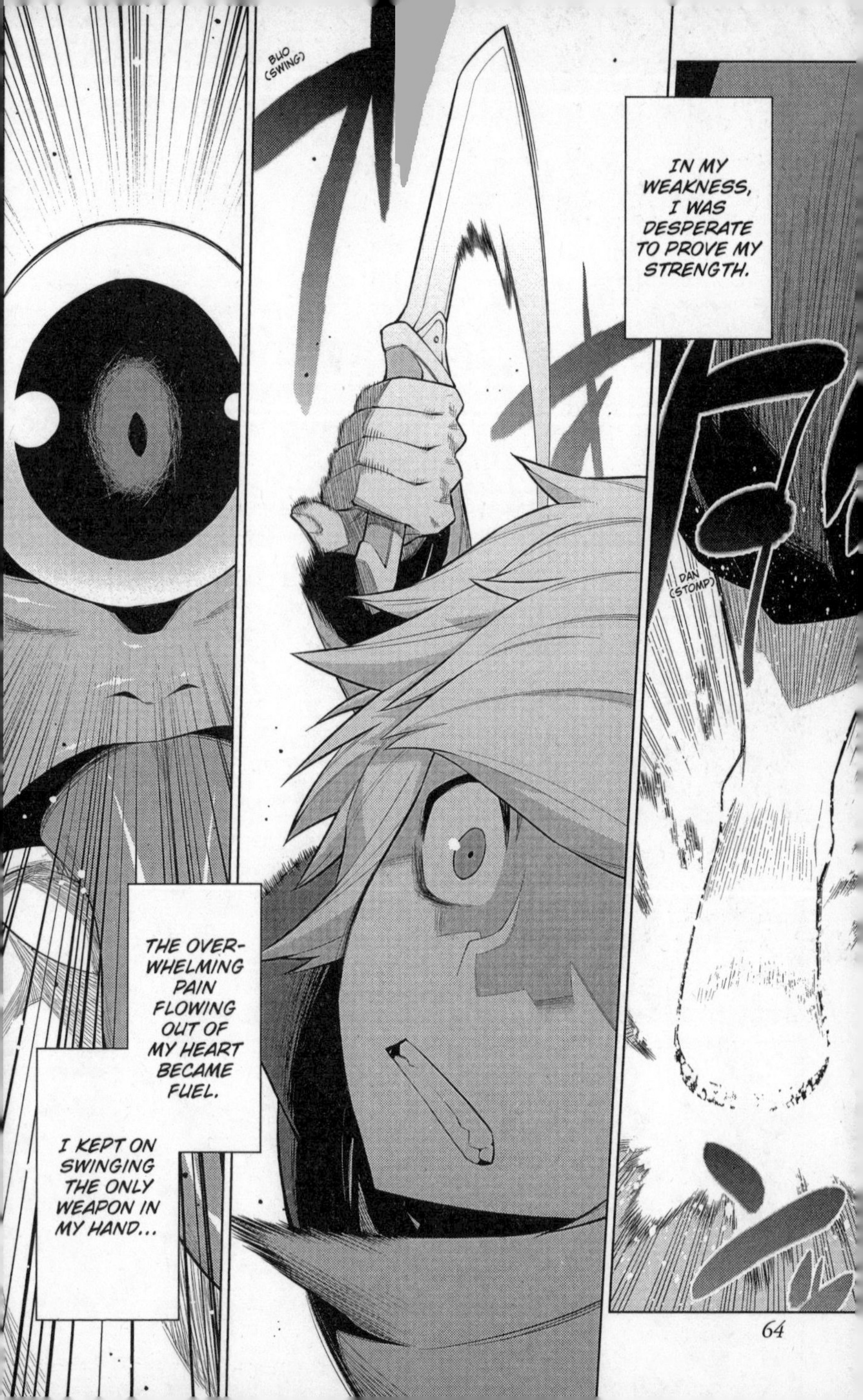
IN MY WEAKNESS, I WAS DESPERATE TO PROVE MY STRENGTH.
DAN (STOMP)
BUO (SWING)
THE OVER-WHELMING PAIN FLOWING OUT OF MY HEART BECAME FUEL.
I KEPT ON SWINGING THE ONLY WEAPON IN MY HAND...

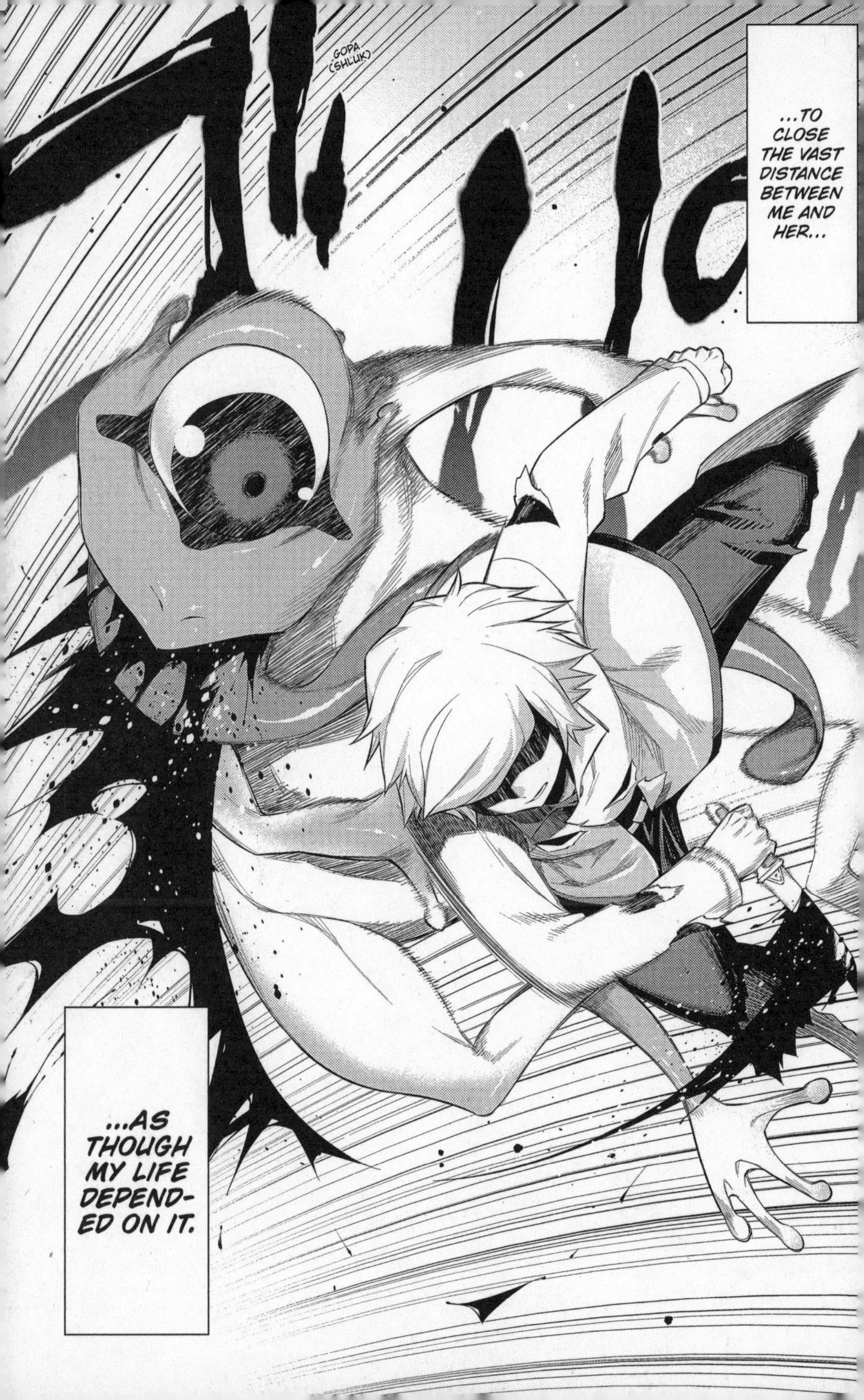
...TO CLOSE THE VAST DISTANCE BETWEEN ME AND HER...
GOPA (SHLUK)
...AS THOUGH MY LIFE DEPEND-ED ON IT.

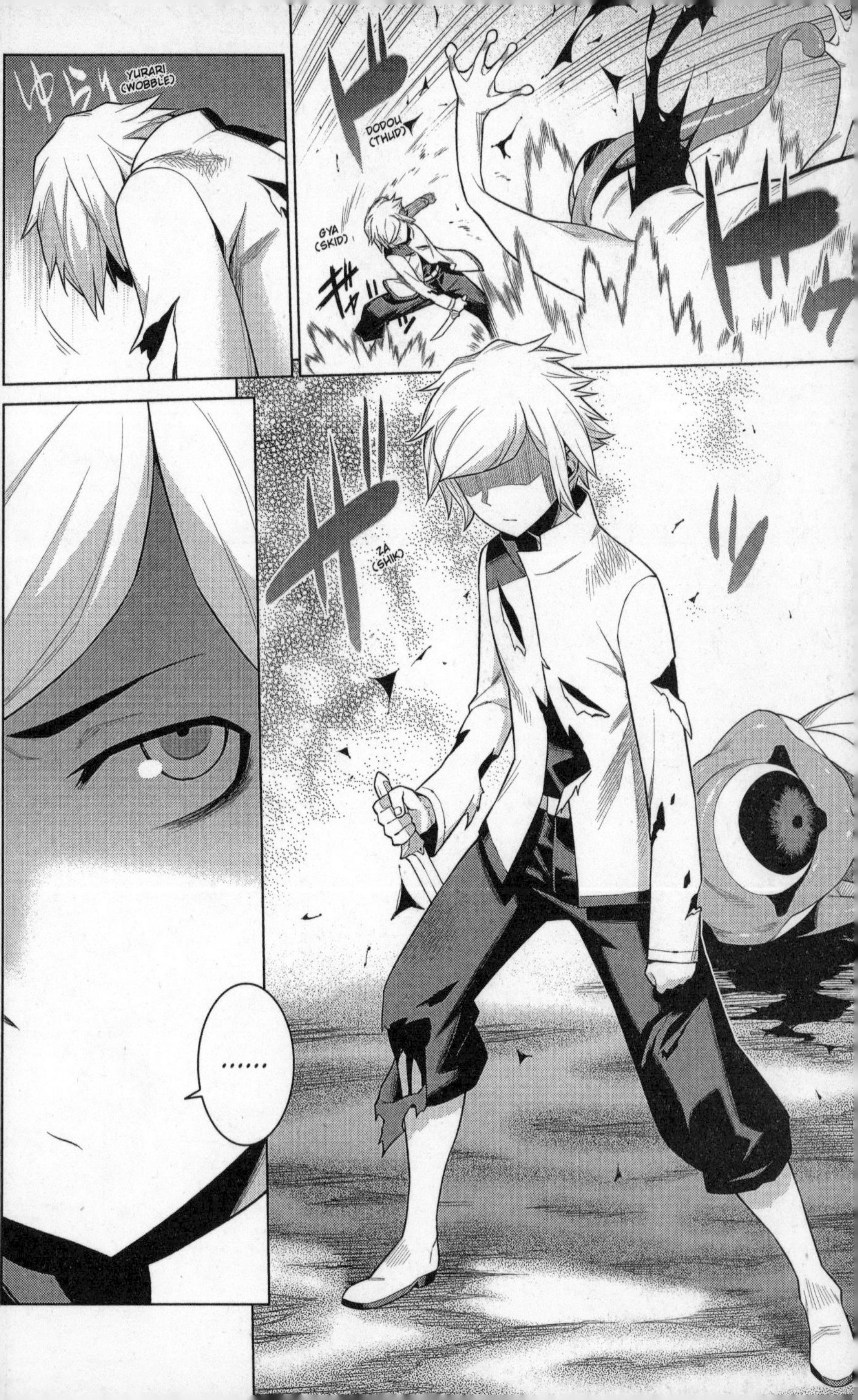
DODOU (THUD)
GYA (SKID)
YURARI (WOBBLE)
ZA (SHIK)
......

WHERE...

...AM I...?

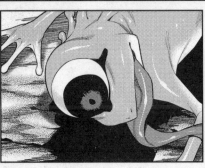

THE
SIXTH.

THE FIFTH
LEVEL...?
NO...

ZARI
(KRUNCH)

ZARI
(KRUNCH)

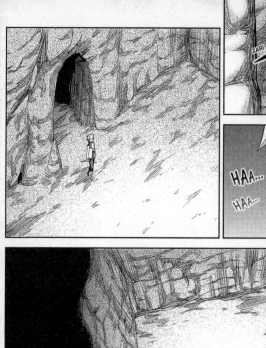

HAA...

HAA...

...A
DEAD
END?

BIKI
(CRACK)

BA
(WHF)

—

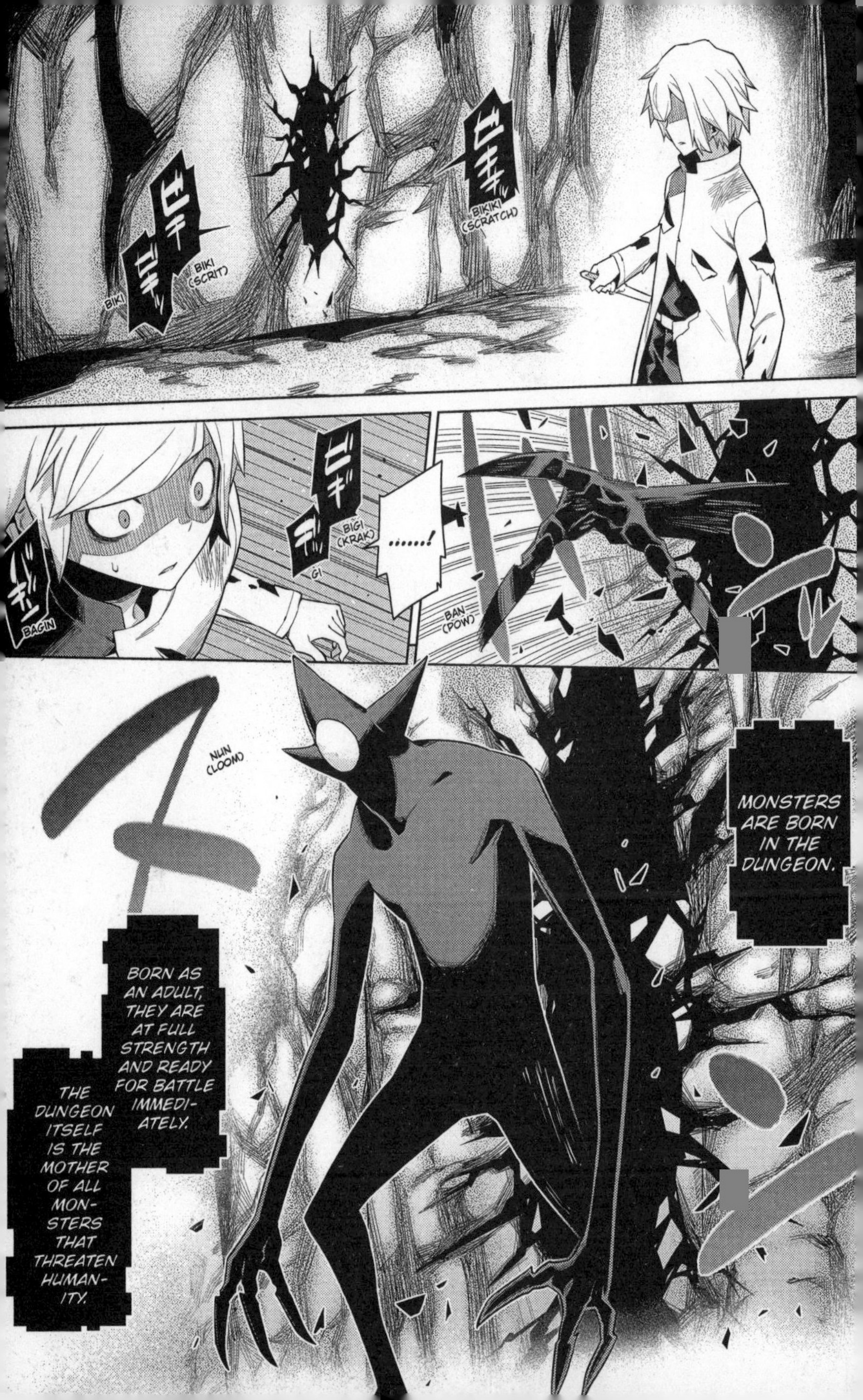
BIKIKI (SCRATCH)
BIKI (SCRIT)
BIKI
BAN (POW)
BIGI (KRAK)
GI
......!
BAGIN
MONSTERS ARE BORN IN THE DUNGEON.
NUN (LOOM)
BORN AS AN ADULT, THEY ARE AT FULL STRENGTH AND READY FOR BATTLE IMMEDI-ATELY.
THE DUNGEON ITSELF IS THE MOTHER OF ALL MON-STERS THAT THREATEN HUMAN-ITY.

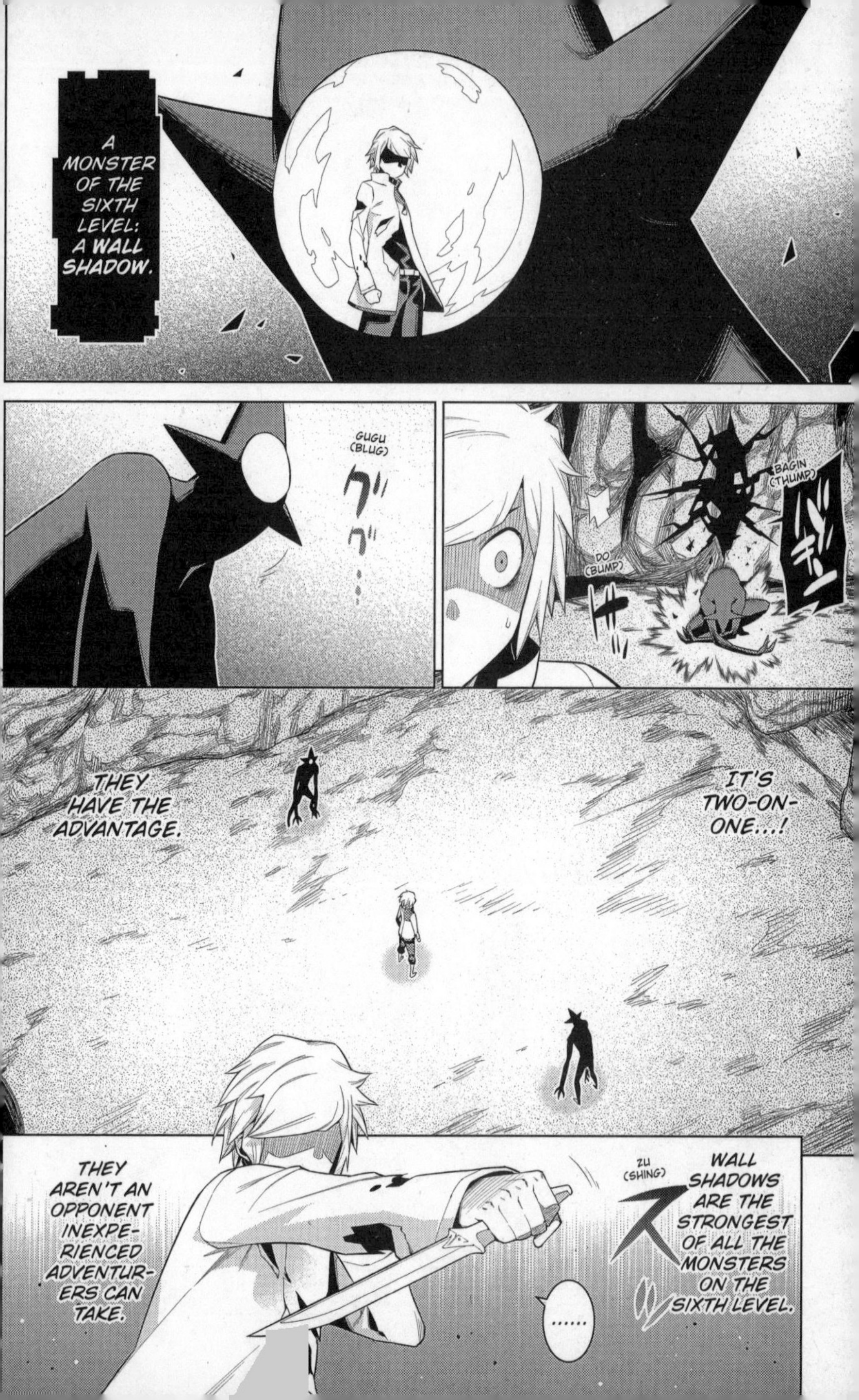
A MONSTER OF THE SIXTH LEVEL: A WALL SHADOW.
BAGIN (THUMP)
DO (BUMP)
GUGU (BLUG)
IT'S TWO-ON-ONE...!
THEY HAVE THE ADVANTAGE.
ZU (SHING)
WALL SHADOWS ARE THE STRONGEST OF ALL THE MONSTERS ON THE SIXTH LEVEL.
......
THEY AREN'T AN OPPONENT INEXPE-RIENCED ADVENTURER-ERS CAN TAKE.

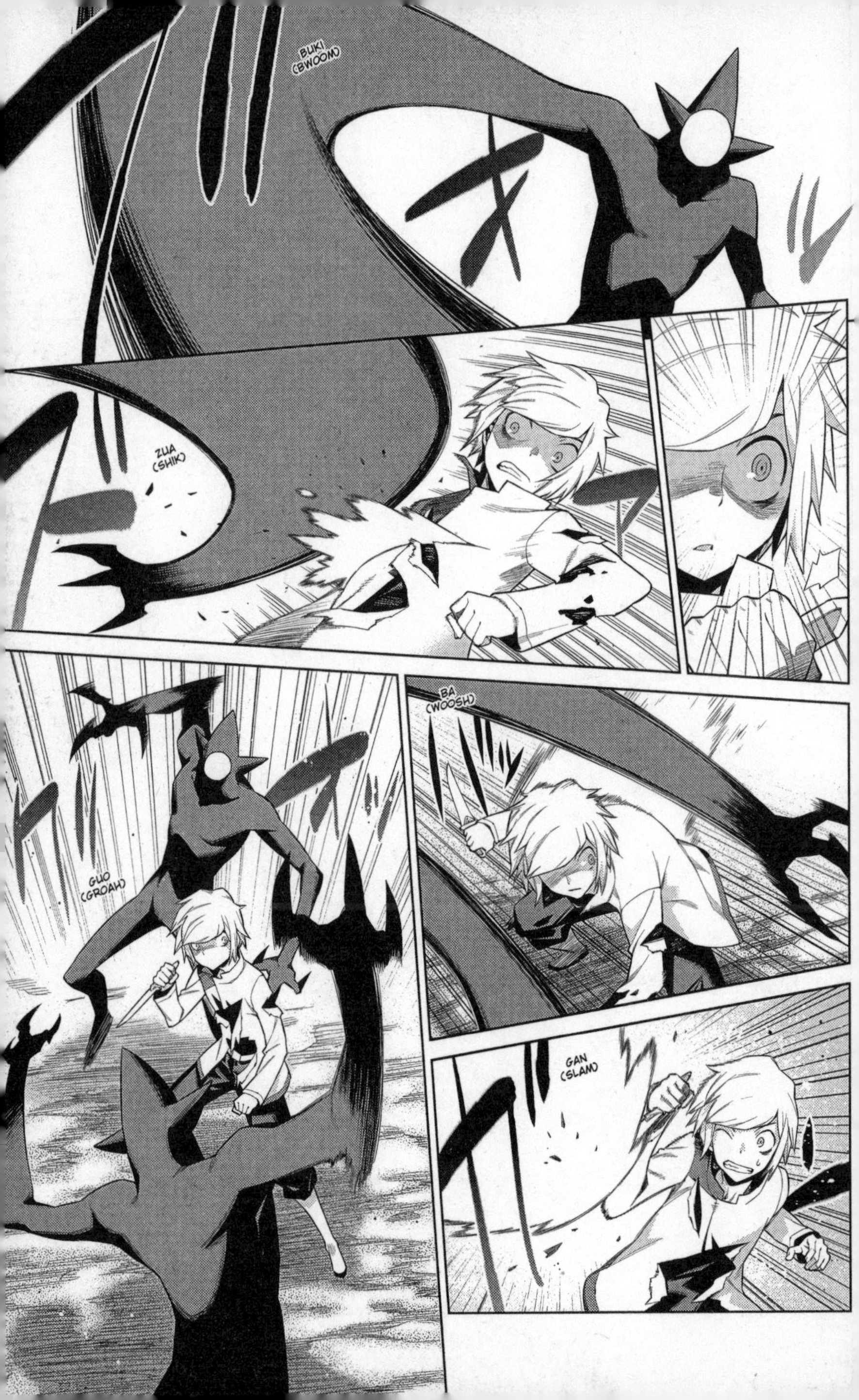
BUKI (BWOOM)
ZUA (SHIK)
BA (WOOSH)
GAN (SLAM)
GUO (GROAH)

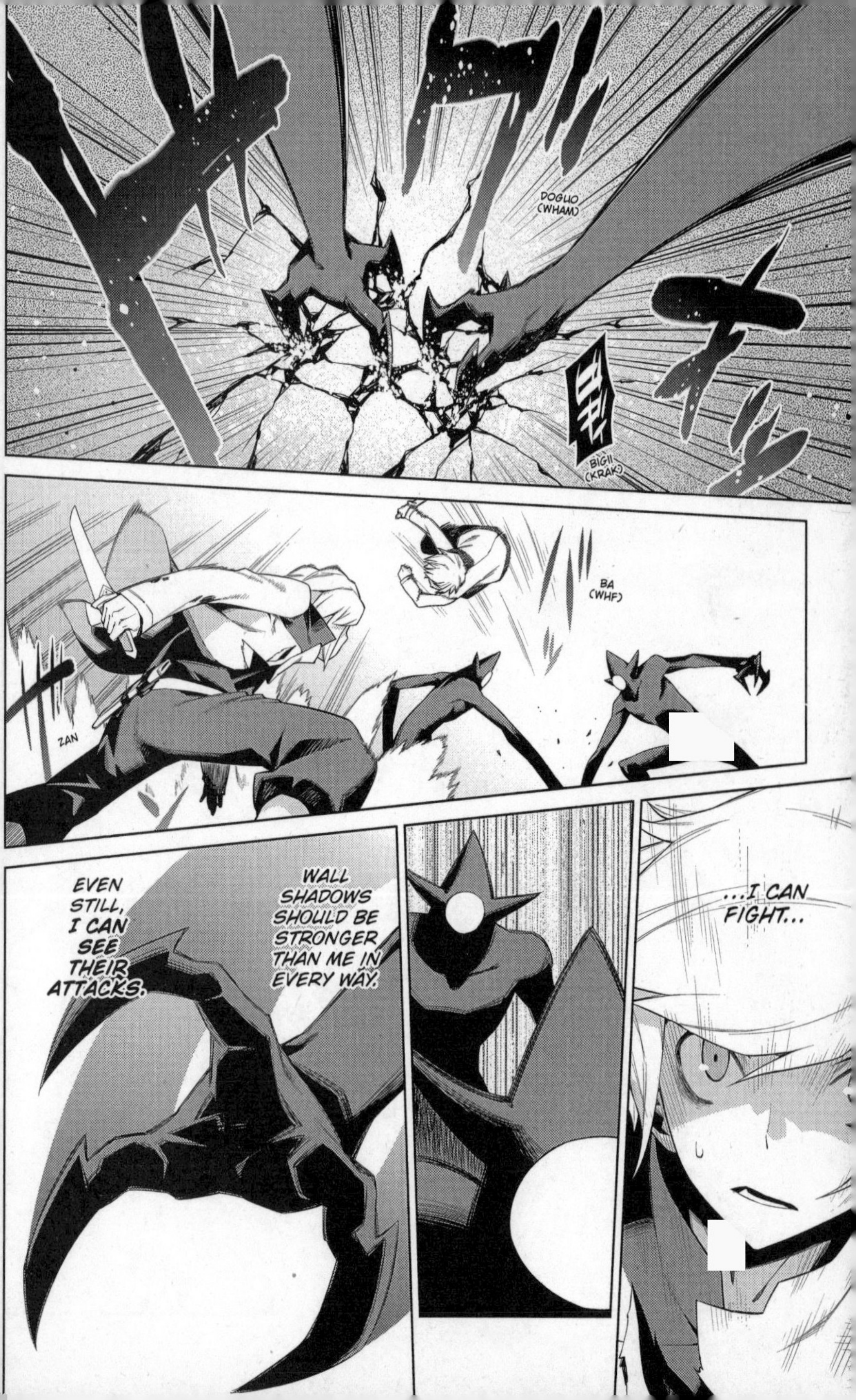
DOGUO (WHAM)
BIGII (KRAK)
BA (WHF)
ZAN
...I CAN FIGHT...
WALL SHADOWS SHOULD BE STRONGER THAN ME IN EVERY WAY.
EVEN STILL, I CAN SEE THEIR ATTACKS.

I MAY BE AN ADVENTURER WITH LESS THAN TWO WEEKS' EXPERIENCE...

BA

BA

BA

BA

BA

BA

...BUT I'M ON PAR WITH THESE MONSTERS— AS STRONG AS THEM.

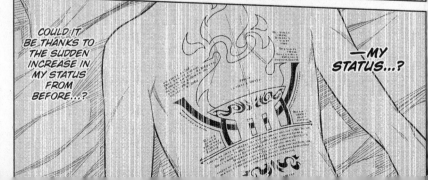

OVER-NIGHT...?

HYUBO (WHOOSH)

DID I GET STRONGER?

COULD IT BE THANKS TO THE SUDDEN INCREASE IN MY STATUS FROM BEFORE...?

—MY STATUS...?

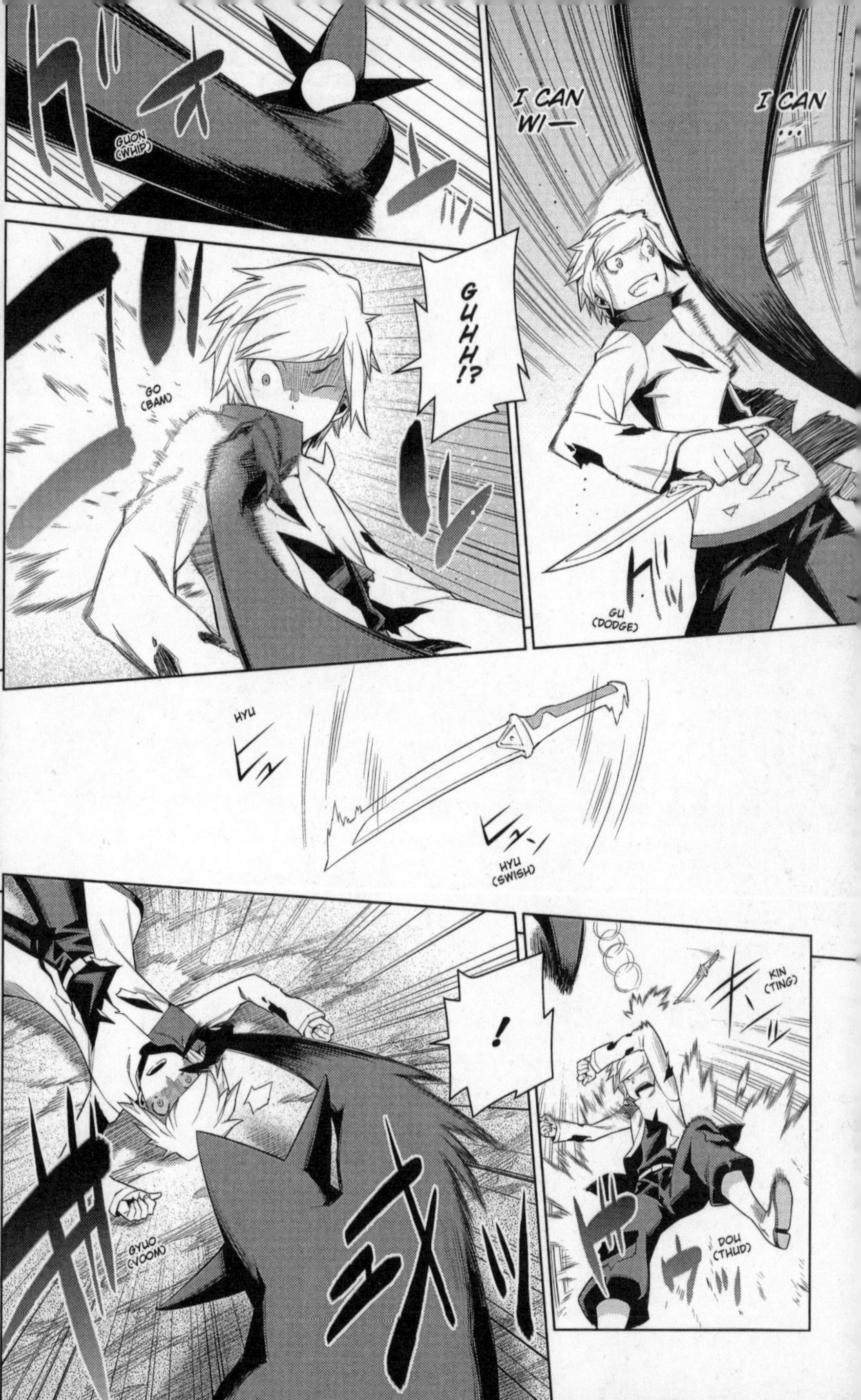
I CAN...
I CAN WI—
GUON (WHIP)
GU (DODGE)
GUHH!?
GO (BAM)
HYU
HYU (SWISH)
KIN (TING)
DOU (THUD)
!
GYUO (VOOM)

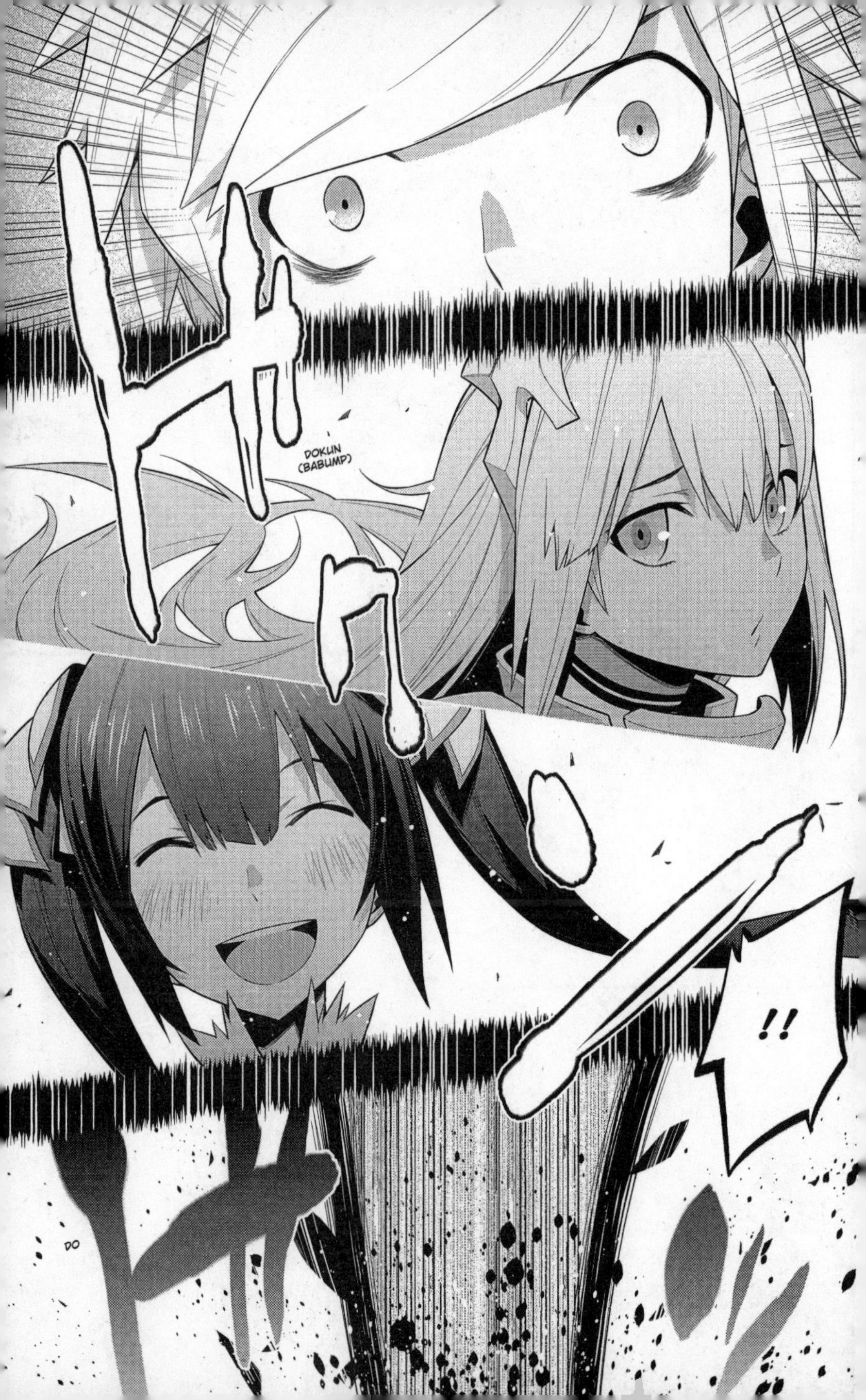
DOKUN
(BABUMP)
!!
DO

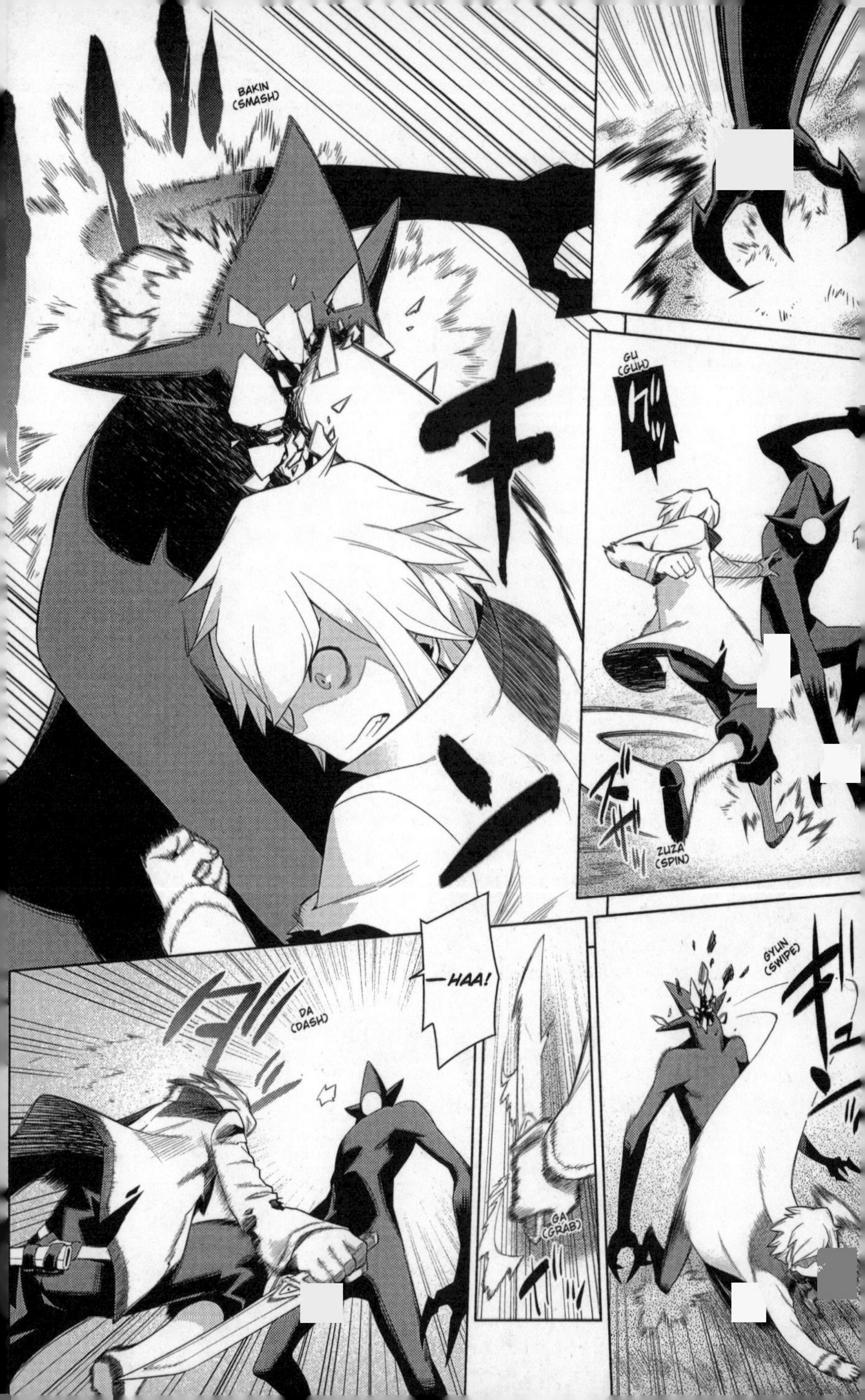
GU
(GUH)
ZUZA
(SPIN)
BAKIN
(SMASH)
GYUN
(SWIPE)
—HAA!
GA
(GRAB)
DA
(DASH)

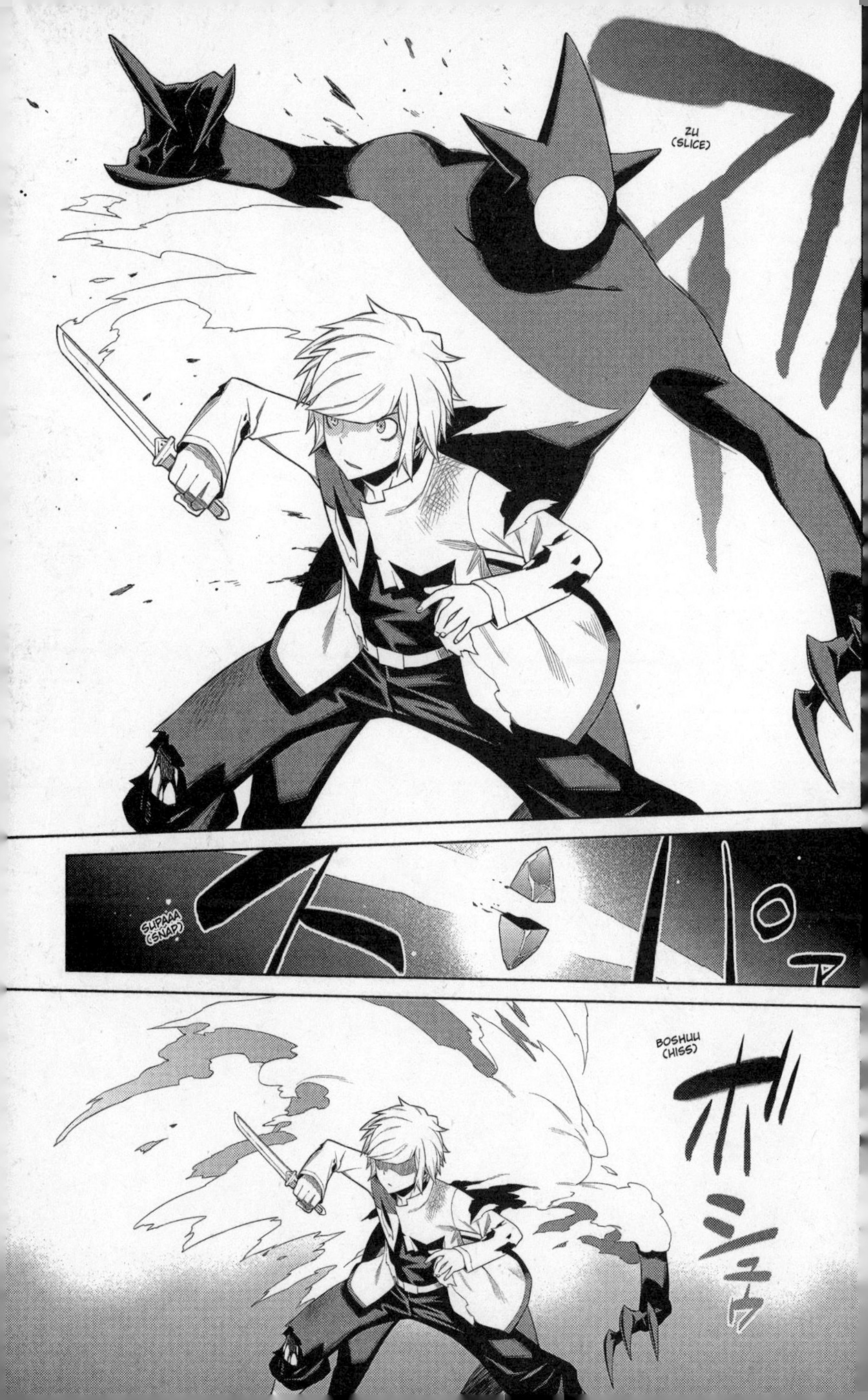
ZU
(SLICE)
SUPAAA
(SNAP)
BOSHUU
(HISS)

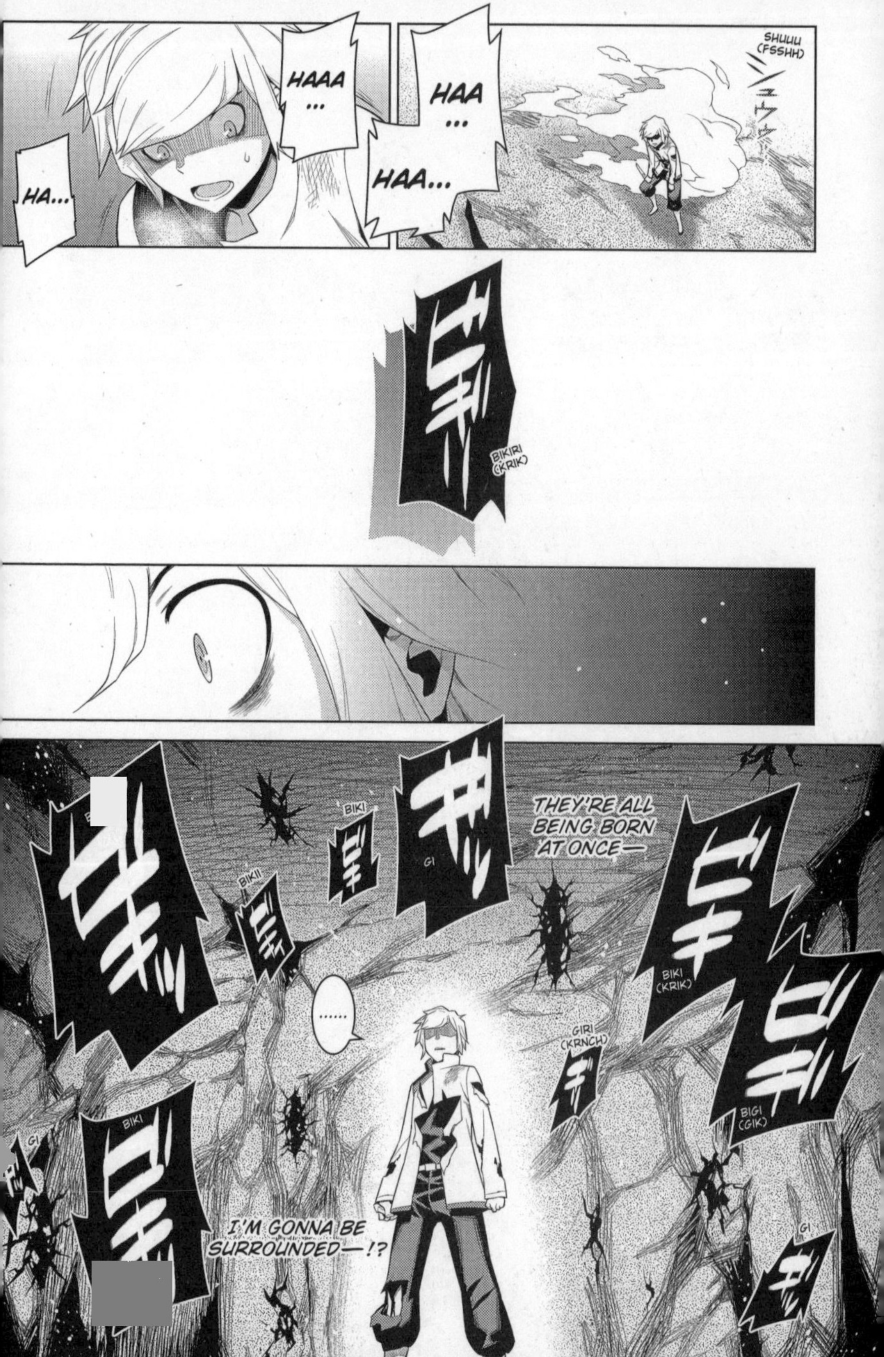
SHUUU (FSSHH)
HAAA...
HAA...
HAA...
HA...
BIKIRI (KRIK)
THEY'RE ALL BEING BORN AT ONCE—
BIKI (KRIK)
BIGI (GIK)
GIRI (KRNCH)
GI
BIKI
GI
BIKII
......
BIKI
GI
I'M GONNA BE SURROUNDED—!?

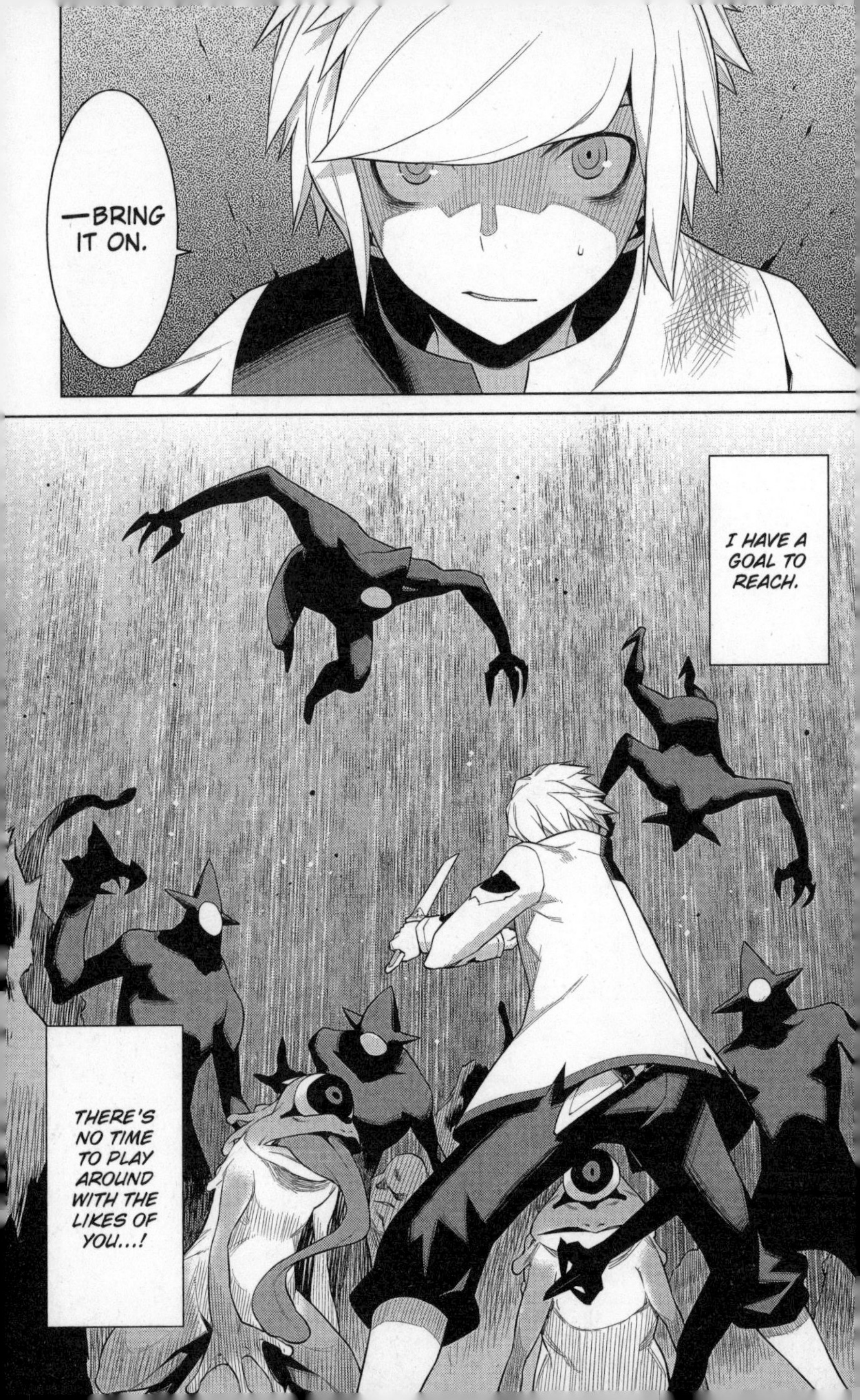
—BRING IT ON.
I HAVE A GOAL TO REACH.
THERE'S NO TIME TO PLAY AROUND WITH THE LIKES OF YOU...!

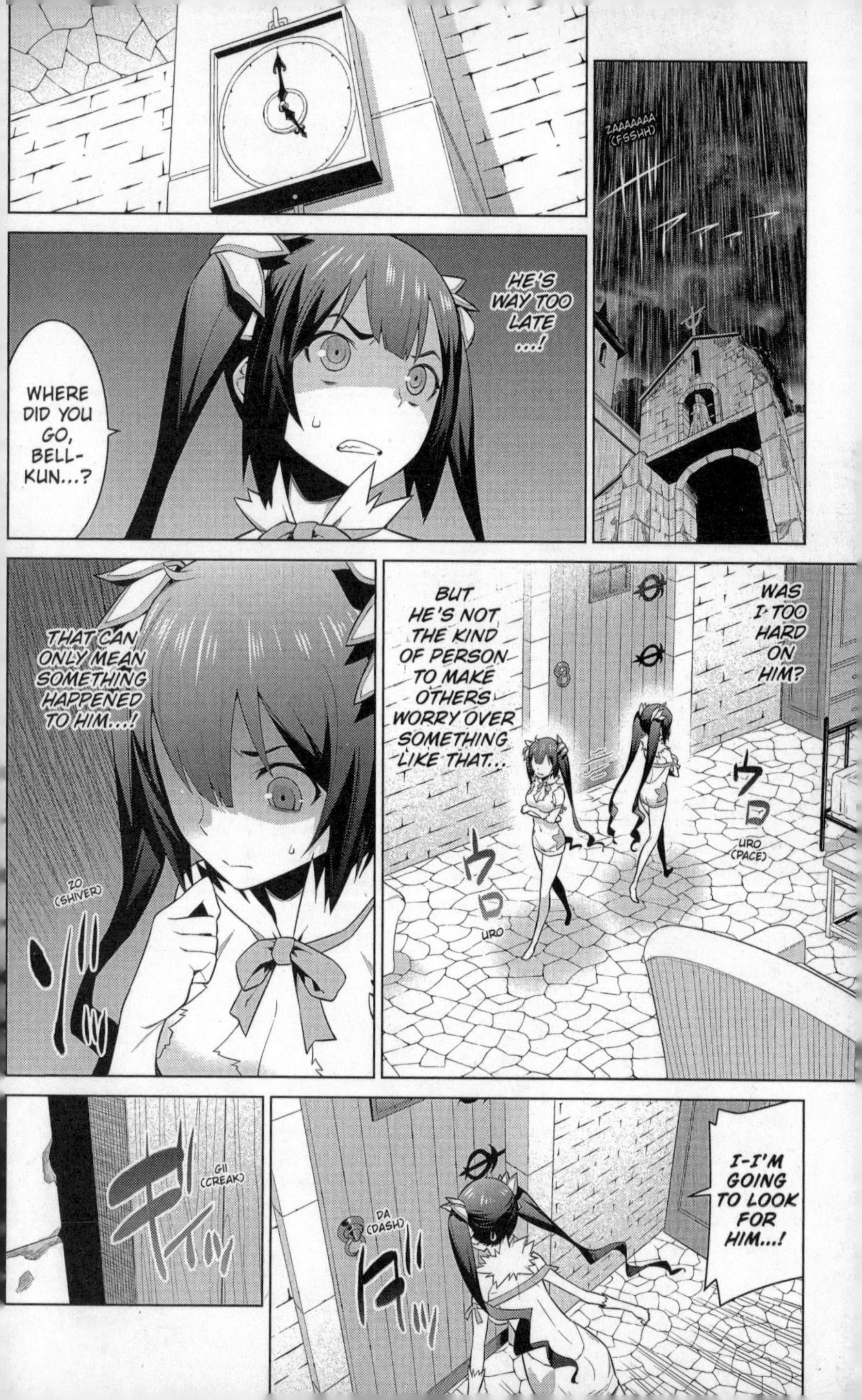
ZAAAAAAA
(FSSHH)
HE'S WAY TOO LATE ...!
WHERE DID YOU GO, BELL-KUN...?
WAS I TOO HARD ON HIM?
BUT HE'S NOT THE KIND OF PERSON TO MAKE OTHERS WORRY OVER SOMETHING LIKE THAT...
URO
(PACE)
URO
THAT CAN ONLY MEAN SOMETHING HAPPENED TO HIM...!
ZO
(SHIVER)
I-I'M GOING TO LOOK FOR HIM...!
DA
(DASH)
GII
(CREAK)

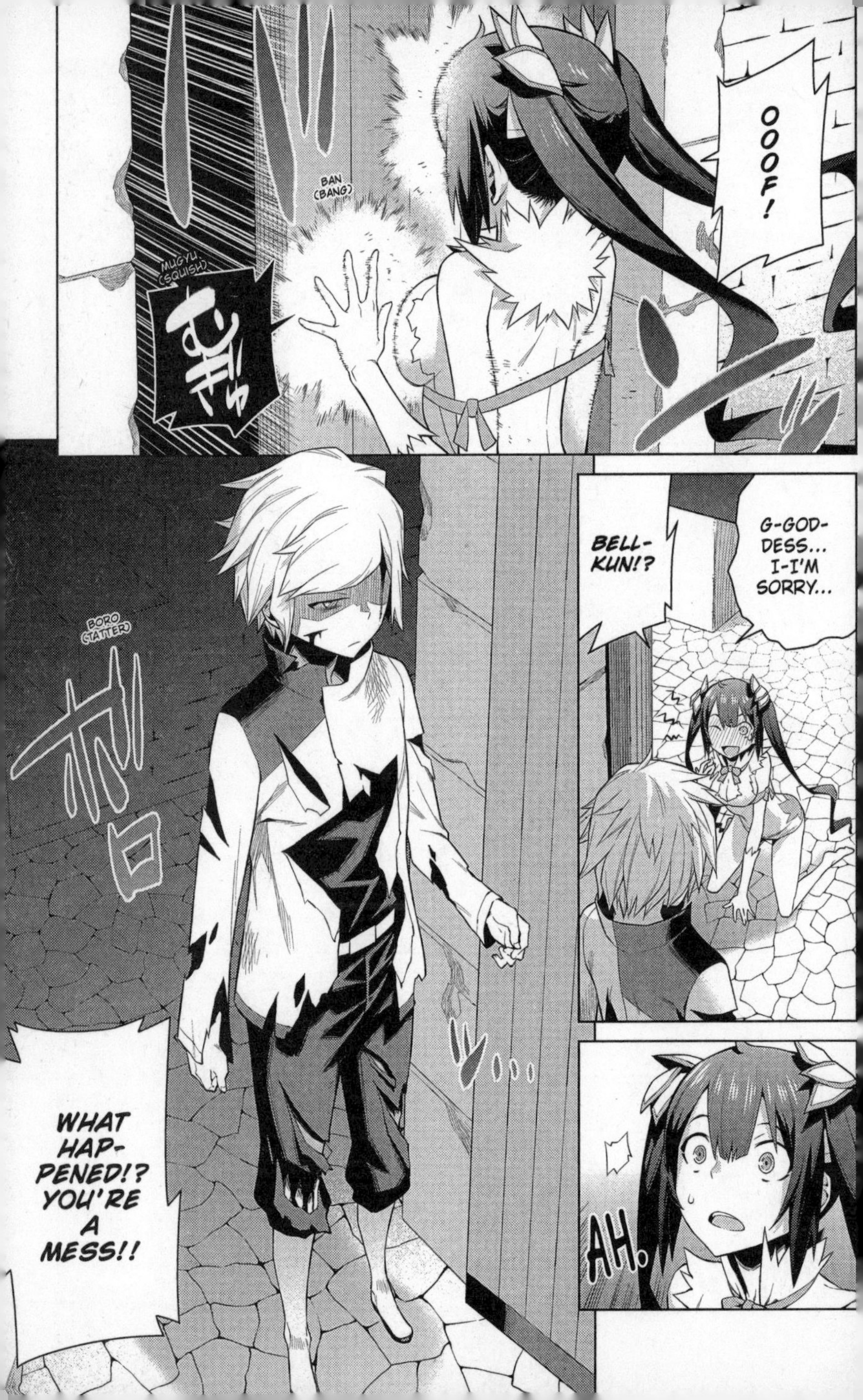
OOOF!
BAN (BANG)
MUGYU (SQUISH)
G-GOD-DESS... I-I'M SORRY...
BELL-KUN!?
AH.
BORO (TATTER)
WHAT HAP-PENED!? YOU'RE A MESS!!

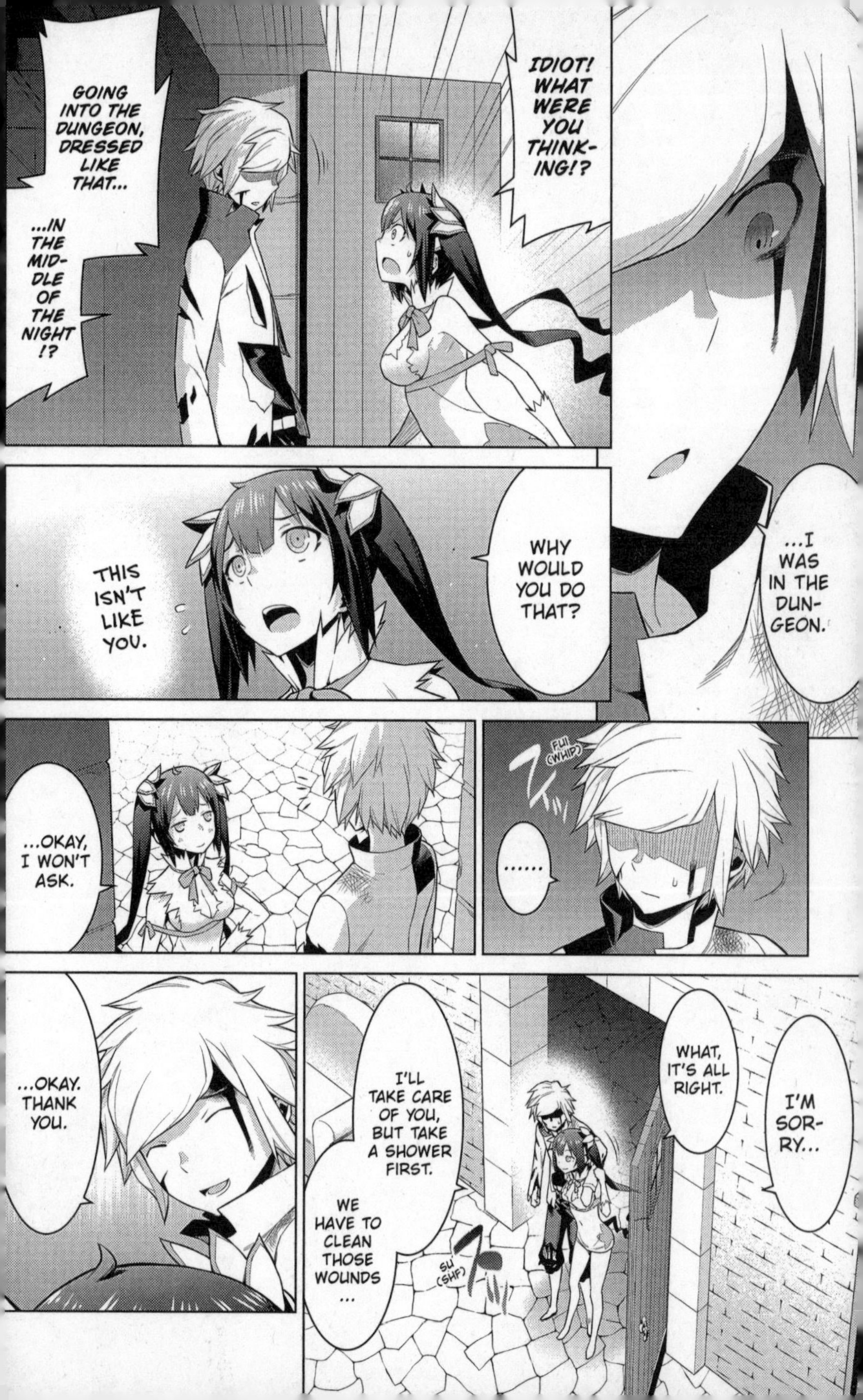
IDIOT! WHAT WERE YOU THINKING!?
GOING INTO THE DUNGEON, DRESSED LIKE THAT...
...IN THE MIDDLE OF THE NIGHT!?
...I WAS IN THE DUNGEON.
WHY WOULD YOU DO THAT?
THIS ISN'T LIKE YOU.
FUI (WHIP)
......
...OKAY, I WON'T ASK.
I'M SORRY...
WHAT, IT'S ALL RIGHT.
I'LL TAKE CARE OF YOU, BUT TAKE A SHOWER FIRST.
WE HAVE TO CLEAN THOSE WOUNDS...
SU (SHF)
...OKAY. THANK YOU.

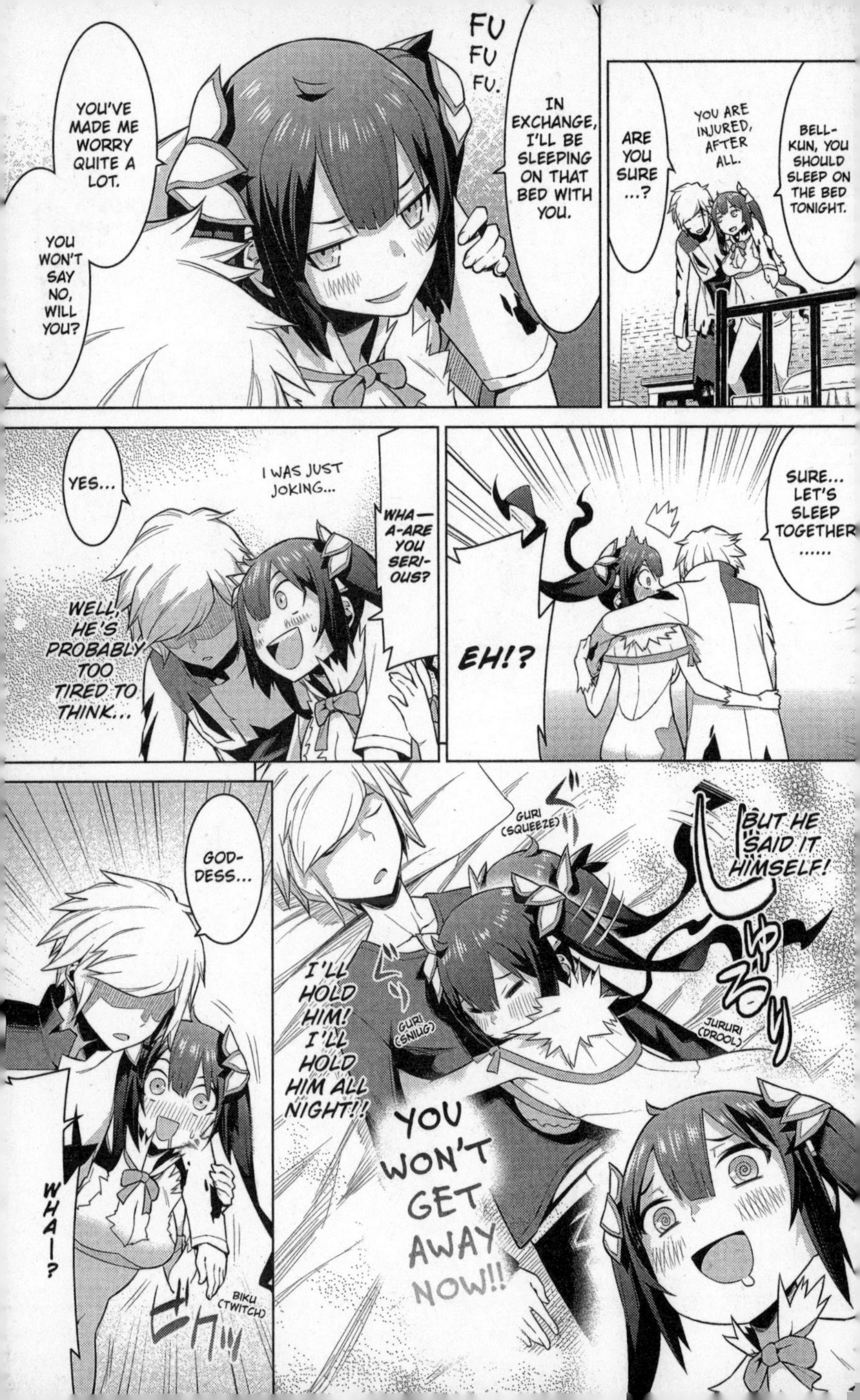
BELL-KUN, YOU SHOULD SLEEP ON THE BED TONIGHT.
YOU ARE INJURED, AFTER ALL.
ARE YOU SURE ...?
FU FU FU.
IN EXCHANGE, I'LL BE SLEEPING ON THAT BED WITH YOU.
YOU'VE MADE ME WORRY QUITE A LOT.
YOU WON'T SAY NO, WILL YOU?
SURE... LET'S SLEEP TOGETHER ......
EH!?
WHA— A-ARE YOU SERI-OUS?
I WAS JUST JOKING...
YES...
WELL, HE'S PROBABLY TOO TIRED TO THINK...
BUT HE SAID IT HIMSELF!
JURURI (DROOL)
GURI (SQUEEZE)
I'LL HOLD HIM! I'LL HOLD HIM ALL NIGHT!!
GURI (SNUG)
YOU WON'T GET AWAY NOW!!
GOD-DESS...
WHA—?
BIKU (TWITCH)

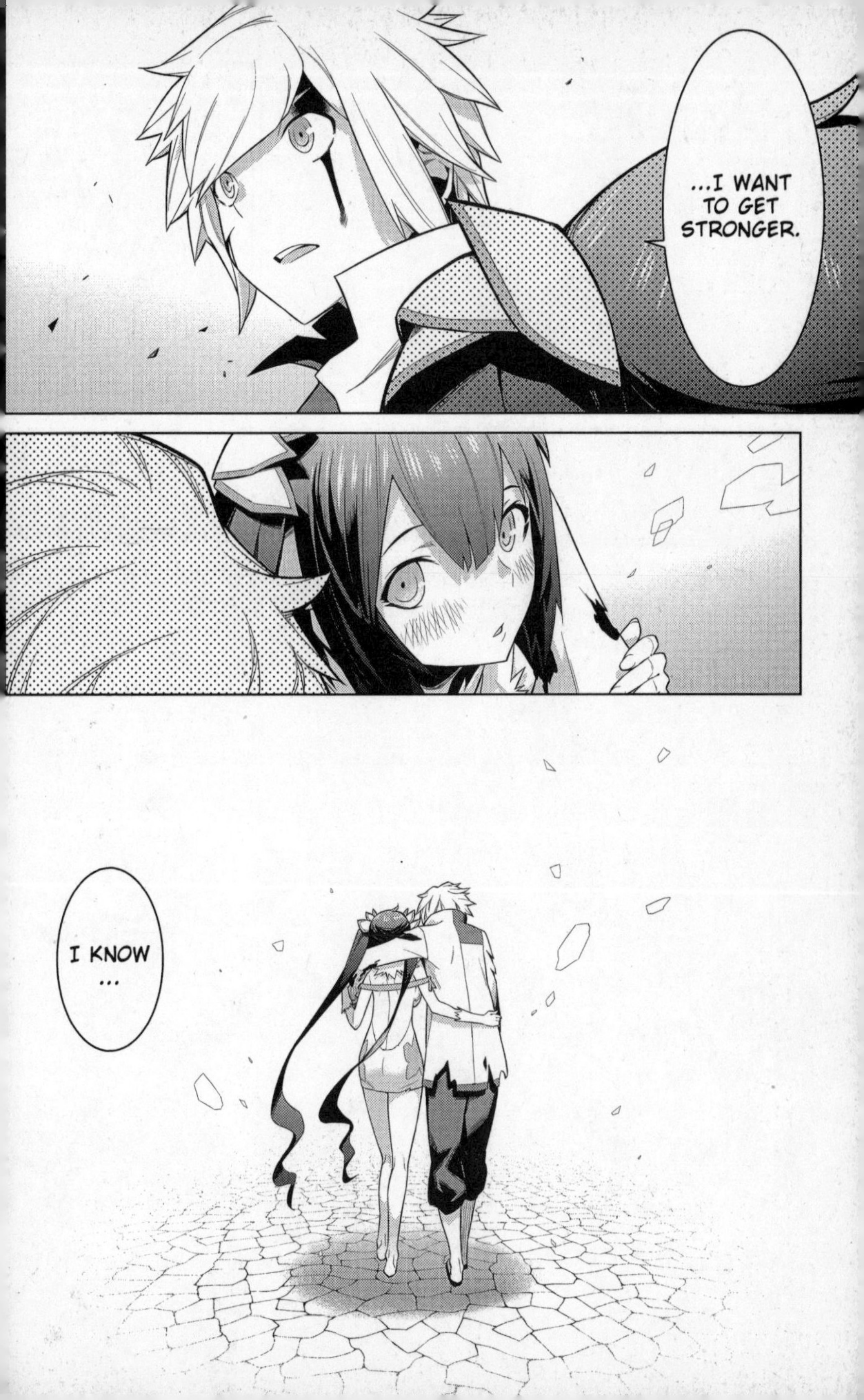
...I WANT TO GET STRONGER.
I KNOW ...

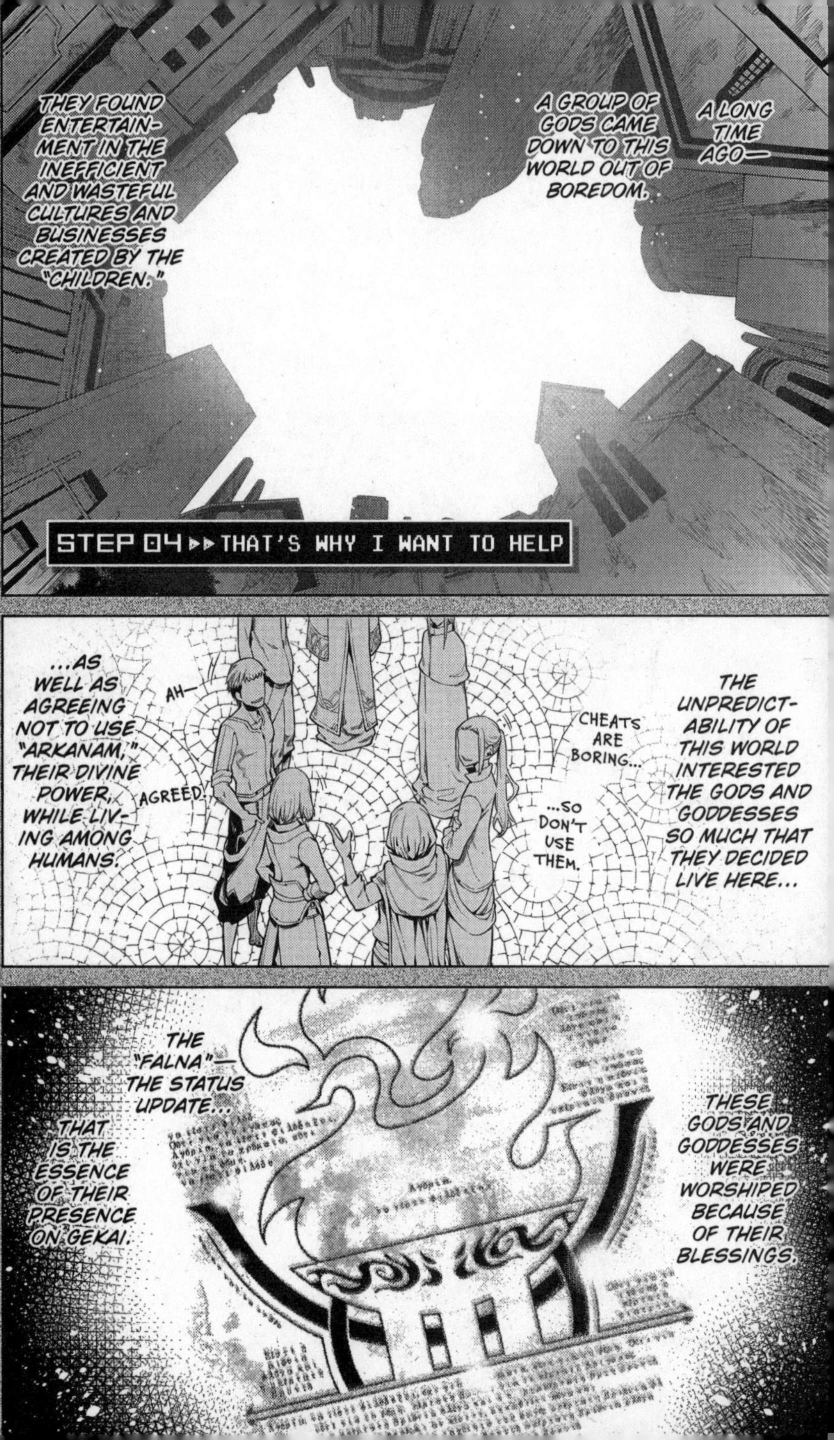
A LONG TIME AGO—
A GROUP OF GODS CAME DOWN TO THIS WORLD OUT OF BOREDOM.
THEY FOUND ENTERTAINMENT IN THE INEFFICIENT AND WASTEFUL CULTURES AND BUSINESSES CREATED BY THE "CHILDREN."
STEP 04 ▸▸ THAT'S WHY I WANT TO HELP
THE UNPREDICTABILITY OF THIS WORLD INTERESTED THE GODS AND GODDESSES SO MUCH THAT THEY DECIDED LIVE HERE…
CHEATS ARE BORING…
…SO DON'T USE THEM.
AH—
AGREED.
…AS WELL AS AGREEING NOT TO USE "ARKANAM," THEIR DIVINE POWER, WHILE LIVING AMONG HUMANS.
THESE GODS AND GODDESSES WERE WORSHIPED BECAUSE OF THEIR BLESSINGS.
THE "FALNA"—THE STATUS UPDATE…
THAT IS THE ESSENCE OF THEIR PRESENCE ON GEKAI.

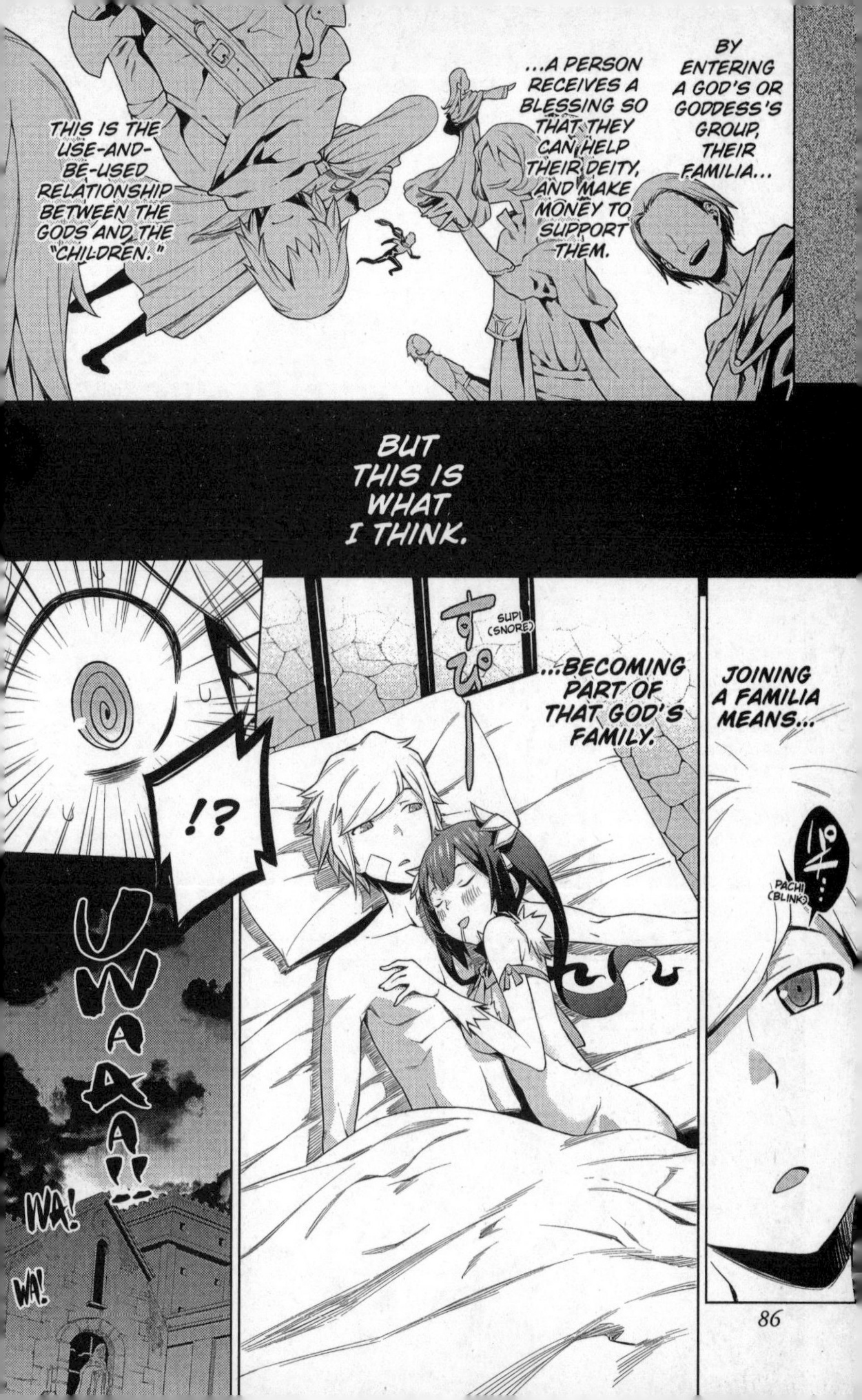
BY ENTERING A GOD'S OR GODDESS'S GROUP, THEIR FAMILIA...
...A PERSON RECEIVES A BLESSING SO THAT THEY CAN HELP THEIR DEITY, AND MAKE MONEY TO SUPPORT THEM.
THIS IS THE USE-AND-BE-USED RELATIONSHIP BETWEEN THE GODS AND THE "CHILDREN."
BUT THIS IS WHAT I THINK.
JOINING A FAMILIA MEANS...
ぱち…
PACHI (BLINK)
...BECOMING PART OF THAT GOD'S FAMILY.
すぴー
SUPI (SNORE)
!?
UWAAAA!!
WA!
WA!

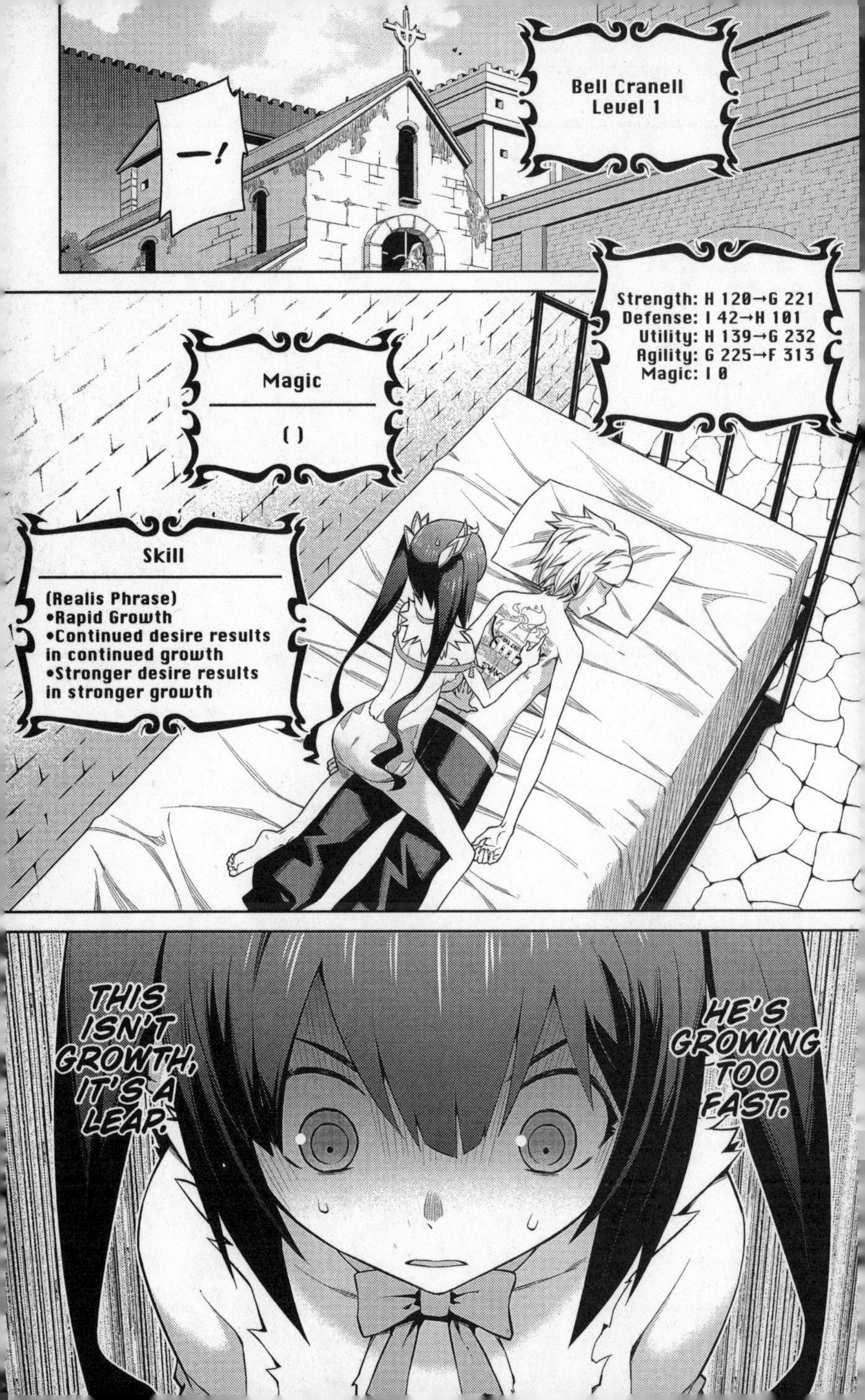
Bell Cranell
Level 1
—!
Strength: H 120→G 221
Defense: I 42→H 101
Utility: H 139→G 232
Agility: G 225→F 313
Magic: I 0
Magic
( )
Skill
(Realis Phrase)
•Rapid Growth
•Continued desire results in continued growth
•Stronger desire results in stronger growth
HE'S GROWING TOO FAST.
THIS ISN'T GROWTH, IT'S A LEAP.

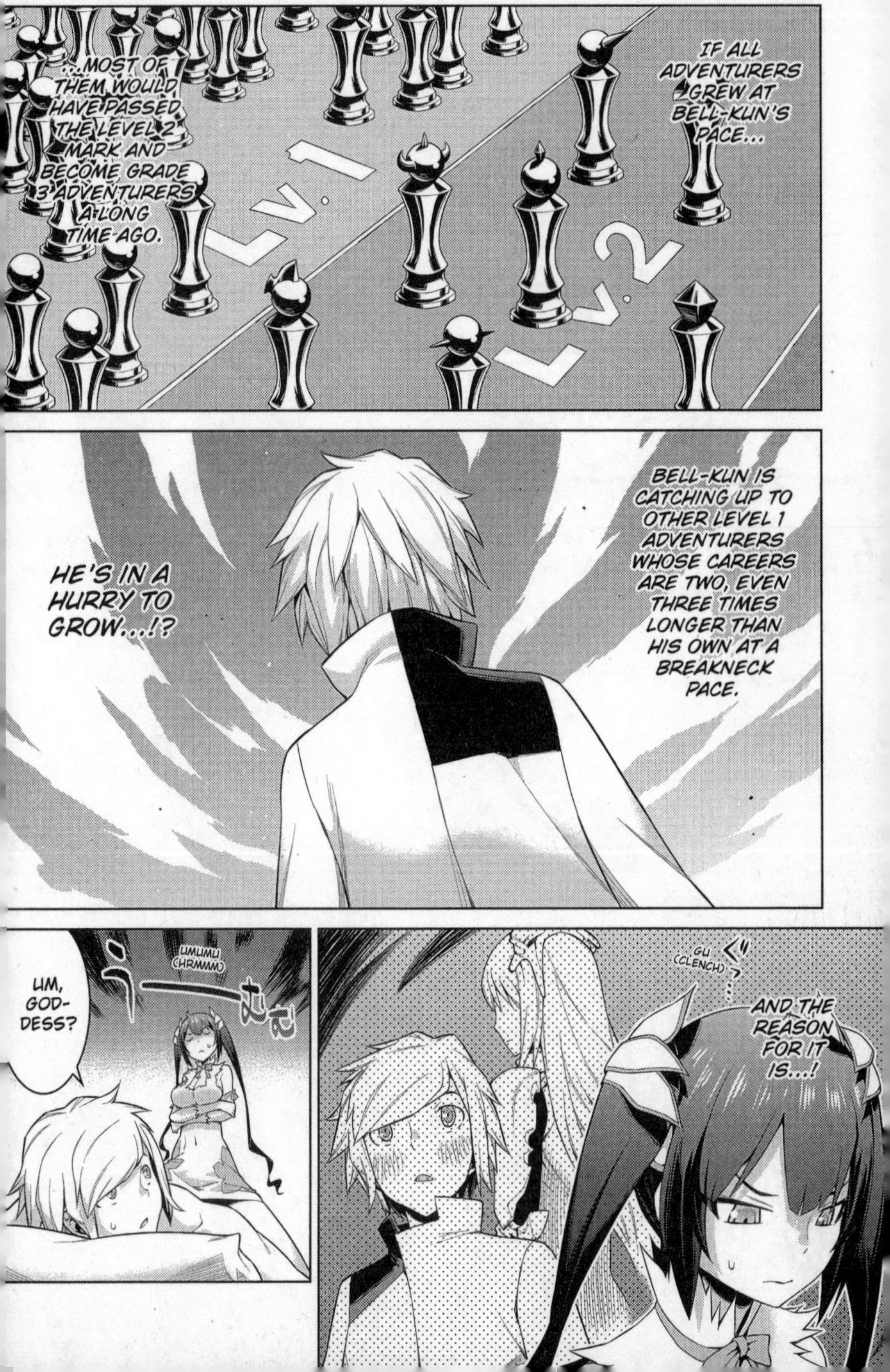
IF ALL ADVENTURERS GREW AT BELL-KUN'S PACE...
...MOST OF THEM WOULD HAVE PASSED THE LEVEL 2 MARK AND BECOME GRADE 3 ADVENTURERS A LONG TIME AGO.
Lv.2
Lv.1
BELL-KUN IS CATCHING UP TO OTHER LEVEL 1 ADVENTURERS WHOSE CAREERS ARE TWO, EVEN THREE TIMES LONGER THAN HIS OWN AT A BREAKNECK PACE.
HE'S IN A HURRY TO GROW...!?
GU (CLENCH)
AND THE REASON FOR IT IS...!
UMUMU (HRMMM)
UM, GODDESS?

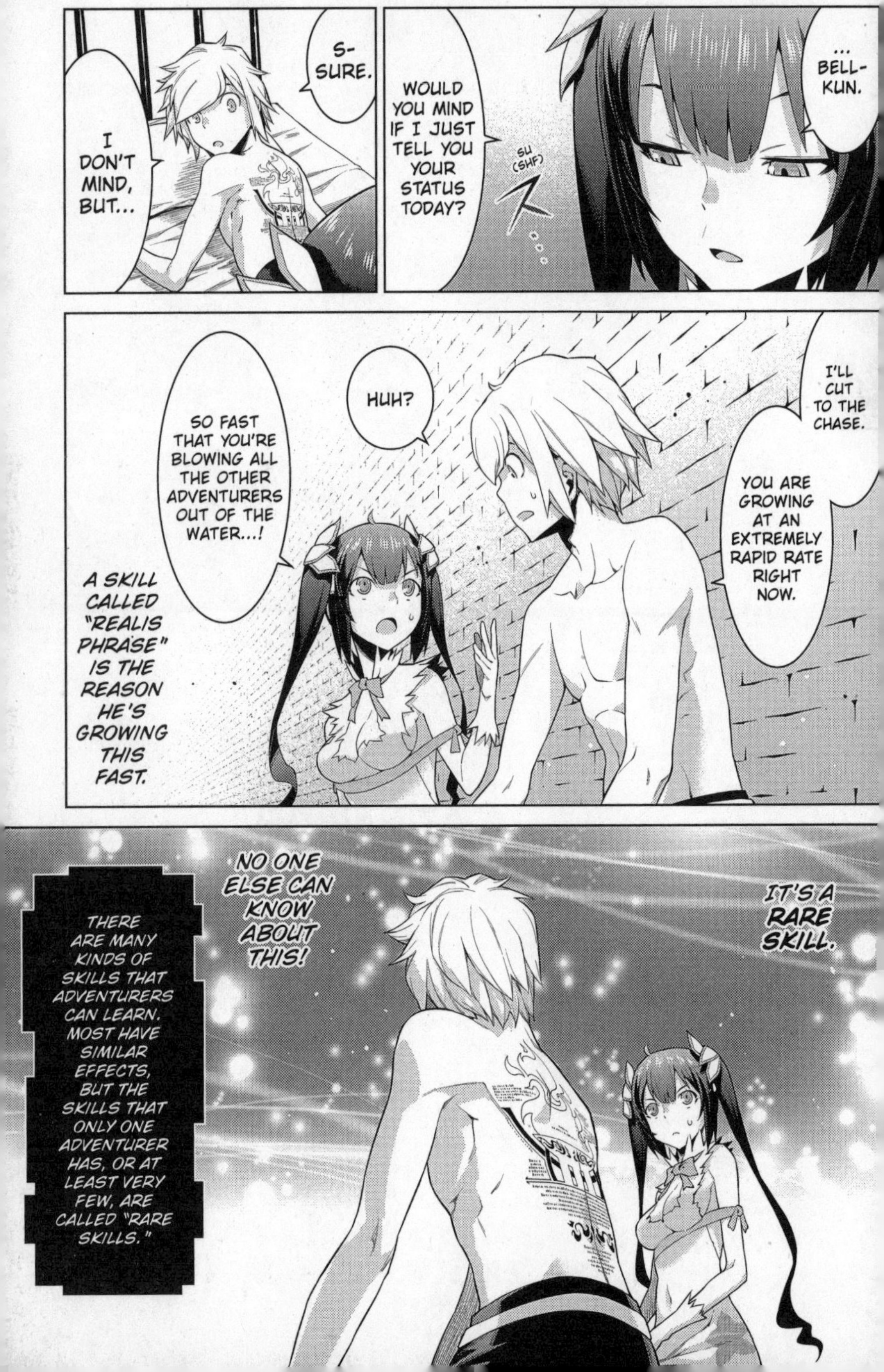
...BELL-KUN.
WOULD YOU MIND IF I JUST TELL YOU YOUR STATUS TODAY?
SU (SHF)
S-SURE.
I DON'T MIND, BUT...
I'LL CUT TO THE CHASE.
YOU ARE GROWING AT AN EXTREMELY RAPID RATE RIGHT NOW.
HUH?
SO FAST THAT YOU'RE BLOWING ALL THE OTHER ADVENTURERS OUT OF THE WATER...!
A SKILL CALLED "REALIS PHRASE" IS THE REASON HE'S GROWING THIS FAST.
IT'S A RARE SKILL.
NO ONE ELSE CAN KNOW ABOUT THIS!
THERE ARE MANY KINDS OF SKILLS THAT ADVENTURERS CAN LEARN. MOST HAVE SIMILAR EFFECTS, BUT THE SKILLS THAT ONLY ONE ADVENTURER HAS, OR AT LEAST VERY FEW, ARE CALLED "RARE SKILLS."

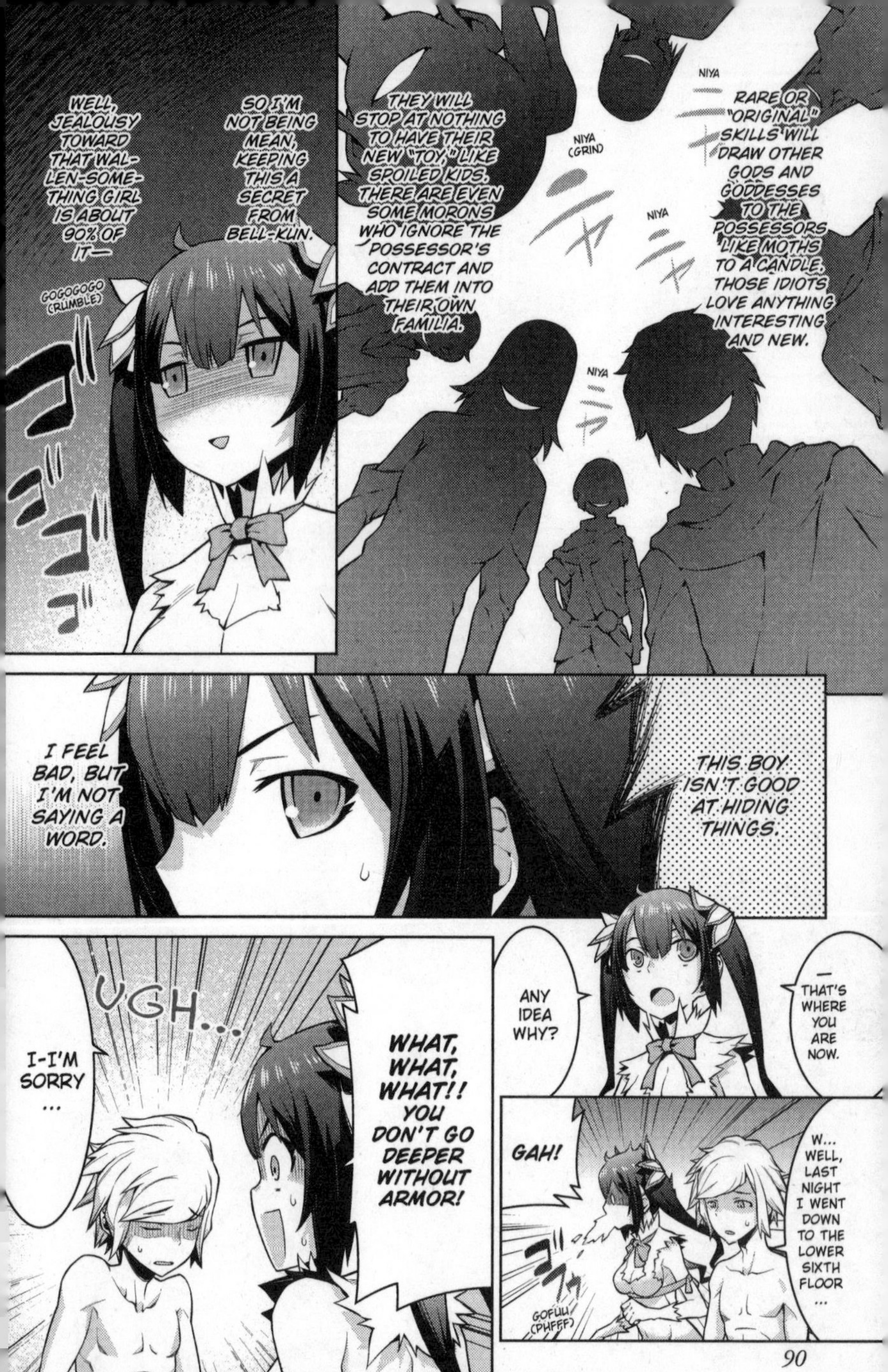
RARE OR "ORIGINAL" SKILLS WILL DRAW OTHER GODS AND GODDESSES TO THE POSSESSORS LIKE MOTHS TO A CANDLE. THOSE IDIOTS LOVE ANYTHING INTERESTING AND NEW.
NIYA
THEY WILL STOP AT NOTHING TO HAVE THEIR NEW "TOY," LIKE SPOILED KIDS. THERE ARE EVEN SOME MORONS WHO IGNORE THE POSSESSOR'S CONTRACT AND ADD THEM INTO THEIR OWN FAMILIA.
NIYA (GRIN)
NIYA
NIYA
SO I'M NOT BEING MEAN, KEEPING THIS A SECRET FROM BELL-KUN.
WELL, JEALOUSY TOWARD THAT WALLEN-SOMETHING GIRL IS ABOUT 90% OF IT—
GOGOGOGO (RUMBLE)
THIS BOY ISN'T GOOD AT HIDING THINGS.
I FEEL BAD, BUT I'M NOT SAYING A WORD.
—THAT'S WHERE YOU ARE NOW.
ANY IDEA WHY?
W... WELL, LAST NIGHT I WENT DOWN TO THE LOWER SIXTH FLOOR...
GAH!
GOFUU (PHFFF)
WHAT, WHAT, WHAT!! YOU DON'T GO DEEPER WITHOUT ARMOR!
UGH...
I-I'M SORRY ...

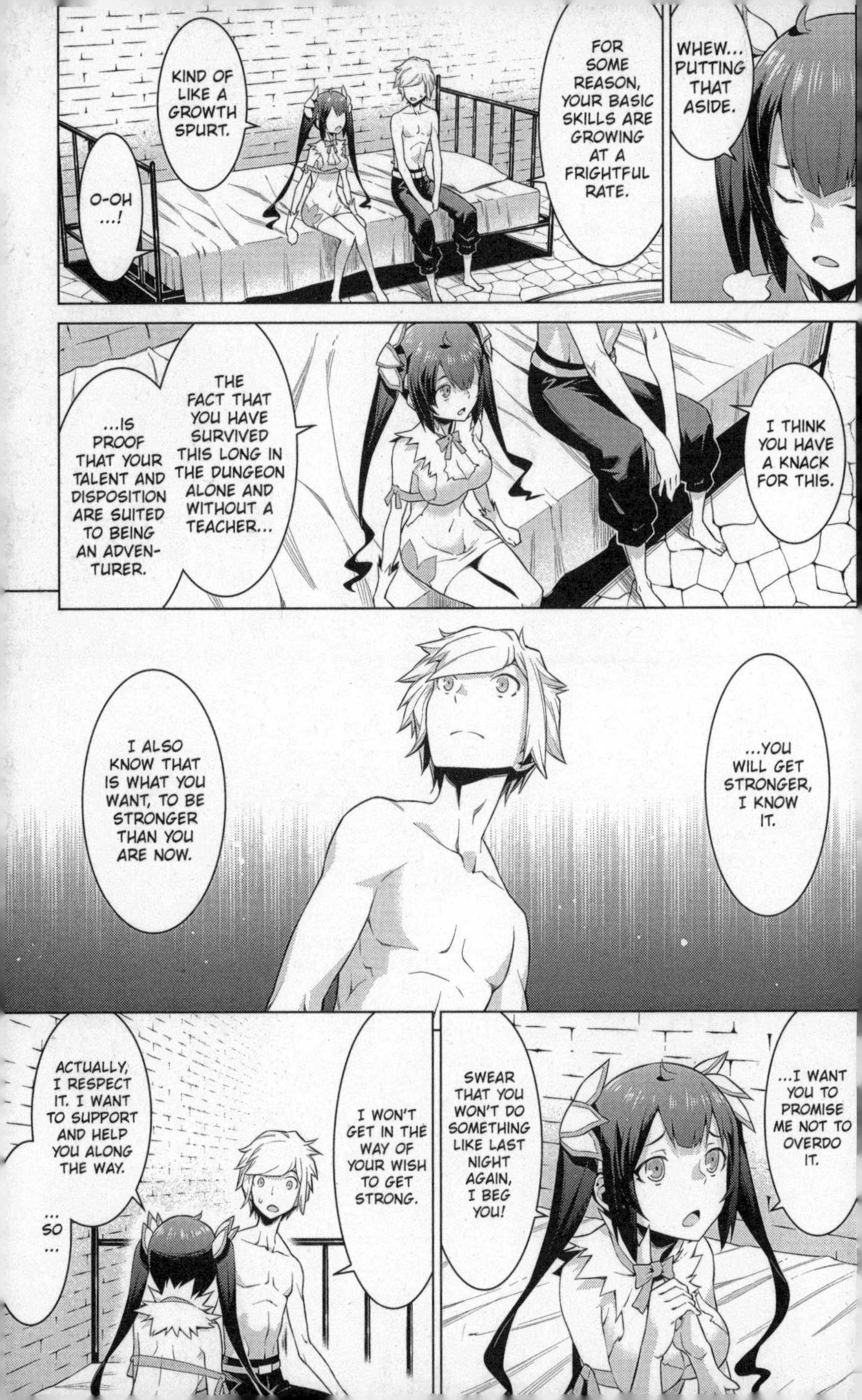
WHEW... PUTTING THAT ASIDE.
FOR SOME REASON, YOUR BASIC SKILLS ARE GROWING AT A FRIGHTFUL RATE.
KIND OF LIKE A GROWTH SPURT.
O-OH ...!
I THINK YOU HAVE A KNACK FOR THIS.
THE FACT THAT YOU HAVE SURVIVED THIS LONG IN THE DUNGEON ALONE AND WITHOUT A TEACHER...
...IS PROOF THAT YOUR TALENT AND DISPOSITION ARE SUITED TO BEING AN ADVEN-TURER.
...YOU WILL GET STRONGER, I KNOW IT.
I ALSO KNOW THAT IS WHAT YOU WANT, TO BE STRONGER THAN YOU ARE NOW.
...I WANT YOU TO PROMISE ME NOT TO OVERDO IT.
SWEAR THAT YOU WON'T DO SOMETHING LIKE LAST NIGHT AGAIN, I BEG YOU!
I WON'T GET IN THE WAY OF YOUR WISH TO GET STRONG.
ACTUALLY, I RESPECT IT. I WANT TO SUPPORT AND HELP YOU ALONG THE WAY.
... SO ...

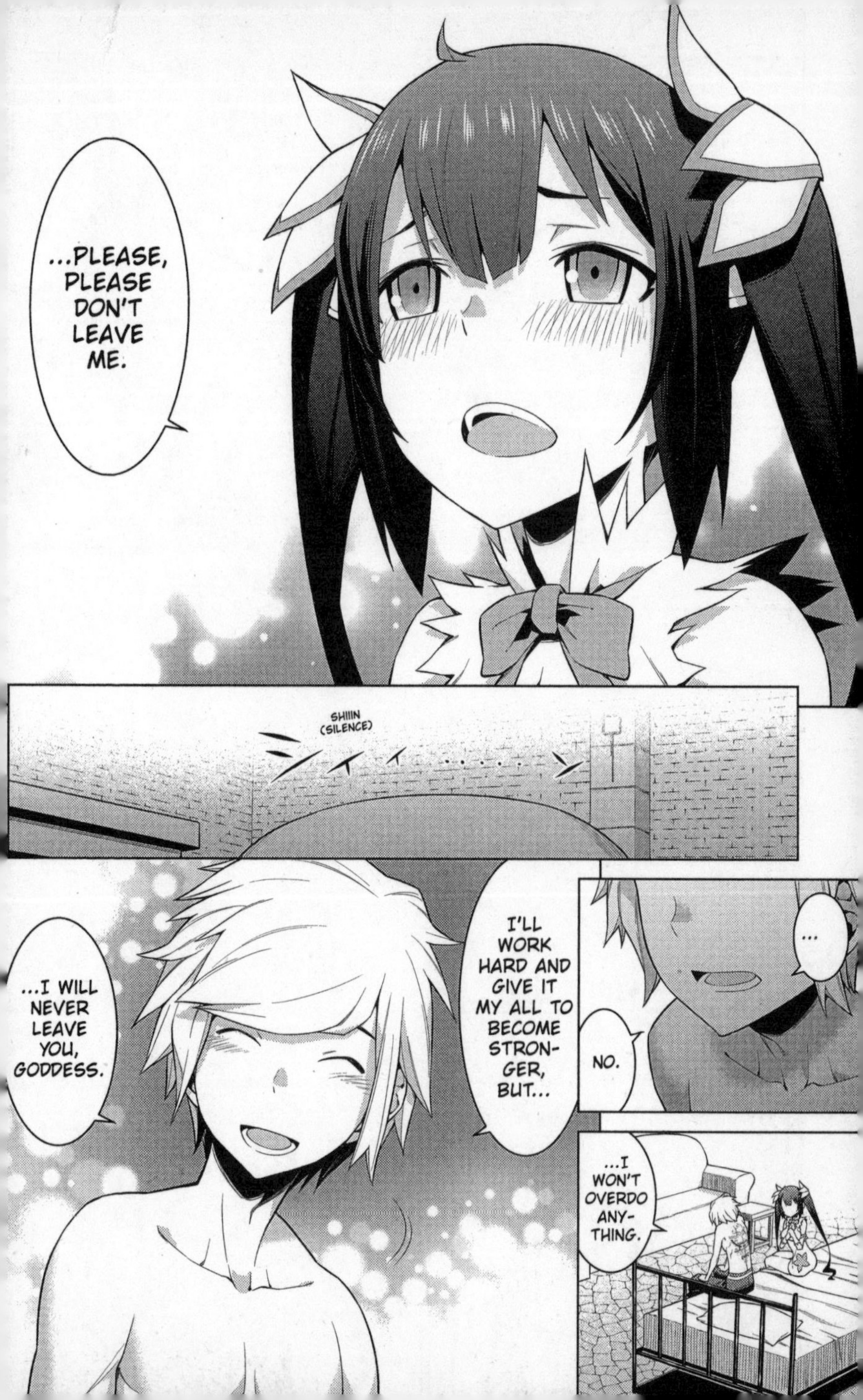
...PLEASE, PLEASE DON'T LEAVE ME.
SHIIIN (SILENCE)
...
NO.
...I WON'T OVERDO ANYTHING.
I'LL WORK HARD AND GIVE IT MY ALL TO BECOME STRONGER, BUT...
...I WILL NEVER LEAVE YOU, GODDESS.

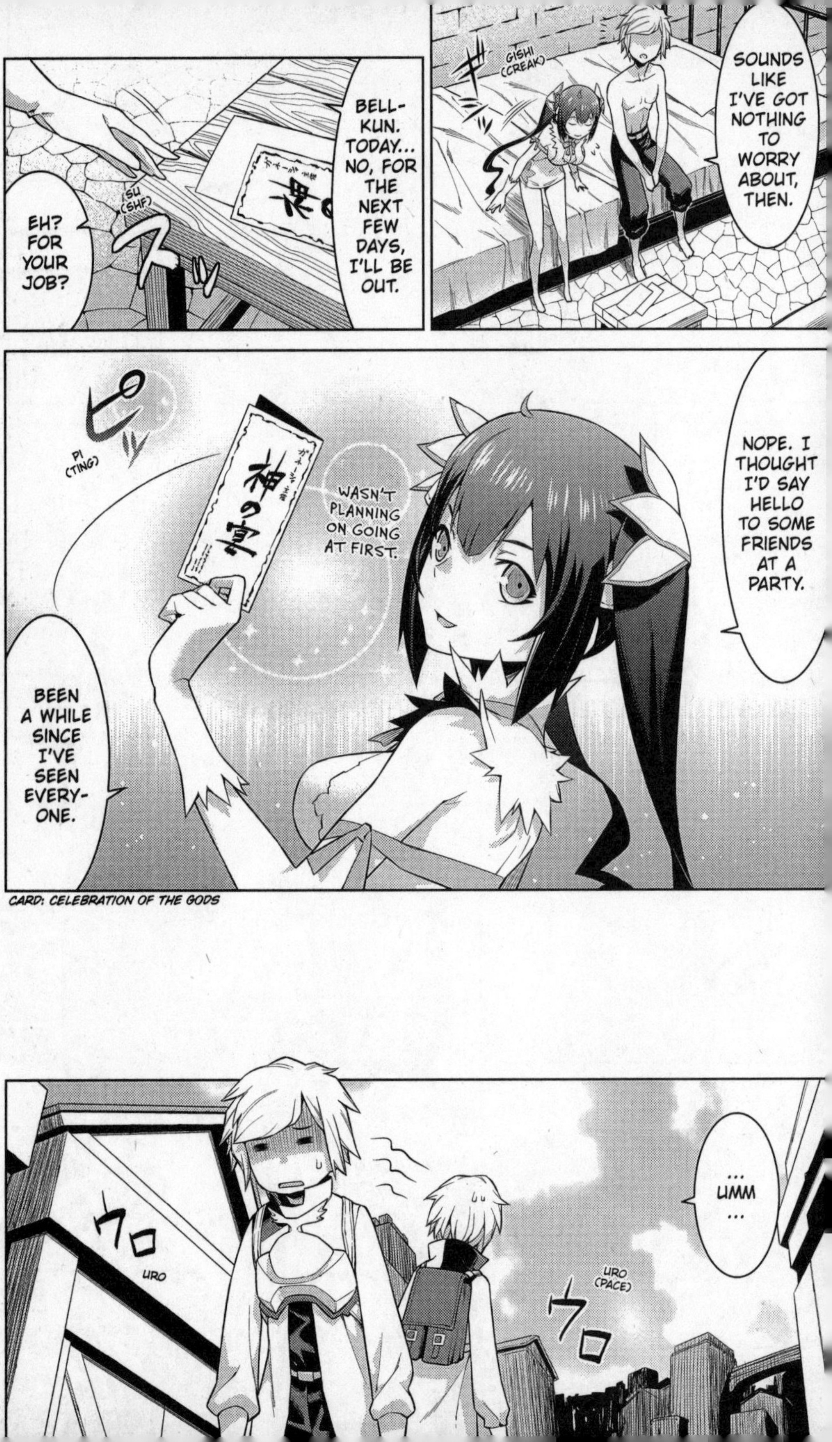
GISHI (CREAK)
SOUNDS LIKE I'VE GOT NOTHING TO WORRY ABOUT, THEN.
BELL-KUN. TODAY... NO, FOR THE NEXT FEW DAYS, I'LL BE OUT.
SU (SHF)
EH? FOR YOUR JOB?
NOPE. I THOUGHT I'D SAY HELLO TO SOME FRIENDS AT A PARTY.
WASN'T PLANNING ON GOING AT FIRST.
PI (TING)
BEEN A WHILE SINCE I'VE SEEN EVERY-ONE.
神の宴
CARD: CELEBRATION OF THE GODS
... UMM ...
URO (PACE)
URO

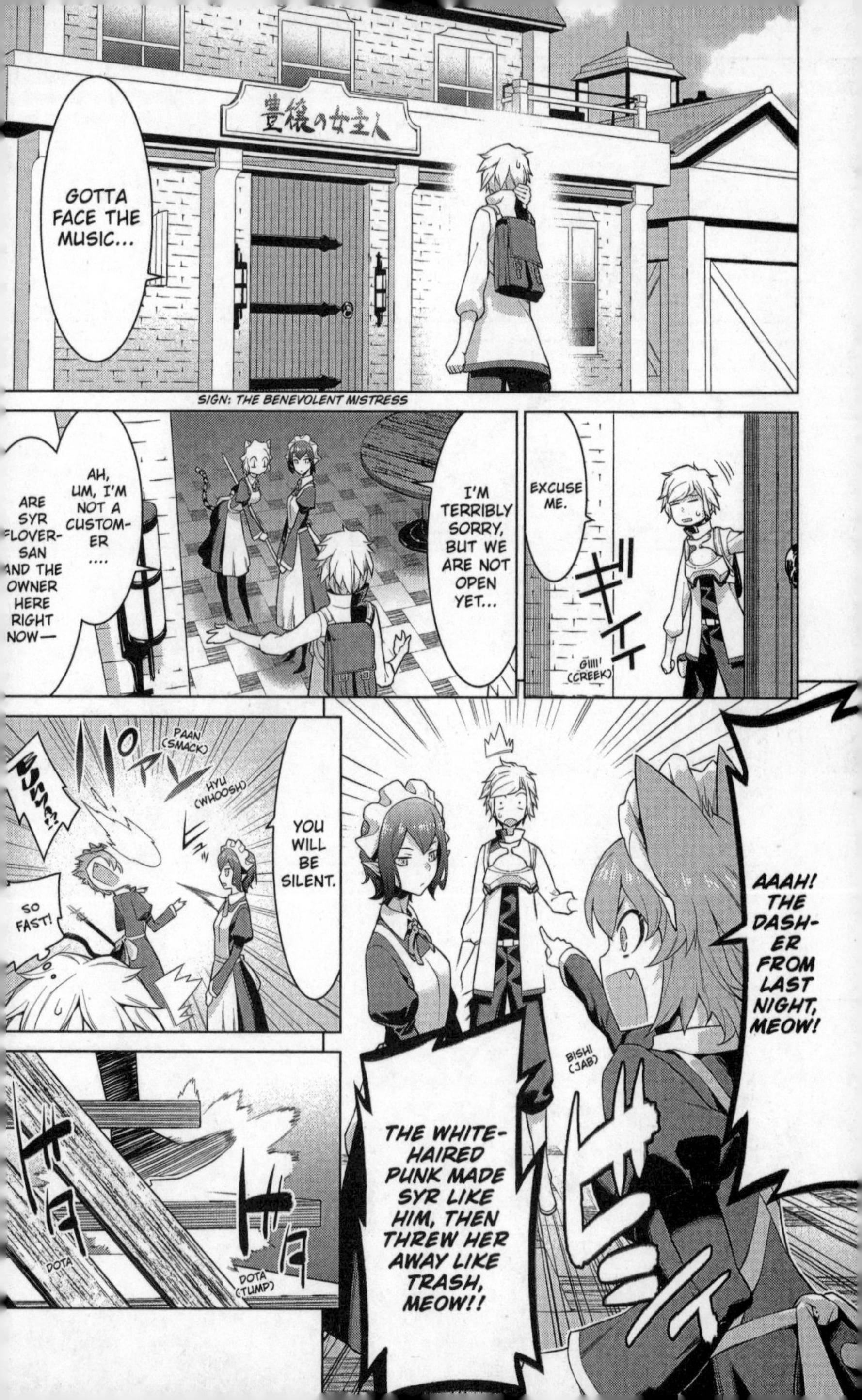
GOTTA FACE THE MUSIC...
SIGN: THE BENEVOLENT MISTRESS
EXCUSE ME.
GIIII (CREEK)
I'M TERRIBLY SORRY, BUT WE ARE NOT OPEN YET...
AH, UM, I'M NOT A CUSTOMER ....
ARE SYR FLOVER-SAN AND THE OWNER HERE RIGHT NOW—
AAAH! THE DASHER FROM LAST NIGHT, MEOW!
BISHI (JAB)
THE WHITE-HAIRED PUNK MADE SYR LIKE HIM, THEN THREW HER AWAY LIKE TRASH, MEOW!!
YOU WILL BE SILENT.
PAAN (SMACK)
HYU (WHOOSH)
BUNYA!?
SO FAST!
DOTA
DOTA (TUMP)

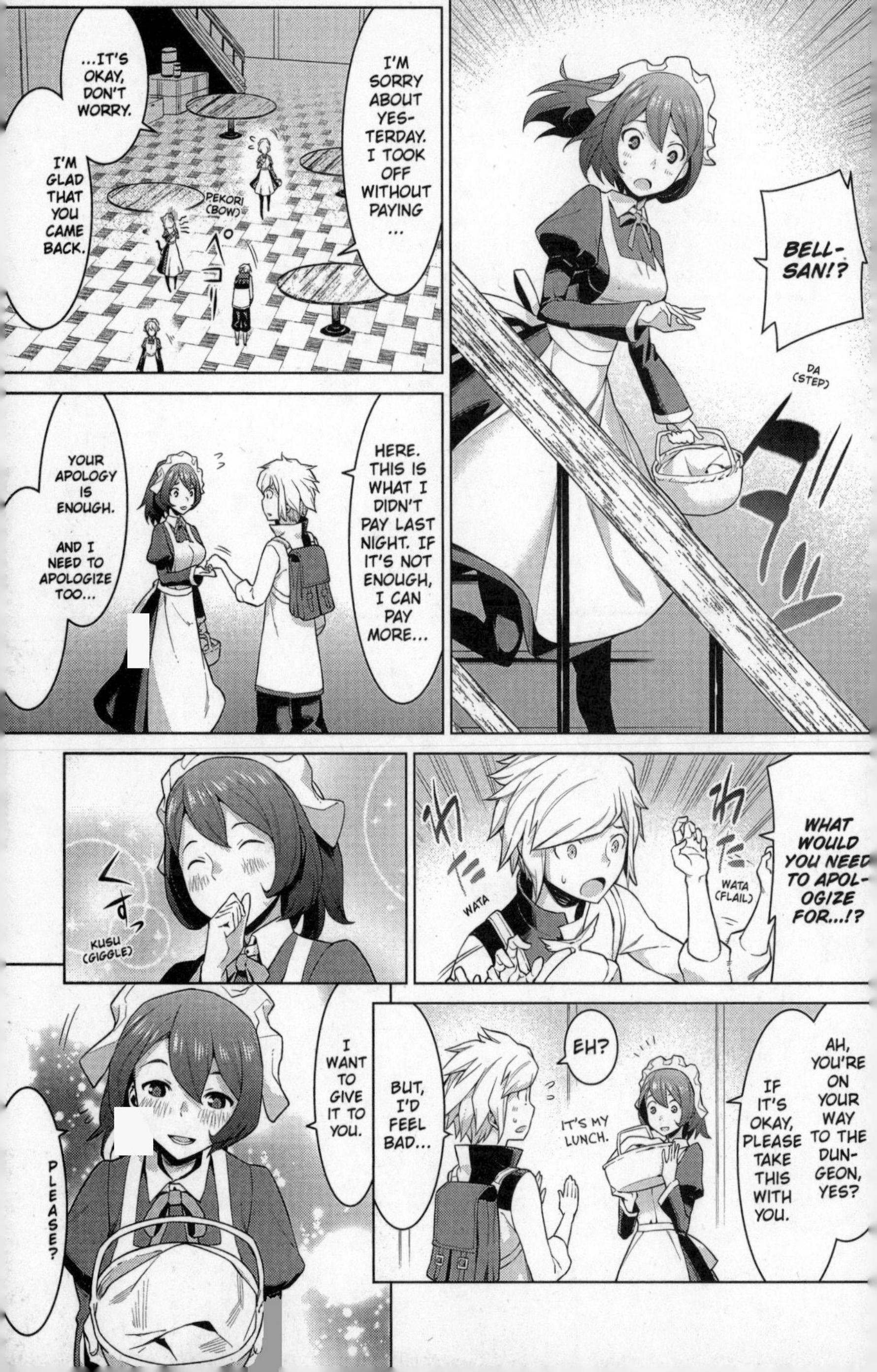
BELL-SAN!?
DA (STEP)
I'M SORRY ABOUT YESTERDAY. I TOOK OFF WITHOUT PAYING...
PEKORI (BOW)
...IT'S OKAY, DON'T WORRY.
I'M GLAD THAT YOU CAME BACK.
HERE. THIS IS WHAT I DIDN'T PAY LAST NIGHT. IF IT'S NOT ENOUGH, I CAN PAY MORE...
YOUR APOLOGY IS ENOUGH.
AND I NEED TO APOLOGIZE TOO...
WHAT WOULD YOU NEED TO APOLOGIZE FOR...!?
WATA (FLAIL)
WATA
KUSU (GIGGLE)
AH, YOU'RE ON YOUR WAY TO THE DUNGEON, YES?
IF IT'S OKAY, PLEASE TAKE THIS WITH YOU.
EH?
IT'S MY LUNCH.
BUT, I'D FEEL BAD...
I WANT TO GIVE IT TO YOU.
PLEASE?

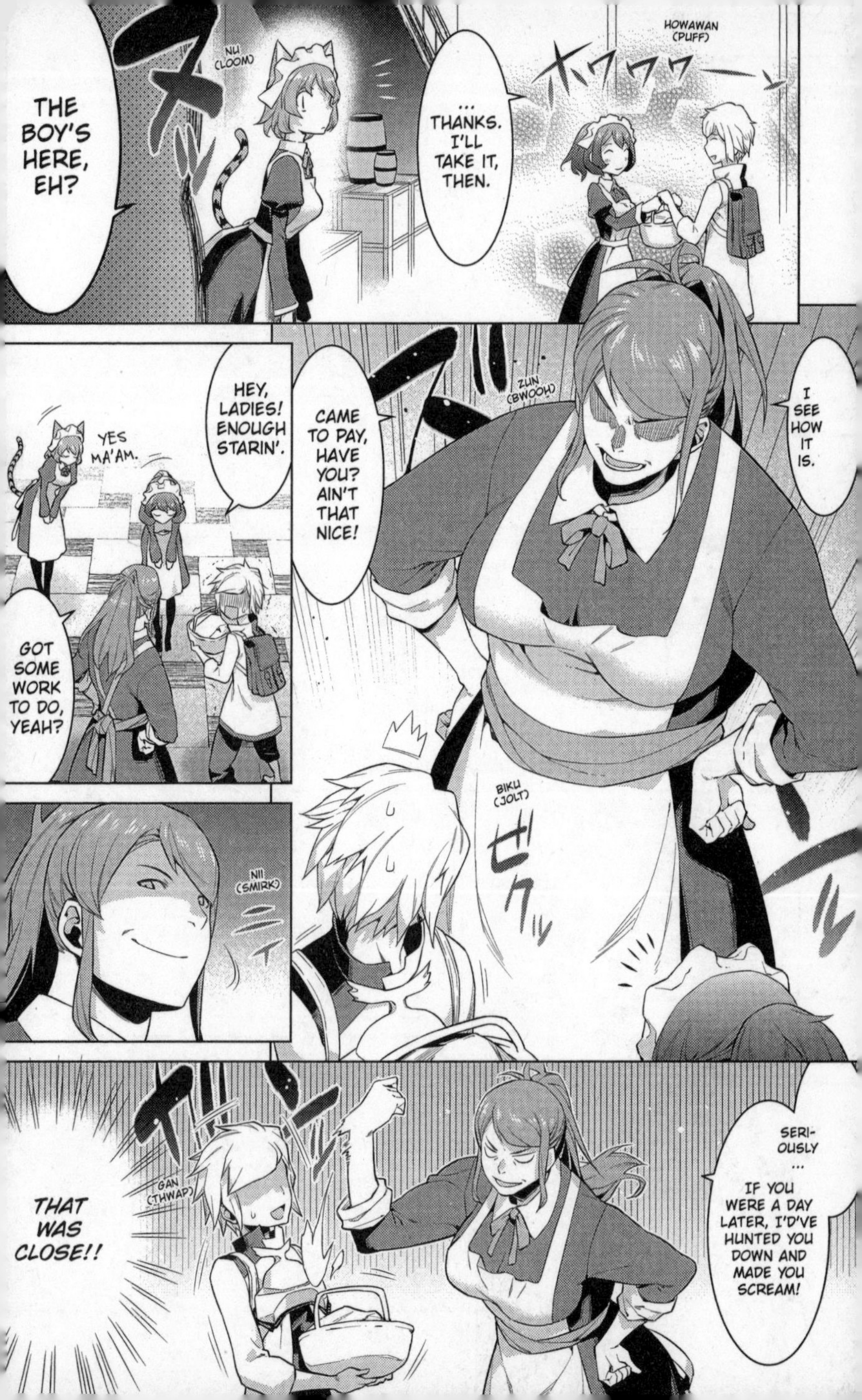
HOWAWAN (PUFF)
... THANKS. I'LL TAKE IT, THEN.
NU (LOOM)
THE BOY'S HERE, EH?
I SEE HOW IT IS.
ZUN (BWOOH)
CAME TO PAY, HAVE YOU? AIN'T THAT NICE!
BIKU (JOLT)
HEY, LADIES! ENOUGH STARIN'.
YES MA'AM.
GOT SOME WORK TO DO, YEAH?
NII (SMIRK)
SERI-OUSLY ... IF YOU WERE A DAY LATER, I'D'VE HUNTED YOU DOWN AND MADE YOU SCREAM!
GAN (THWAP)
THAT WAS CLOSE!!

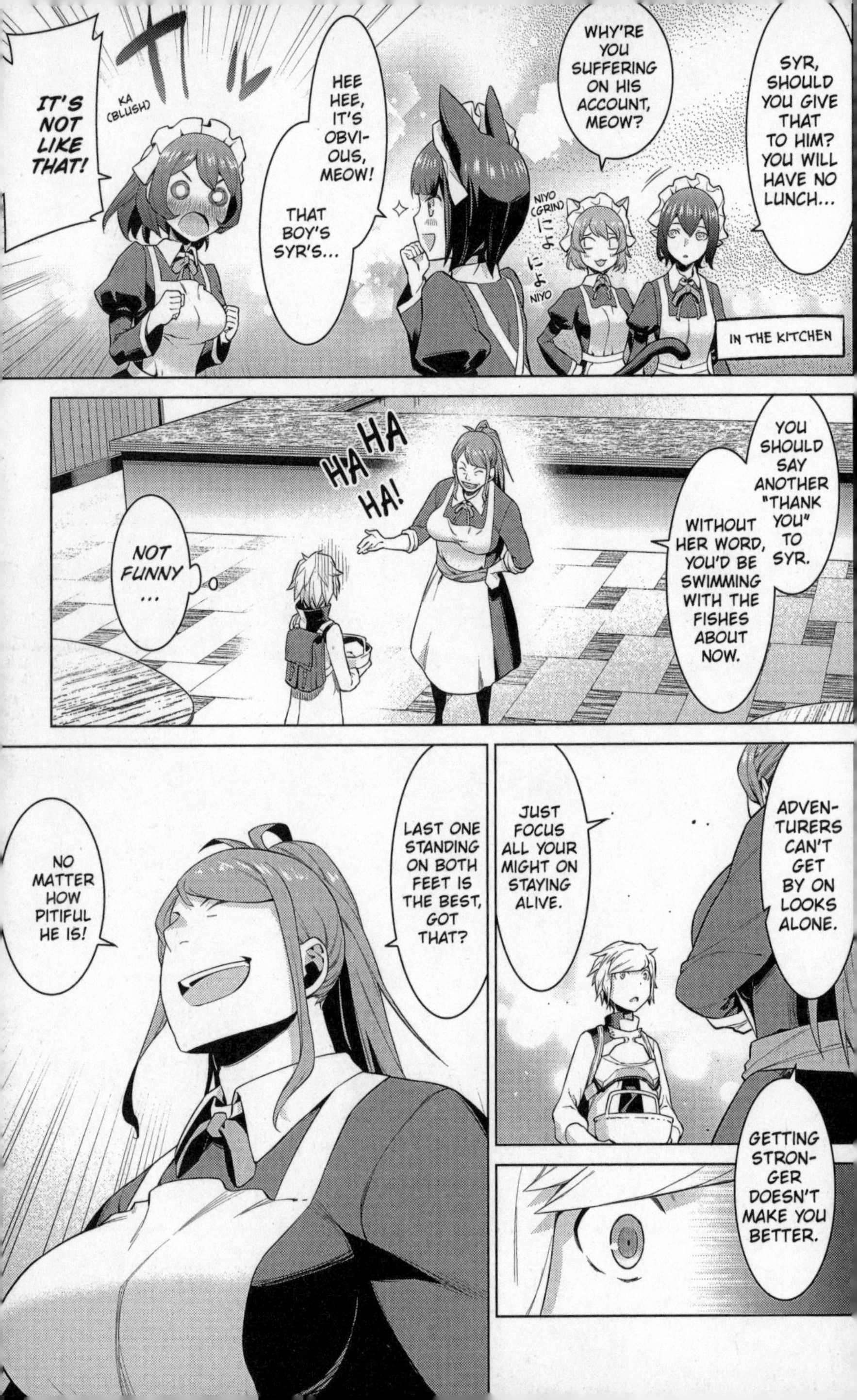
IN THE KITCHEN
SYR, SHOULD YOU GIVE THAT TO HIM? YOU WILL HAVE NO LUNCH...
WHY'RE YOU SUFFERING ON HIS ACCOUNT, MEOW?
NIYO (GRIN)
にょにょ
NIYO
HEE HEE, IT'S OBVIOUS, MEOW!
THAT BOY'S SYR'S...
KA (BLUSH)
IT'S NOT LIKE THAT!
YOU SHOULD SAY ANOTHER "THANK YOU" TO SYR.
WITHOUT HER WORD, YOU'D BE SWIMMING WITH THE FISHES ABOUT NOW.
HA HA HA!
NOT FUNNY...
ADVENTURERS CAN'T GET BY ON LOOKS ALONE.
JUST FOCUS ALL YOUR MIGHT ON STAYING ALIVE.
GETTING STRONGER DOESN'T MAKE YOU BETTER.
LAST ONE STANDING ON BOTH FEET IS THE BEST, GOT THAT?
NO MATTER HOW PITIFUL HE IS!

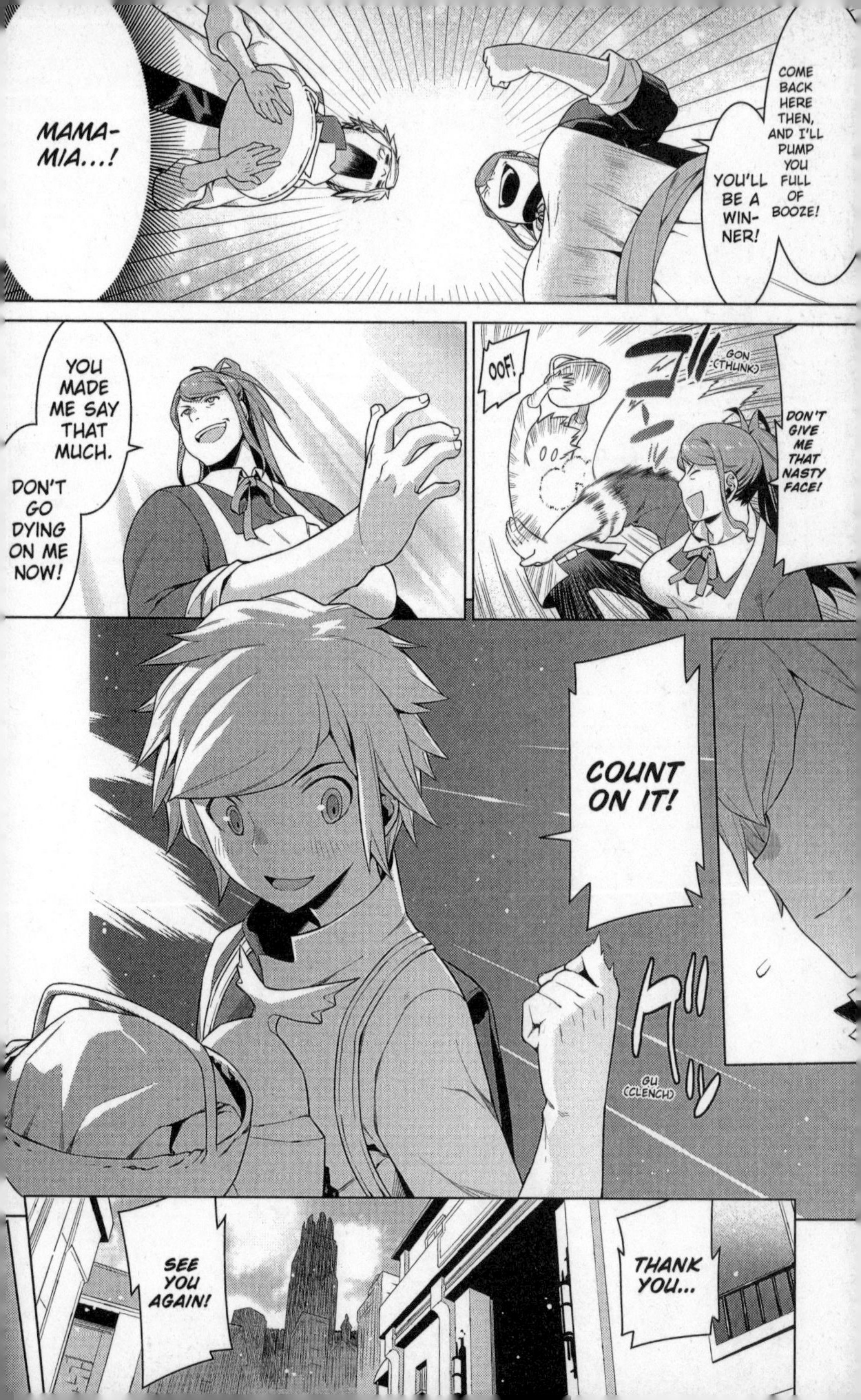
COME BACK HERE THEN, AND I'LL PUMP YOU FULL OF BOOZE!
YOU'LL BE A WIN-NER!
MAMA-MIA...!
GON (THUNK)
DON'T GIVE ME THAT NASTY FACE!
OOF!
YOU MADE ME SAY THAT MUCH.
DON'T GO DYING ON ME NOW!
COUNT ON IT!
GU (CLENCH)
THANK YOU...
SEE YOU AGAIN!

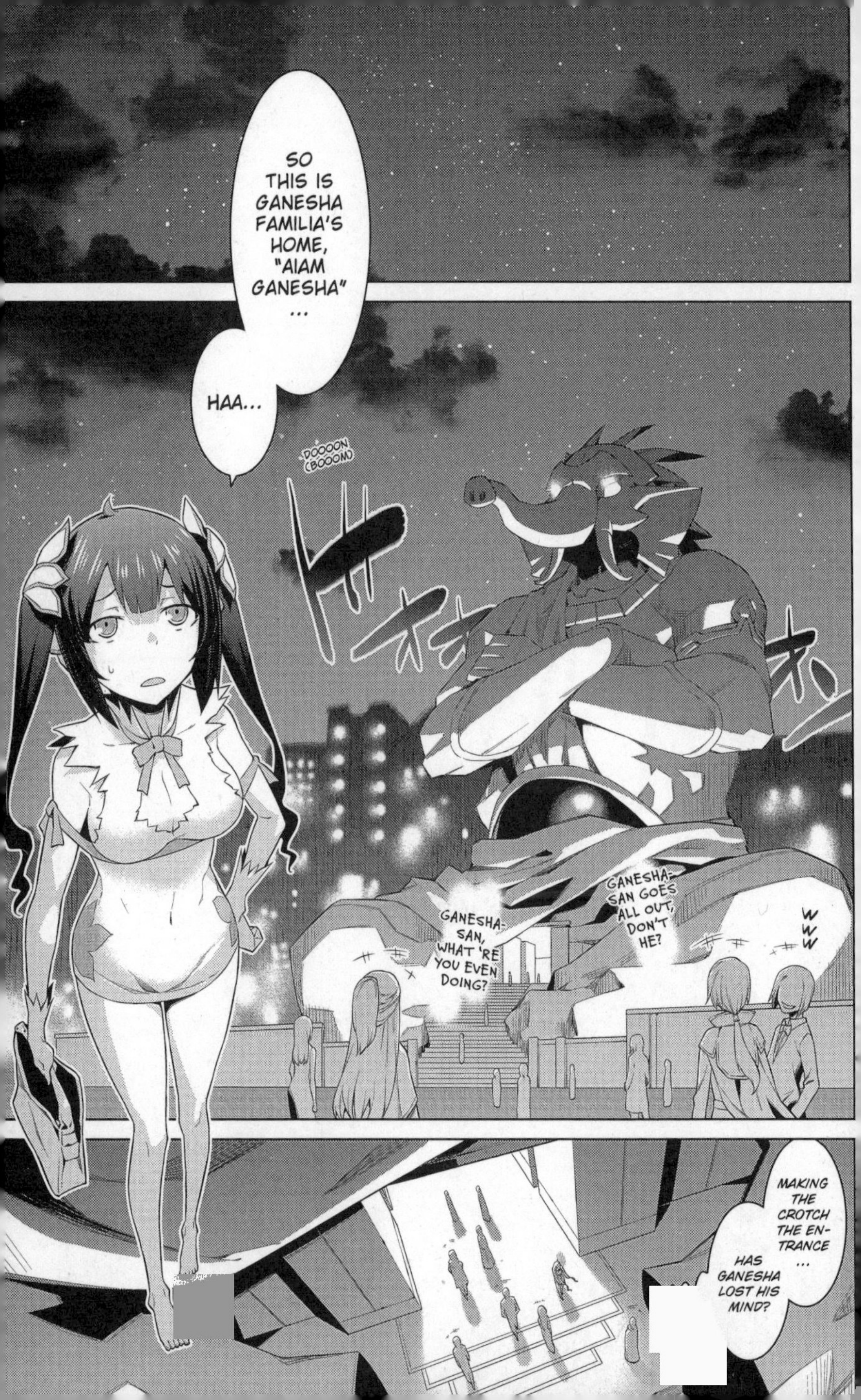
SO THIS IS GANESHA FAMILIA'S HOME, "AIAM GANESHA"...
HAA...
DOOOON (BOOOM)
WWW
GANESHA-SAN GOES ALL OUT, DON'T HE?
GANESHA-SAN, WHAT'RE YOU EVEN DOING?
MAKING THE CROTCH THE EN-TRANCE...
HAS GANESHA LOST HIS MIND?

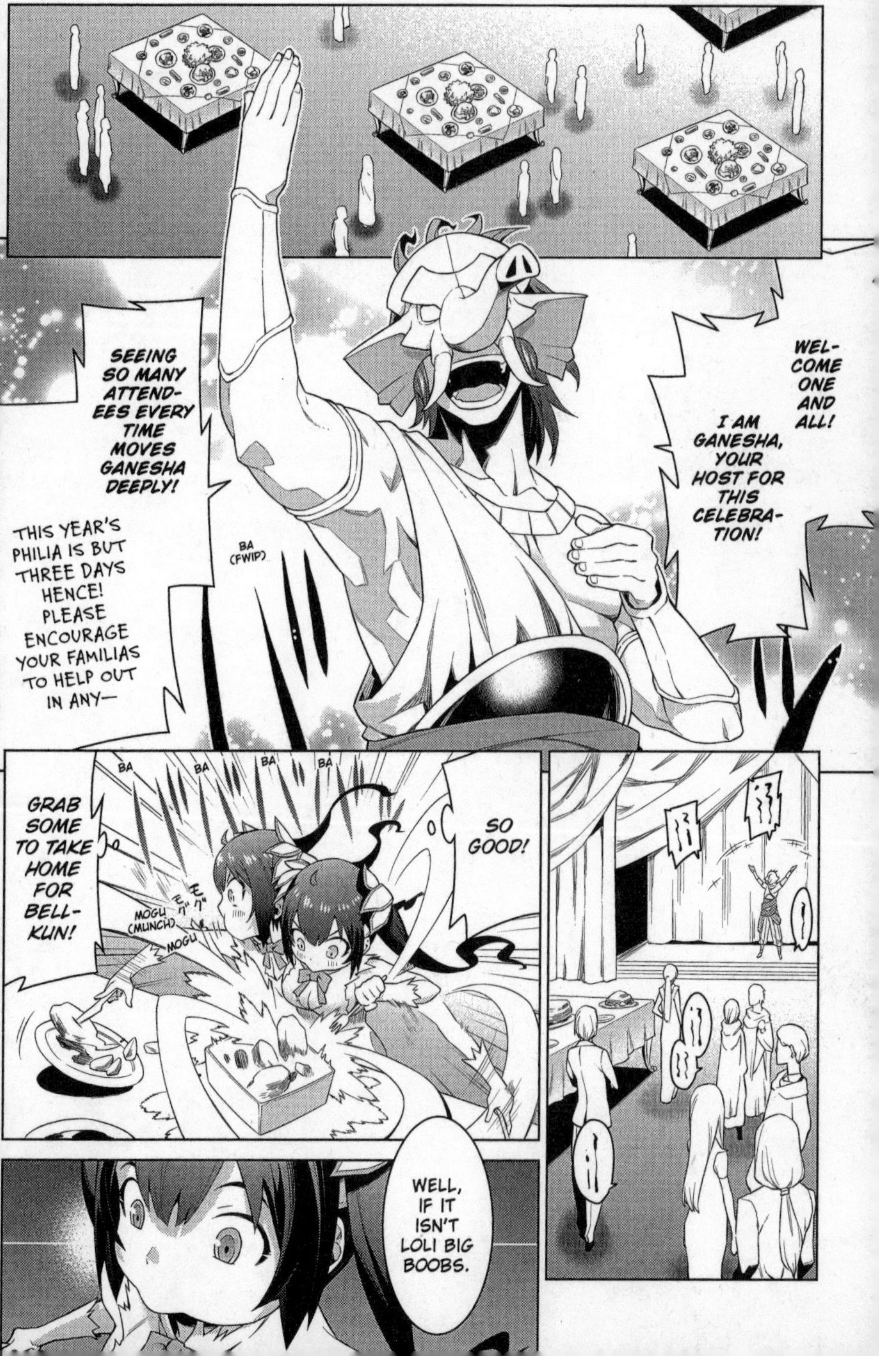
WELCOME ONE AND ALL!
I AM GANESHA, YOUR HOST FOR THIS CELEBRATION!
SEEING SO MANY ATTENDEES EVERY TIME MOVES GANESHA DEEPLY!
BA (FWIP)
THIS YEAR'S PHILIA IS BUT THREE DAYS HENCE! PLEASE ENCOURAGE YOUR FAMILIAS TO HELP OUT IN ANY—
BA BA BA BA
SO GOOD!
GRAB SOME TO TAKE HOME FOR BELL-KUN!
モグ
MOGU (MUNCH)
MOGU
WELL, IF IT ISN'T LOLI BIG BOOBS.

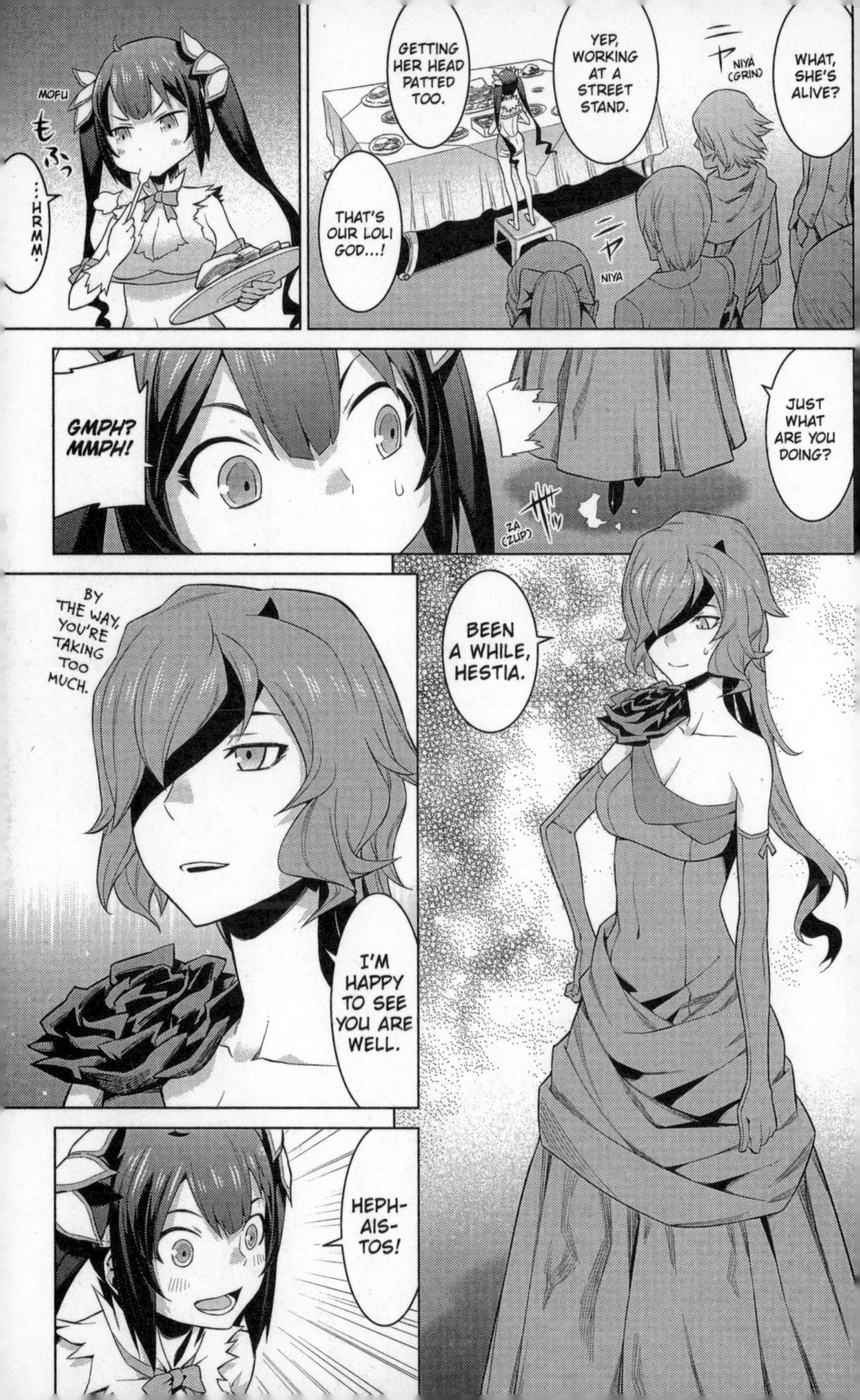
WHAT, SHE'S ALIVE?
ニヤ NIYA (GRIN)
YEP, WORKING AT A STREET STAND.
GETTING HER HEAD PATTED TOO.
THAT'S OUR LOLI GOD...!
ニヤ NIYA
もふっ MOFU
...HRMM.
JUST WHAT ARE YOU DOING?
ZA (ZUP)
GMPH? MMPH!
BEEN A WHILE, HESTIA.
I'M HAPPY TO SEE YOU ARE WELL.
BY THE WAY, YOU'RE TAKING TOO MUCH.
HEPH-AISTOS!

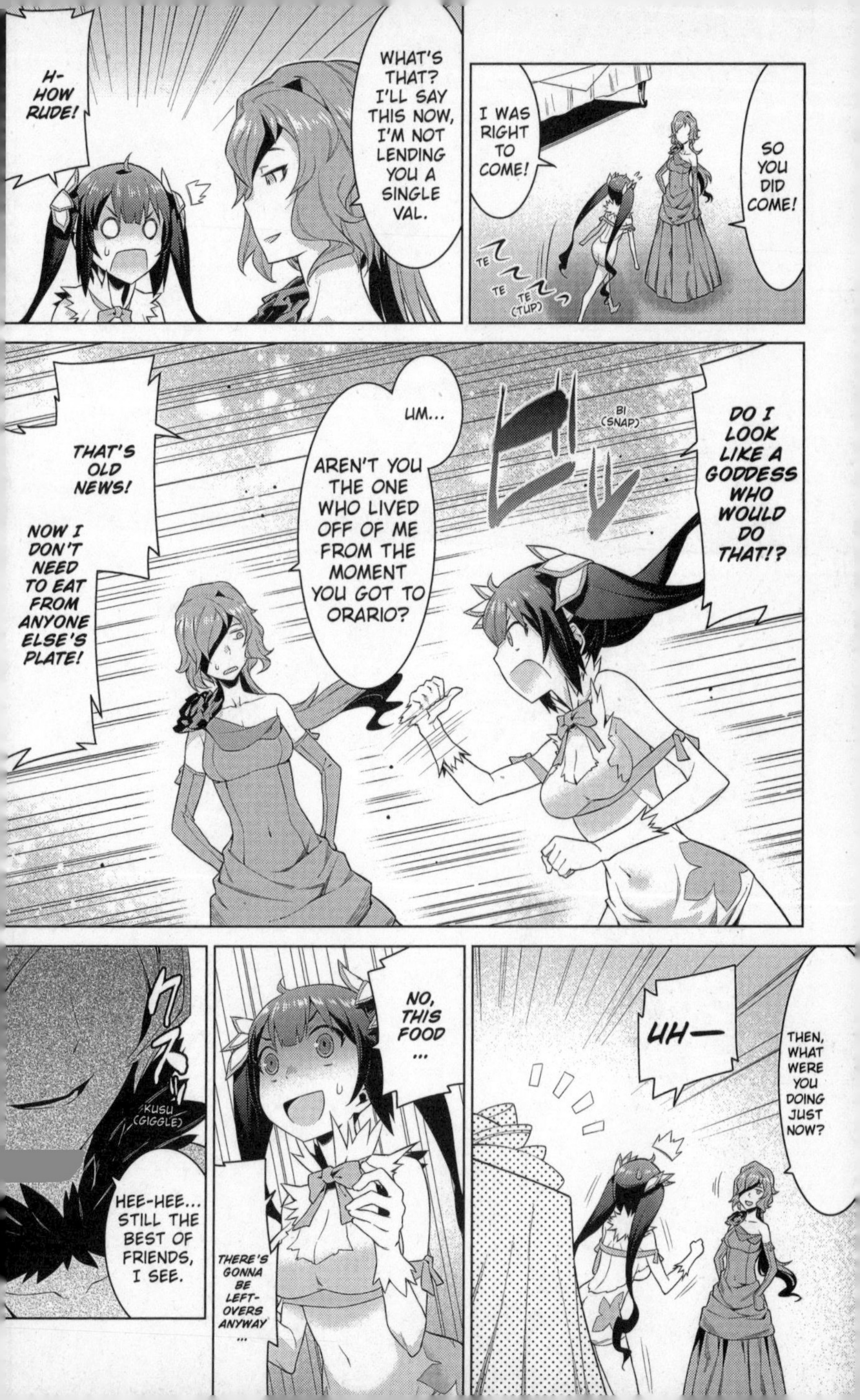
SO YOU DID COME!
I WAS RIGHT TO COME!
TE TE TE (TUP)
WHAT'S THAT? I'LL SAY THIS NOW, I'M NOT LENDING YOU A SINGLE VAL.
H-HOW RUDE!
DO I LOOK LIKE A GODDESS WHO WOULD DO THAT!?
BI (SNAP)
UM...
AREN'T YOU THE ONE WHO LIVED OFF OF ME FROM THE MOMENT YOU GOT TO ORARIO?
THAT'S OLD NEWS!
NOW I DON'T NEED TO EAT FROM ANYONE ELSE'S PLATE!
THEN, WHAT WERE YOU DOING JUST NOW?
UH—
NO, THIS FOOD ...
THERE'S GONNA BE LEFT-OVERS ANYWAY ...
KUSU (GIGGLE)
HEE-HEE... STILL THE BEST OF FRIENDS, I SEE.

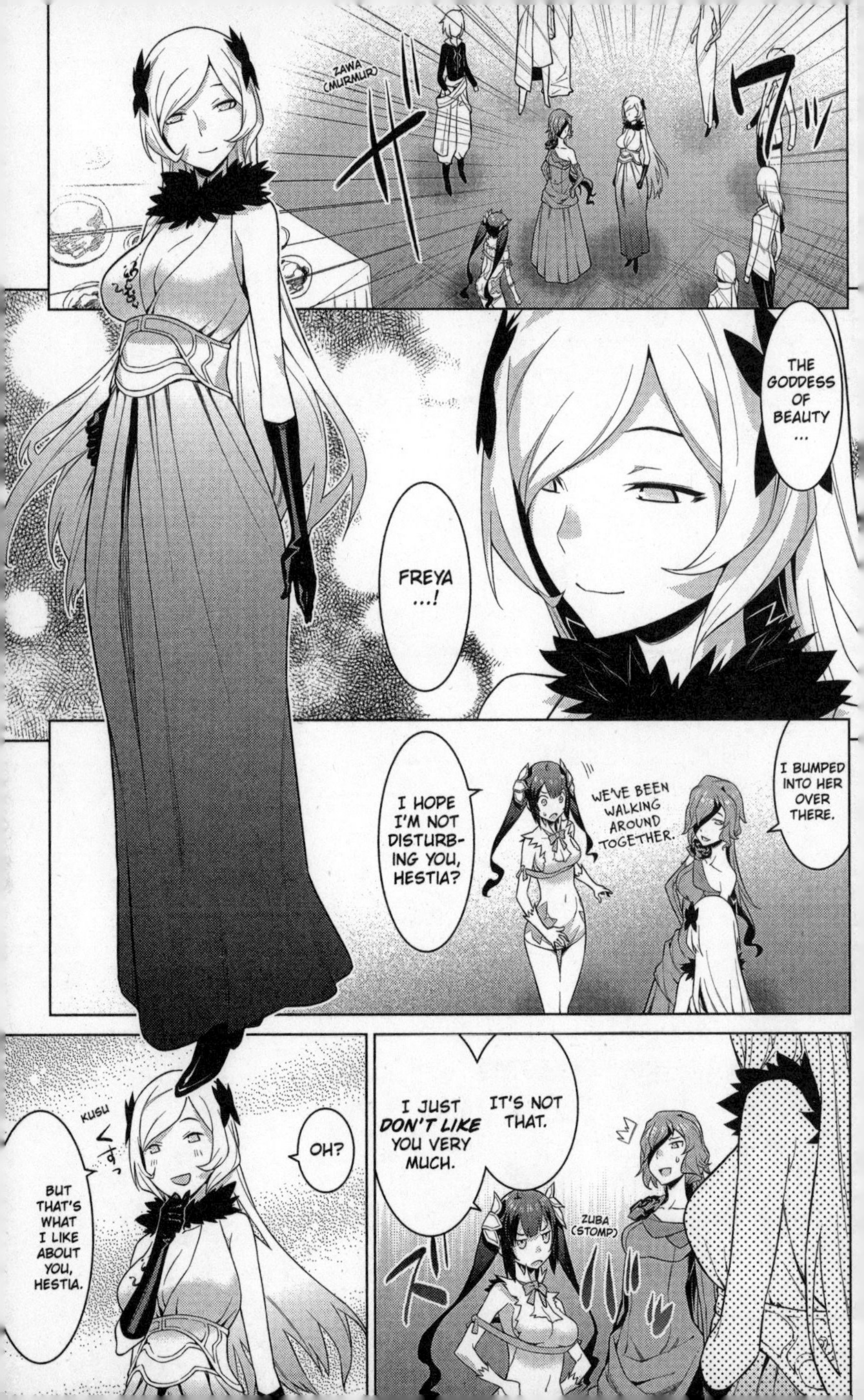
ZAWA (MURMUR)
THE GODDESS OF BEAUTY...
FREYA...!
I BUMPED INTO HER OVER THERE.
WE'VE BEEN WALKING AROUND TOGETHER.
I HOPE I'M NOT DISTURBING YOU, HESTIA?
IT'S NOT THAT.
I JUST ***DON'T LIKE*** YOU VERY MUCH.
ZUBA (STOMP)
OH?
KUSU
BUT THAT'S WHAT I LIKE ABOUT YOU, HESTIA.

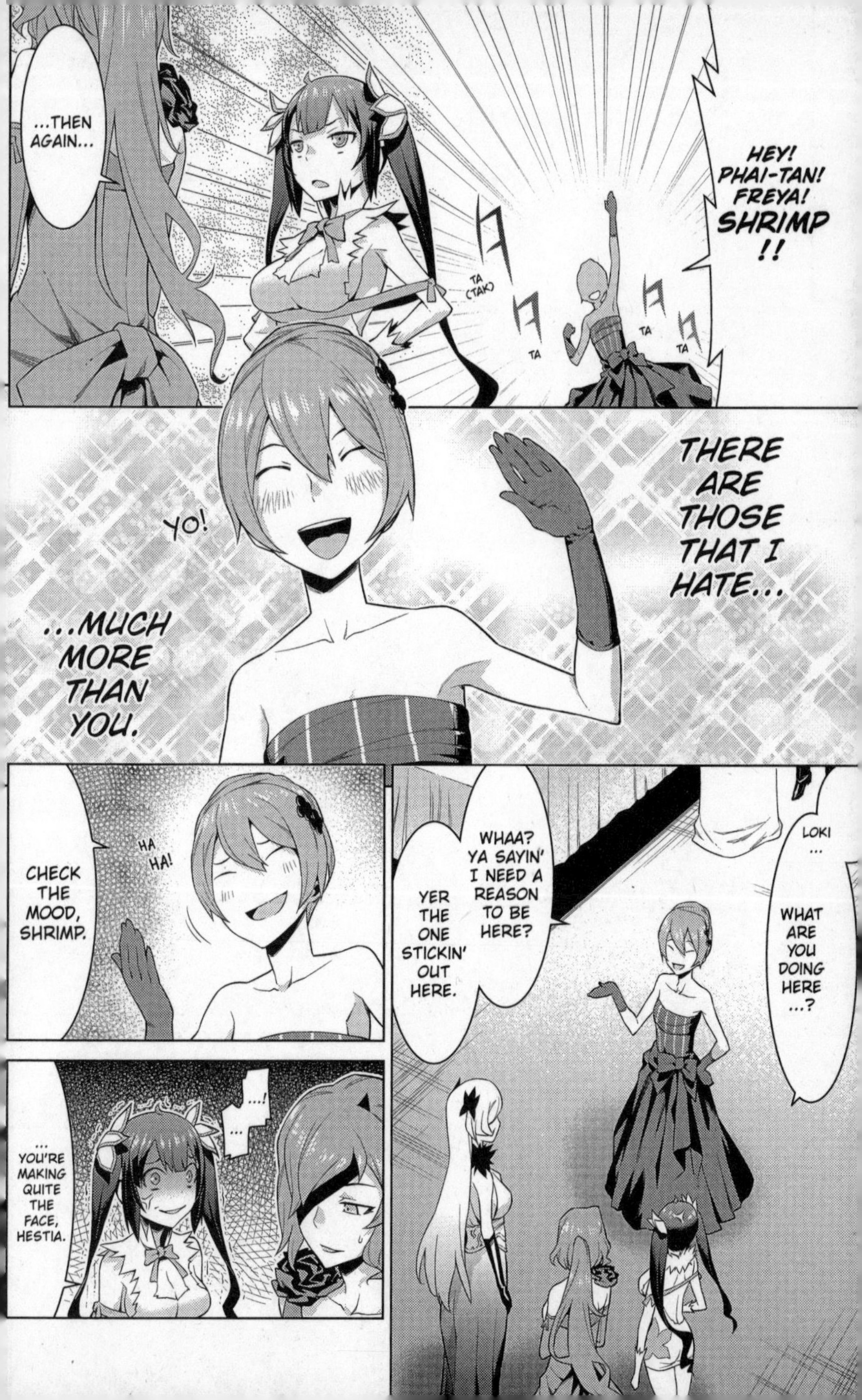
HEY! PHAI-TAN! FREYA! SHRIMP!!
TA (TAK)
TA
TA
TA
...THEN AGAIN...
THERE ARE THOSE THAT I HATE...
YO!
...MUCH MORE THAN YOU.
LOKI... WHAT ARE YOU DOING HERE...?
WHAA? YA SAYIN' I NEED A REASON TO BE HERE?
YER THE ONE STICKIN' OUT HERE.
HA HA!
CHECK THE MOOD, SHRIMP.
...!
...
... YOU'RE MAKING QUITE THE FACE, HESTIA.

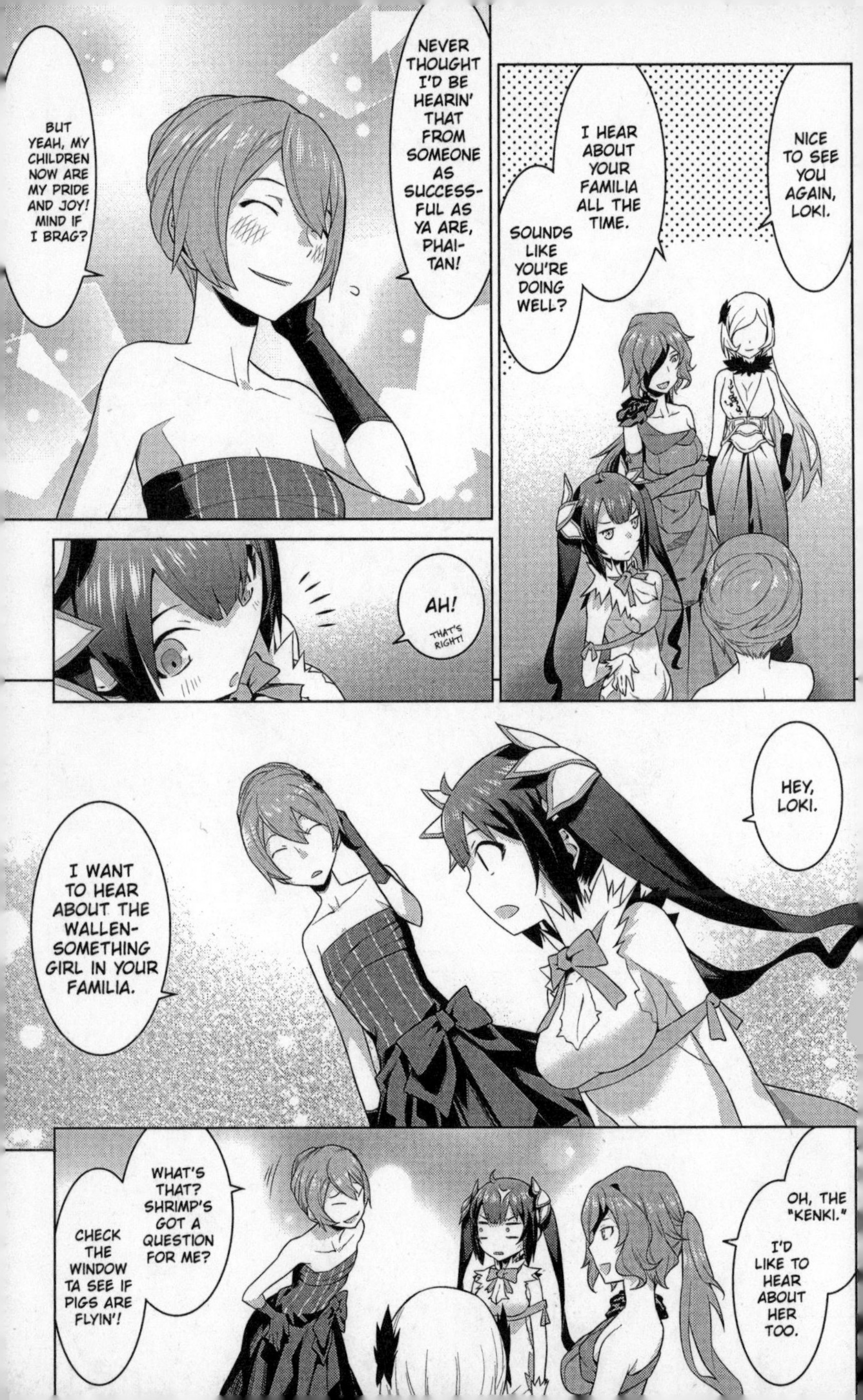
NICE TO SEE YOU AGAIN, LOKI.
I HEAR ABOUT YOUR FAMILIA ALL THE TIME.
SOUNDS LIKE YOU'RE DOING WELL?
NEVER THOUGHT I'D BE HEARIN' THAT FROM SOMEONE AS SUCCESS-FUL AS YA ARE, PHAI-TAN!
BUT YEAH, MY CHILDREN NOW ARE MY PRIDE AND JOY! MIND IF I BRAG?
AH!
THAT'S RIGHT!
HEY, LOKI.
I WANT TO HEAR ABOUT THE WALLEN-SOMETHING GIRL IN YOUR FAMILIA.
OH, THE "KENKI."
I'D LIKE TO HEAR ABOUT HER TOO.
WHAT'S THAT? SHRIMP'S GOT A QUESTION FOR ME?
CHECK THE WINDOW TA SEE IF PIGS ARE FLYIN'!

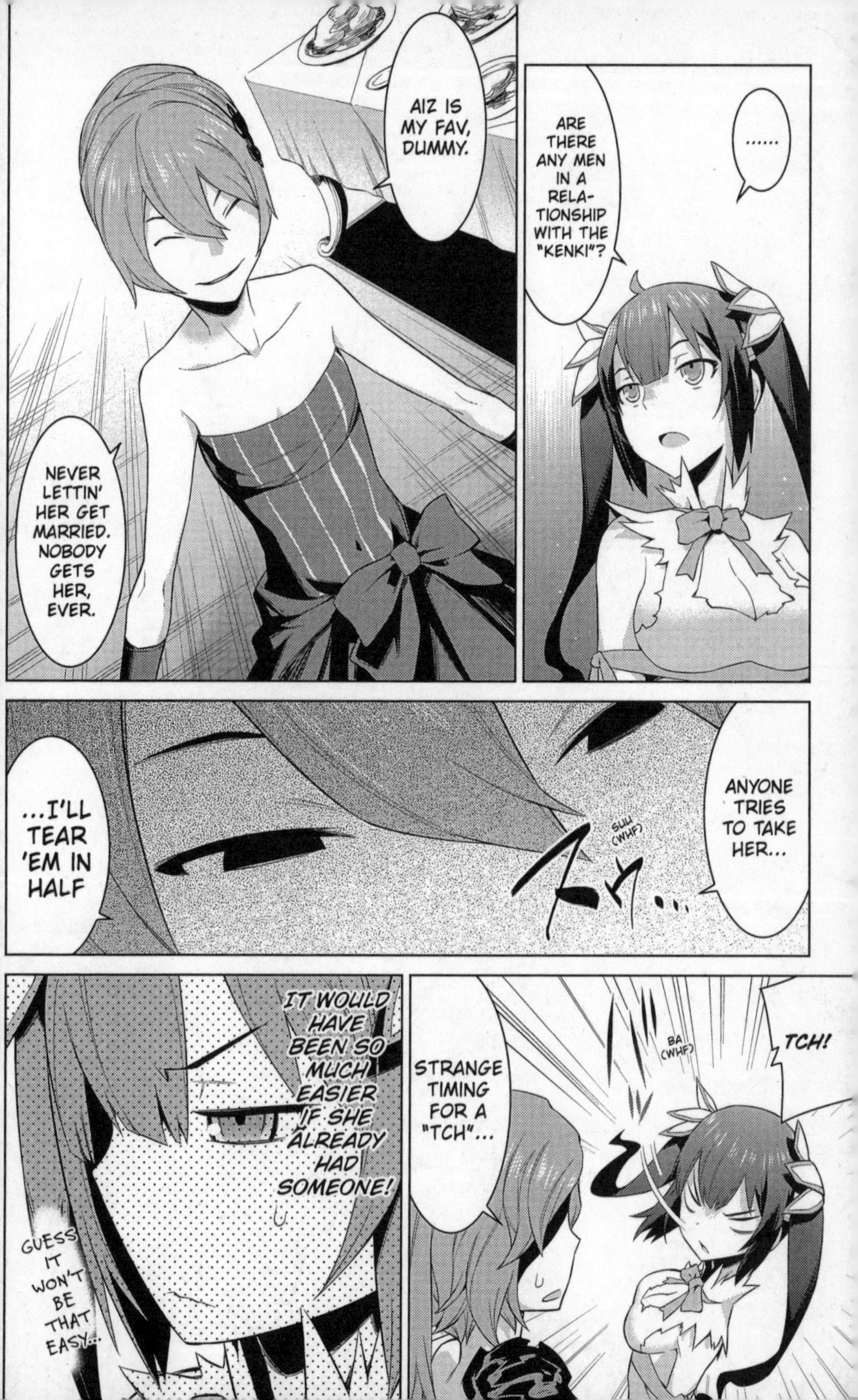
......
ARE THERE ANY MEN IN A RELATIONSHIP WITH THE "KENKI"?
AIZ IS MY FAV, DUMMY.
NEVER LETTIN' HER GET MARRIED. NOBODY GETS HER, EVER.
ANYONE TRIES TO TAKE HER...
SUU (WHF)
...I'LL TEAR 'EM IN HALF
TCH!
BA (WHF)
STRANGE TIMING FOR A "TCH"...
IT WOULD HAVE BEEN SO MUCH EASIER IF SHE ALREADY HAD SOMEONE!
GUESS IT WON'T BE THAT EASY...

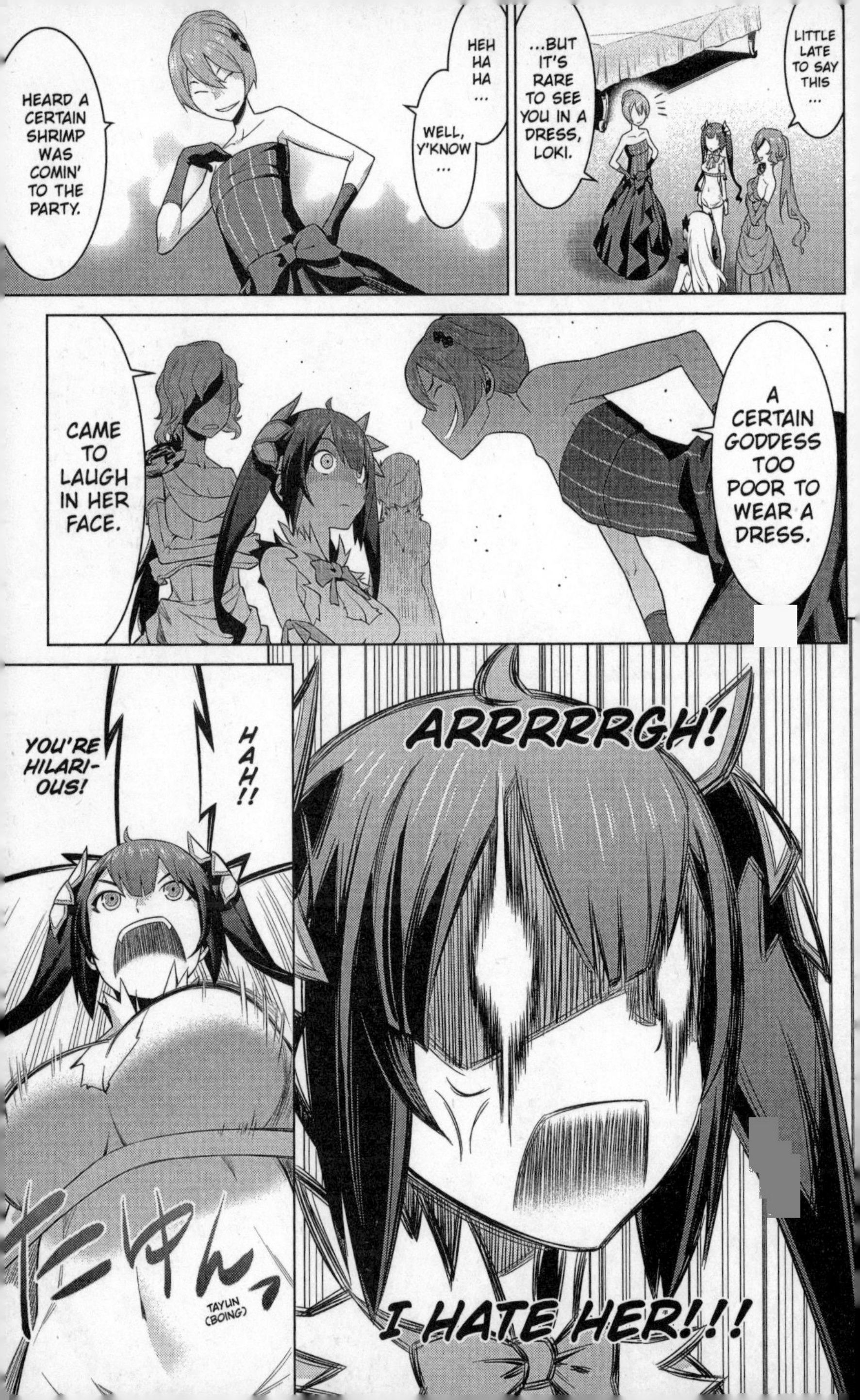
LITTLE LATE TO SAY THIS ...
...BUT IT'S RARE TO SEE YOU IN A DRESS, LOKI.
HEH HA HA ...
WELL, Y'KNOW ...
HEARD A CERTAIN SHRIMP WAS COMIN' TO THE PARTY.
A CERTAIN GODDESS TOO POOR TO WEAR A DRESS.
CAME TO LAUGH IN HER FACE.
ARRRRRGH!
I HATE HER!!!
HAH!!
YOU'RE HILARI-OUS!
たゆんっ
TAYUN (BOING)

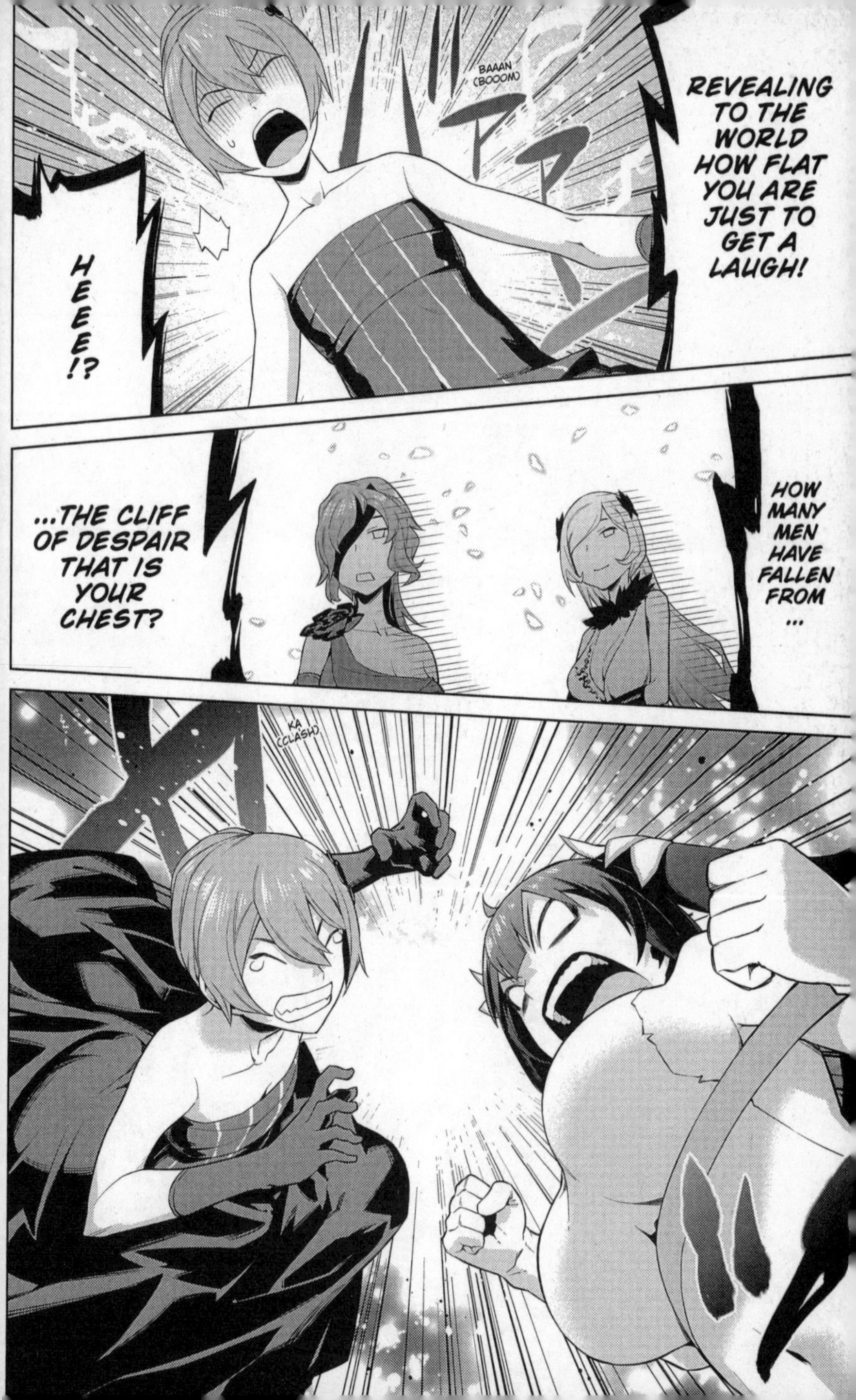
REVEALING TO THE WORLD HOW FLAT YOU ARE JUST TO GET A LAUGH!
BAAAN (BOOOM)
HEEEE!?
HOW MANY MEN HAVE FALLEN FROM ...
...THE CLIFF OF DESPAIR THAT IS YOUR CHEST?
KA (CLASH)

ADVENTURER'S GUIDE ❸

FAMILIA

➤ *A god's family. The god blesses members of their own group to create a Familia.*

➤ *A Familia's activities revolve around their god's hobbies and making money.*

➤ *Examples include conducting business, founding a country, prowling the dungeon, etc.*

➤ *When two gods are in conflict, their Familias may go to war.*

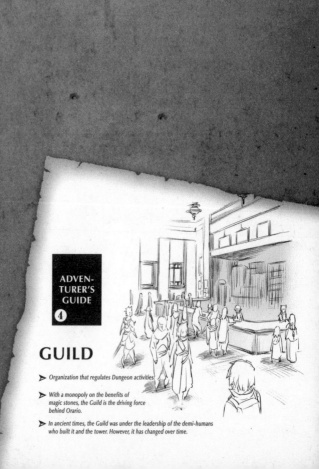

ADVENTURER'S GUIDE ④

GUILD

➤ *Organization that regulates Dungeon activities.*

➤ *With a monopoly on the benefits of magic stones, the Guild is the driving force behind Orario.*

➤ *In ancient times, the Guild was under the leadership of the demi-humans who built it and the tower. However, it has changed over time.*

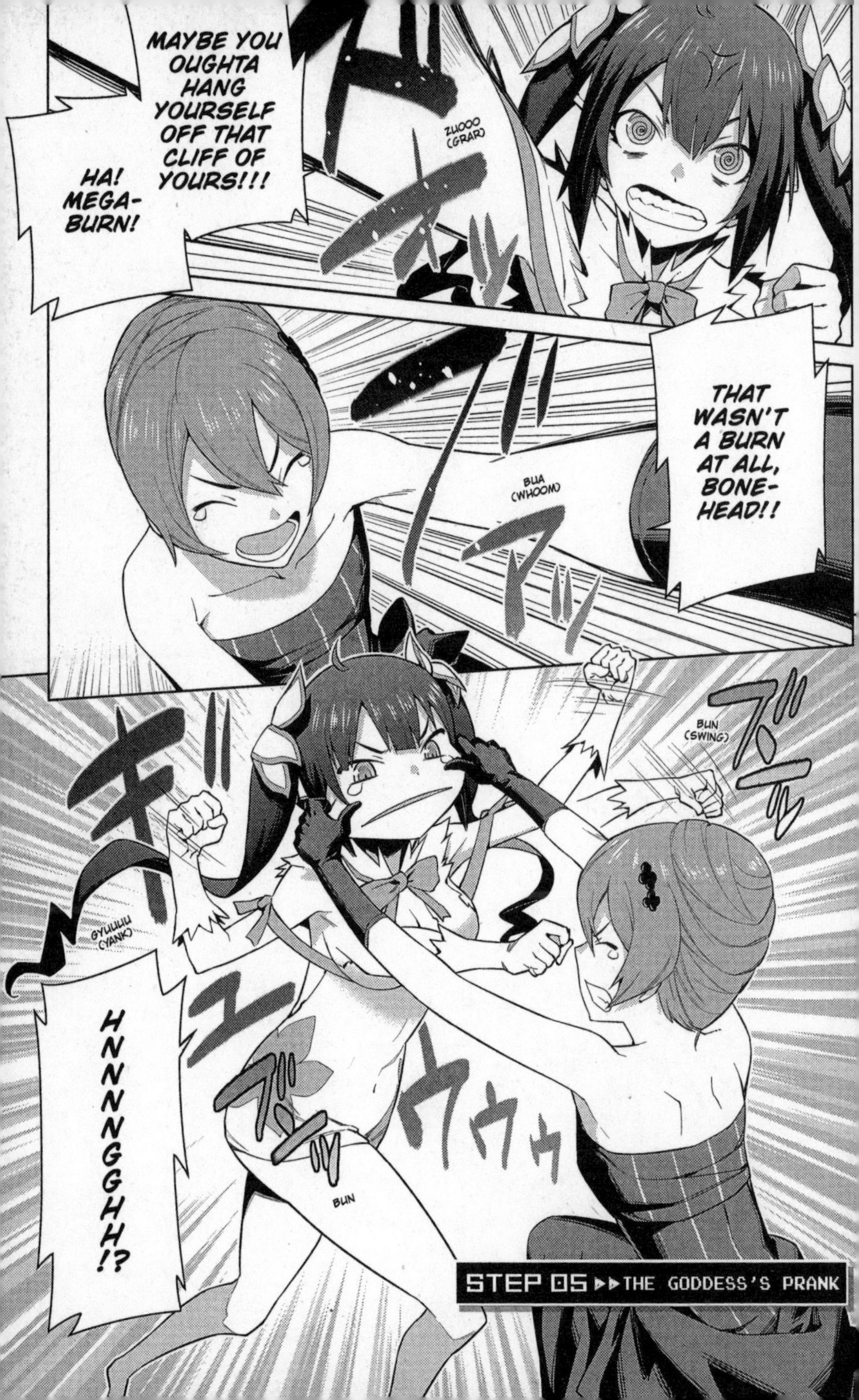

MAYBE YOU OUGHTA HANG YOURSELF OFF THAT CLIFF OF YOURS!!!
HA! MEGA-BURN!
ZUOOO (GRAR)
THAT WASN'T A BURN AT ALL, BONE-HEAD!!
BUA (WHOOM)
BUN (SWING)
GYUUUU (YANK)
HNNNNGGHH!?
BUN
STEP 05 ▶▶ THE GODDESS'S PRANK

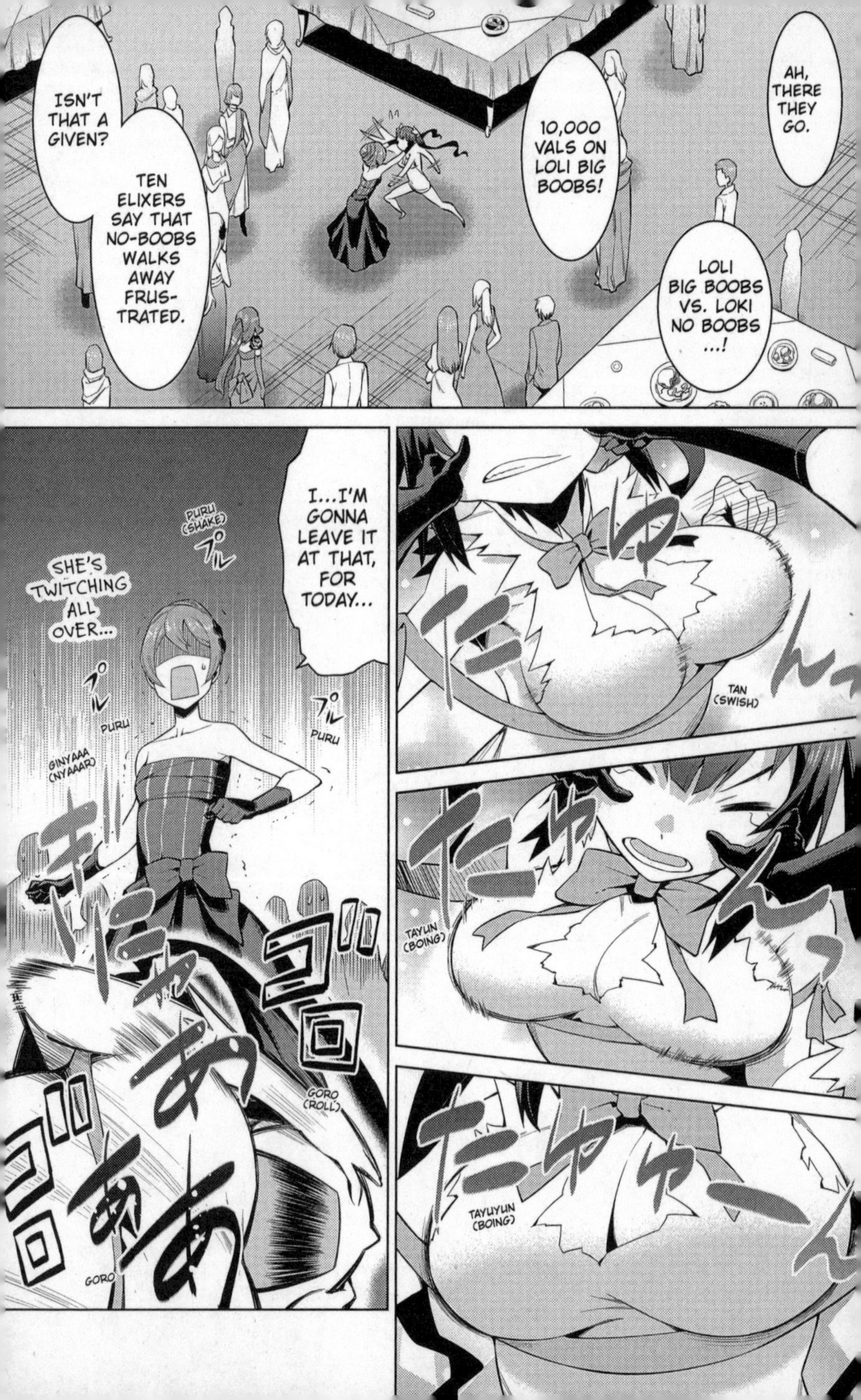
AH, THERE THEY GO.
10,000 VALS ON LOLI BIG BOOBS!
LOLI BIG BOOBS VS. LOKI NO BOOBS ...!
ISN'T THAT A GIVEN?
TEN ELIXERS SAY THAT NO-BOOBS WALKS AWAY FRUS-TRATED.
TAN (SWISH)
TAYUN (BOING)
TAYUYUN (BOING)
I...I'M GONNA LEAVE IT AT THAT, FOR TODAY...
PURU (SHAKE)
SHE'S TWITCHING ALL OVER...
PURU
PURU
GINYAAA (NYAAAR)
GORO (ROLL)
GORO

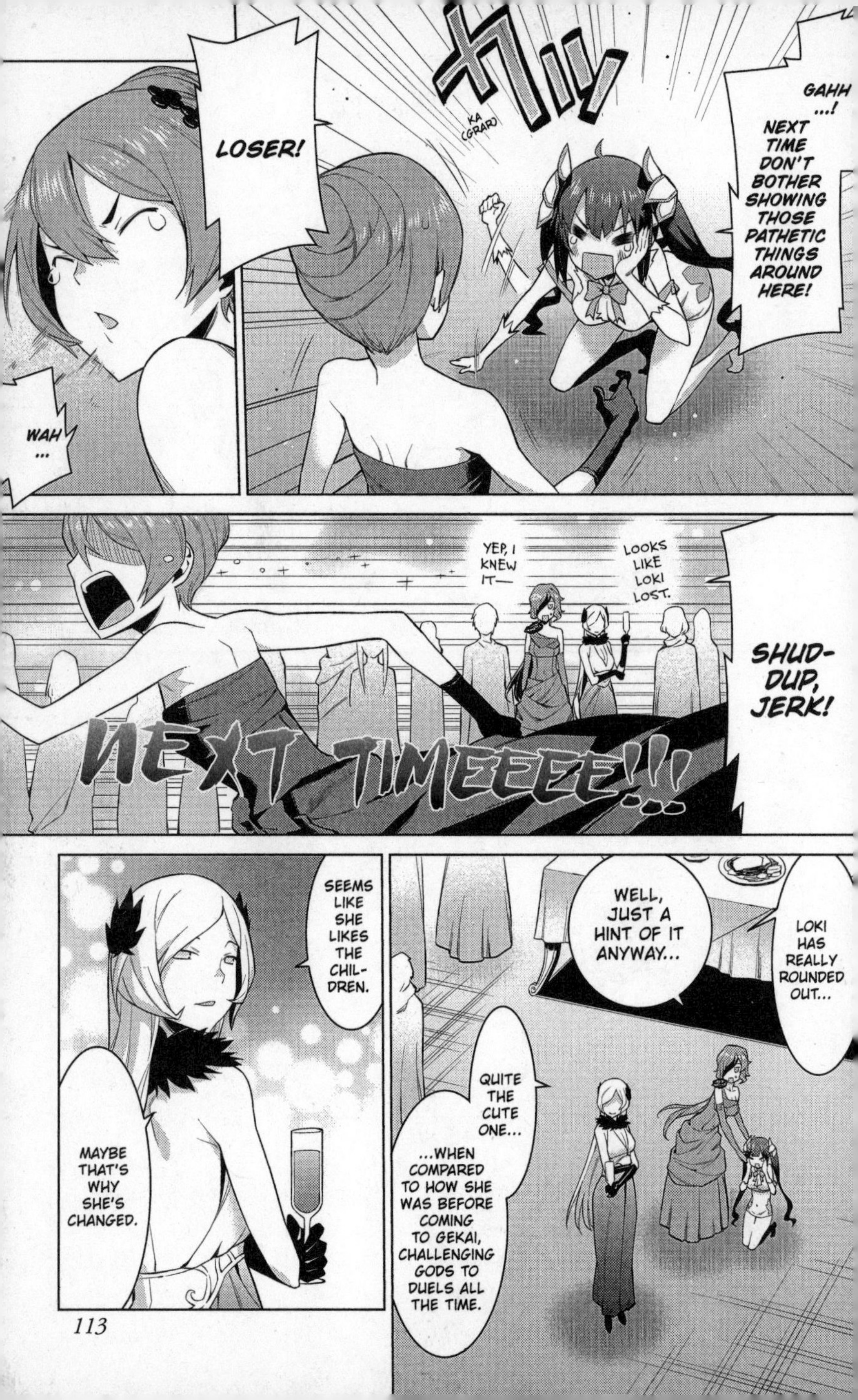
KA (GRAP)
GAHH...! NEXT TIME DON'T BOTHER SHOWING THOSE PATHETIC THINGS AROUND HERE!
LOSER!
WAH...
SHUD-DUP, JERK!
LOOKS LIKE LOKI LOST.
YEP, I KNEW IT—
NEXT TIMEEEE!!!
LOKI HAS REALLY ROUNDED OUT...
WELL, JUST A HINT OF IT ANYWAY...
QUITE THE CUTE ONE...
...WHEN COMPARED TO HOW SHE WAS BEFORE COMING TO GEKAI, CHALLENGING GODS TO DUELS ALL THE TIME.
SEEMS LIKE SHE LIKES THE CHIL-DREN.
MAYBE THAT'S WHY SHE'S CHANGED.

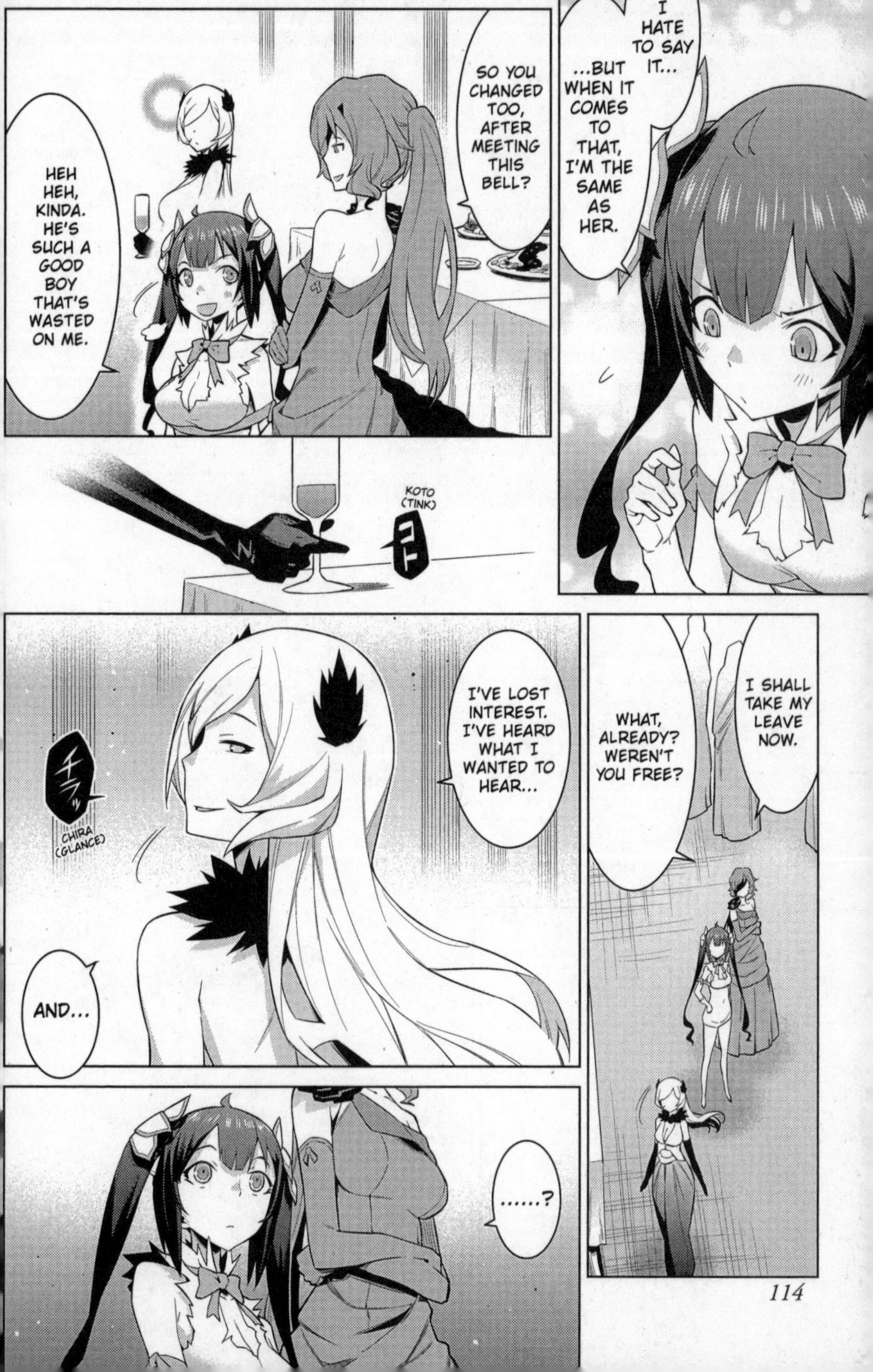
I HATE TO SAY IT...
...BUT WHEN IT COMES TO THAT, I'M THE SAME AS HER.
SO YOU CHANGED TOO, AFTER MEETING THIS BELL?
HEH HEH, KINDA. HE'S SUCH A GOOD BOY THAT'S WASTED ON ME.
コト
KOTO (TINK)
I SHALL TAKE MY LEAVE NOW.
WHAT, ALREADY? WEREN'T YOU FREE?
I'VE LOST INTEREST. I'VE HEARD WHAT I WANTED TO HEAR...
チラッ
CHIRA (GLANCE)
AND...
......?

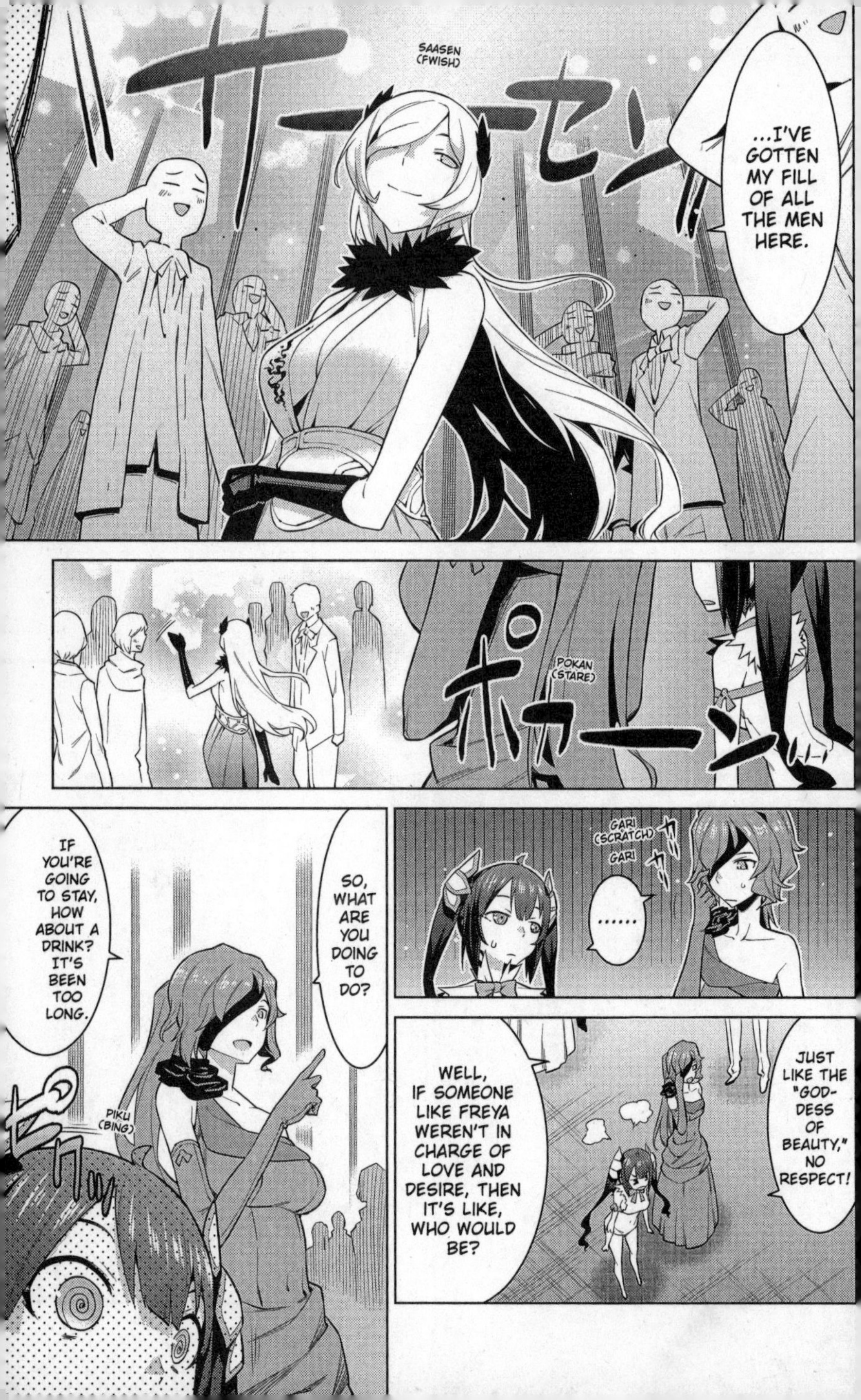
...I'VE GOTTEN MY FILL OF ALL THE MEN HERE.
SAASEN (FWISH)
POKAN (STARE)
GARI (SCRATCH) GARI
......
JUST LIKE THE "GODDESS OF BEAUTY," NO RESPECT!
WELL, IF SOMEONE LIKE FREYA WEREN'T IN CHARGE OF LOVE AND DESIRE, THEN IT'S LIKE, WHO WOULD BE?
SO, WHAT ARE YOU DOING TO DO?
IF YOU'RE GOING TO STAY, HOW ABOUT A DRINK? IT'S BEEN TOO LONG.
PIKU (BING)

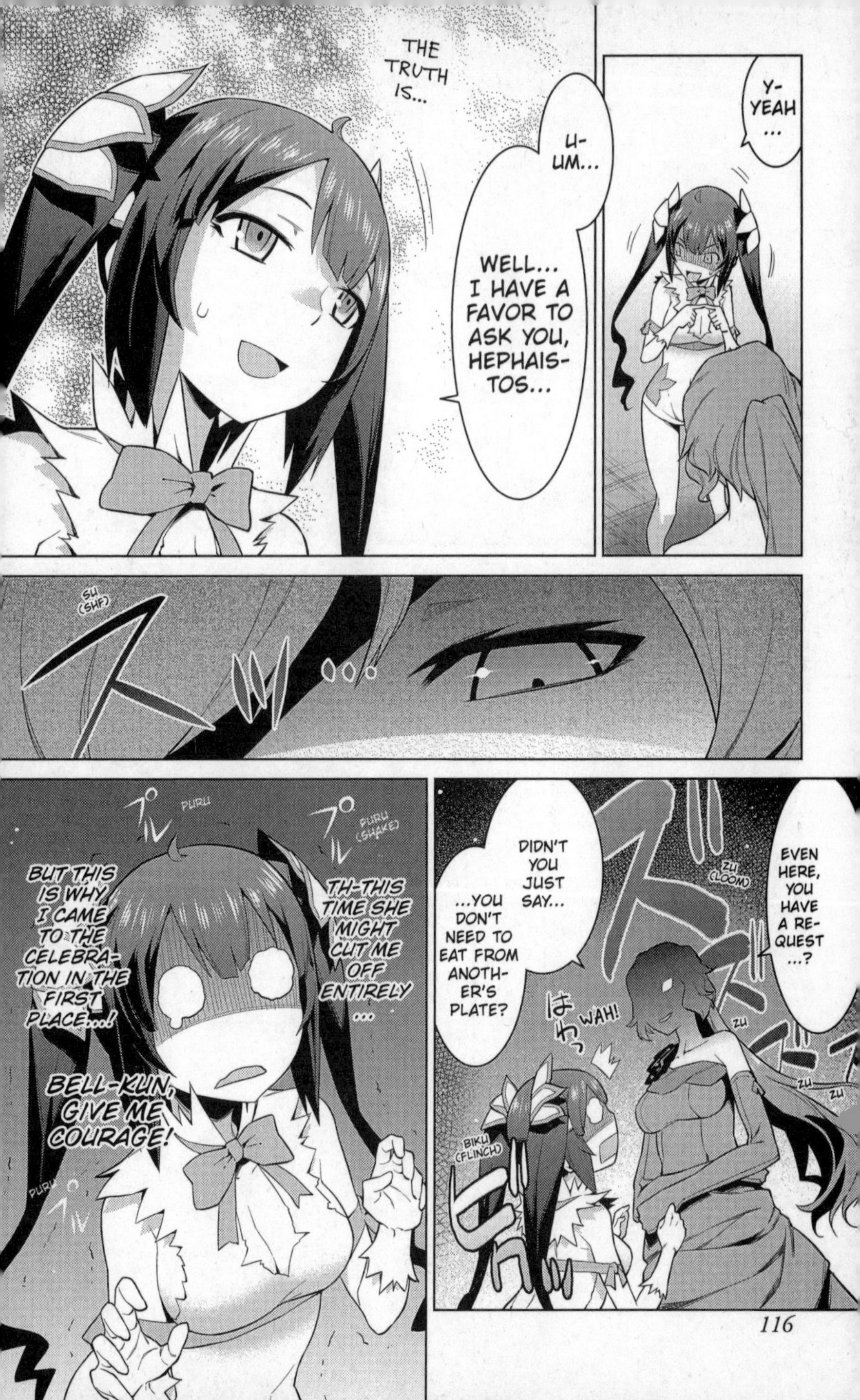
Y-YEAH...
U-UM...
THE TRUTH IS...
WELL... I HAVE A FAVOR TO ASK YOU, HEPHAISTOS...
SU (SHF)
EVEN HERE, YOU HAVE A REQUEST...?
ZU (LOOM)
DIDN'T YOU JUST SAY...
...YOU DON'T NEED TO EAT FROM ANOTHER'S PLATE?
WAH!
ZU
ZU
ZU
BIKU (FLINCH)
PURU (SHAKE)
PURU
TH-THIS TIME SHE MIGHT CUT ME OFF ENTIRELY...
BUT THIS IS WHY I CAME TO THE CELEBRATION IN THE FIRST PLACE...!
BELL-KUN, GIVE ME COURAGE!
PURU

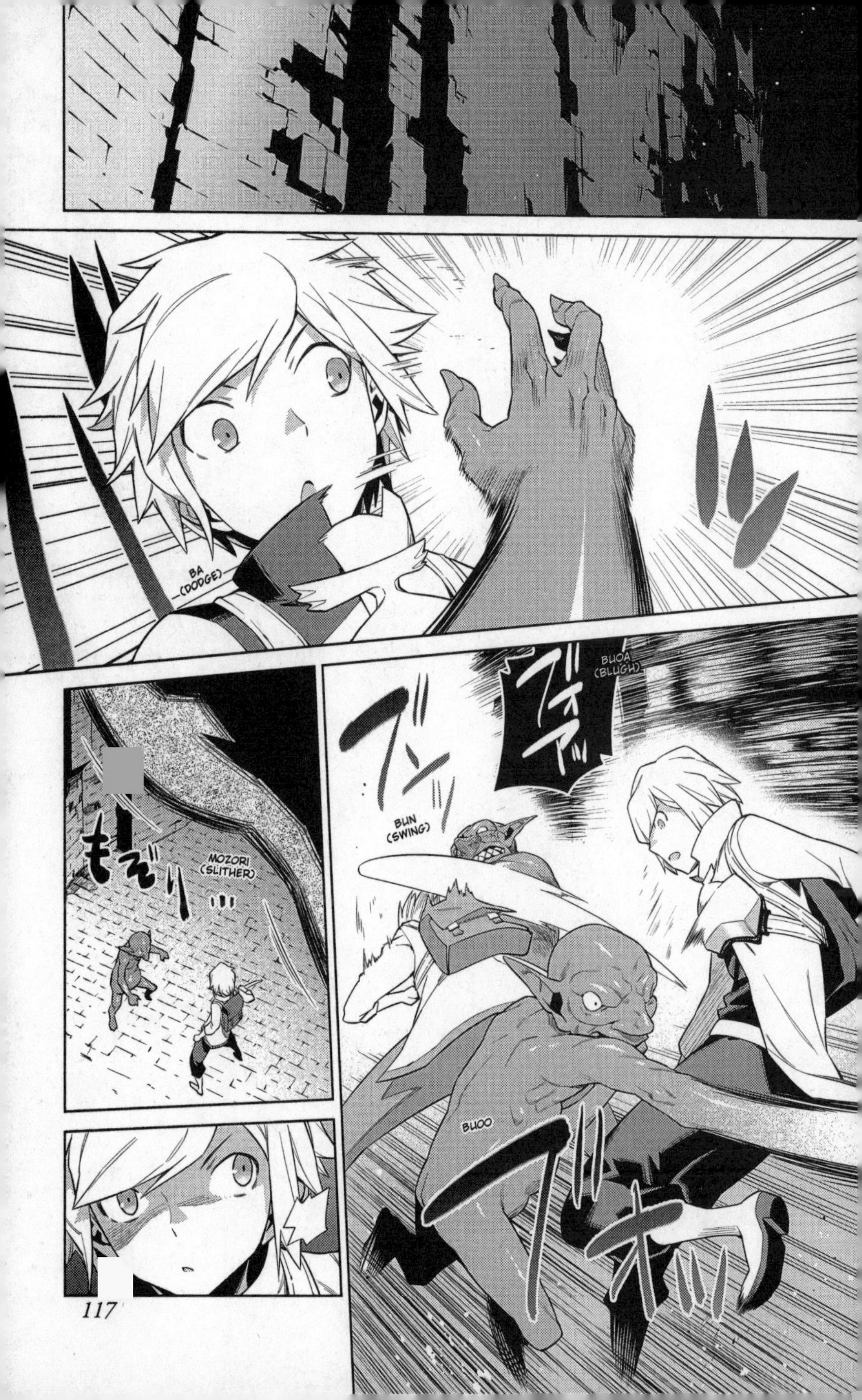
BA
(DODGE)
BUOA
(BLUGH)
BUN
(SWING)
BUOO
MOZORI
(SLITHER)

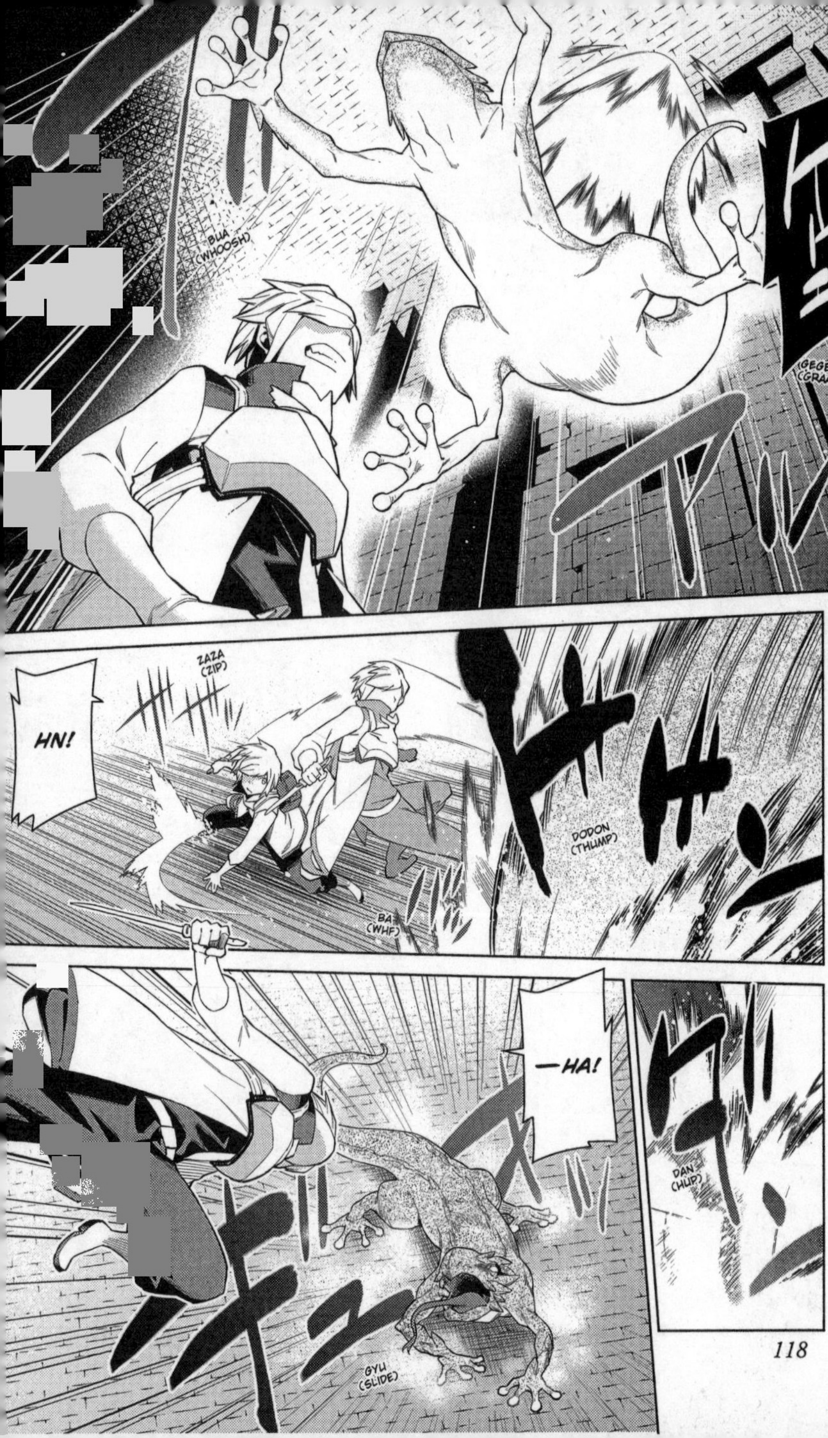
GEGEEE
(GRAAH)
BUA
(WHOOSH)
DODON
(THUMP)
BA
(WHF)
ZAZA
(ZIP)
HN!
DAN
(HUP)
—HA!
GYU
(SLIDE)

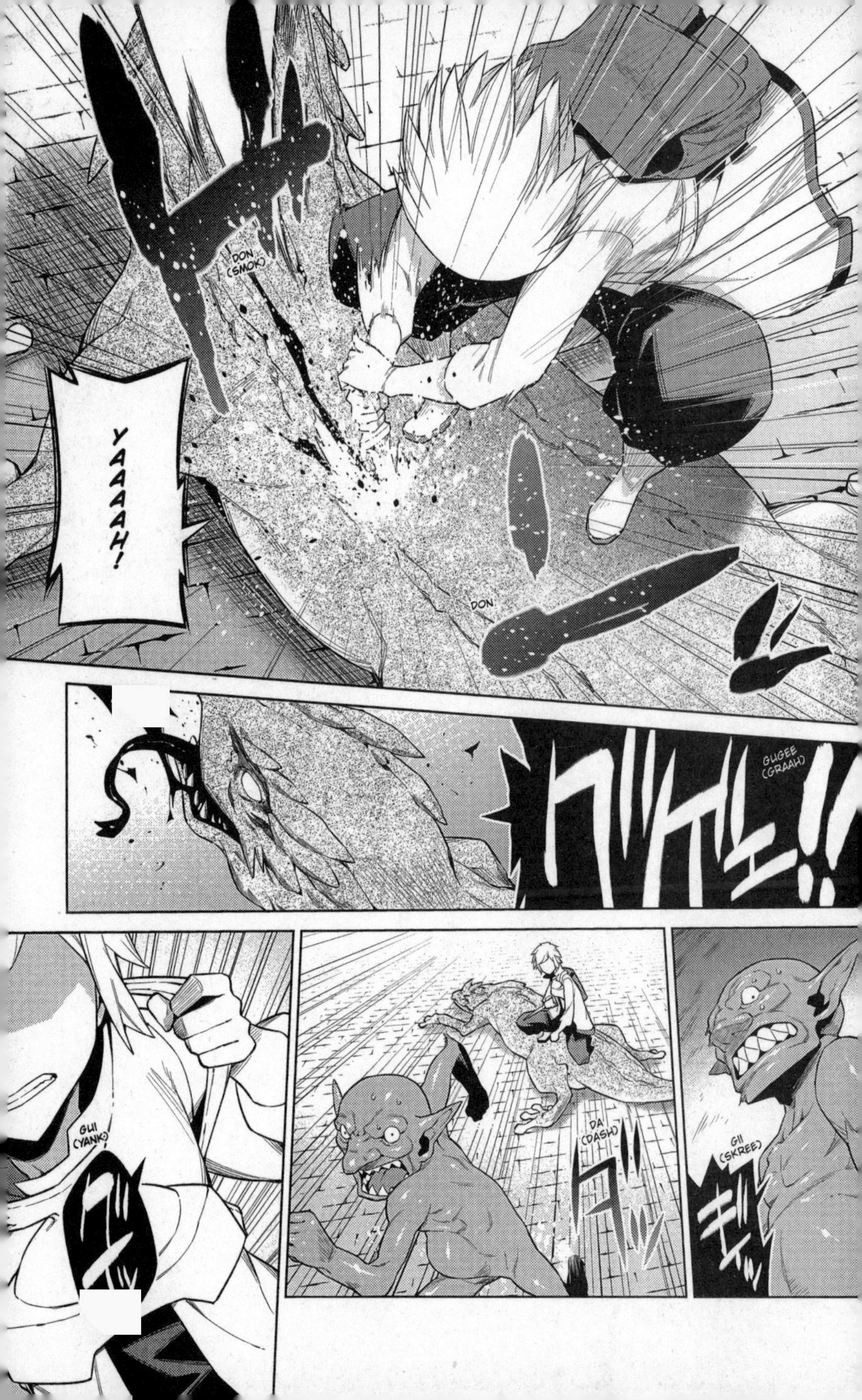
DON (SMOK)
YAAAAAH!
DON
GUGEE (GRAAH)
GII (SKREE)
DA (DASH)
GUI (YANK)

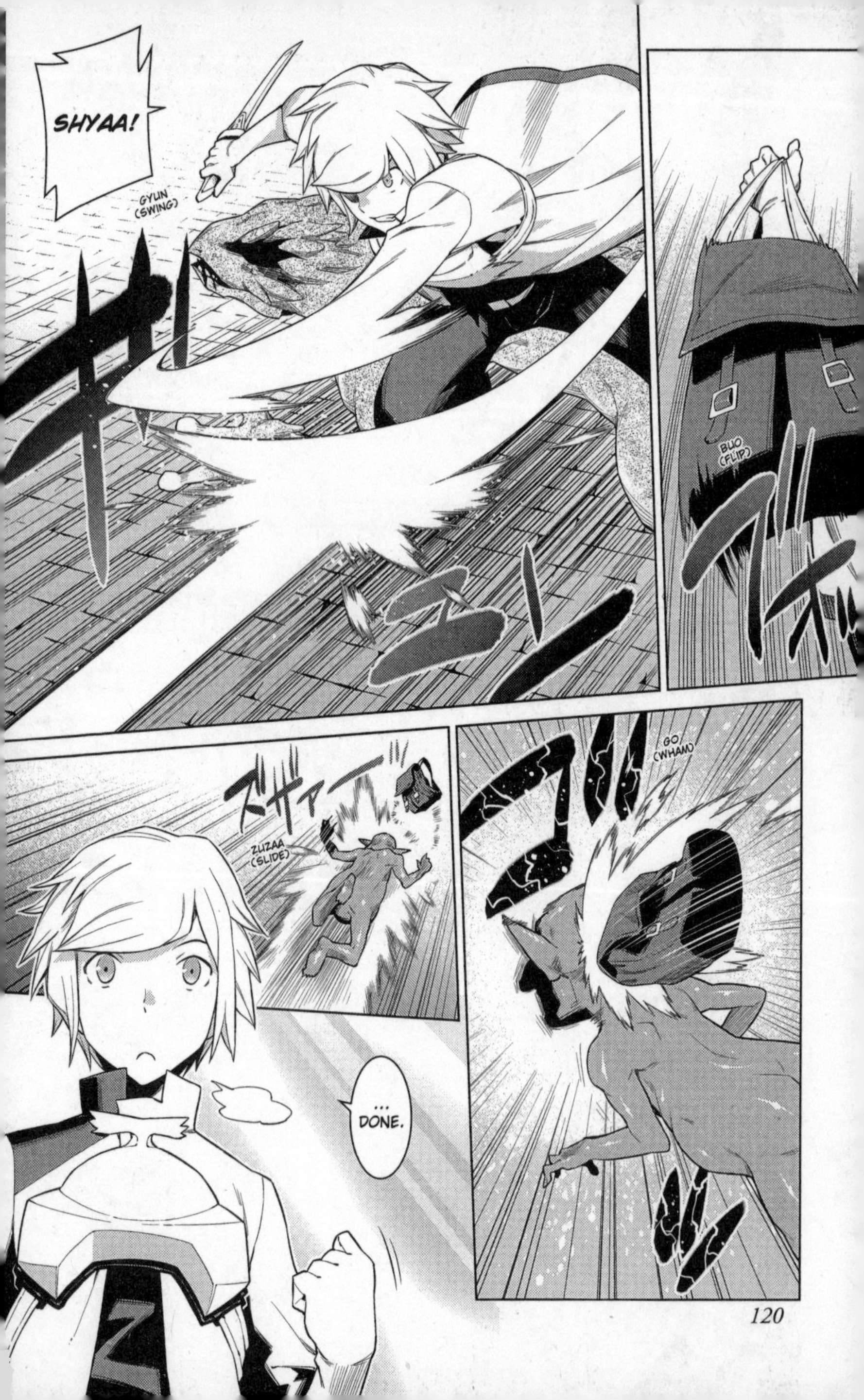
BUO (FLIP)
SHYAA!
GYUN (SWING)
GO (WHAM)
ZUZAA (SLIDE)
... DONE.

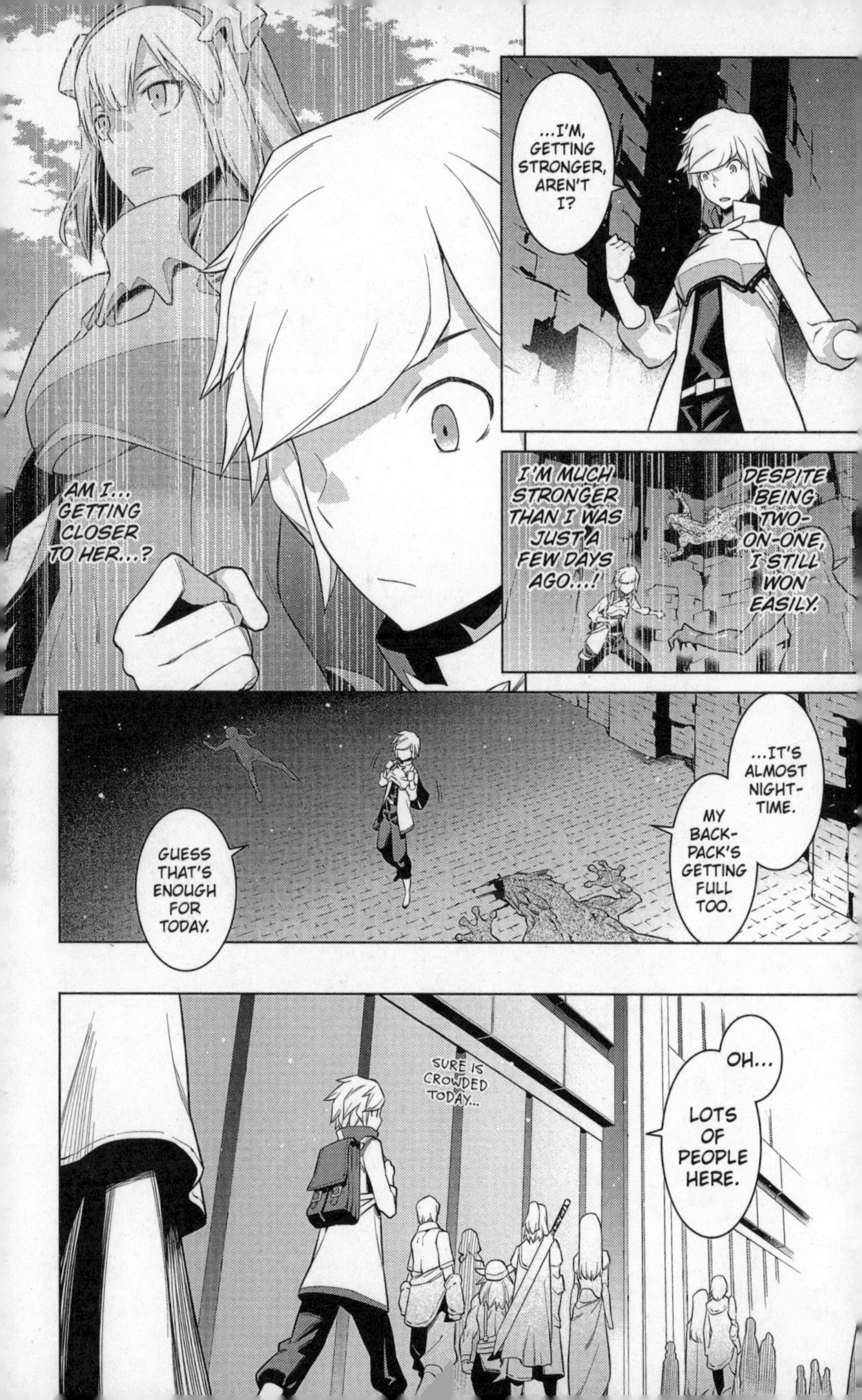
...I'M, GETTING STRONGER, AREN'T I?
DESPITE BEING TWO-ON-ONE, I STILL WON EASILY.
I'M MUCH STRONGER THAN I WAS JUST A FEW DAYS AGO...!
AM I... GETTING CLOSER TO HER...?
...IT'S ALMOST NIGHT-TIME.
MY BACK-PACK'S GETTING FULL TOO.
GUESS THAT'S ENOUGH FOR TODAY.
OH...
LOTS OF PEOPLE HERE.
SURE IS CROWDED TODAY...

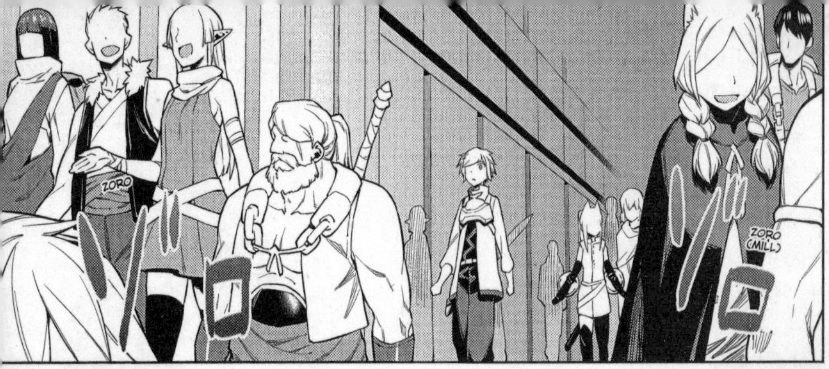
ZORO
(MILL)
ZORO
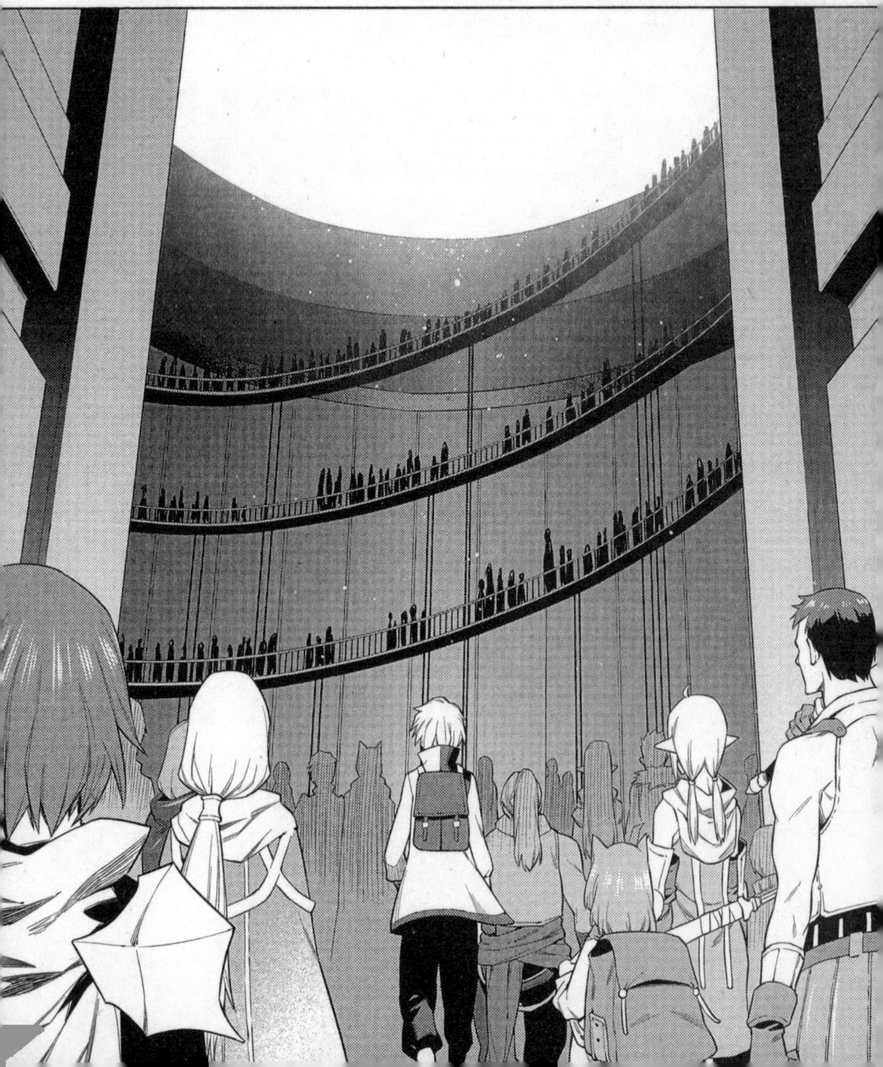

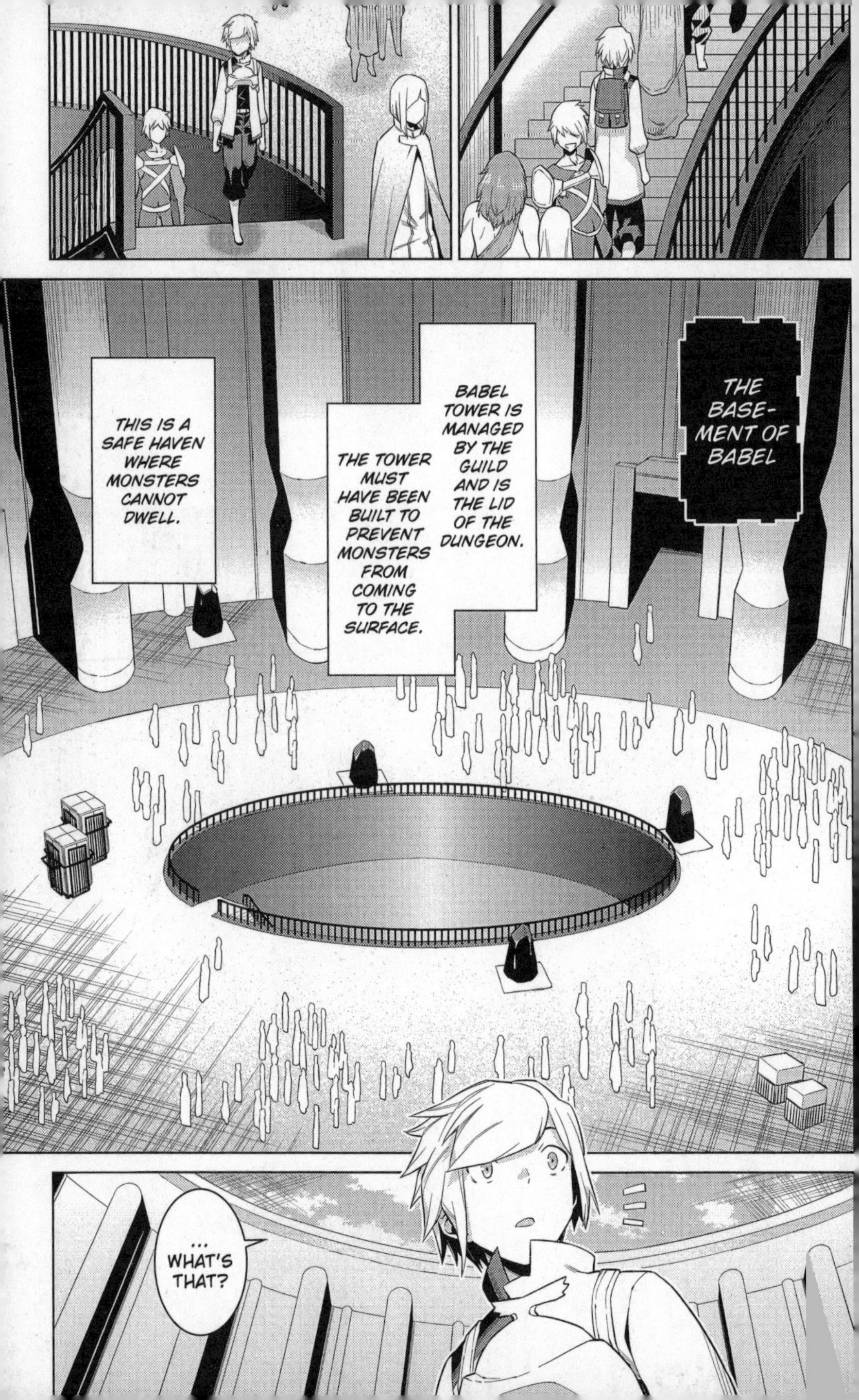
THE BASEMENT OF BABEL
BABEL TOWER IS MANAGED BY THE GUILD AND IS THE LID OF THE DUNGEON.
THE TOWER MUST HAVE BEEN BUILT TO PREVENT MONSTERS FROM COMING TO THE SURFACE.
THIS IS A SAFE HAVEN WHERE MONSTERS CANNOT DWELL.
... WHAT'S THAT?

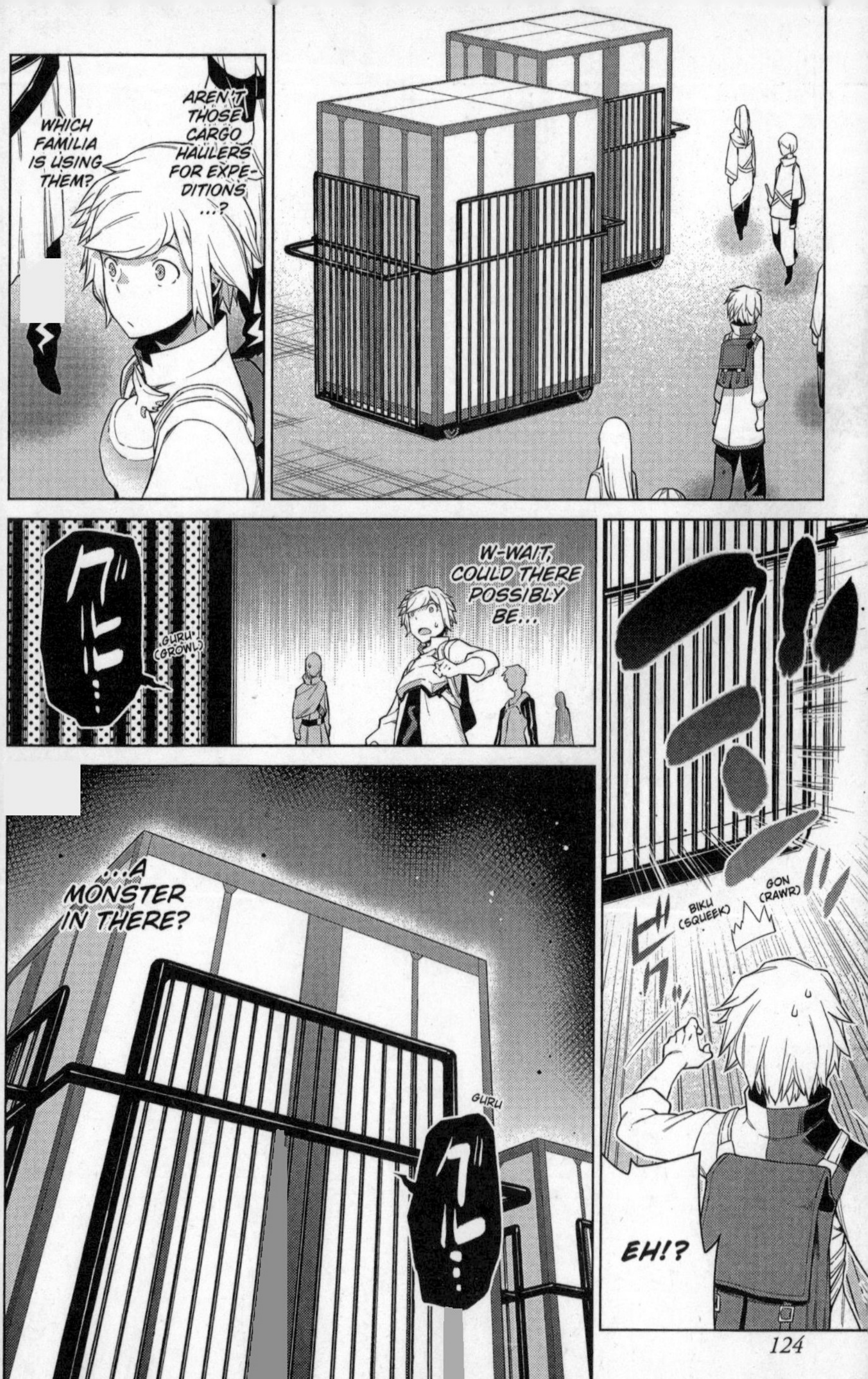
AREN'T THOSE CARGO HAULERS FOR EXPEDITIONS ...?
WHICH FAMILIA IS USING THEM?
GON (RAWR)
BIKU (SQUEEK)
EH!?
W-WAIT, COULD THERE POSSIBLY BE...
GURU (GROWL)
...A MONSTER IN THERE?
GURU

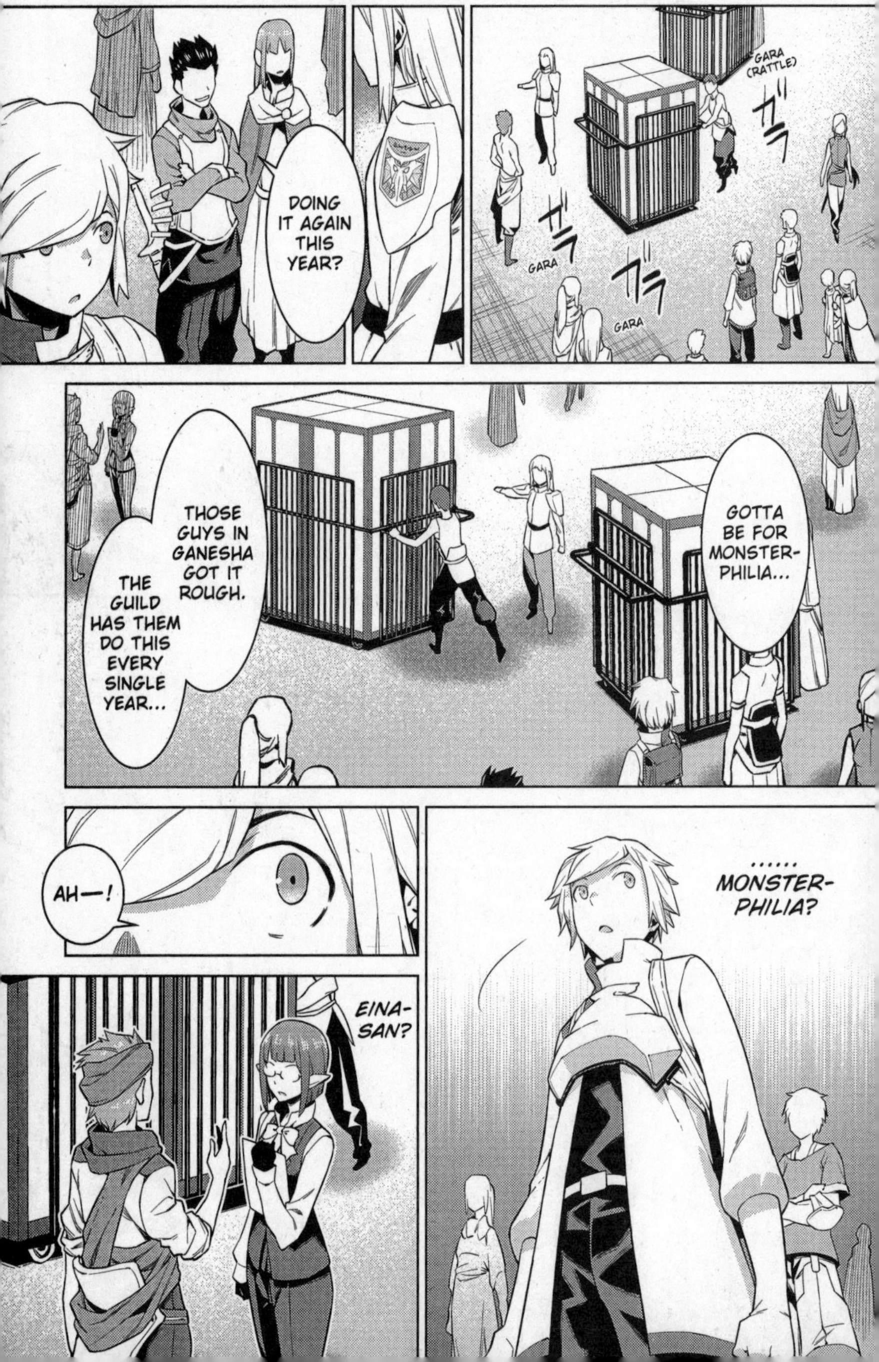
GARA (RATTLE)
GARA
GARA
DOING IT AGAIN THIS YEAR?
GOTTA BE FOR MONSTER-PHILIA...
THOSE GUYS IN GANESHA GOT IT ROUGH.
THE GUILD HAS THEM DO THIS EVERY SINGLE YEAR...
...... MONSTER-PHILIA?
AH—!
EINA-SAN?

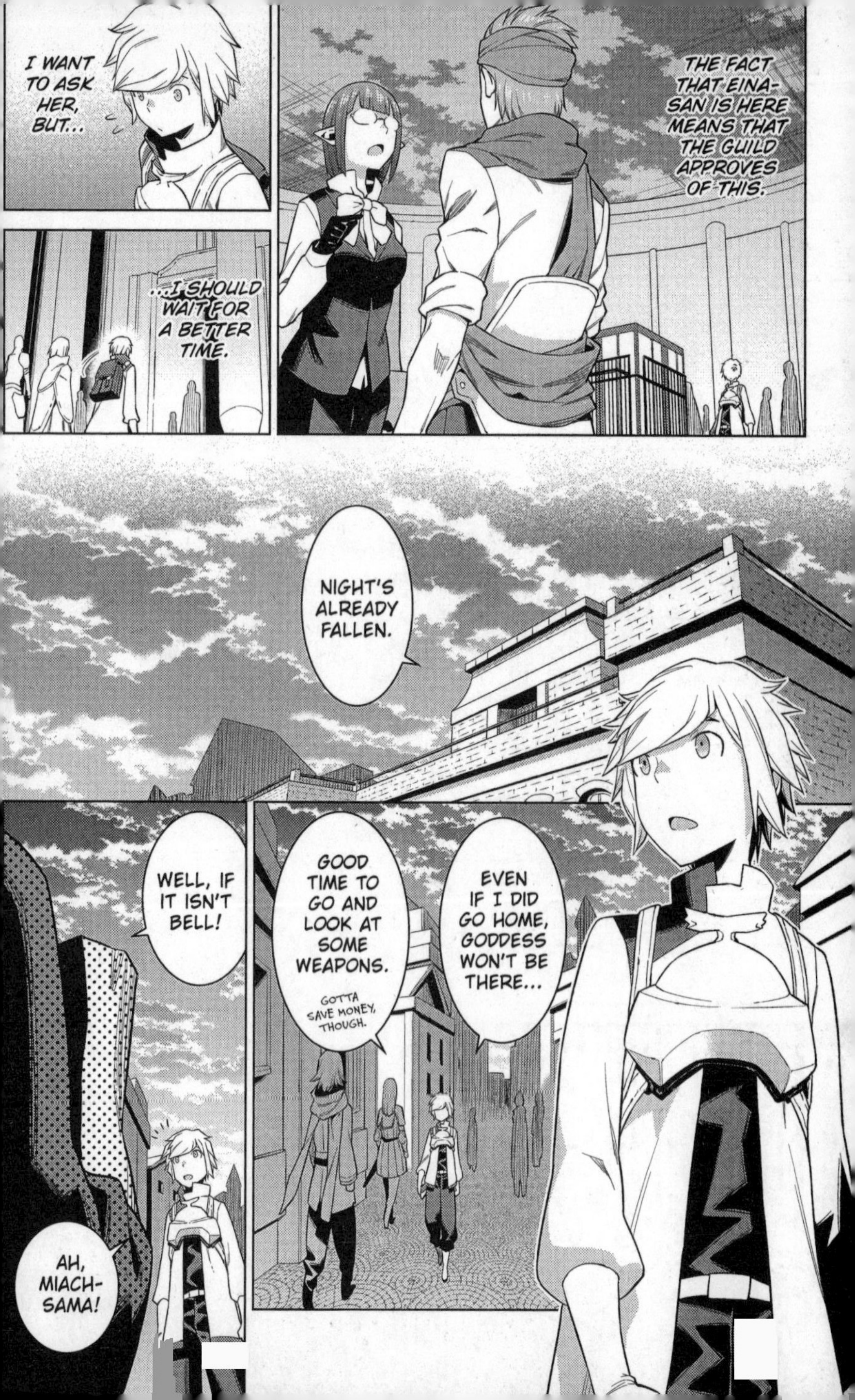
THE FACT THAT EINA-SAN IS HERE MEANS THAT THE GUILD APPROVES OF THIS.
I WANT TO ASK HER, BUT...
...I SHOULD WAIT FOR A BETTER TIME.
NIGHT'S ALREADY FALLEN.
EVEN IF I DID GO HOME, GODDESS WON'T BE THERE...
GOOD TIME TO GO AND LOOK AT SOME WEAPONS.
GOTTA SAVE MONEY, THOUGH.
WELL, IF IT ISN'T BELL!
AH, MIACH-SAMA!

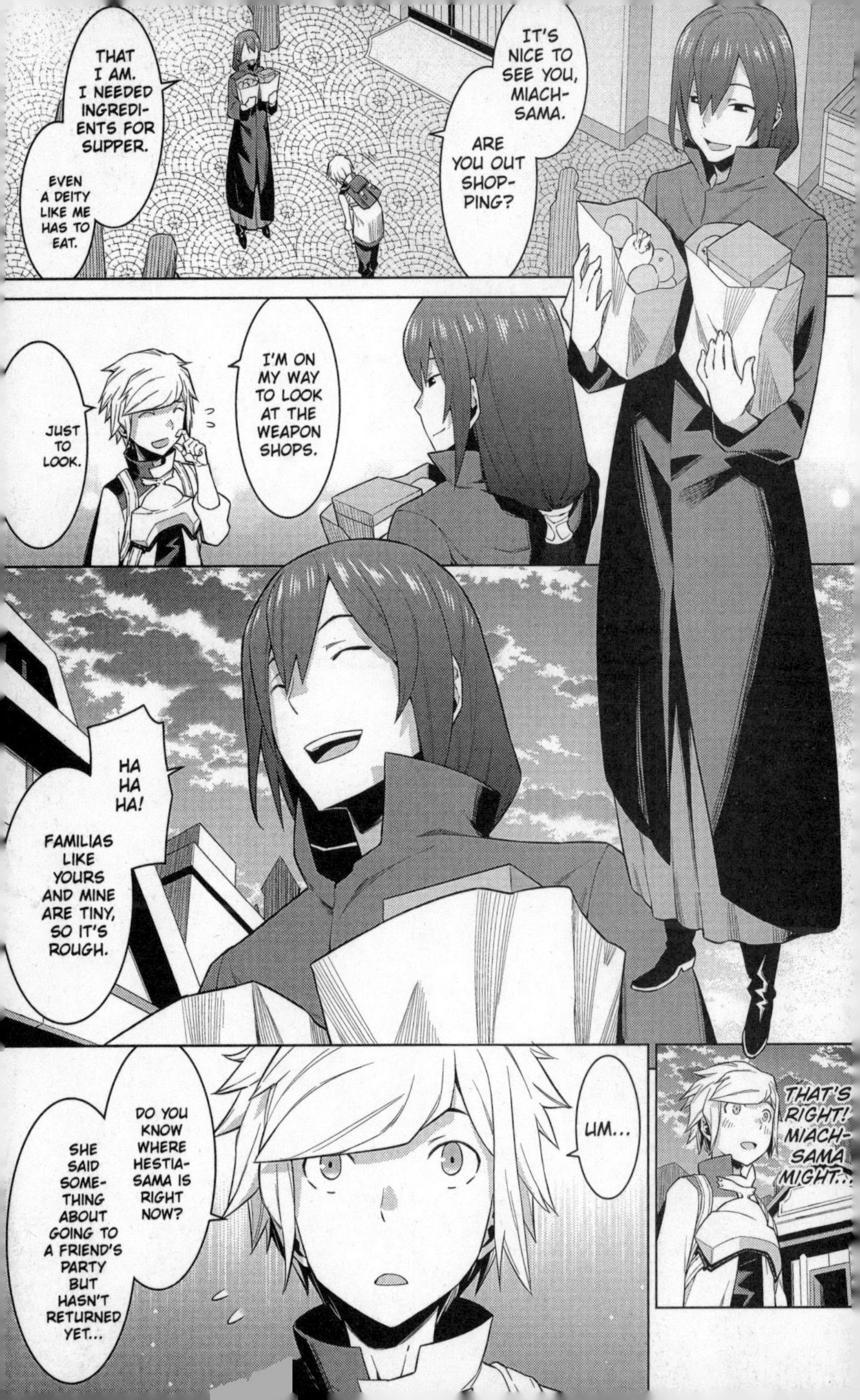
IT'S NICE TO SEE YOU, MIACH-SAMA.
ARE YOU OUT SHOP-PING?
THAT I AM. I NEEDED INGREDI-ENTS FOR SUPPER.
EVEN A DEITY LIKE ME HAS TO EAT.
I'M ON MY WAY TO LOOK AT THE WEAPON SHOPS.
JUST TO LOOK.
HA HA HA!
FAMILIAS LIKE YOURS AND MINE ARE TINY, SO IT'S ROUGH.
THAT'S RIGHT! MIACH-SAMA MIGHT...
UM...
DO YOU KNOW WHERE HESTIA-SAMA IS RIGHT NOW?
SHE SAID SOME-THING ABOUT GOING TO A FRIEND'S PARTY BUT HASN'T RETURNED YET...

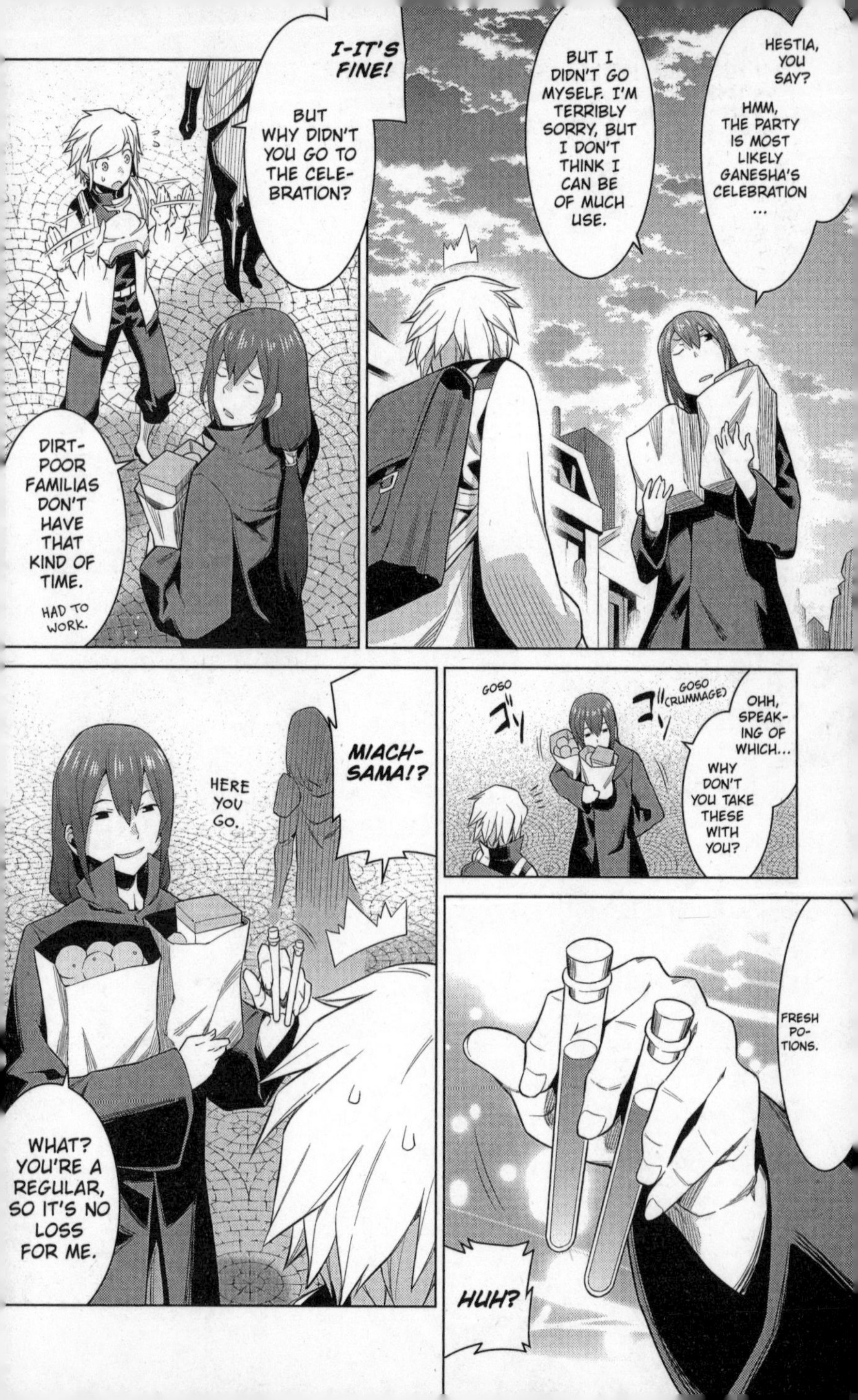
HESTIA, YOU SAY? HMM, THE PARTY IS MOST LIKELY GANESHA'S CELEBRATION ...
BUT I DIDN'T GO MYSELF. I'M TERRIBLY SORRY, BUT I DON'T THINK I CAN BE OF MUCH USE.
I-IT'S FINE!
BUT WHY DIDN'T YOU GO TO THE CELE-BRATION?
DIRT-POOR FAMILIAS DON'T HAVE THAT KIND OF TIME.
HAD TO WORK.
GOSO (RUMMAGE)
GOSO
OHH, SPEAK-ING OF WHICH... WHY DON'T YOU TAKE THESE WITH YOU?
FRESH PO-TIONS.
HUH?
MIACH-SAMA!?
HERE YOU GO.
WHAT? YOU'RE A REGULAR, SO IT'S NO LOSS FOR ME.

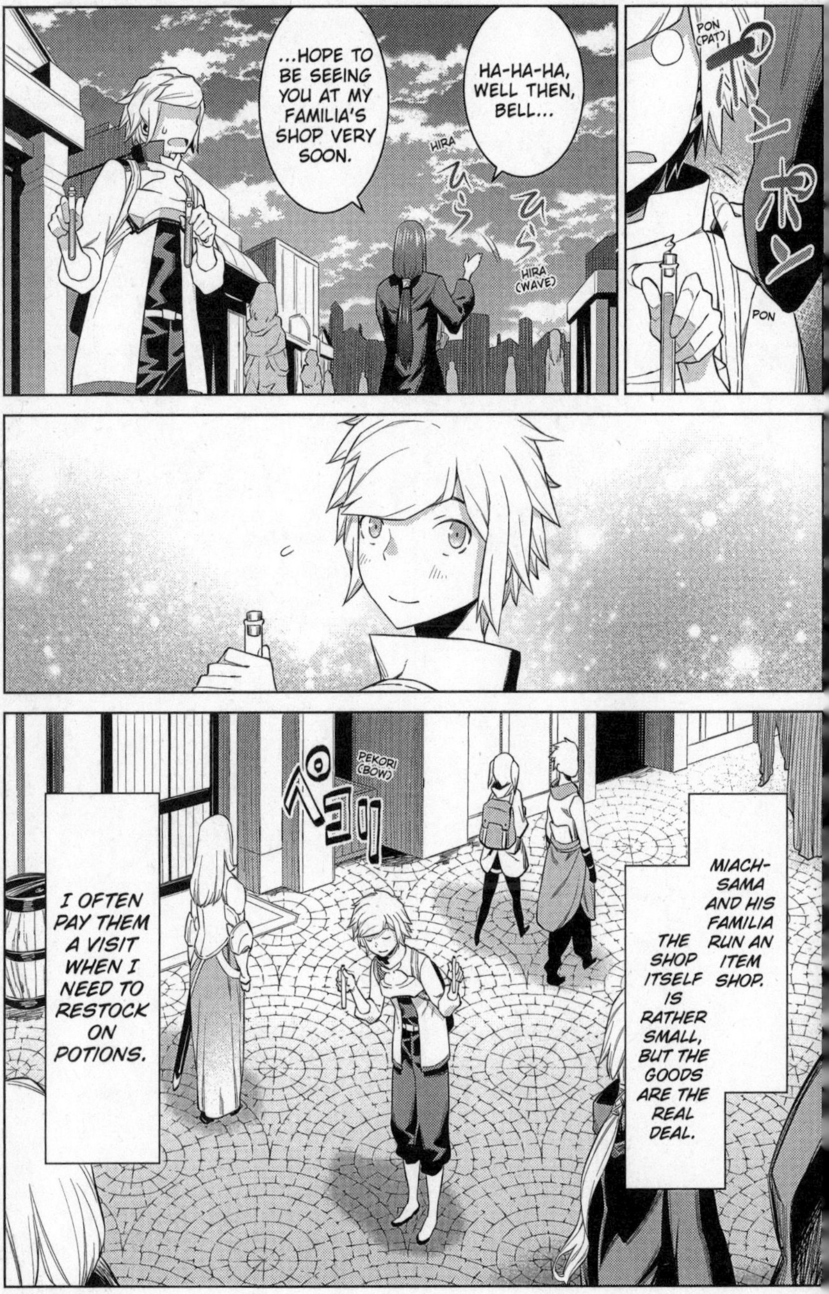
PON (PAT)
PON
HA-HA-HA, WELL THEN, BELL...
...HOPE TO BE SEEING YOU AT MY FAMILIA'S SHOP VERY SOON.
HIRA
HIRA (WAVE)
MIACH-SAMA AND HIS FAMILIA RUN AN ITEM SHOP.
THE SHOP ITSELF IS RATHER SMALL, BUT THE GOODS ARE THE REAL DEAL.
PEKORI (BOW)
I OFTEN PAY THEM A VISIT WHEN I NEED TO RESTOCK ON POTIONS.

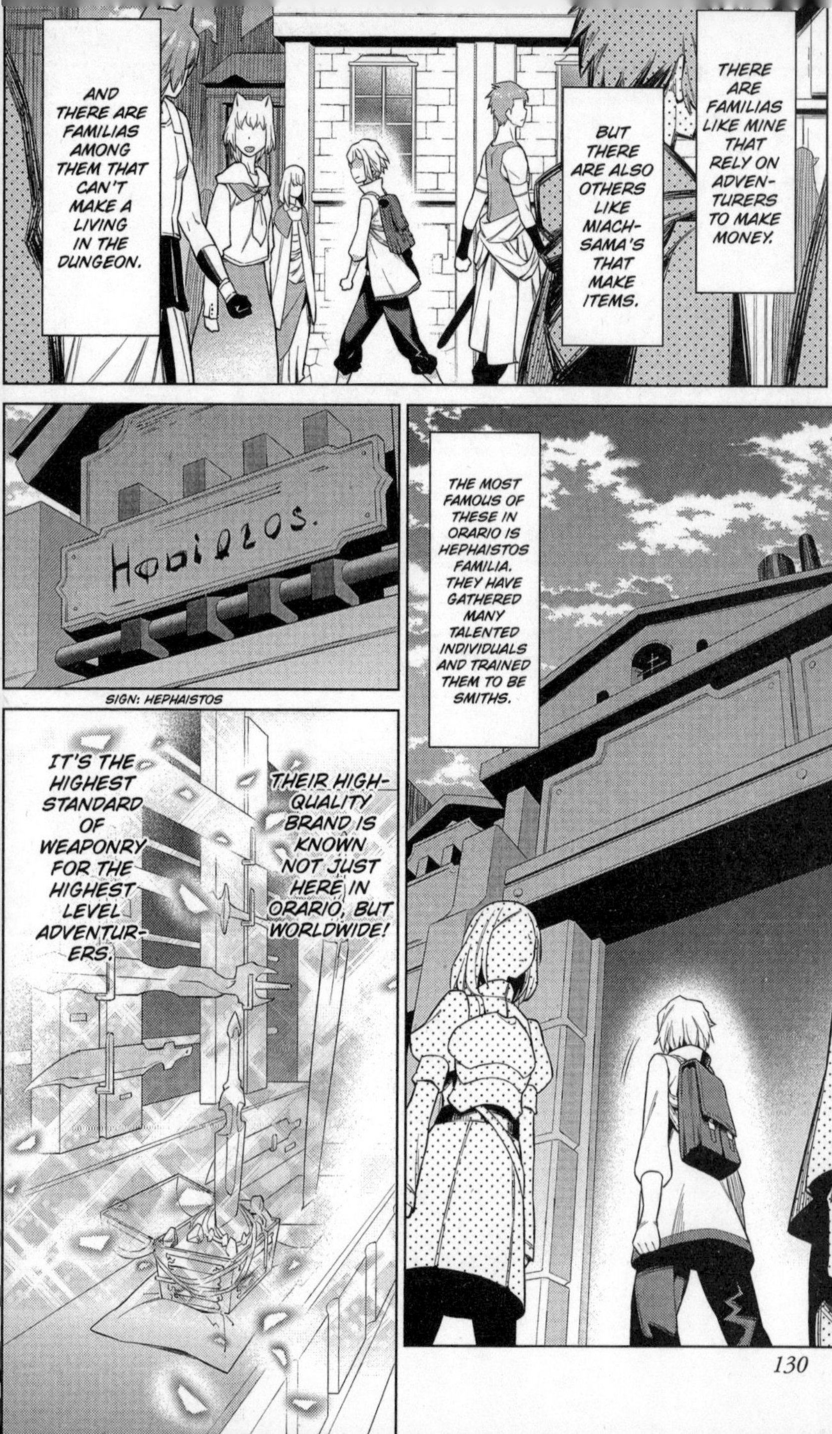

THERE ARE FAMILIAS LIKE MINE THAT RELY ON ADVEN-TURERS TO MAKE MONEY.
BUT THERE ARE ALSO OTHERS LIKE MIACH-SAMA'S THAT MAKE ITEMS.
AND THERE ARE FAMILIAS AMONG THEM THAT CAN'T MAKE A LIVING IN THE DUNGEON.
THE MOST FAMOUS OF THESE IN ORARIO IS HEPHAISTOS FAMILIA. THEY HAVE GATHERED MANY TALENTED INDIVIDUALS AND TRAINED THEM TO BE SMITHS.
SIGN: HEPHAISTOS
THEIR HIGH-QUALITY BRAND IS KNOWN NOT JUST HERE IN ORARIO, BUT WORLDWIDE!
IT'S THE HIGHEST STANDARD OF WEAPONRY FOR THE HIGHEST LEVEL ADVENTUR-ERS.

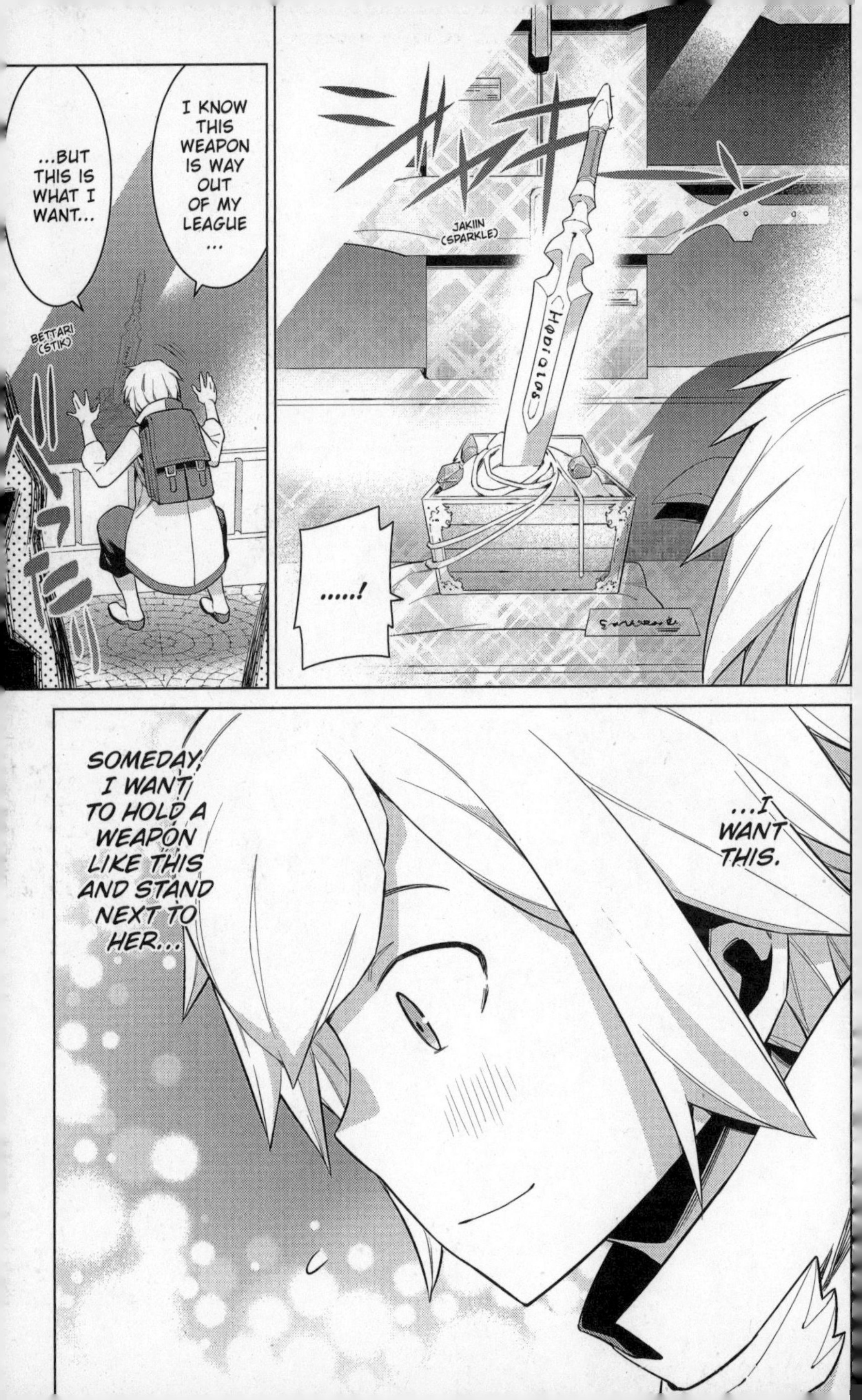
JAKIIN (SPARKLE)
.....!
I KNOW THIS WEAPON IS WAY OUT OF MY LEAGUE ...
...BUT THIS IS WHAT I WANT...
BETTARI (STIK)
...I WANT THIS.
SOMEDAY, I WANT TO HOLD A WEAPON LIKE THIS AND STAND NEXT TO HER...

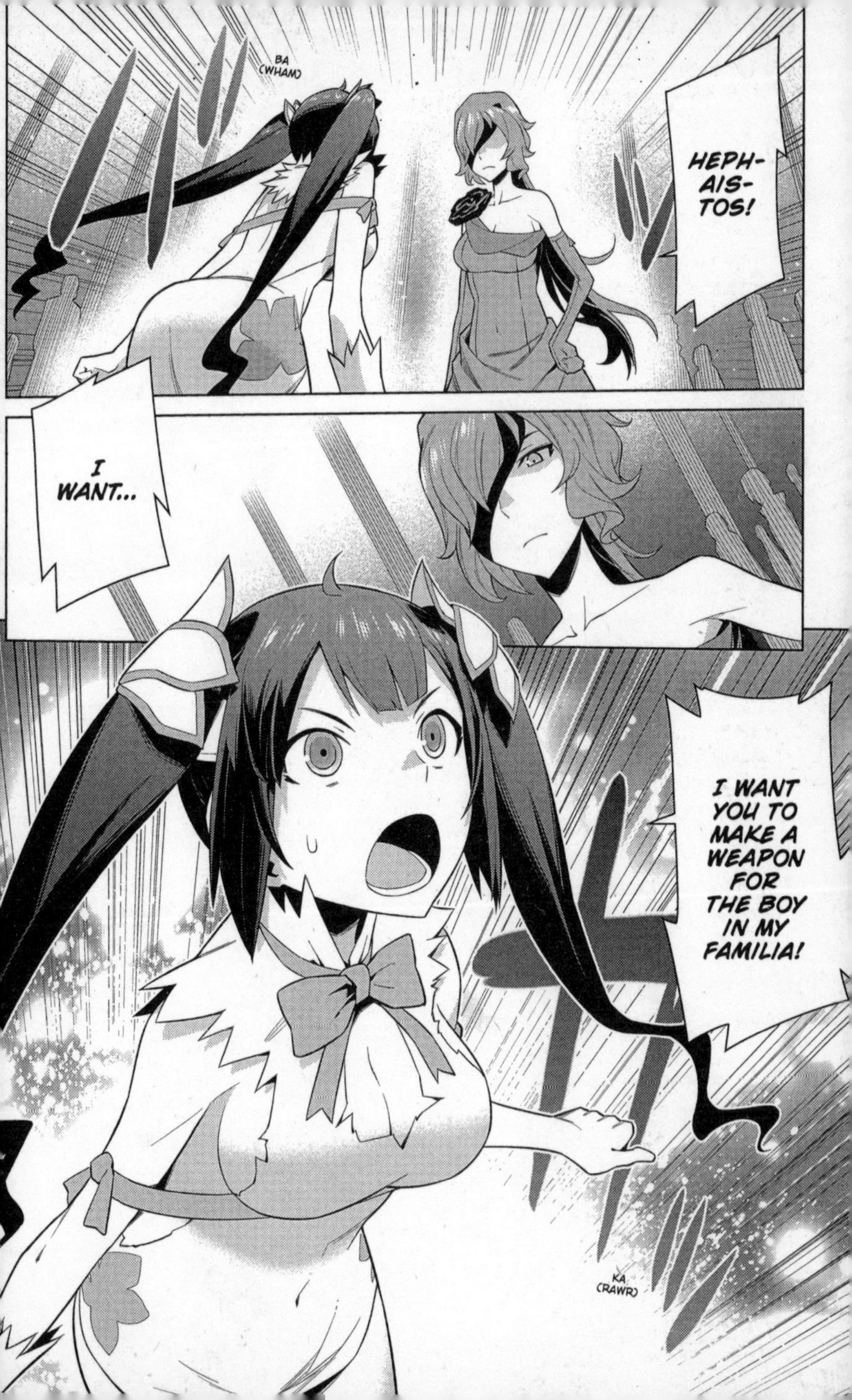
BA (WHAM)
HEPH-AIS-TOS!
I WANT...
I WANT YOU TO MAKE A WEAPON FOR THE BOY IN MY FAMILIA!
KA (RAWR)

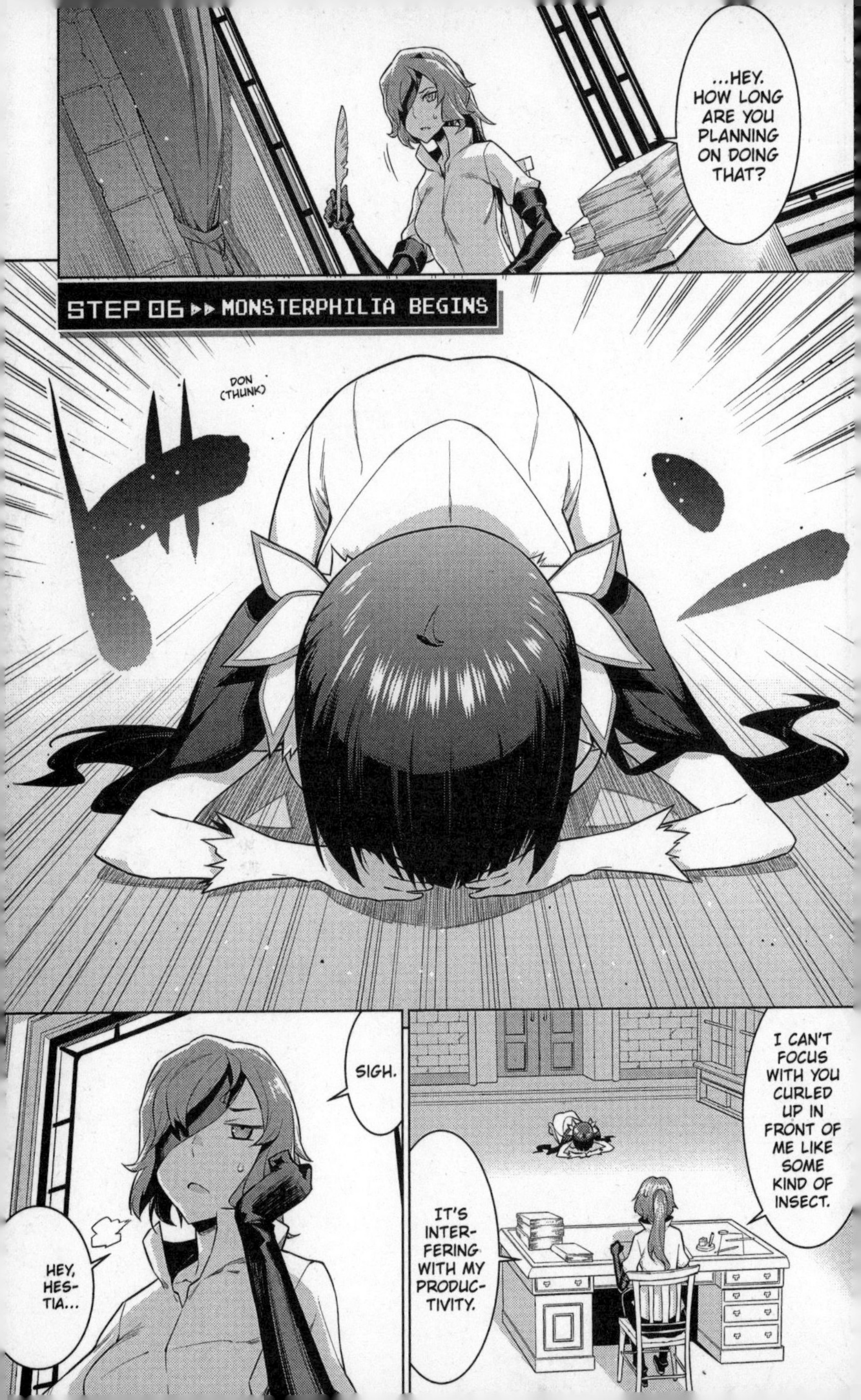
...HEY. HOW LONG ARE YOU PLANNING ON DOING THAT?
STEP 06 ▸▸ MONSTERPHILIA BEGINS
DON (THUNK)
I CAN'T FOCUS WITH YOU CURLED UP IN FRONT OF ME LIKE SOME KIND OF INSECT.
IT'S INTER-FERING WITH MY PRODUC-TIVITY.
SIGH.
HEY, HES-TIA...

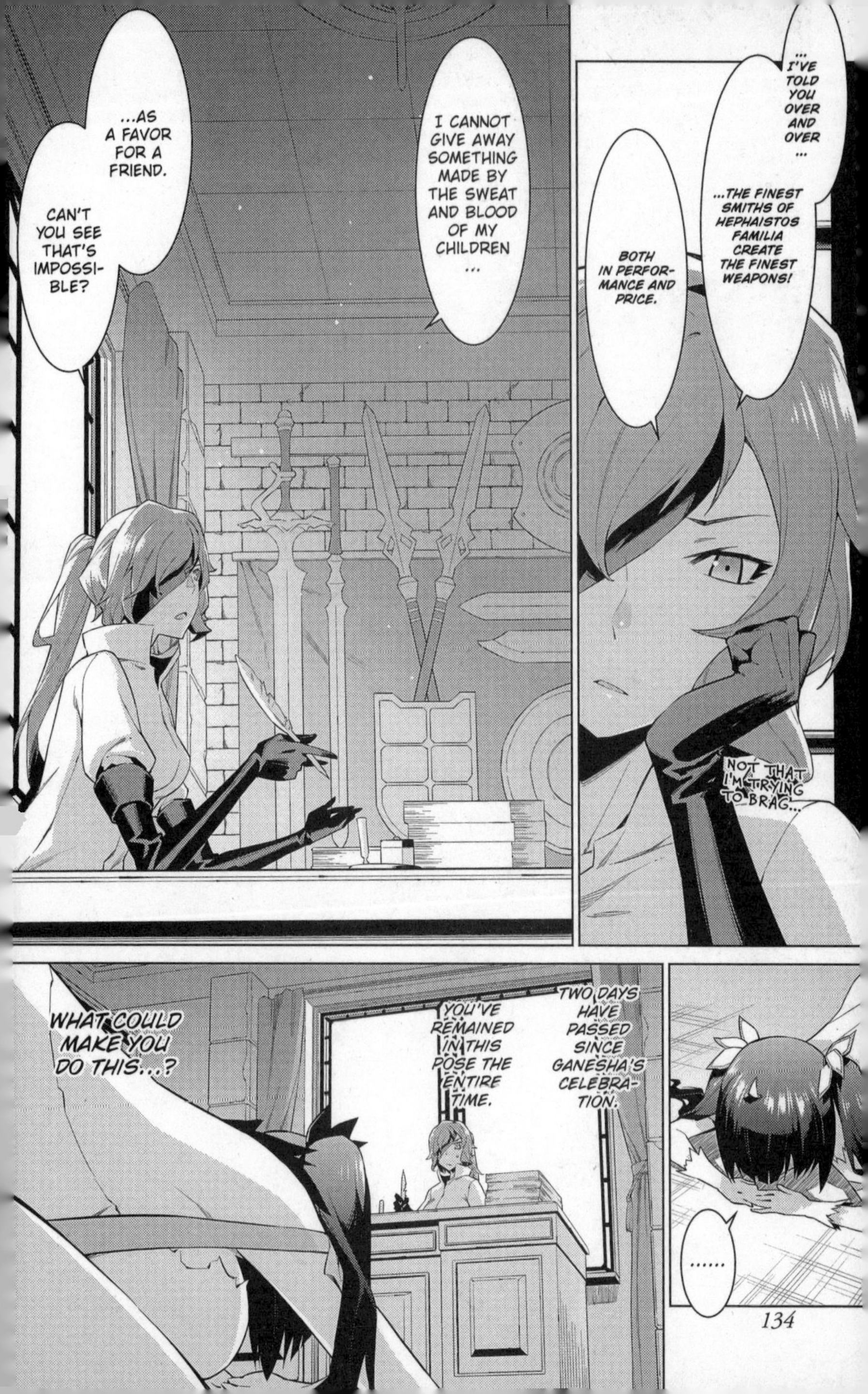

... I'VE TOLD YOU OVER AND OVER ...
...THE FINEST SMITHS OF HEPHAISTOS FAMILIA CREATE THE FINEST WEAPONS!
BOTH IN PERFORMANCE AND PRICE.
NOT THAT I'M TRYING TO BRAG...
I CANNOT GIVE AWAY SOMETHING MADE BY THE SWEAT AND BLOOD OF MY CHILDREN ...
...AS A FAVOR FOR A FRIEND.
CAN'T YOU SEE THAT'S IMPOSSI-BLE?
......
TWO DAYS HAVE PASSED SINCE GANESHA'S CELEBRA-TION.
YOU'VE REMAINED IN THIS POSE THE ENTIRE TIME.
WHAT COULD MAKE YOU DO THIS...?

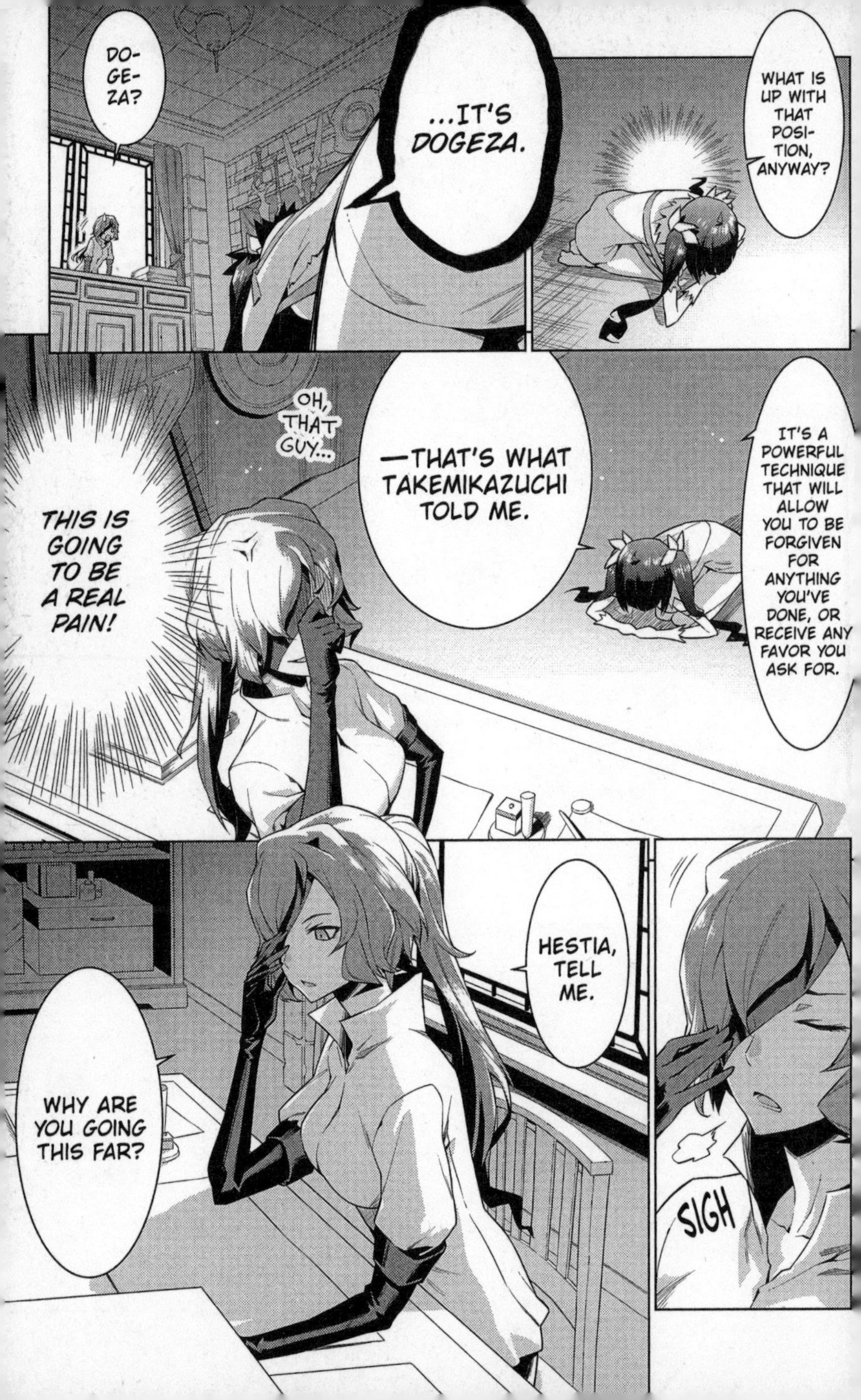
WHAT IS UP WITH THAT POSITION, ANYWAY?
...IT'S DOGEZA.
DO-GE-ZA?
IT'S A POWERFUL TECHNIQUE THAT WILL ALLOW YOU TO BE FORGIVEN FOR ANYTHING YOU'VE DONE, OR RECEIVE ANY FAVOR YOU ASK FOR.
—THAT'S WHAT TAKEMIKAZUCHI TOLD ME.
OH, THAT GUY...
THIS IS GOING TO BE A REAL PAIN!
SIGH
HESTIA, TELL ME.
WHY ARE YOU GOING THIS FAR?

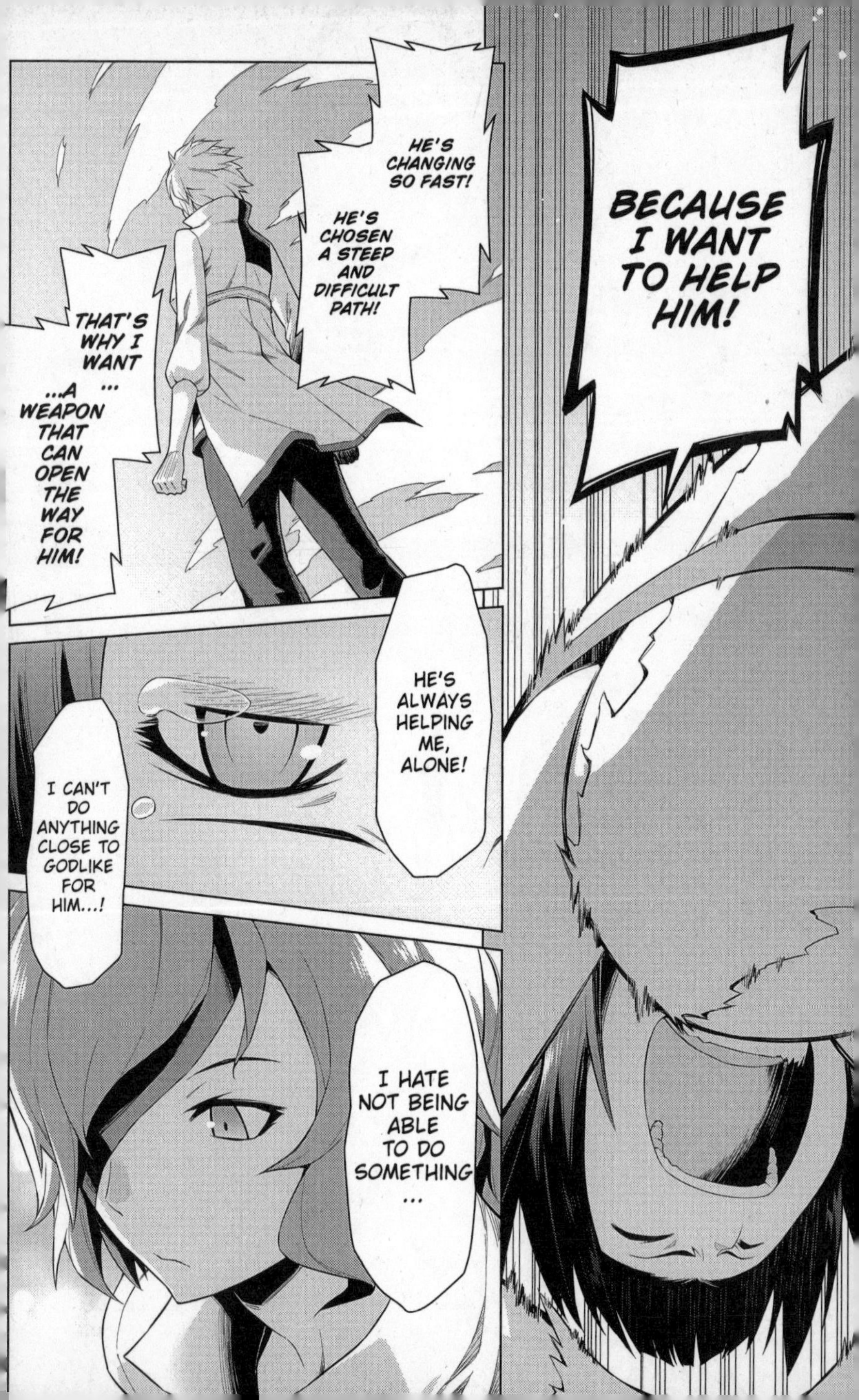
BECAUSE I WANT TO HELP HIM!
HE'S CHANGING SO FAST!
HE'S CHOSEN A STEEP AND DIFFICULT PATH!
THAT'S WHY I WANT ...
...A WEAPON THAT CAN OPEN THE WAY FOR HIM!
HE'S ALWAYS HELPING ME, ALONE!
I CAN'T DO ANYTHING CLOSE TO GODLIKE FOR HIM...!
I HATE NOT BEING ABLE TO DO SOMETHING...

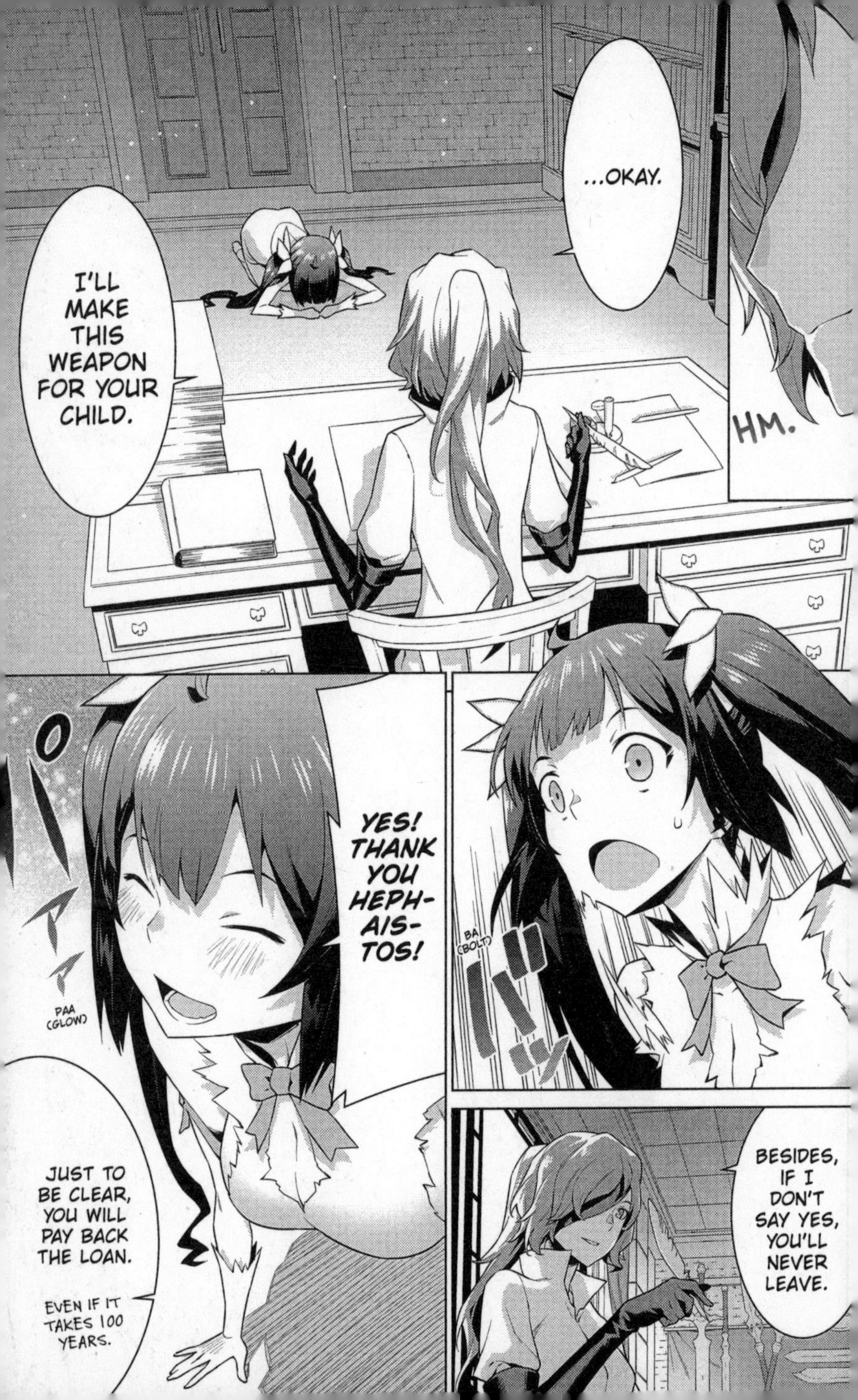
HM.
...OKAY.
I'LL MAKE THIS WEAPON FOR YOUR CHILD.
BA (BOLT)
BESIDES, IF I DON'T SAY YES, YOU'LL NEVER LEAVE.
YES! THANK YOU HEPH-AIS-TOS!
PAA (GLOW)
JUST TO BE CLEAR, YOU WILL PAY BACK THE LOAN.
EVEN IF IT TAKES 100 YEARS.

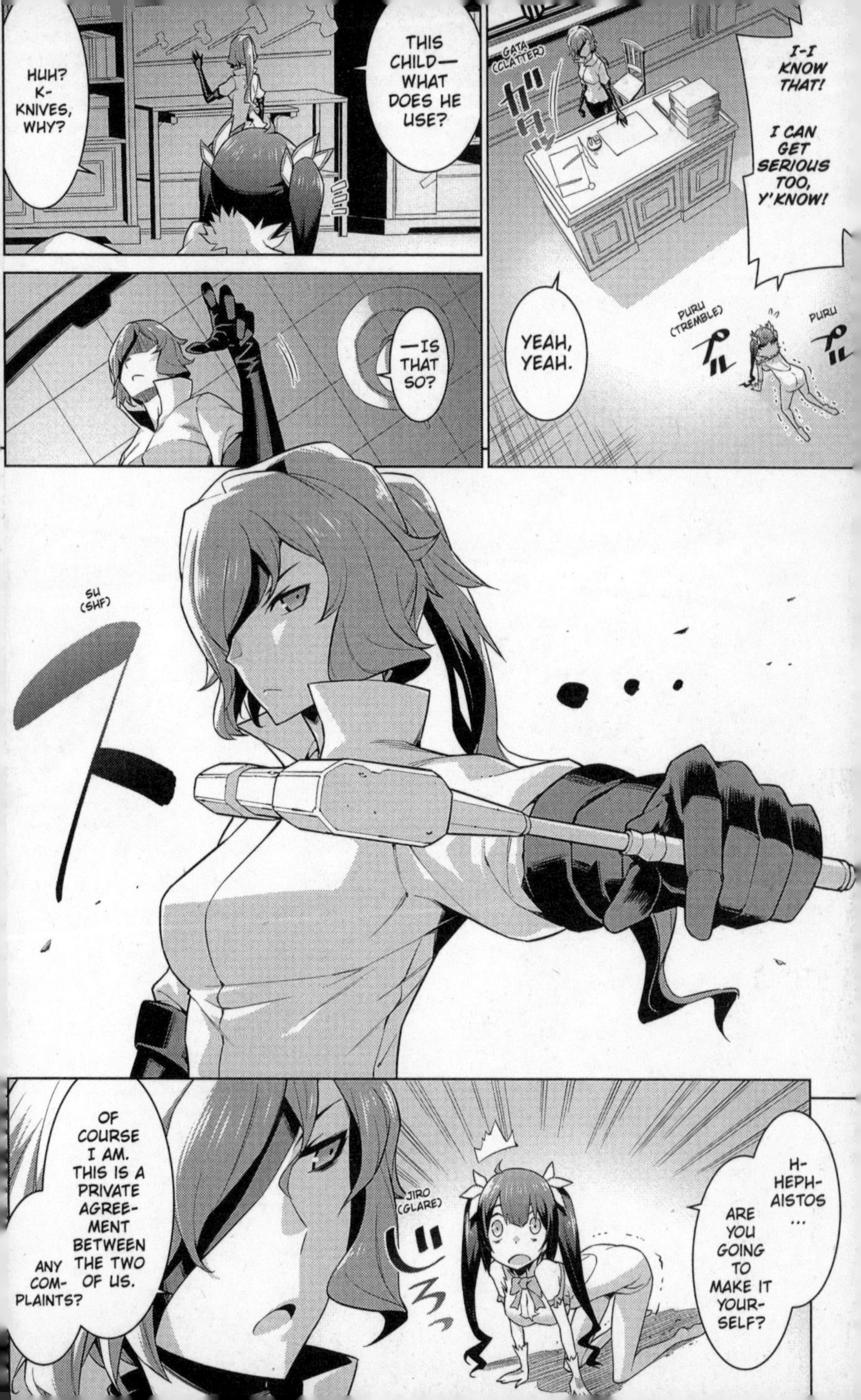

GATA (CLATTER)
I-I KNOW THAT!
I CAN GET SERIOUS TOO, Y'KNOW!
YEAH, YEAH.
PURU (TREMBLE)
PURU
THIS CHILD— WHAT DOES HE USE?
HUH? K-KNIVES, WHY?
—IS THAT SO?
SU (SHF)
...
H-HEPHAISTOS...
ARE YOU GOING TO MAKE IT YOURSELF?
JIRO (GLARE)
OF COURSE I AM. THIS IS A PRIVATE AGREEMENT BETWEEN THE TWO OF US.
ANY COMPLAINTS?

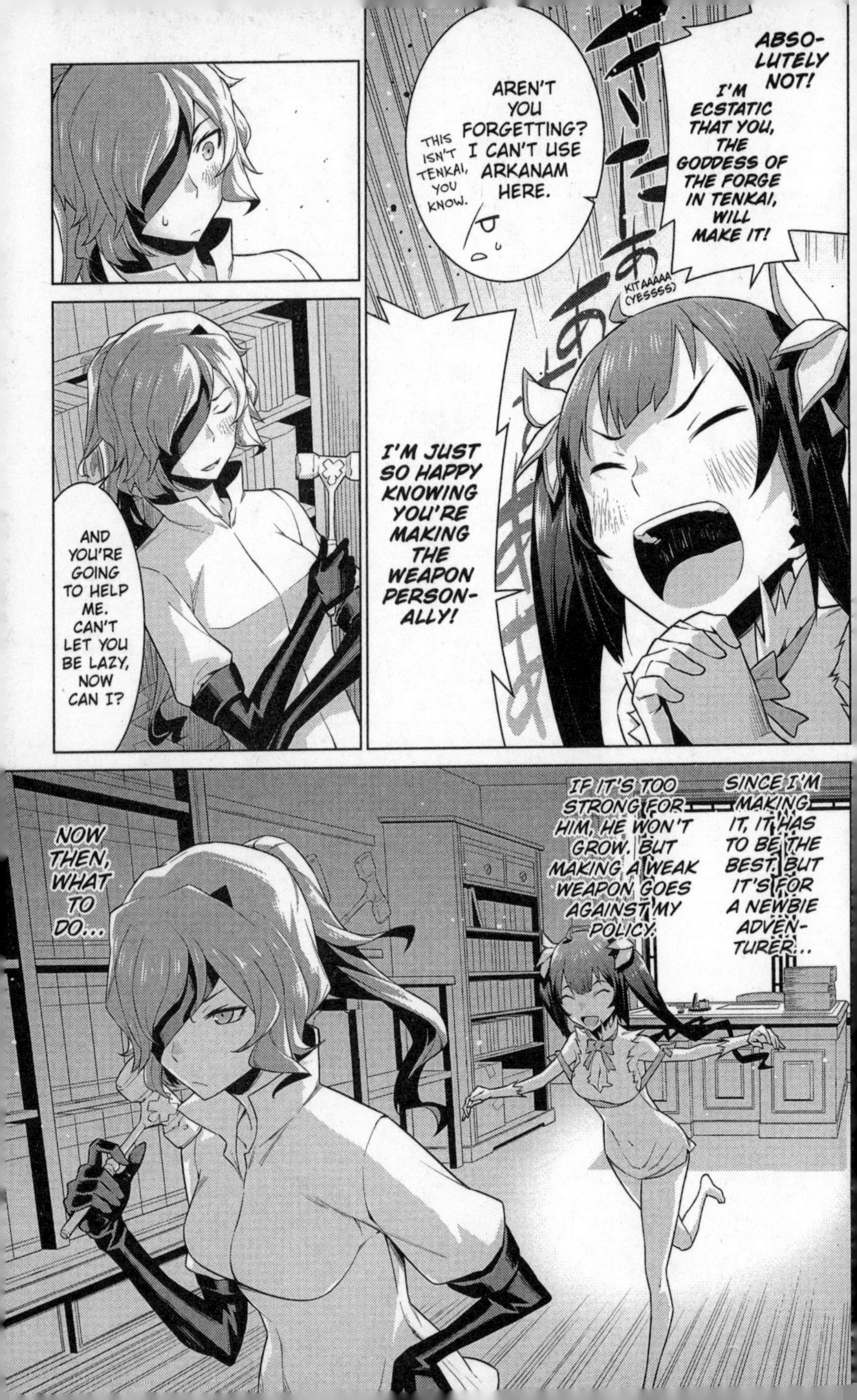
ABSOLUTELY NOT!
I'M ECSTATIC THAT YOU, THE GODDESS OF THE FORGE IN TENKAI, WILL MAKE IT!
KITAAAAA (YESSSSS)
AREN'T YOU FORGETTING? I CAN'T USE ARKANAM HERE.
THIS ISN'T TENKAI, YOU KNOW.
I'M JUST SO HAPPY KNOWING YOU'RE MAKING THE WEAPON PERSONALLY!
AND YOU'RE GOING TO HELP ME. CAN'T LET YOU BE LAZY, NOW CAN I?
SINCE I'M MAKING IT, IT HAS TO BE THE BEST. BUT IT'S FOR A NEWBIE ADVENTURER...
IF IT'S TOO STRONG FOR HIM, HE WON'T GROW. BUT MAKING A WEAK WEAPON GOES AGAINST MY POLICY.
NOW THEN, WHAT TO DO...

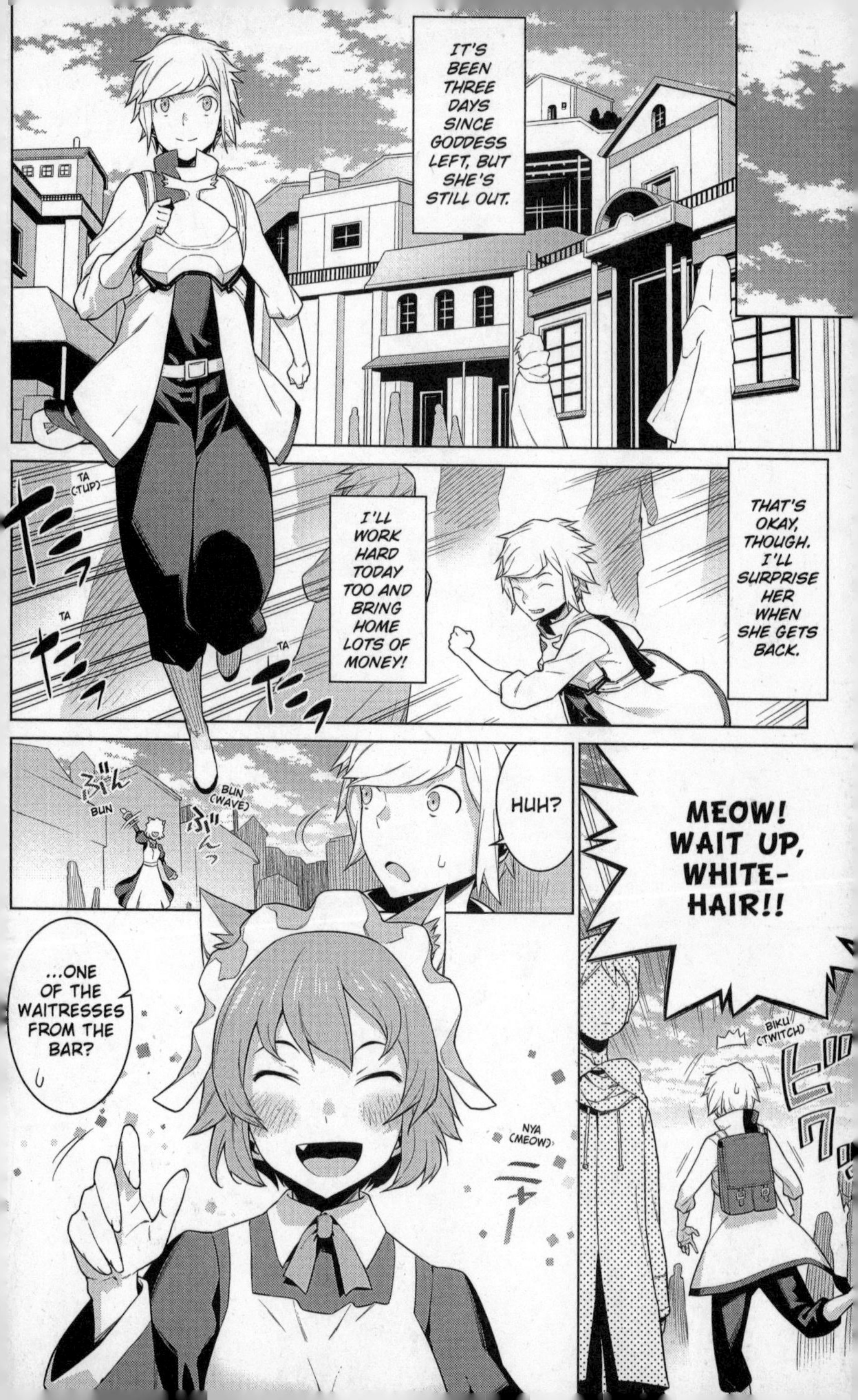

IT'S BEEN THREE DAYS SINCE GODDESS LEFT, BUT SHE'S STILL OUT.
THAT'S OKAY, THOUGH. I'LL SURPRISE HER WHEN SHE GETS BACK.
I'LL WORK HARD TODAY TOO AND BRING HOME LOTS OF MONEY!
TA (TUP)
TA
TA
MEOW! WAIT UP, WHITE-HAIR!!
BIKU (TWITCH)
HUH?
BUN (WAVE)
BUN
...ONE OF THE WAITRESSES FROM THE BAR?
NYA (MEOW)

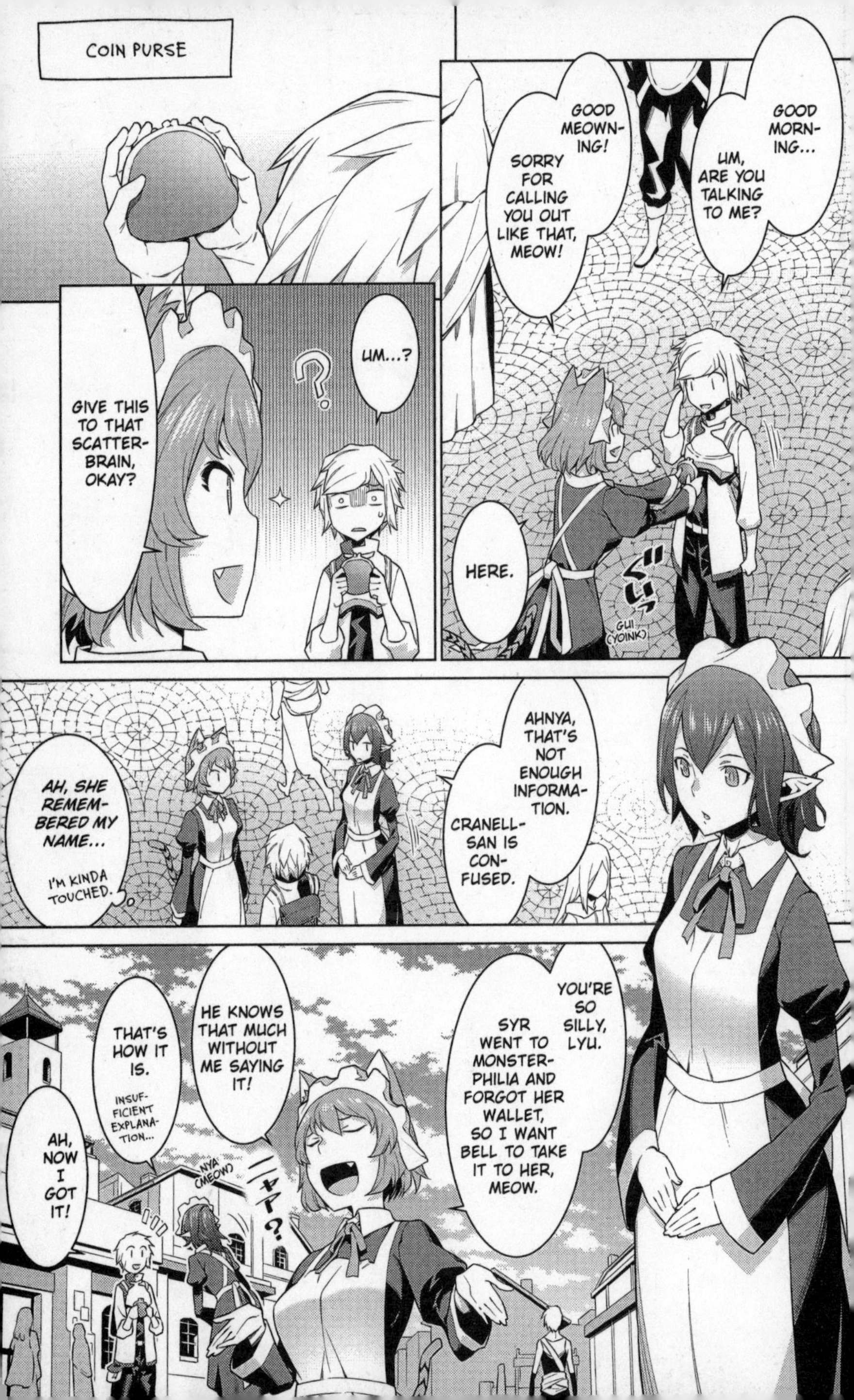
GOOD MORNING...
UM, ARE YOU TALKING TO ME?
GOOD MEOWNING!
SORRY FOR CALLING YOU OUT LIKE THAT, MEOW!
HERE.
GUI (YOINK)
COIN PURSE
UM...?
GIVE THIS TO THAT SCATTER-BRAIN, OKAY?
AHNYA, THAT'S NOT ENOUGH INFORMATION.
CRANELL-SAN IS CONFUSED.
AH, SHE REMEMBERED MY NAME...
I'M KINDA TOUCHED.
YOU'RE SO SILLY, LYU.
SYR WENT TO MONSTERPHILIA AND FORGOT HER WALLET, SO I WANT BELL TO TAKE IT TO HER, MEOW.
NYA (MEOW)
HE KNOWS THAT MUCH WITHOUT ME SAYING IT!
THAT'S HOW IT IS.
INSUFFICIENT EXPLANATION...
AH, NOW I GOT IT!

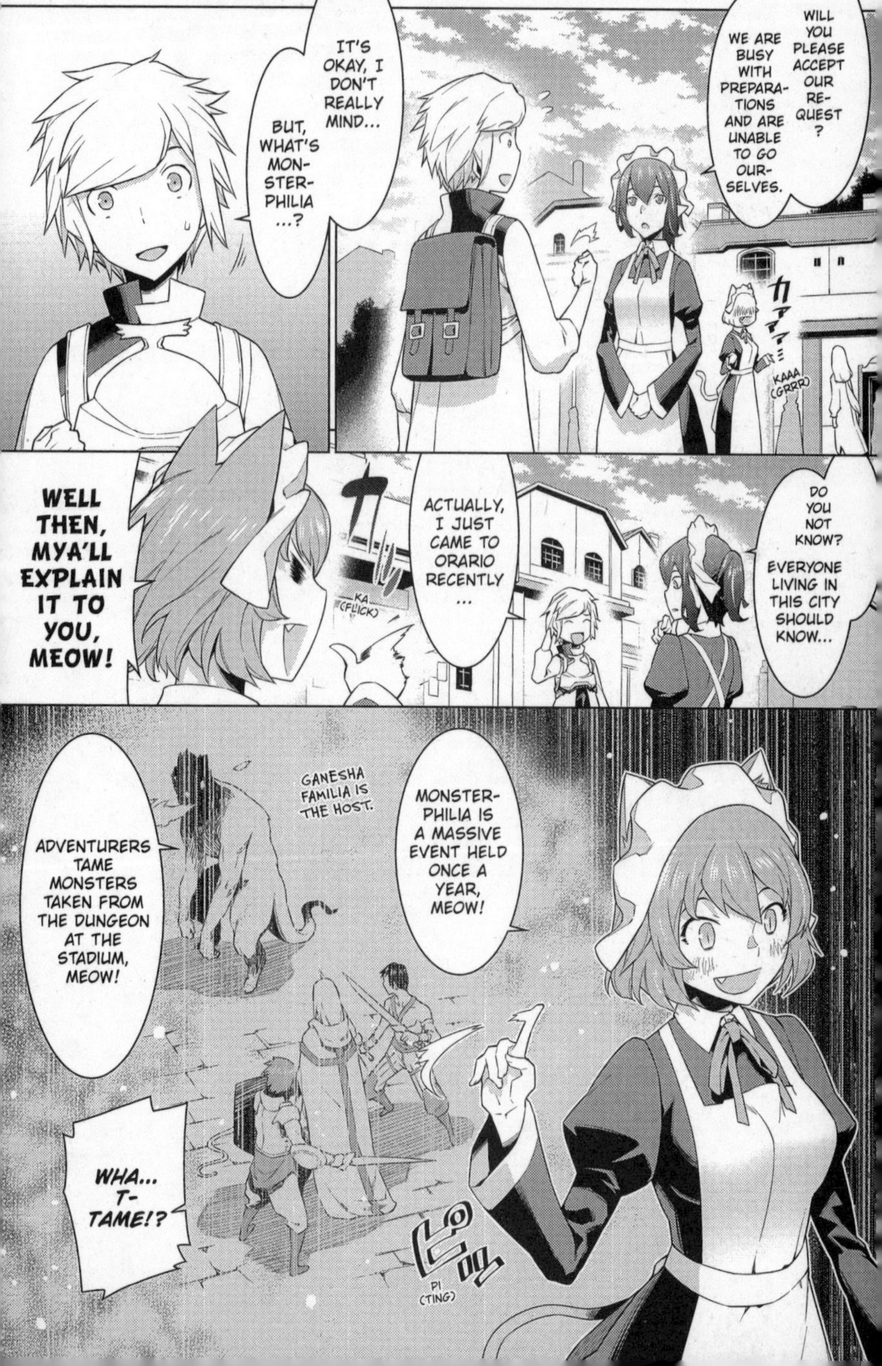
WILL YOU PLEASE ACCEPT OUR REQUEST?
WE ARE BUSY WITH PREPARATIONS AND ARE UNABLE TO GO OURSELVES.
KAAA (GRRR)
IT'S OKAY, I DON'T REALLY MIND...
BUT, WHAT'S MONSTERPHILIA...?
DO YOU NOT KNOW?
EVERYONE LIVING IN THIS CITY SHOULD KNOW...
ACTUALLY, I JUST CAME TO ORARIO RECENTLY...
KA (FLICK)
WELL THEN, MYA'LL EXPLAIN IT TO YOU, MEOW!
MONSTERPHILIA IS A MASSIVE EVENT HELD ONCE A YEAR, MEOW!
GANESHA FAMILIA IS THE HOST.
ADVENTURERS TAME MONSTERS TAKEN FROM THE DUNGEON AT THE STADIUM, MEOW!
PI (TING)
WHA... T-TAME!?

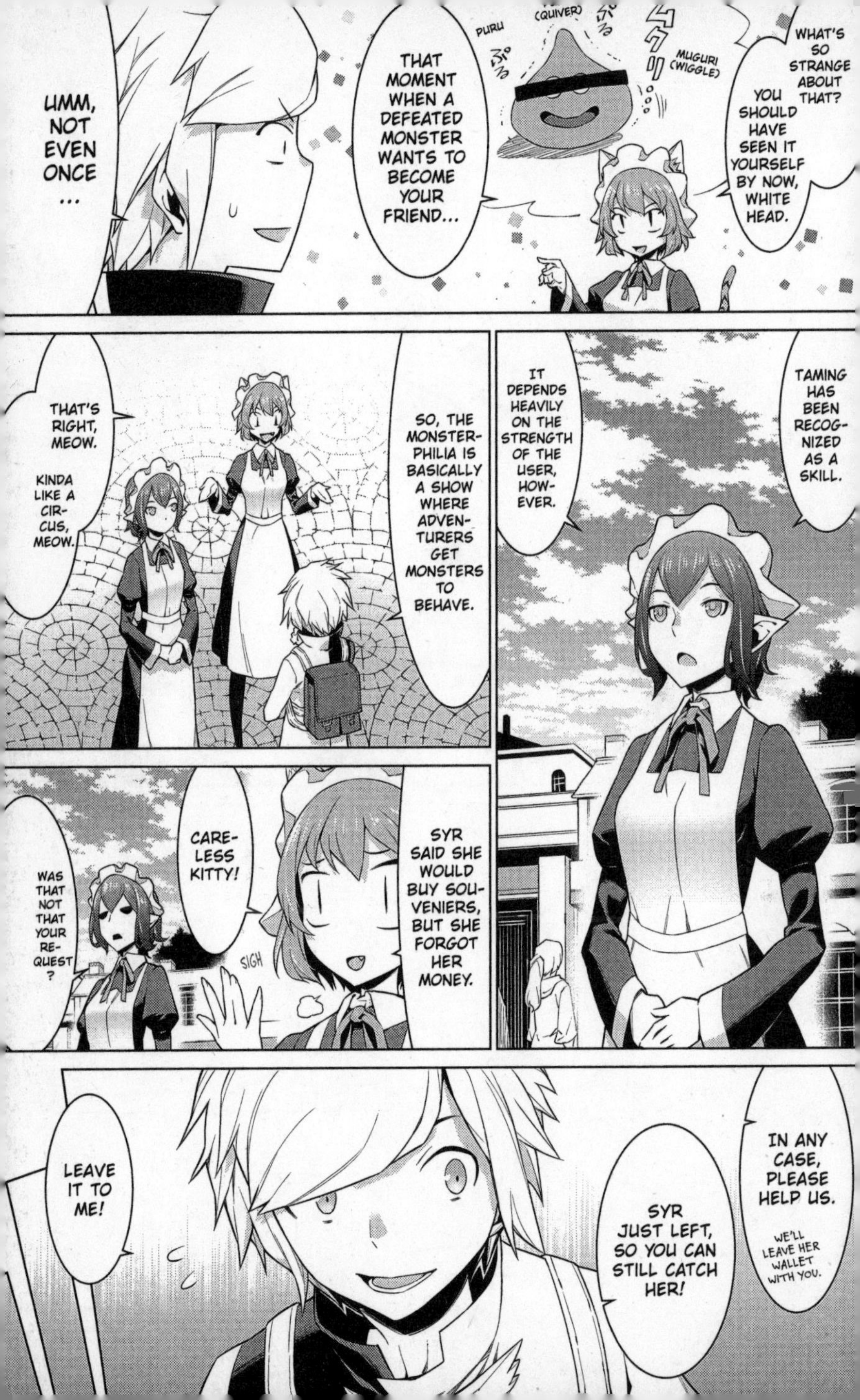
WHAT'S SO STRANGE ABOUT THAT? YOU SHOULD HAVE SEEN IT YOURSELF BY NOW, WHITE HEAD.
MUGURI (WIGGLE)
(QUIVER)
PURU
THAT MOMENT WHEN A DEFEATED MONSTER WANTS TO BECOME YOUR FRIEND...
UMM, NOT EVEN ONCE ...
TAMING HAS BEEN RECOGNIZED AS A SKILL.
IT DEPENDS HEAVILY ON THE STRENGTH OF THE USER, HOWEVER.
SO, THE MONSTERPHILIA IS BASICALLY A SHOW WHERE ADVENTURERS GET MONSTERS TO BEHAVE.
THAT'S RIGHT, MEOW.
KINDA LIKE A CIRCUS, MEOW.
SYR SAID SHE WOULD BUY SOUVENIERS, BUT SHE FORGOT HER MONEY.
SIGH
CARELESS KITTY!
WAS THAT NOT THAT YOUR REQUEST?
IN ANY CASE, PLEASE HELP US.
WE'LL LEAVE HER WALLET WITH YOU.
SYR JUST LEFT, SO YOU CAN STILL CATCH HER!
LEAVE IT TO ME!

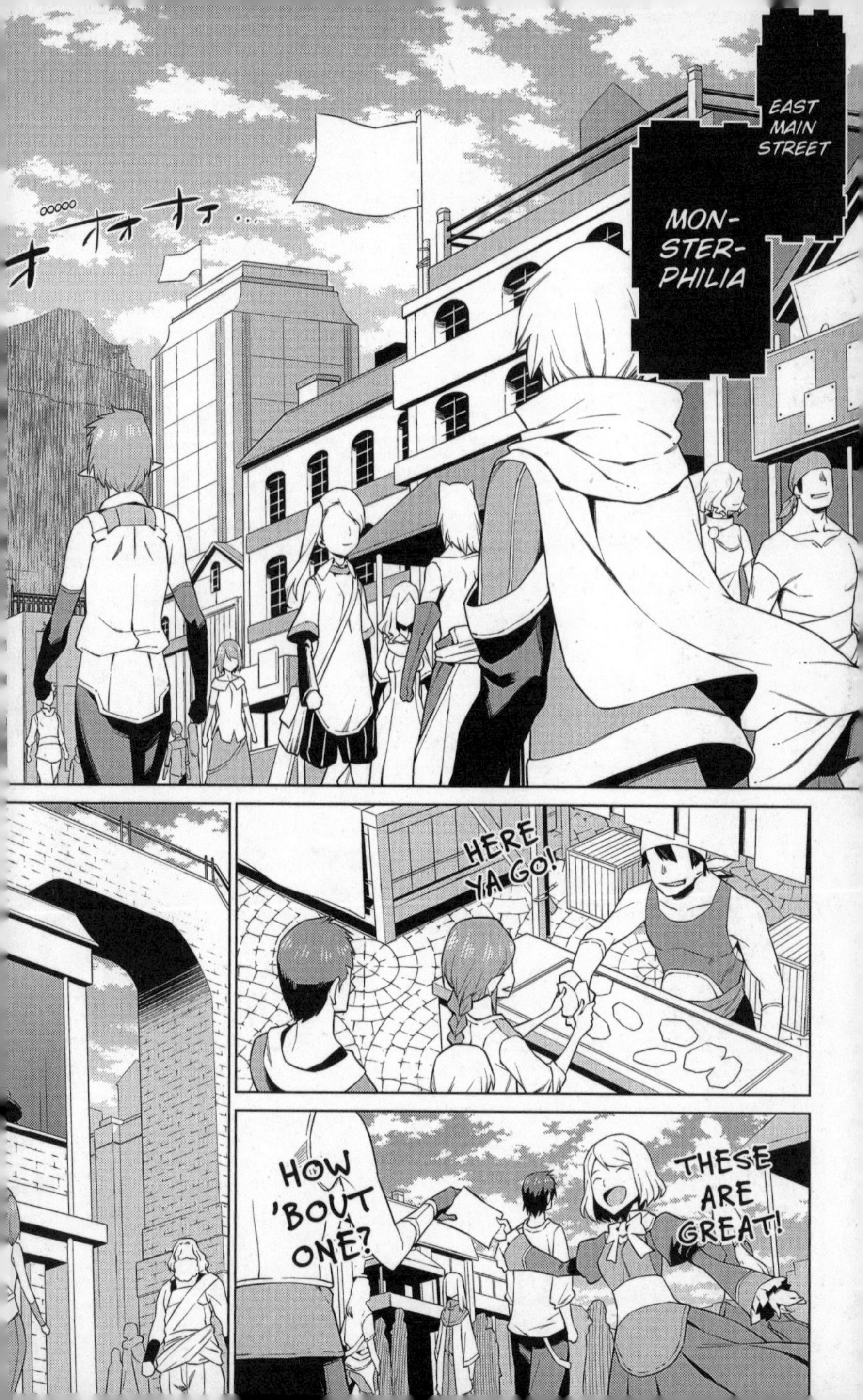
EAST MAIN STREET
MON-STER-PHILIA
OOOOO
オーオォォォ…
HERE YA GO!
THESE ARE GREAT!
HOW 'BOUT ONE?

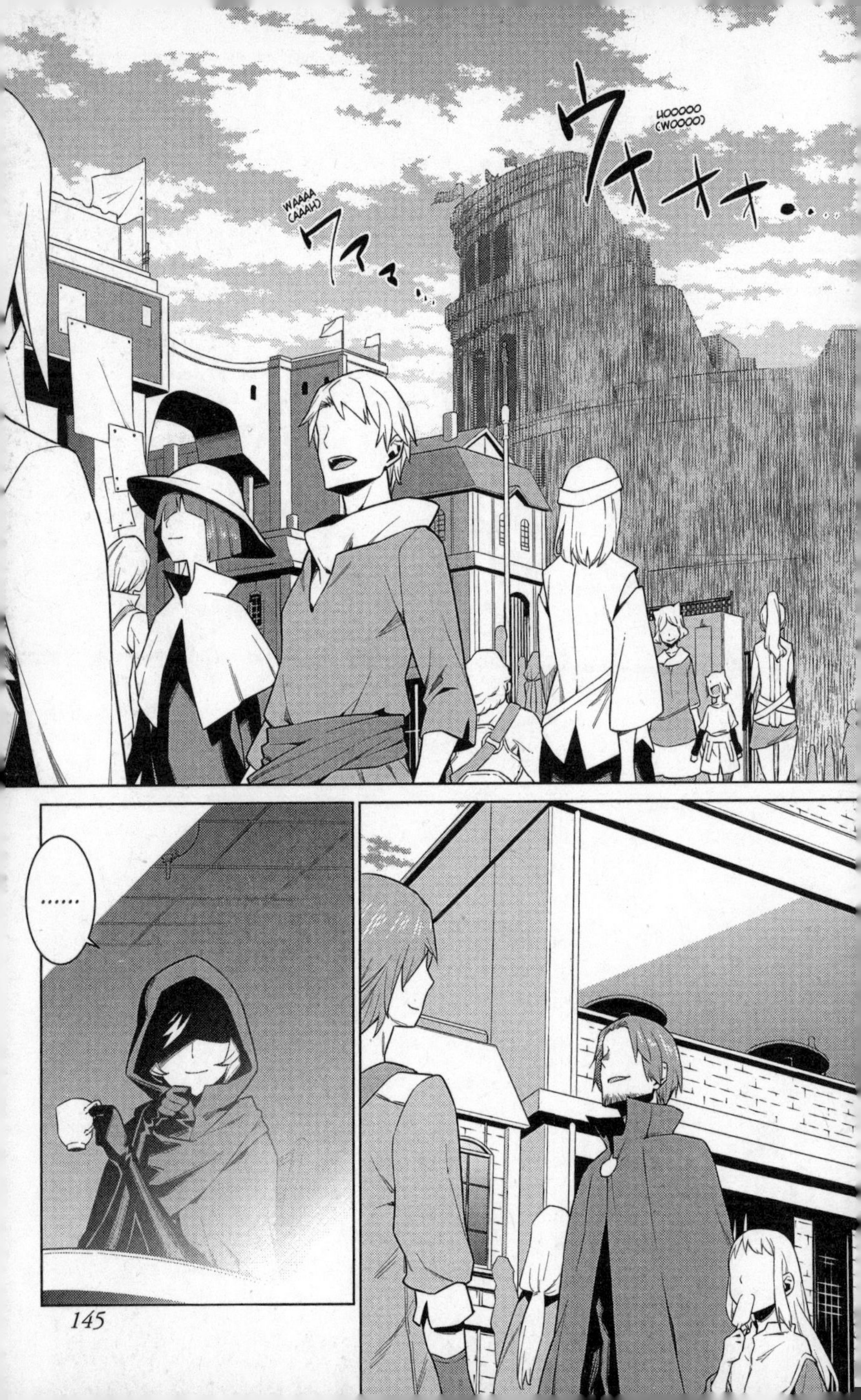
ウォォォ…
HOOOOO (WOOOO)
ワァァ…
WAAAA (AAAH)
……

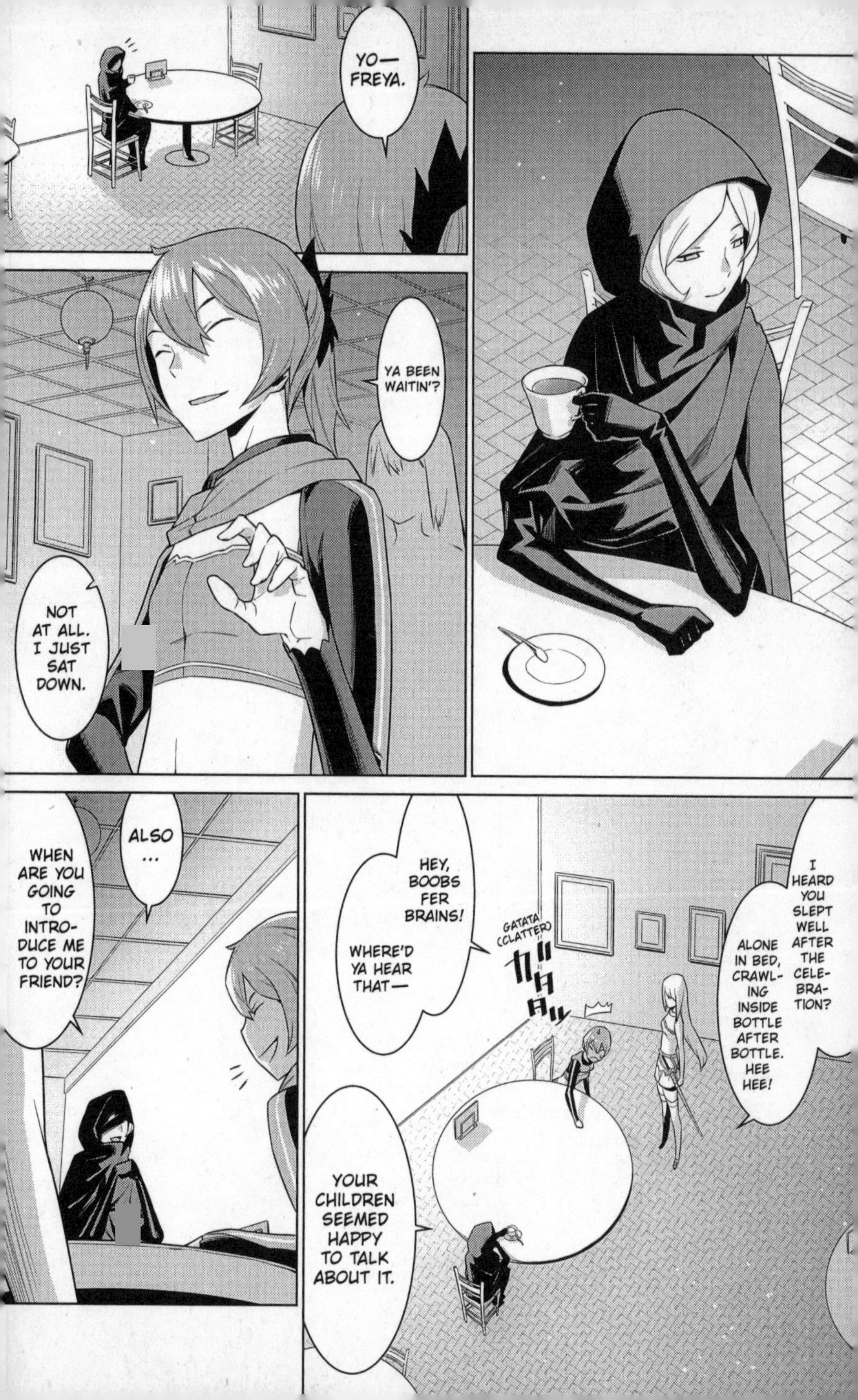
YO— FREYA.
YA BEEN WAITIN'?
NOT AT ALL. I JUST SAT DOWN.
I HEARD YOU SLEPT WELL AFTER THE CELEBRATION?
ALONE IN BED, CRAWLING INSIDE BOTTLE AFTER BOTTLE. HEE HEE!
GATATA (CLATTER)
HEY, BOOBS FER BRAINS!
WHERE'D YA HEAR THAT—
YOUR CHILDREN SEEMED HAPPY TO TALK ABOUT IT.
ALSO...
WHEN ARE YOU GOING TO INTRODUCE ME TO YOUR FRIEND?

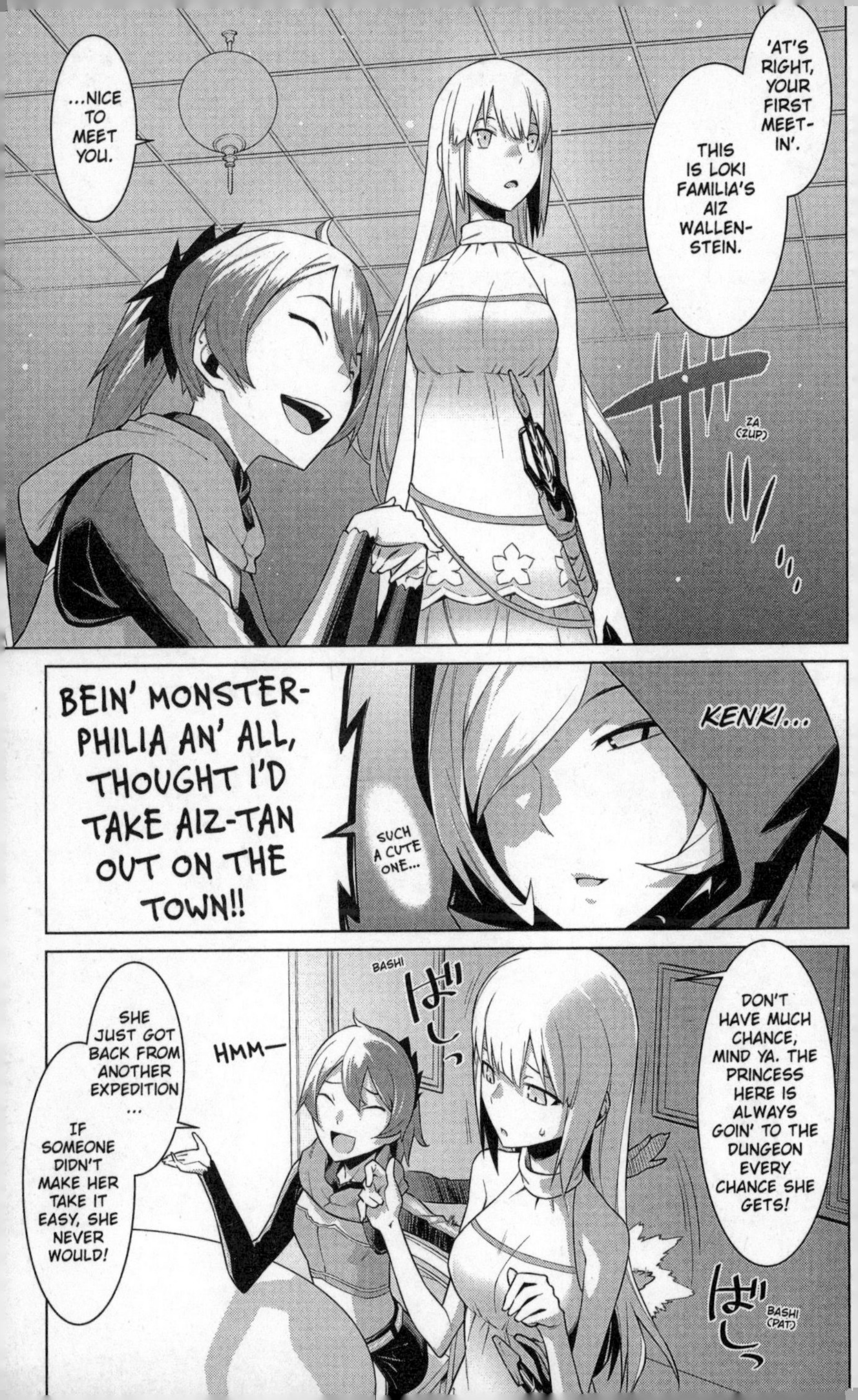
'AT'S RIGHT, YOUR FIRST MEET-IN'.
THIS IS LOKI FAMILIA'S AIZ WALLEN-STEIN.
ZA (ZUP)
...NICE TO MEET YOU.
KENKI...
SUCH A CUTE ONE...
BEIN' MONSTER-PHILIA AN' ALL, THOUGHT I'D TAKE AIZ-TAN OUT ON THE TOWN!!
DON'T HAVE MUCH CHANCE, MIND YA. THE PRINCESS HERE IS ALWAYS GOIN' TO THE DUNGEON EVERY CHANCE SHE GETS!
BASHI
BASHI (PAT)
HMM—
SHE JUST GOT BACK FROM ANOTHER EXPEDITION...
IF SOMEONE DIDN'T MAKE HER TAKE IT EASY, SHE NEVER WOULD!

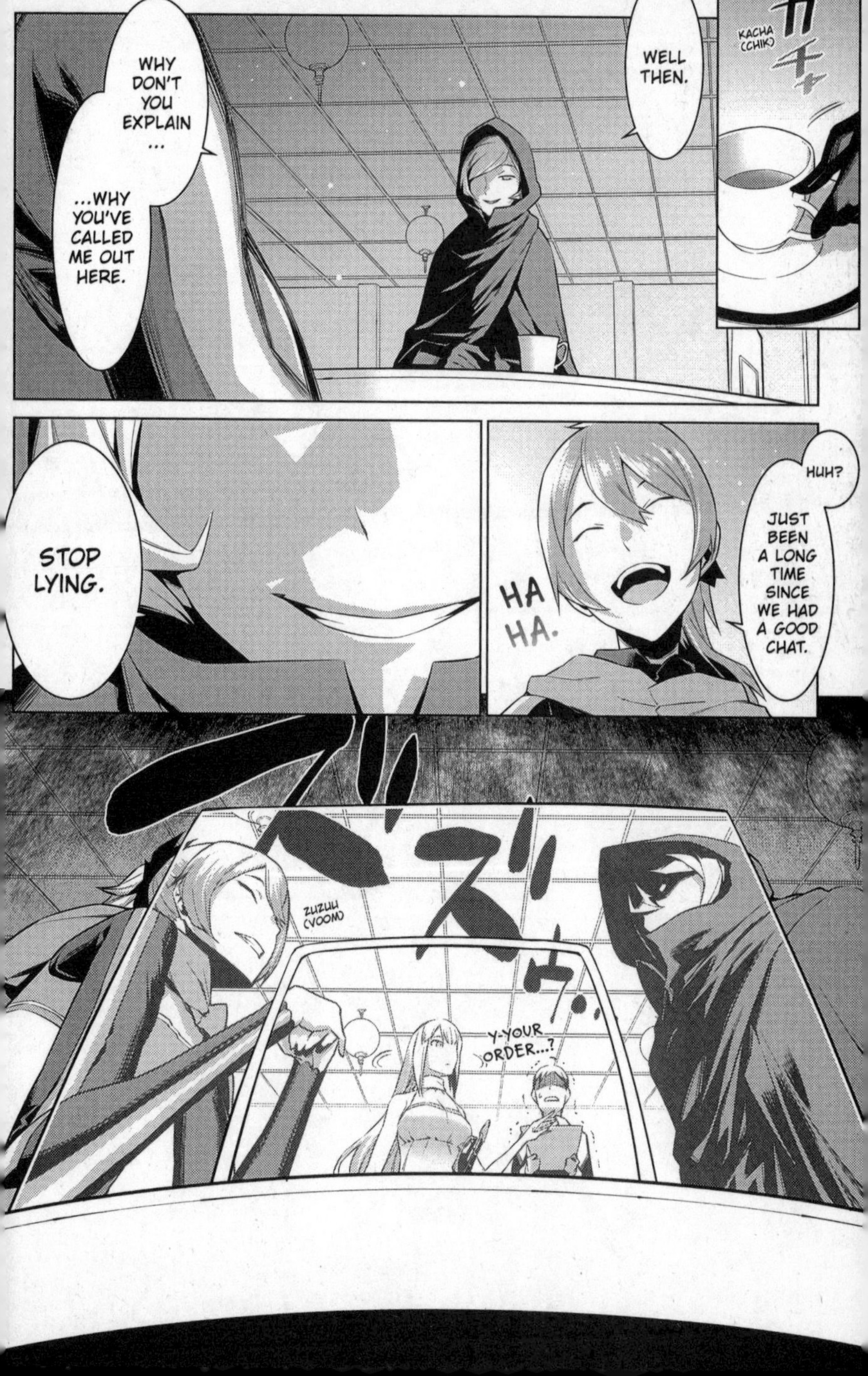
KACHA (CHIK)
WELL THEN.
WHY DON'T YOU EXPLAIN ...
...WHY YOU'VE CALLED ME OUT HERE.
HUH?
JUST BEEN A LONG TIME SINCE WE HAD A GOOD CHAT.
HA HA.
STOP LYING.
ZUZUU (VOOM)
Y-YOUR ORDER...?

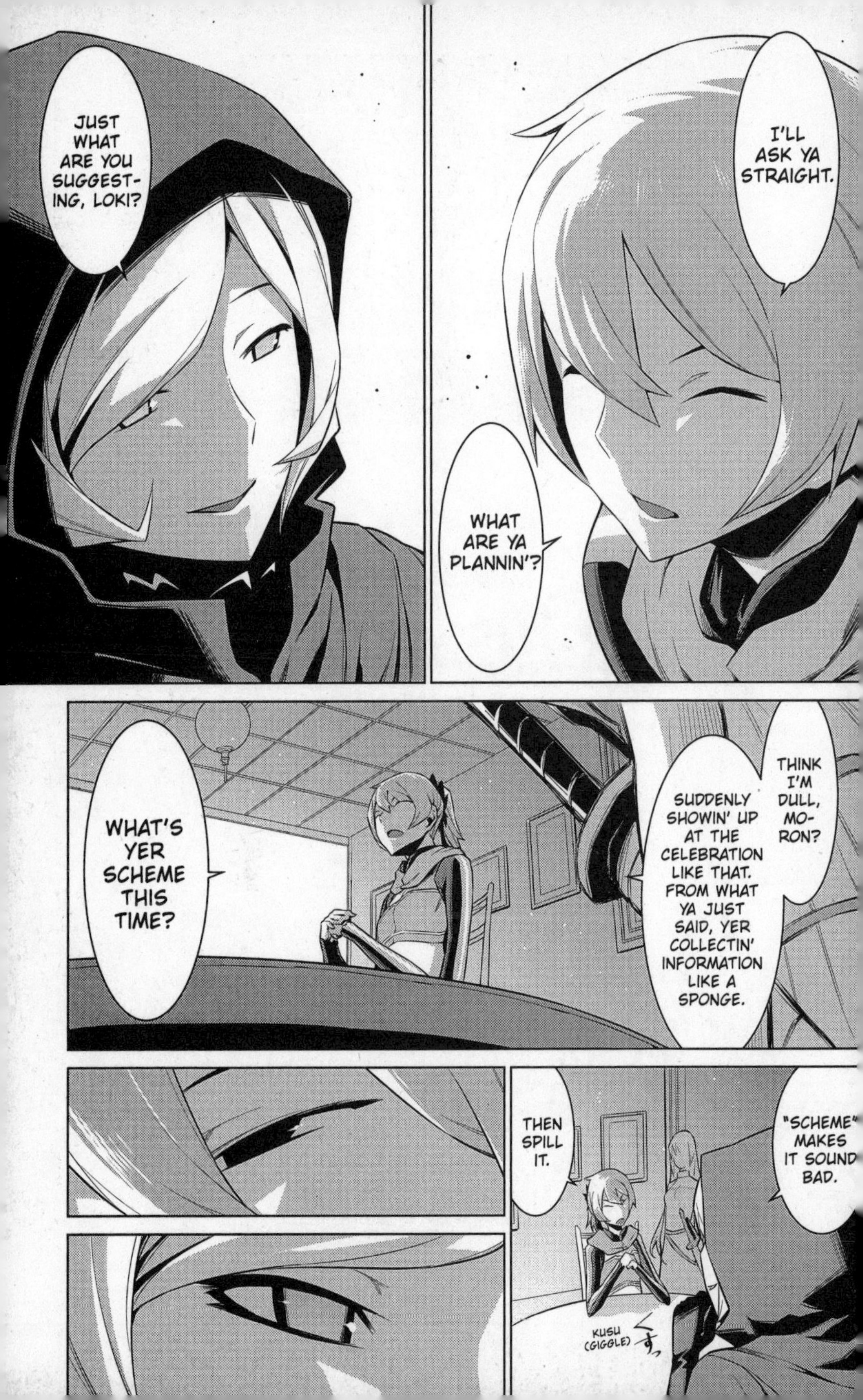
I'LL ASK YA STRAIGHT.
WHAT ARE YA PLANNIN'?
JUST WHAT ARE YOU SUGGEST-ING, LOKI?
THINK I'M DULL, MO-RON?
SUDDENLY SHOWIN' UP AT THE CELEBRATION LIKE THAT. FROM WHAT YA JUST SAID, YER COLLECTIN' INFORMATION LIKE A SPONGE.
WHAT'S YER SCHEME THIS TIME?
"SCHEME" MAKES IT SOUND BAD.
THEN SPILL IT.
KUSU (GIGGLE)

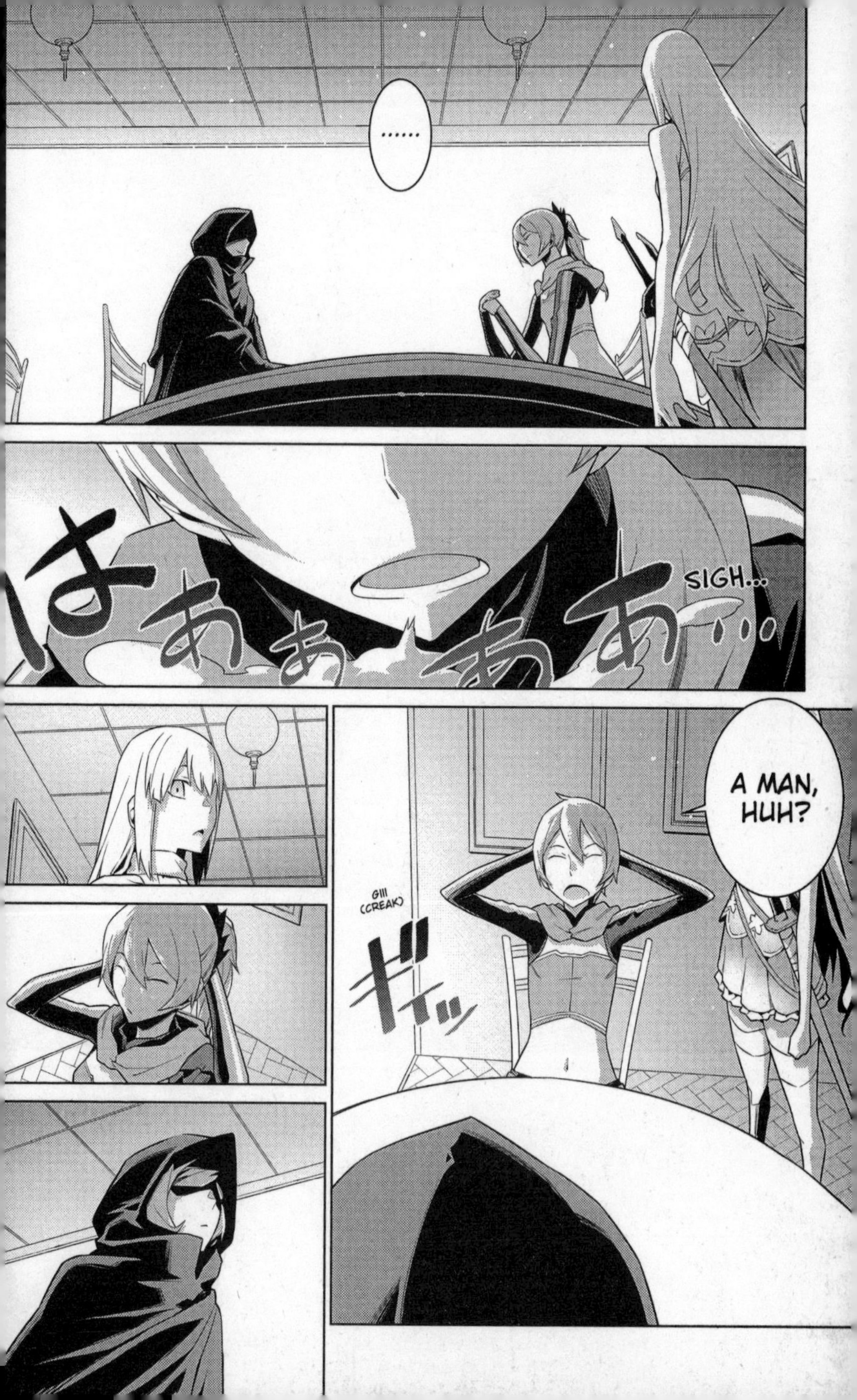
......
はあああ…
SIGH...
A MAN, HUH?
ギイッ
GIII (CREAK)

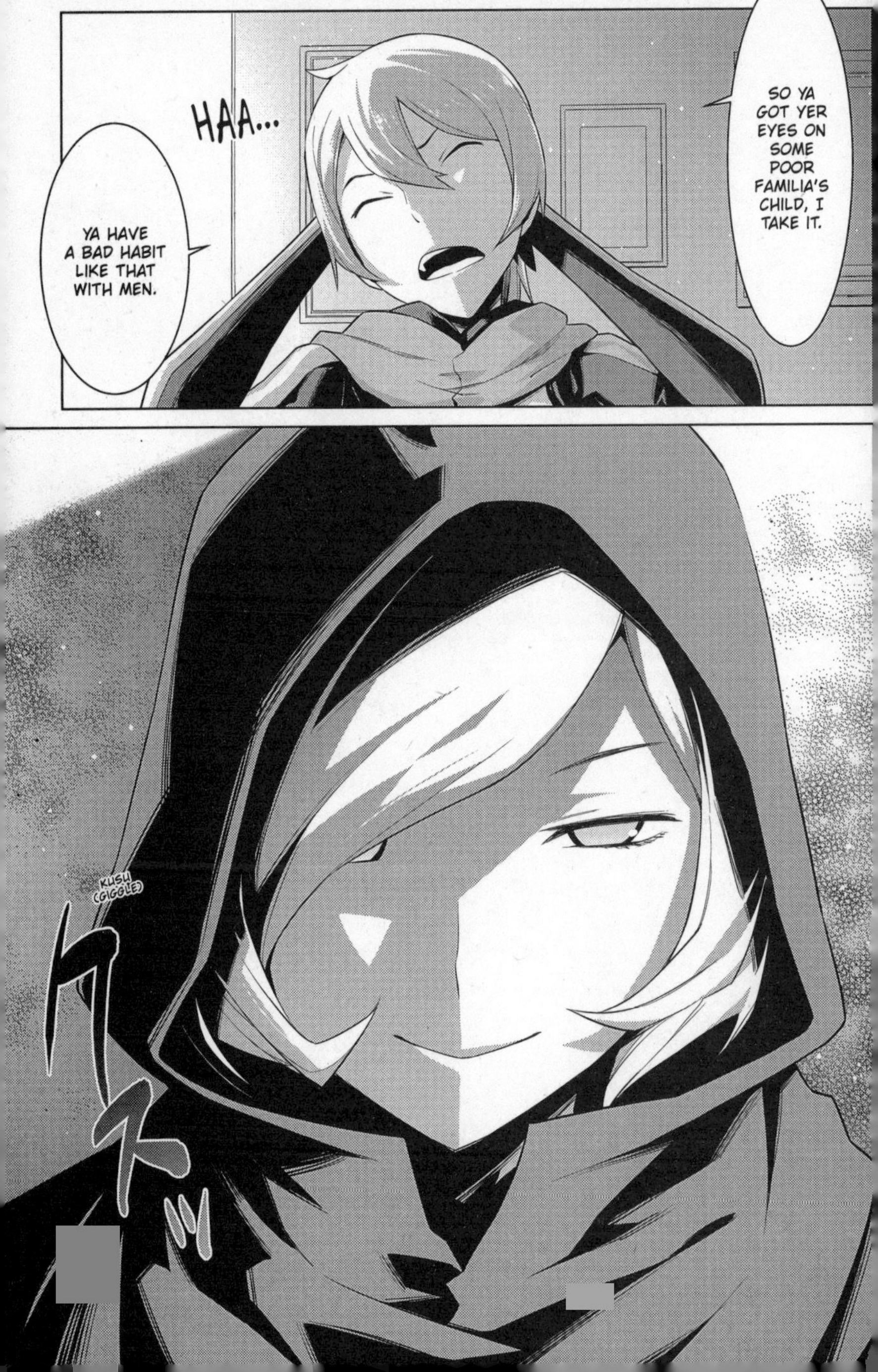
SO YA GOT YER EYES ON SOME POOR FAMILIA'S CHILD, I TAKE IT.
HAA...
YA HAVE A BAD HABIT LIKE THAT WITH MEN.
KUSU (GIGGLE)

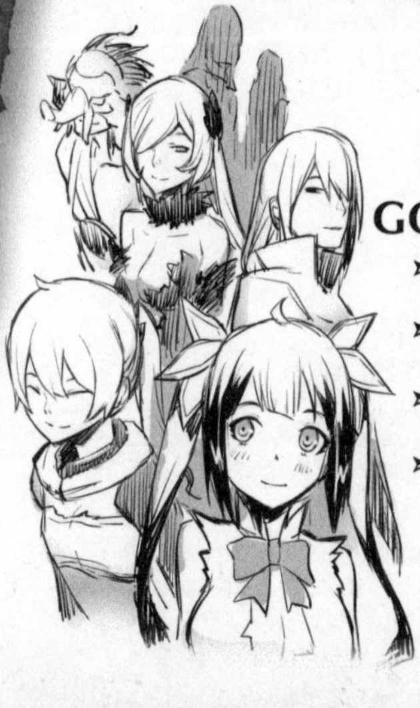

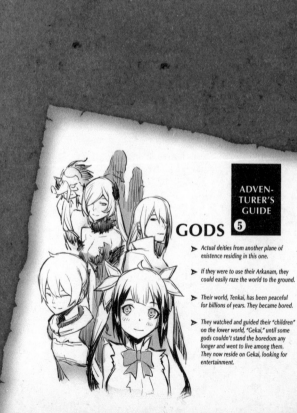

ADVEN-
TURER'S
GUIDE
5

GODS

- *Actual deities from another plane of existence residing in this one.*
- *If they were to use their Arkanam, they could easily raze the world to the ground.*
- *Their world, Tenkai, has been peaceful for billions of years. They became bored.*
- *They watched and guided their "children" on the lower world, "Gekai," until some gods couldn't stand the boredom any longer and went to live among them. They now reside on Gekai, looking for entertainment.*

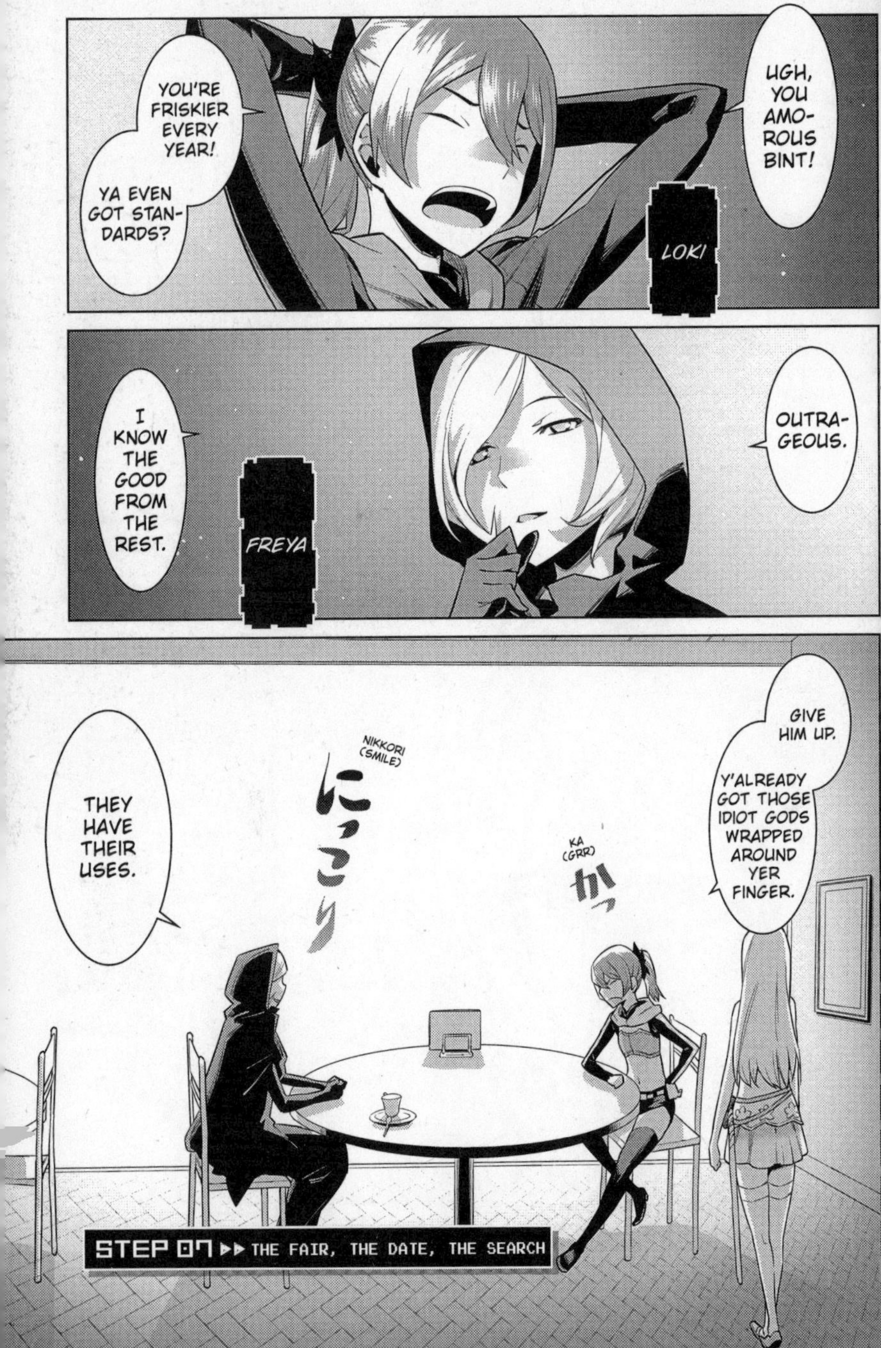
UGH, YOU AMOROUS BINT!
LOKI
YOU'RE FRISKIER EVERY YEAR!
YA EVEN GOT STANDARDS?
OUTRAGEOUS.
FREYA
I KNOW THE GOOD FROM THE REST.
GIVE HIM UP.
Y'ALREADY GOT THOSE IDIOT GODS WRAPPED AROUND YER FINGER.
KA (GRR)
かっ
NIKKORI (SMILE)
にっこり
THEY HAVE THEIR USES.
STEP 07 ▶▶ THE FAIR, THE DATE, THE SEARCH

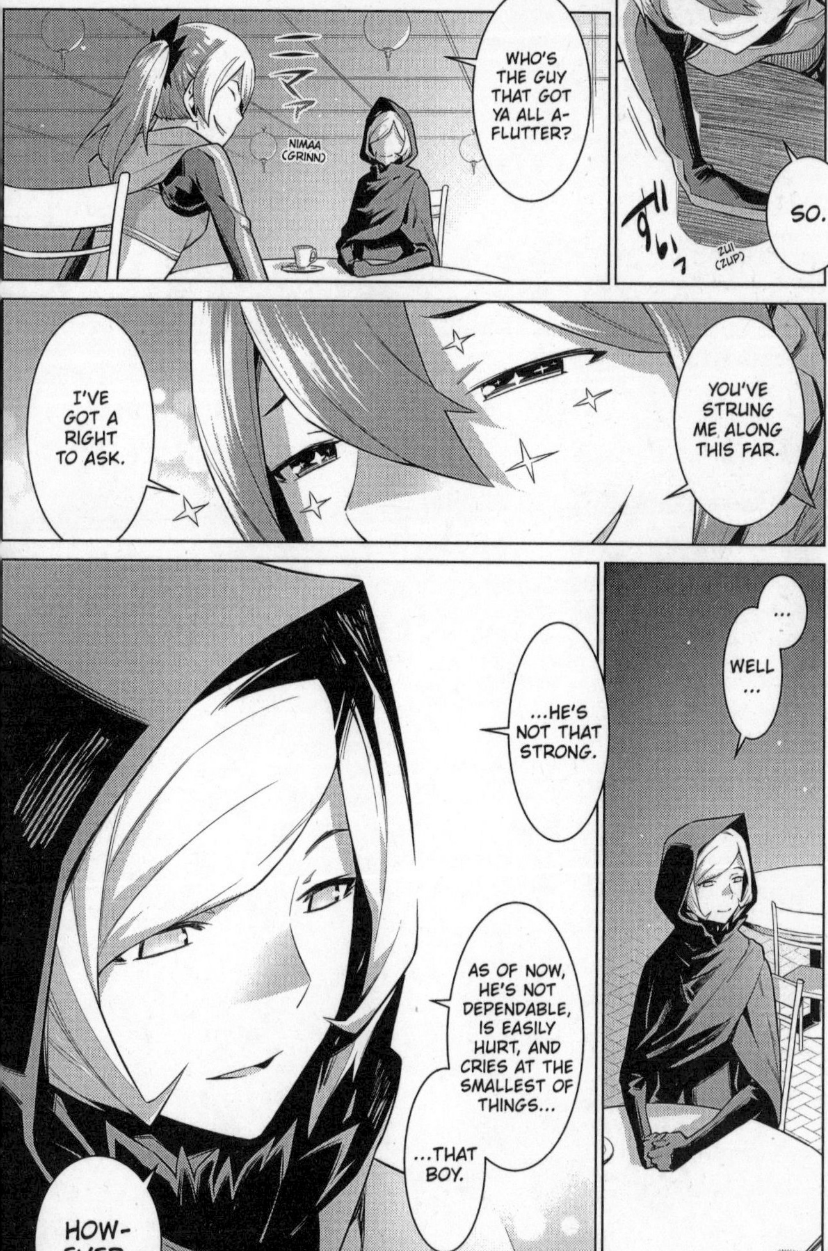
SO.
ZUI (ZUP)
WHO'S THE GUY THAT GOT YA ALL A-FLUTTER?
NIMAA (GRINN)
YOU'VE STRUNG ME ALONG THIS FAR.
I'VE GOT A RIGHT TO ASK.
... WELL ...
...HE'S NOT THAT STRONG.
AS OF NOW, HE'S NOT DEPENDABLE, IS EASILY HURT, AND CRIES AT THE SMALLEST OF THINGS...
...THAT BOY.
HOW-EVER.

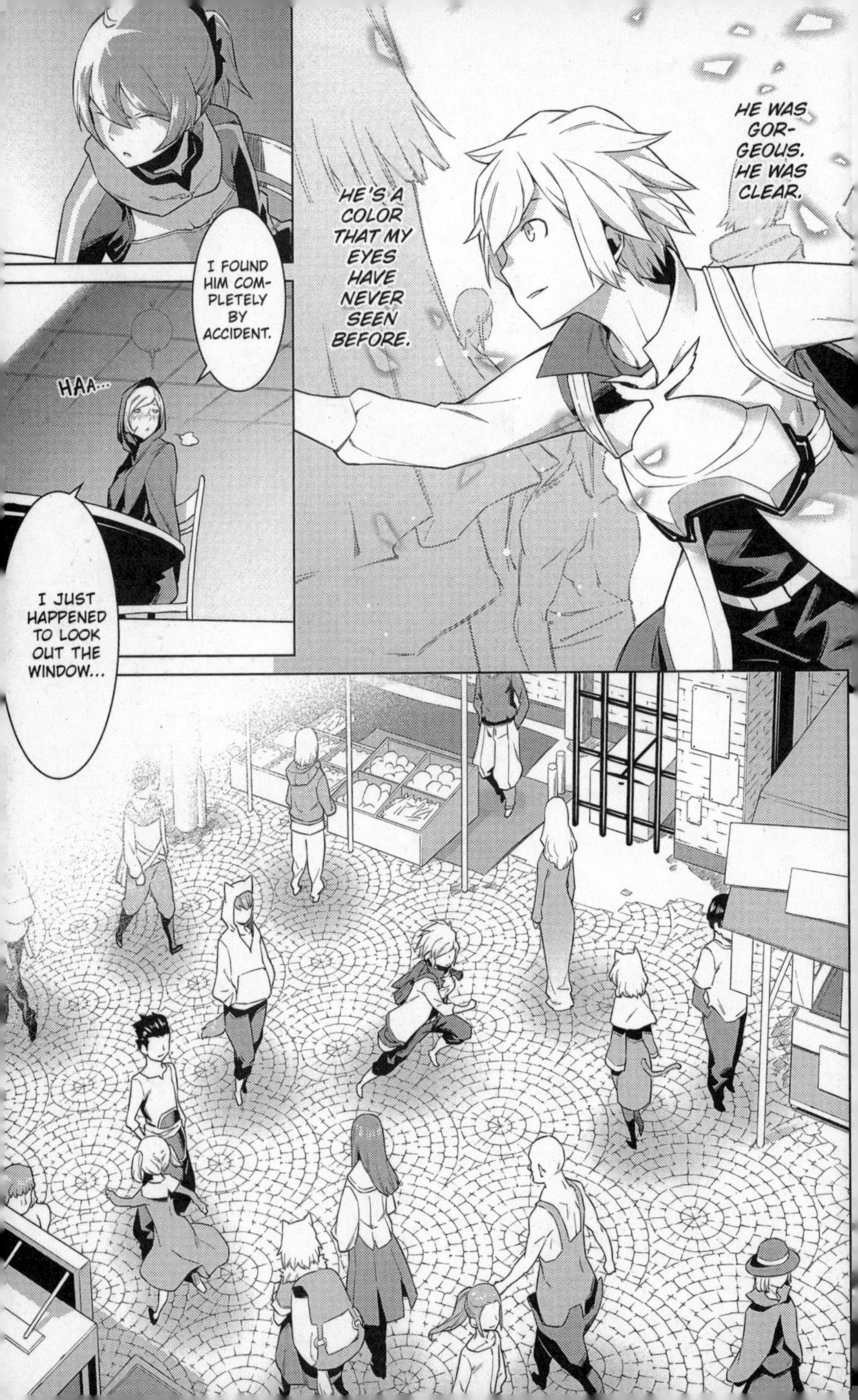
HE WAS GOR-GEOUS. HE WAS CLEAR.
HE'S A COLOR THAT MY EYES HAVE NEVER SEEN BEFORE.
I FOUND HIM COM-PLETELY BY ACCIDENT.
HAA...
I JUST HAPPENED TO LOOK OUT THE WINDOW...

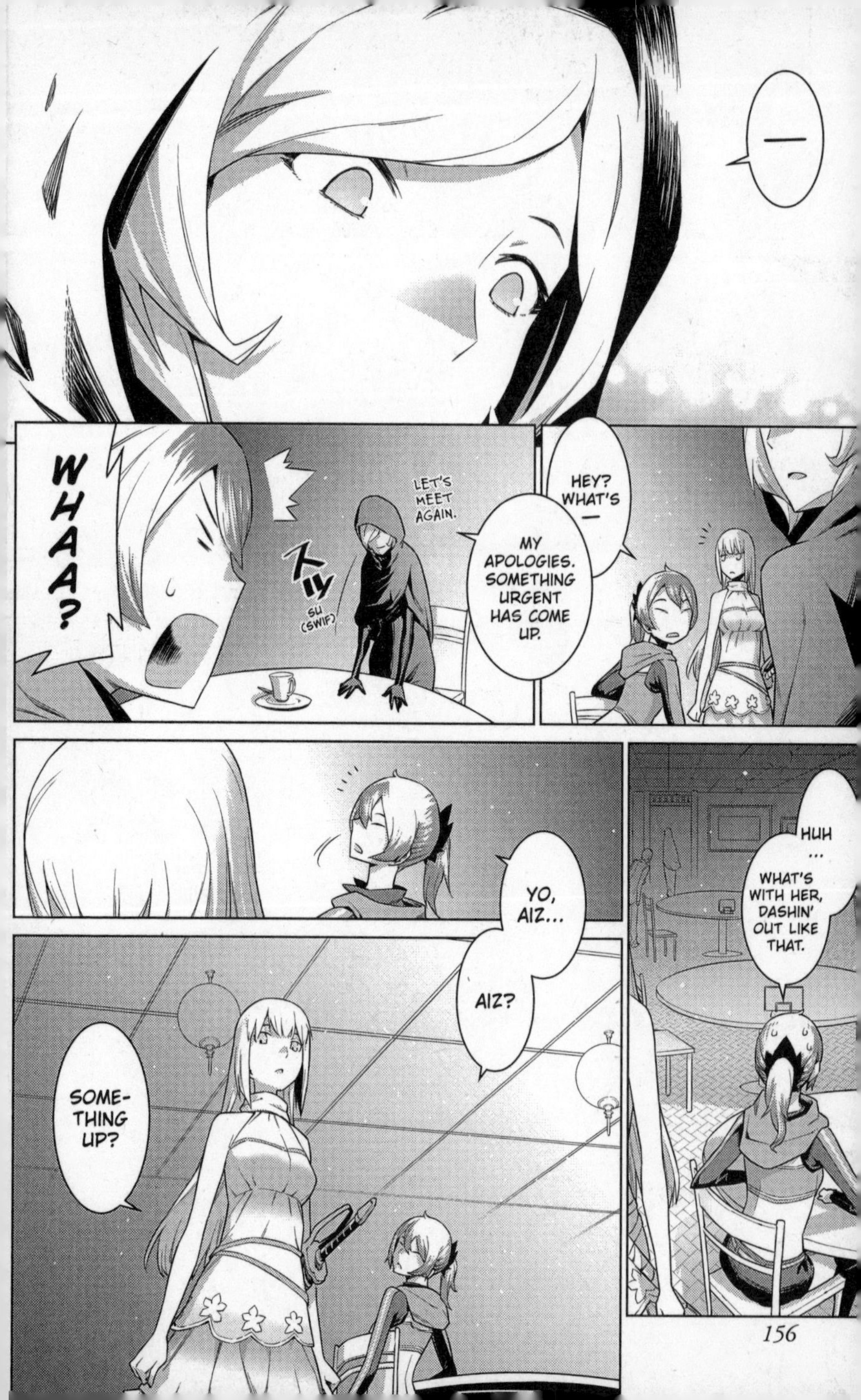
—
HEY? WHAT'S —
MY APOLOGIES. SOMETHING URGENT HAS COME UP.
LET'S MEET AGAIN.
スッ
SU (SWIF)
WHAAA?
HUH... WHAT'S WITH HER, DASHIN' OUT LIKE THAT.
YO, AIZ...
AIZ?
SOME-THING UP?

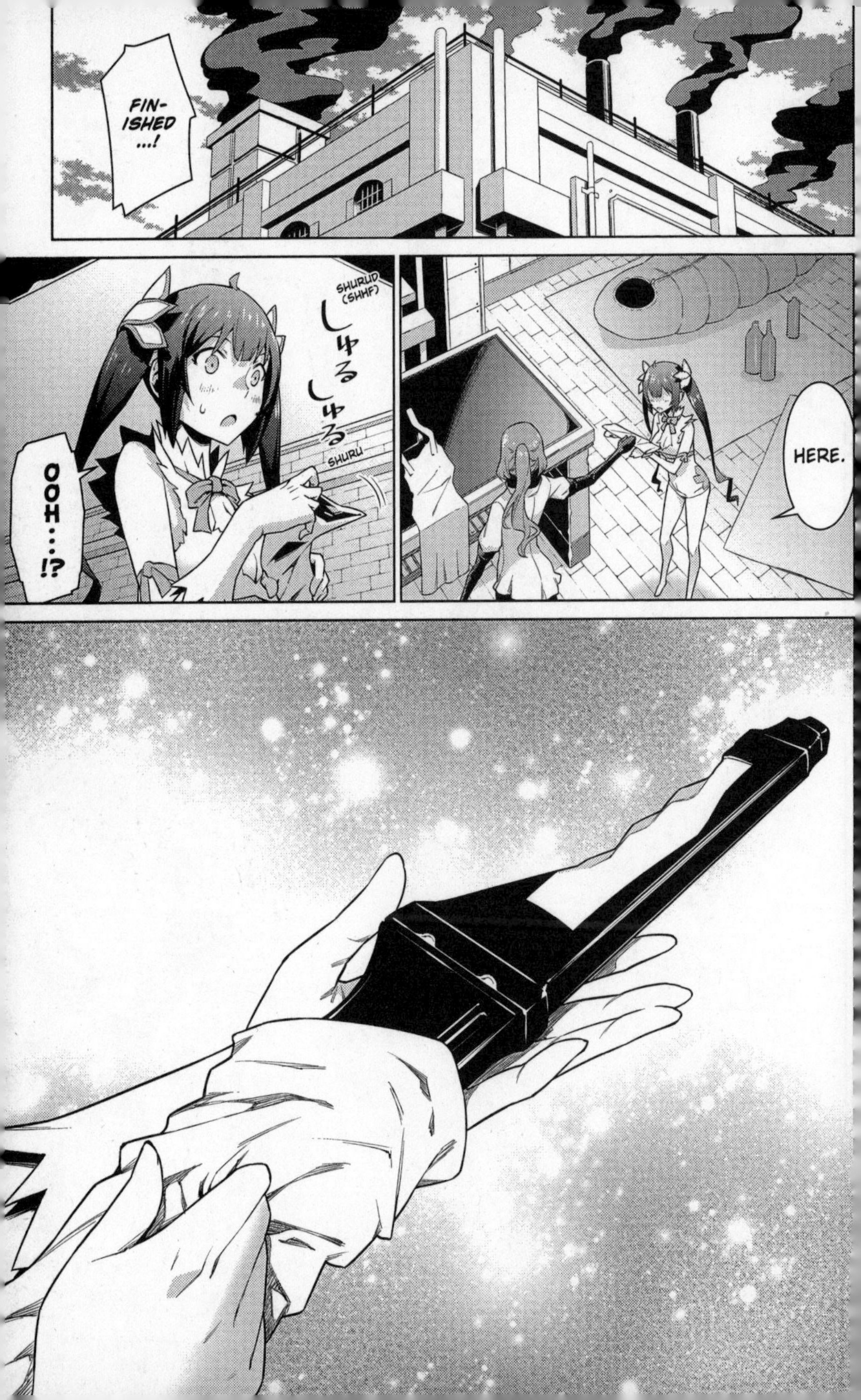
FIN-ISHED ...!
HERE.
SHURUU (SHHF)
しゅるしゅる
SHURU
OOH...!?

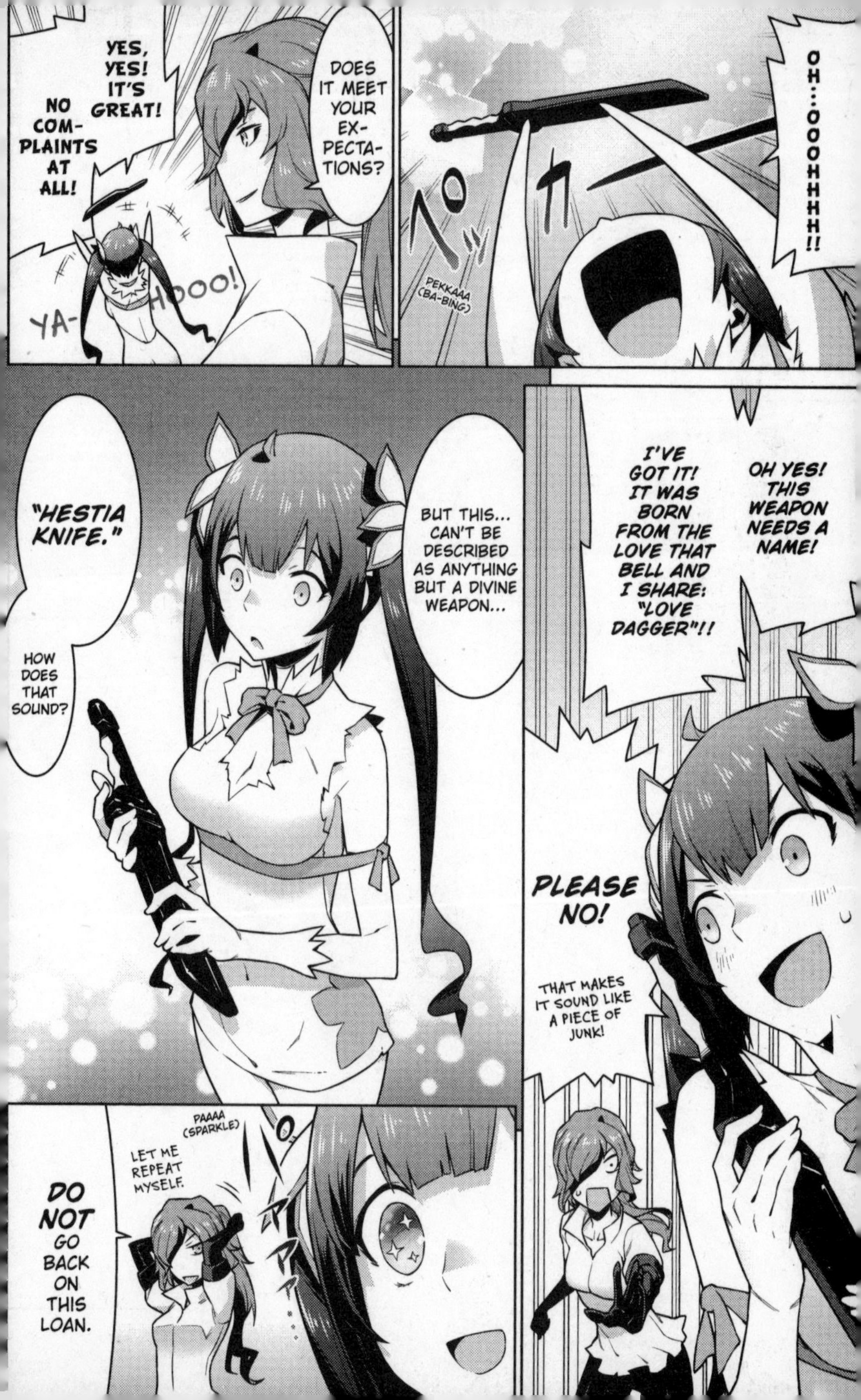
OH...OOOOHHHH!!
PEKKAAA (BA-BING)
DOES IT MEET YOUR EXPECTATIONS?
YES, YES! IT'S GREAT!
NO COMPLAINTS AT ALL!
YA-HOOO!
OH YES! THIS WEAPON NEEDS A NAME!
I'VE GOT IT! IT WAS BORN FROM THE LOVE THAT BELL AND I SHARE: "LOVE DAGGER"!!
PLEASE NO!
THAT MAKES IT SOUND LIKE A PIECE OF JUNK!
BUT THIS... CAN'T BE DESCRIBED AS ANYTHING BUT A DIVINE WEAPON...
"HESTIA KNIFE."
HOW DOES THAT SOUND?
PAAAA (SPARKLE)
LET ME REPEAT MYSELF.
DO NOT GO BACK ON THIS LOAN.

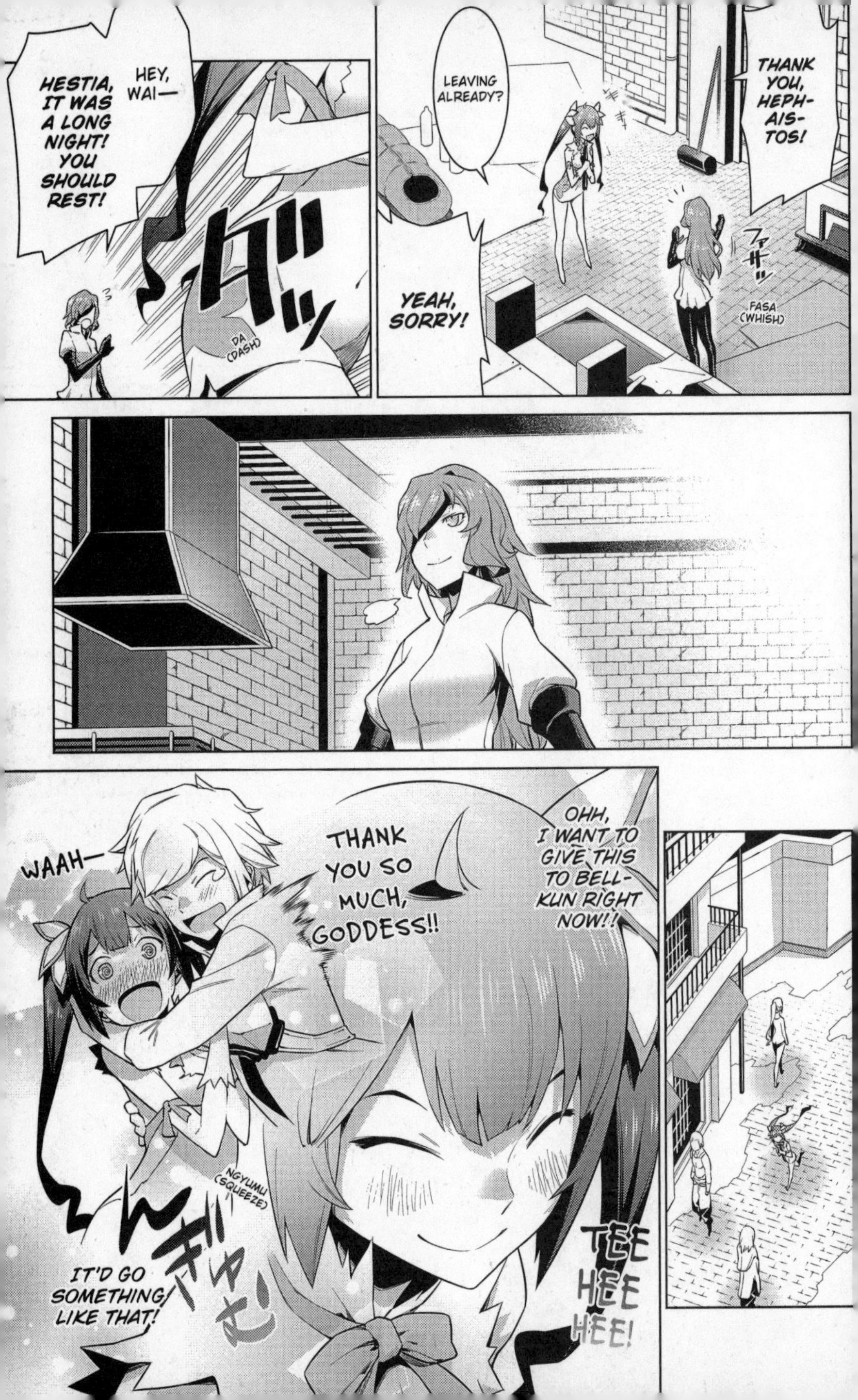
THANK YOU, HEPH-AIS-TOS!
LEAVING ALREADY?
FASA (WHISH)
YEAH, SORRY!
HEY, WAI—
HESTIA, IT WAS A LONG NIGHT! YOU SHOULD REST!
DA (DASH)
OHH, I WANT TO GIVE THIS TO BELL-KUN RIGHT NOW!!
THANK YOU SO MUCH, GODDESS!!
WAAH—
TEE HEE HEE!
NGYUMU (SQUEEZE)
IT'D GO SOMETHING LIKE THAT!

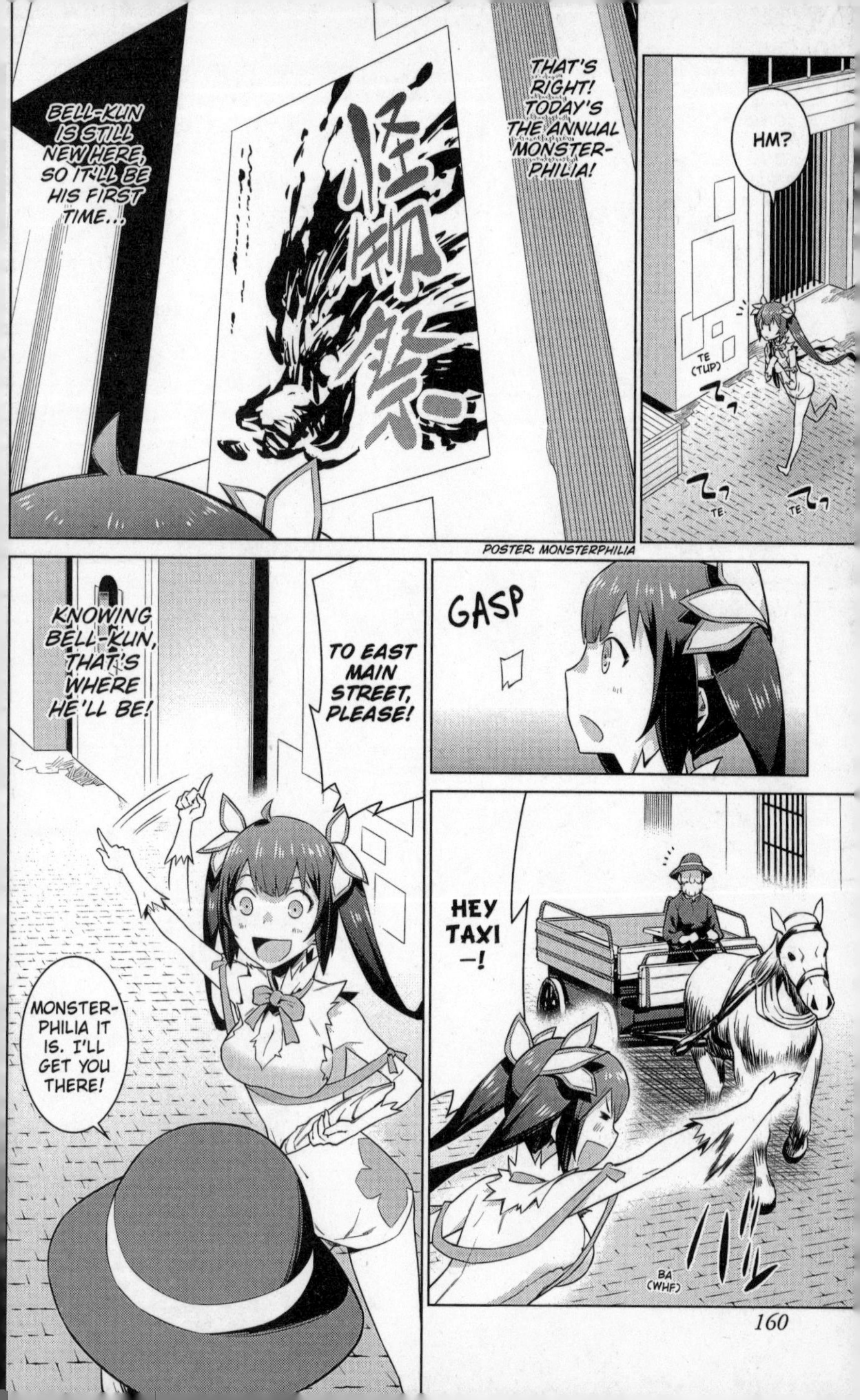
HM?
TE (TUP)
TE
TE
THAT'S RIGHT! TODAY'S THE ANNUAL MONSTER-PHILIA!
BELL-KUN IS STILL NEW HERE, SO IT'LL BE HIS FIRST TIME...
POSTER: MONSTERPHILIA
GASP
HEY TAXI—!
BA (WHF)
TO EAST MAIN STREET, PLEASE!
KNOWING BELL-KUN, THAT'S WHERE HE'LL BE!
MONSTER-PHILIA IT IS. I'LL GET YOU THERE!

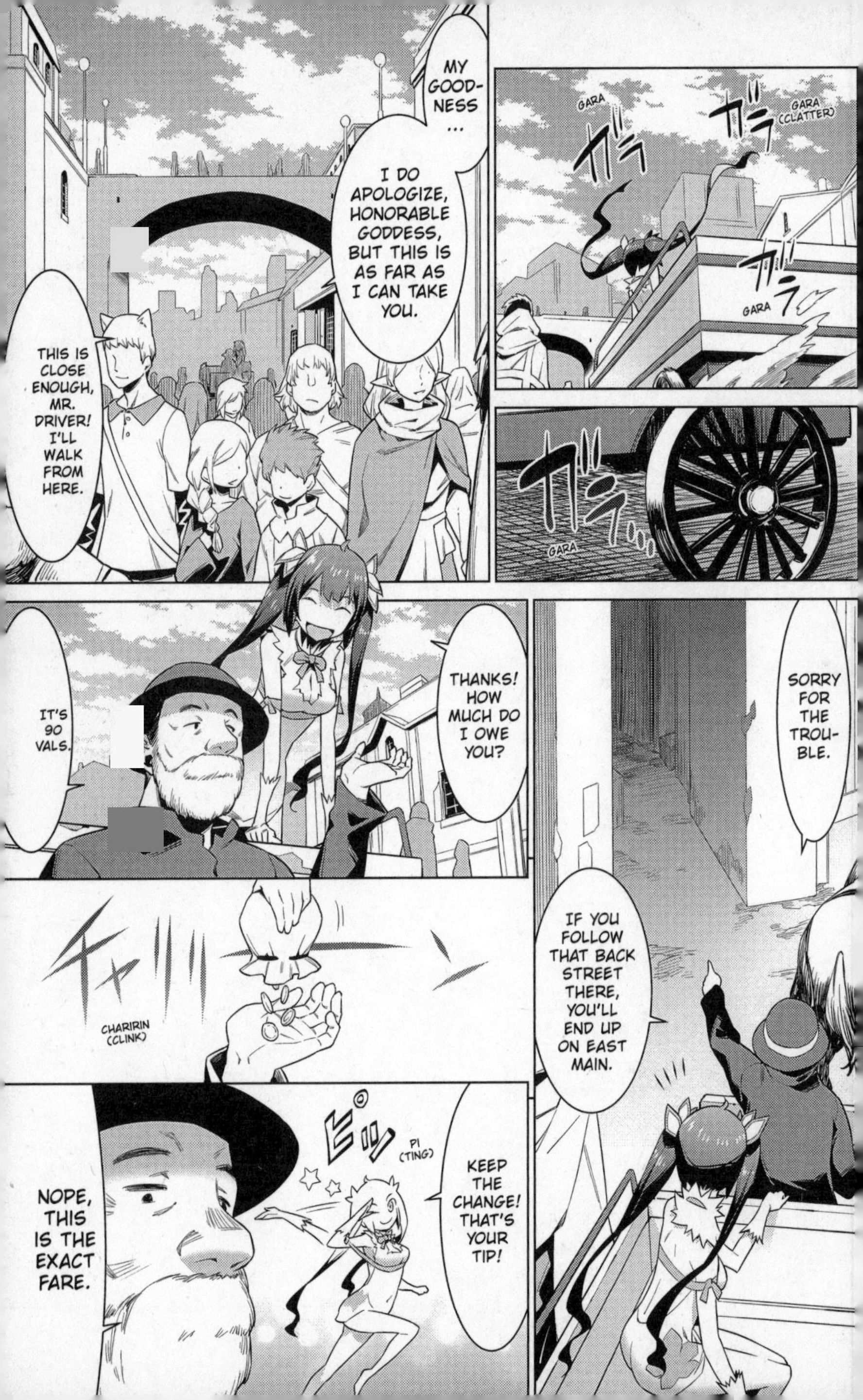
GARA
GARA (CLATTER)
GARA
GARA
MY GOODNESS...
I DO APOLOGIZE, HONORABLE GODDESS, BUT THIS IS AS FAR AS I CAN TAKE YOU.
THIS IS CLOSE ENOUGH, MR. DRIVER! I'LL WALK FROM HERE.
SORRY FOR THE TROUBLE.
IF YOU FOLLOW THAT BACK STREET THERE, YOU'LL END UP ON EAST MAIN.
THANKS! HOW MUCH DO I OWE YOU?
IT'S 90 VALS.
CHARIRIN (CLINK)
PI (TING)
KEEP THE CHANGE! THAT'S YOUR TIP!
NOPE, THIS IS THE EXACT FARE.

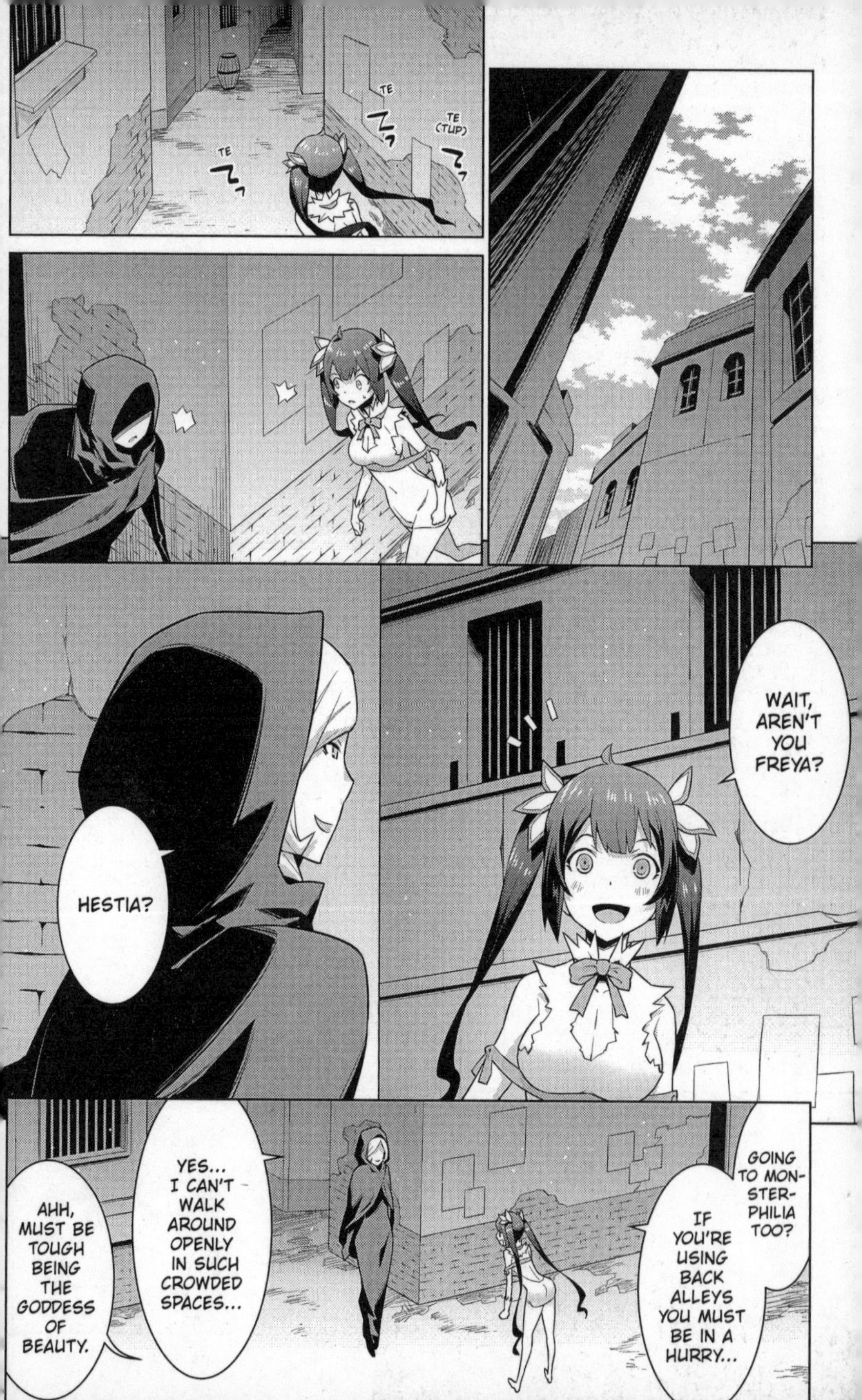

TE (TUP)
TE
TE
WAIT, AREN'T YOU FREYA?
HESTIA?
GOING TO MONSTERPHILIA TOO?
IF YOU'RE USING BACK ALLEYS YOU MUST BE IN A HURRY...
YES... I CAN'T WALK AROUND OPENLY IN SUCH CROWDED SPACES...
AHH, MUST BE TOUGH BEING THE GODDESS OF BEAUTY.

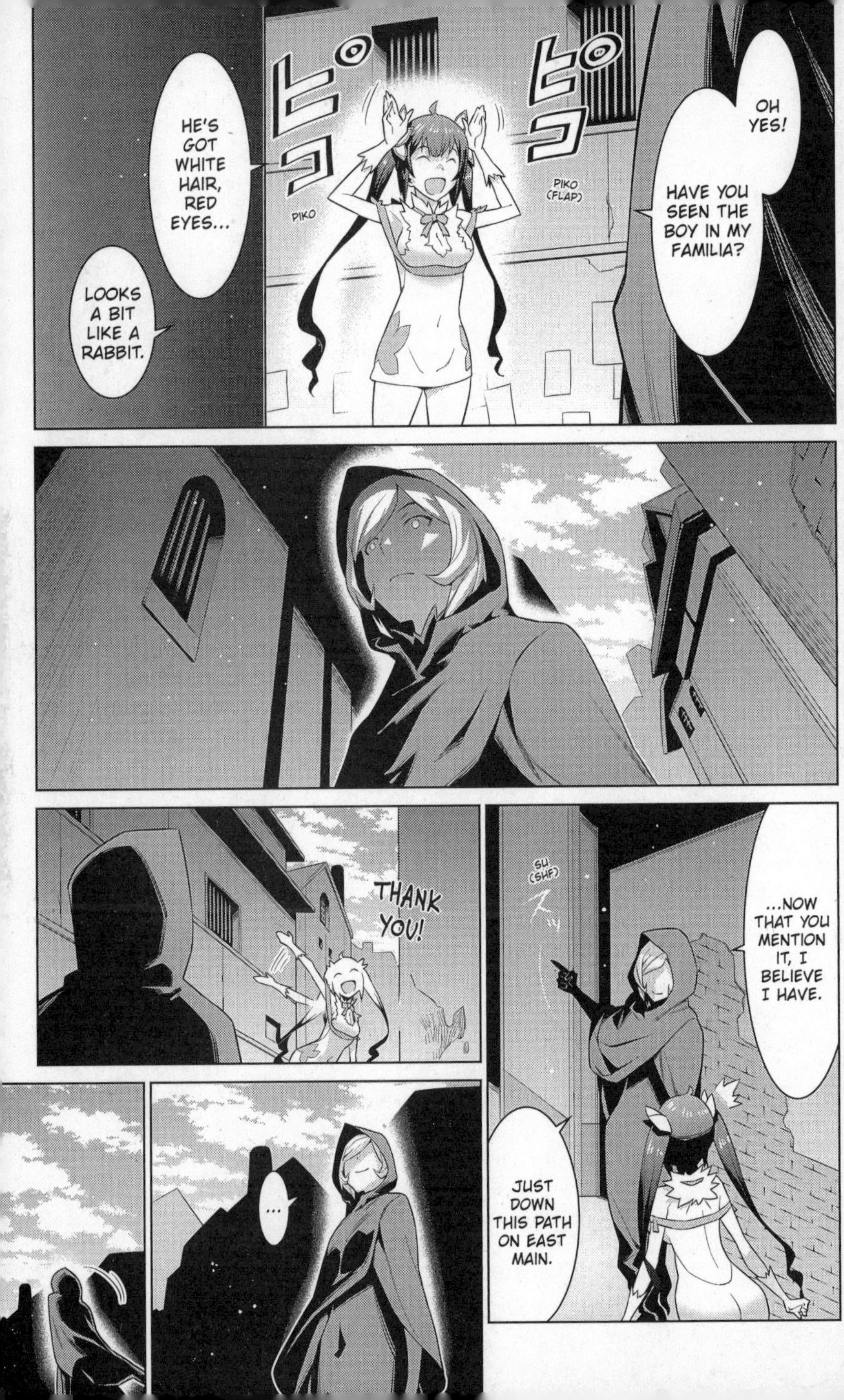
OH YES!
HAVE YOU SEEN THE BOY IN MY FAMILIA?
ピコ
PIKO (FLAP)
ピコ
PIKO
HE'S GOT WHITE HAIR, RED EYES...
LOOKS A BIT LIKE A RABBIT.
SU (SHF)
...NOW THAT YOU MENTION IT, I BELIEVE I HAVE.
JUST DOWN THIS PATH ON EAST MAIN.
THANK YOU!
...

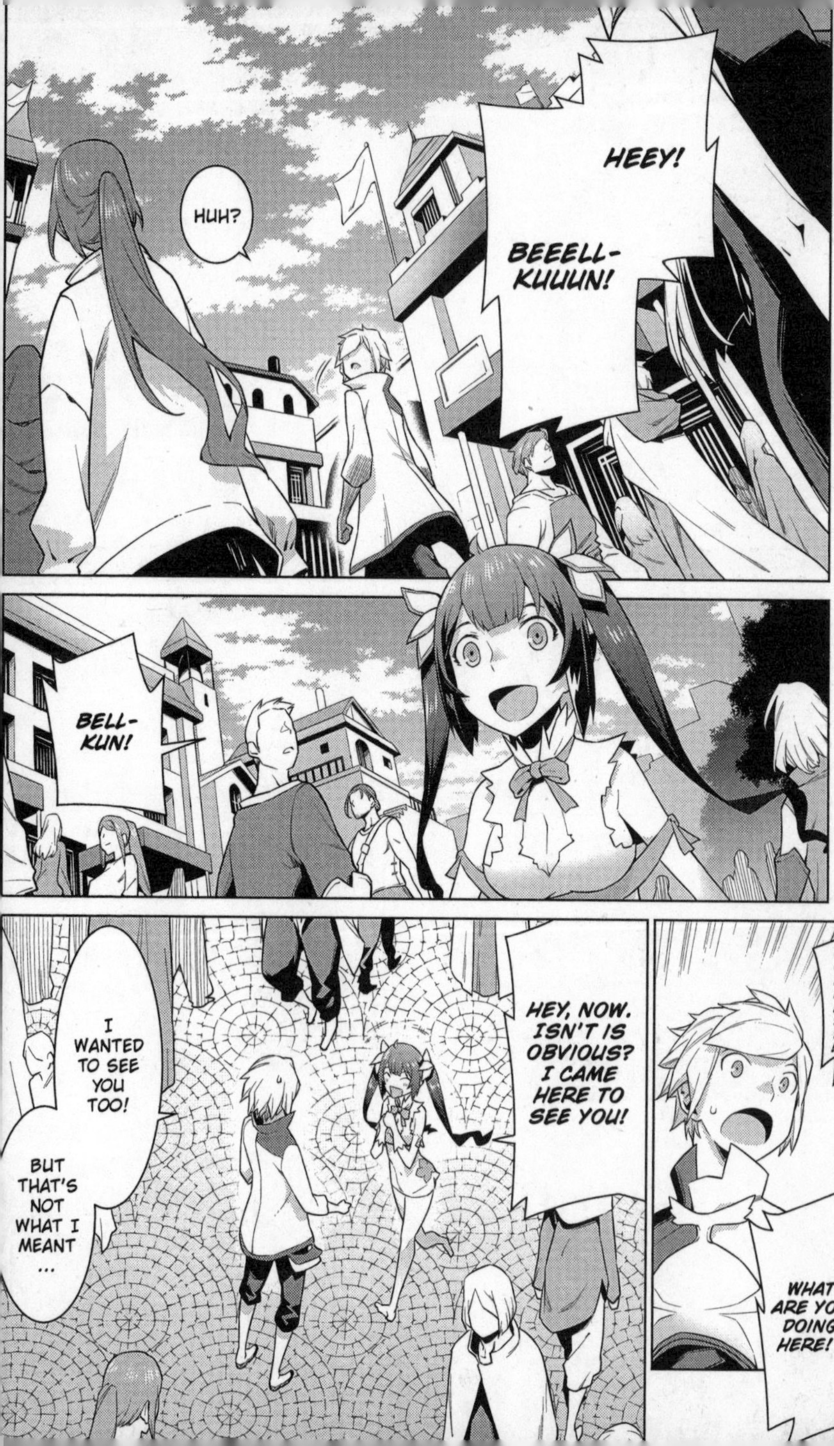
HEEY!
BEEELL-KUUUN!
HUH?
BELL-KUN!
GODDESS!?
WHAT ARE YOU DOING HERE!?
HEY, NOW. ISN'T IS OBVIOUS? I CAME HERE TO SEE YOU!
I WANTED TO SEE YOU TOO!
BUT THAT'S NOT WHAT I MEANT ...

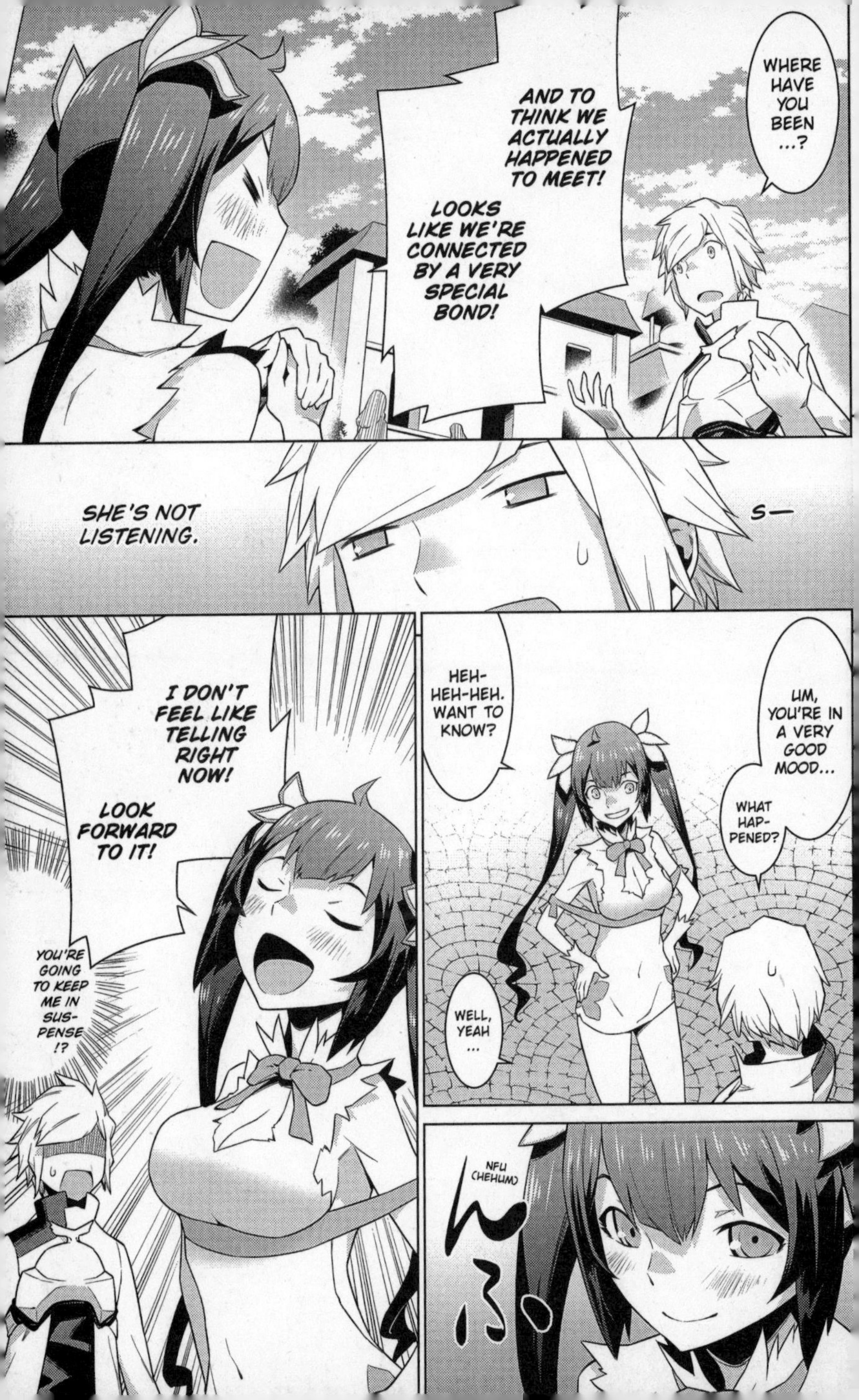
WHERE HAVE YOU BEEN ...?
AND TO THINK WE ACTUALLY HAPPENED TO MEET!
LOOKS LIKE WE'RE CONNECTED BY A VERY SPECIAL BOND!
S—
SHE'S NOT LISTENING.
UM, YOU'RE IN A VERY GOOD MOOD...
WHAT HAP-PENED?
HEH-HEH-HEH. WANT TO KNOW?
WELL, YEAH ...
NFU (HEHUM)
I DON'T FEEL LIKE TELLING RIGHT NOW!
LOOK FORWARD TO IT!
YOU'RE GOING TO KEEP ME IN SUS-PENSE !?

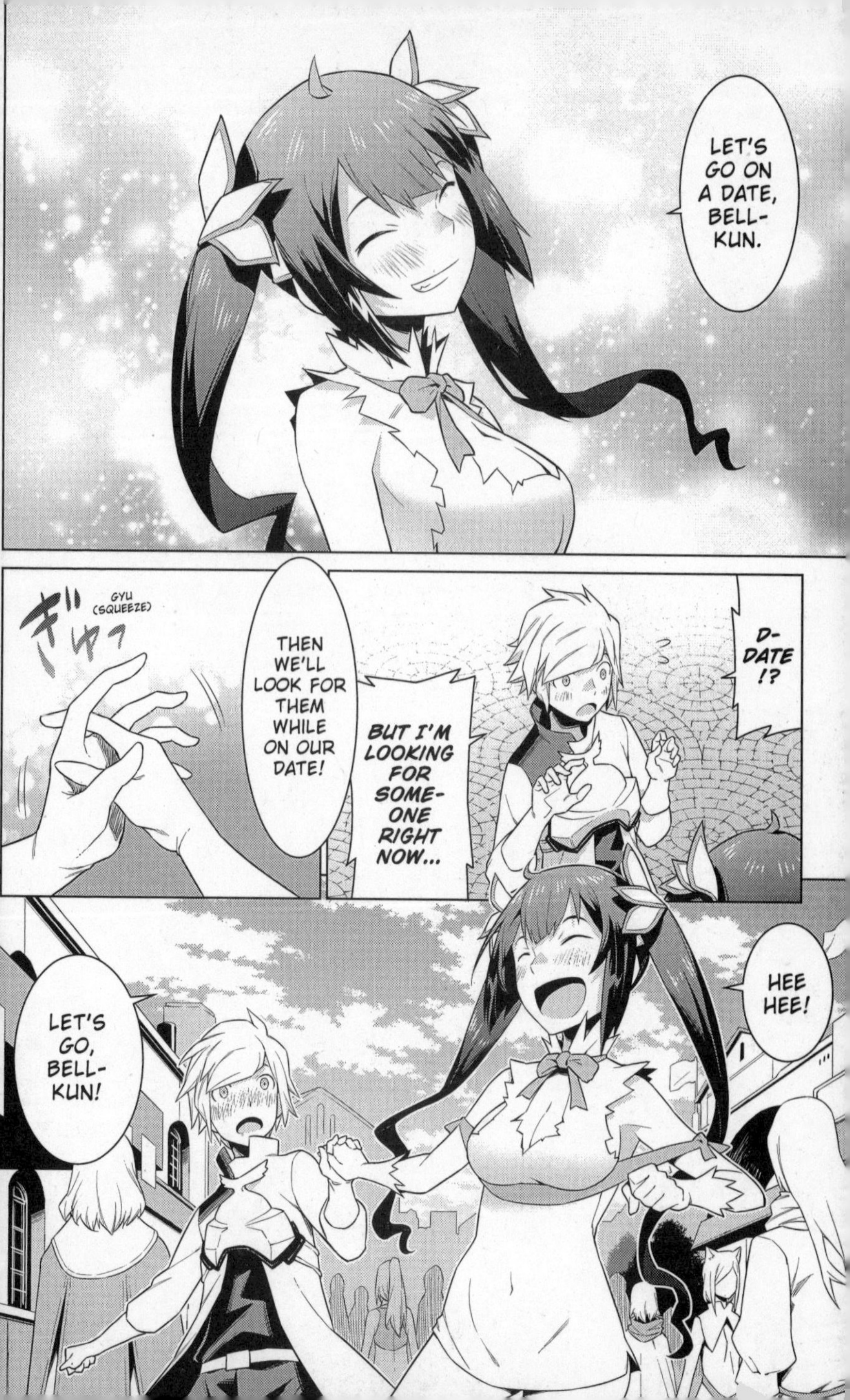

LET'S GO ON A DATE, BELL-KUN.
D-DATE!?
BUT I'M LOOKING FOR SOME-ONE RIGHT NOW...
THEN WE'LL LOOK FOR THEM WHILE ON OUR DATE!
ぎゅっ
GYU (SQUEEZE)
HEE HEE!
LET'S GO, BELL-KUN!

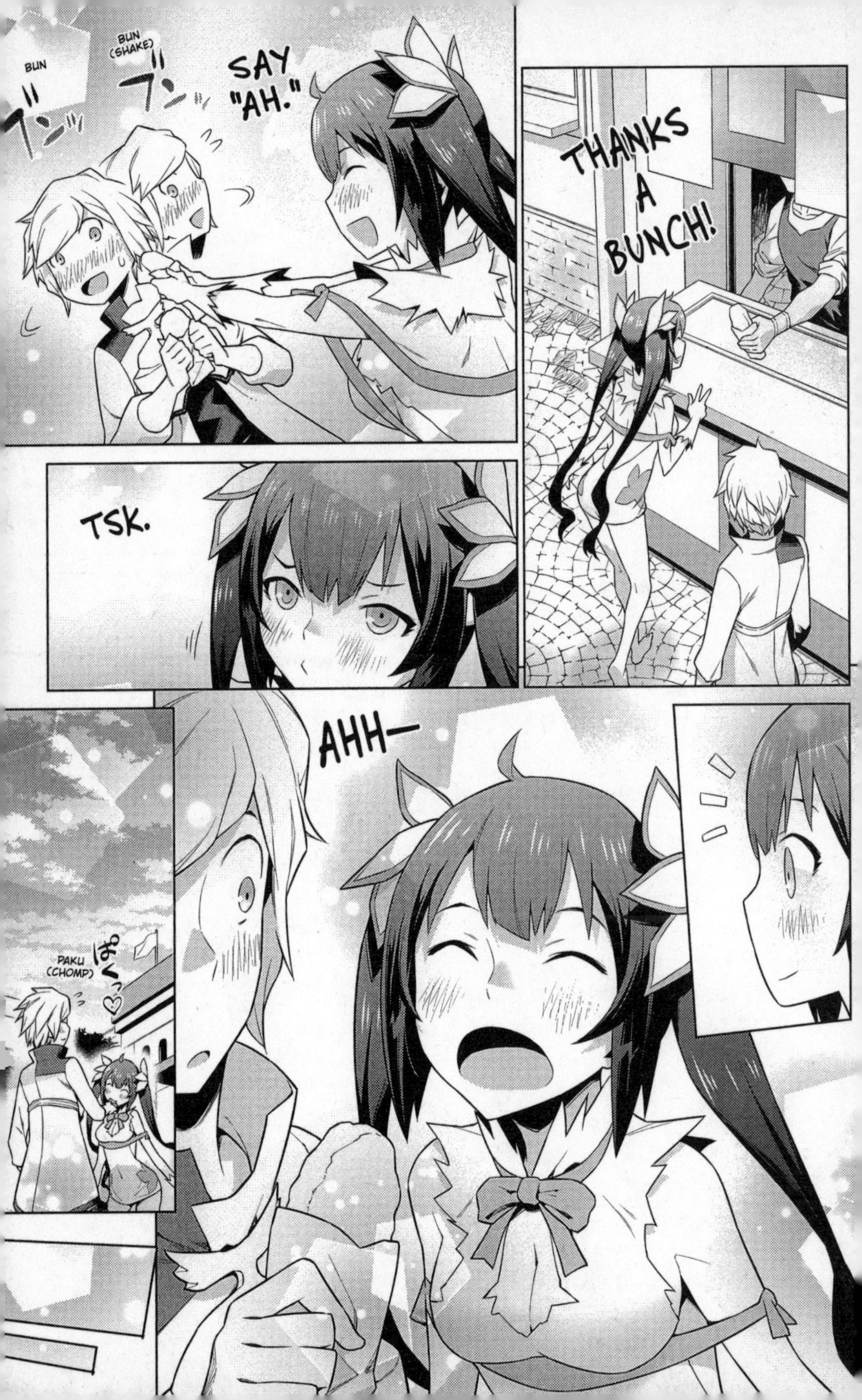
THANKS A BUNCH!
SAY "AH."
BUN (SHAKE)
ブン
BUN
ブンッ
TSK.
AHH—
PAKU (CHOMP)
ぱくっ

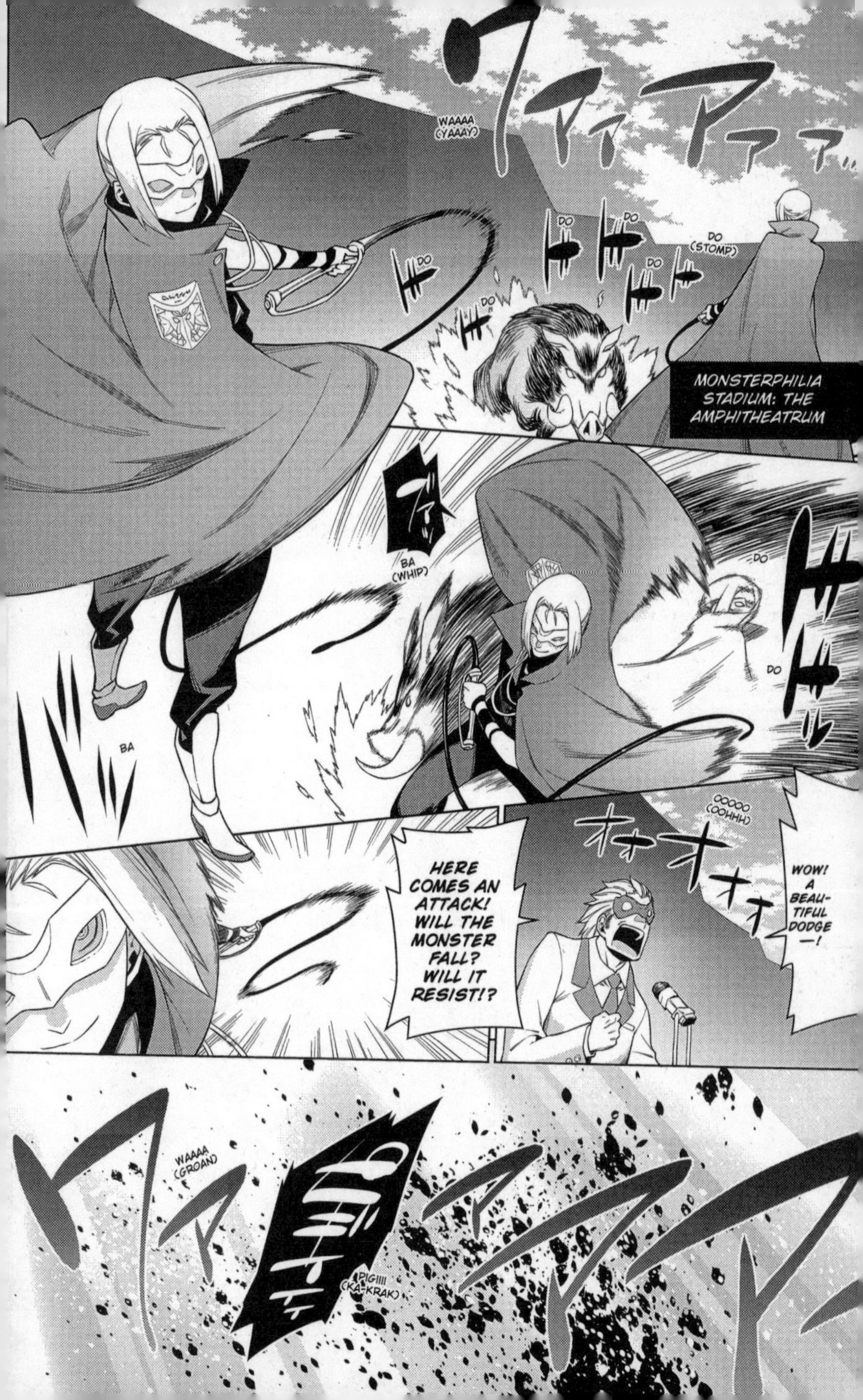
WAAAA (YAAAY)
DO (STOMP)
DO
DO
DO
DO
DO
MONSTERPHILIA STADIUM: THE AMPHITHEATRUM
DO
DO
BA (WHIP)
BA
WOW! A BEAU-TIFUL DODGE—!
OOOOO (OOHHH)
HERE COMES AN ATTACK! WILL THE MONSTER FALL? WILL IT RESIST!?
WAAAA (GROAN)
PIGIII (KA-KRAK)

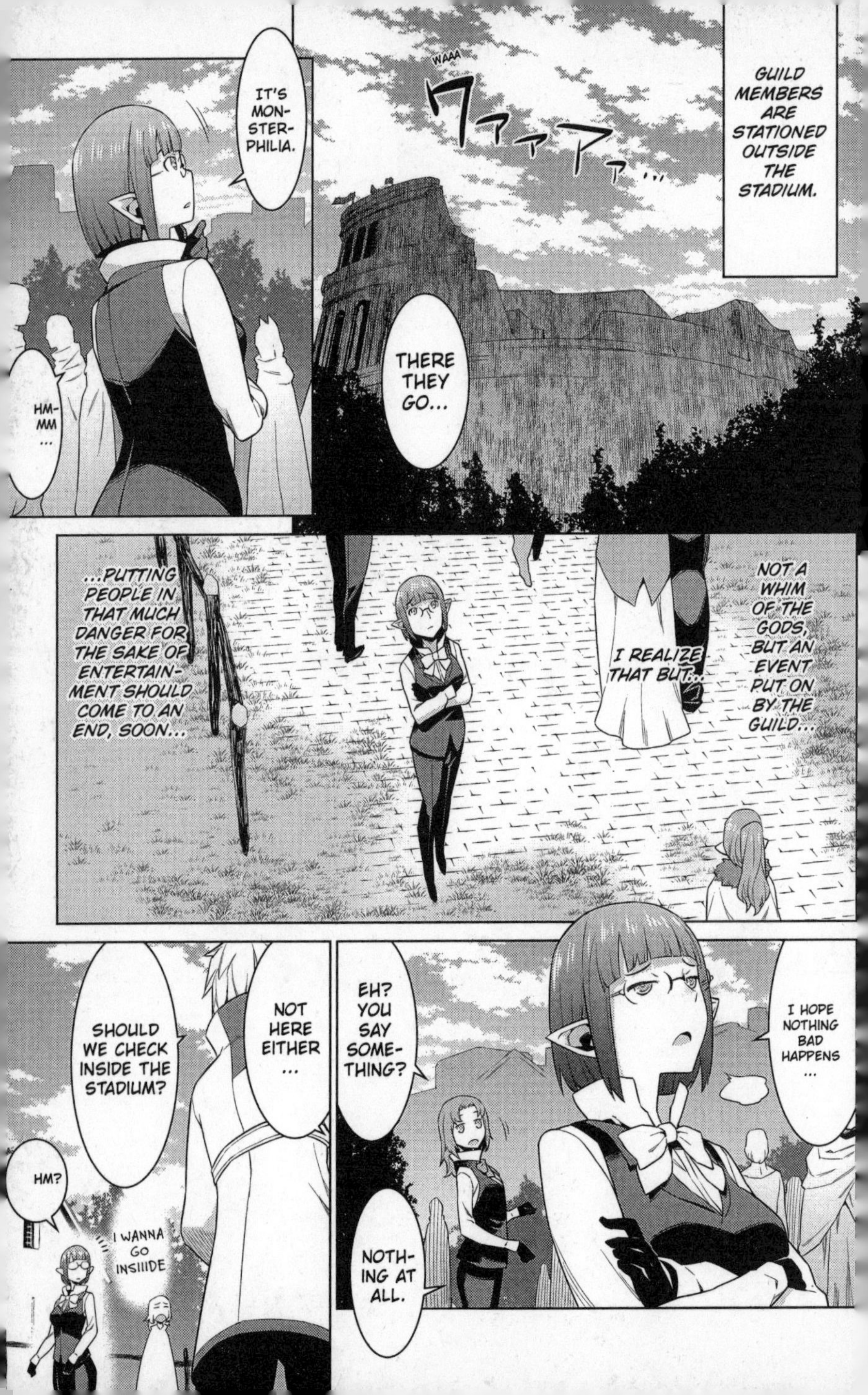
GUILD MEMBERS ARE STATIONED OUTSIDE THE STADIUM.
ワァァァ…
WAAA
THERE THEY GO...
IT'S MONSTERPHILIA.
HMMM...
NOT A WHIM OF THE GODS, BUT AN EVENT PUT ON BY THE GUILD...
I REALIZE THAT BUT...
...PUTTING PEOPLE IN THAT MUCH DANGER FOR THE SAKE OF ENTERTAINMENT SHOULD COME TO AN END, SOON...
I HOPE NOTHING BAD HAPPENS...
EH? YOU SAY SOMETHING?
NOTHING AT ALL.
NOT HERE EITHER...
SHOULD WE CHECK INSIDE THE STADIUM?
HM?
I WANNA GO INSIIIDE

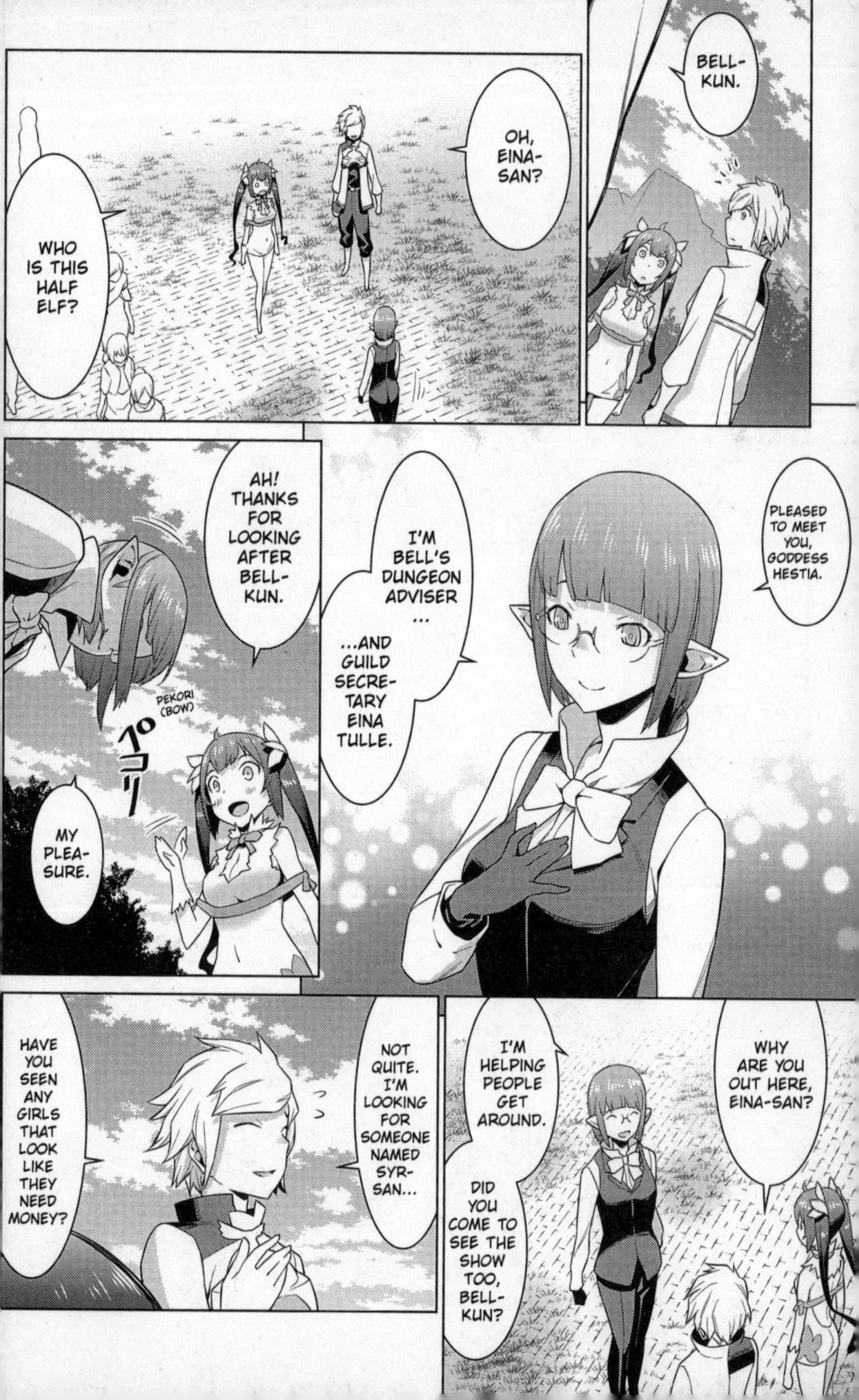
BELL-KUN.
OH, EINA-SAN?
WHO IS THIS HALF ELF?
PLEASED TO MEET YOU, GODDESS HESTIA.
I'M BELL'S DUNGEON ADVISER...
...AND GUILD SECRETARY EINA TULLE.
AH! THANKS FOR LOOKING AFTER BELL-KUN.
PEKORI (BOW)
MY PLEASURE.
WHY ARE YOU OUT HERE, EINA-SAN?
I'M HELPING PEOPLE GET AROUND.
DID YOU COME TO SEE THE SHOW TOO, BELL-KUN?
NOT QUITE. I'M LOOKING FOR SOMEONE NAMED SYR-SAN...
HAVE YOU SEEN ANY GIRLS THAT LOOK LIKE THEY NEED MONEY?

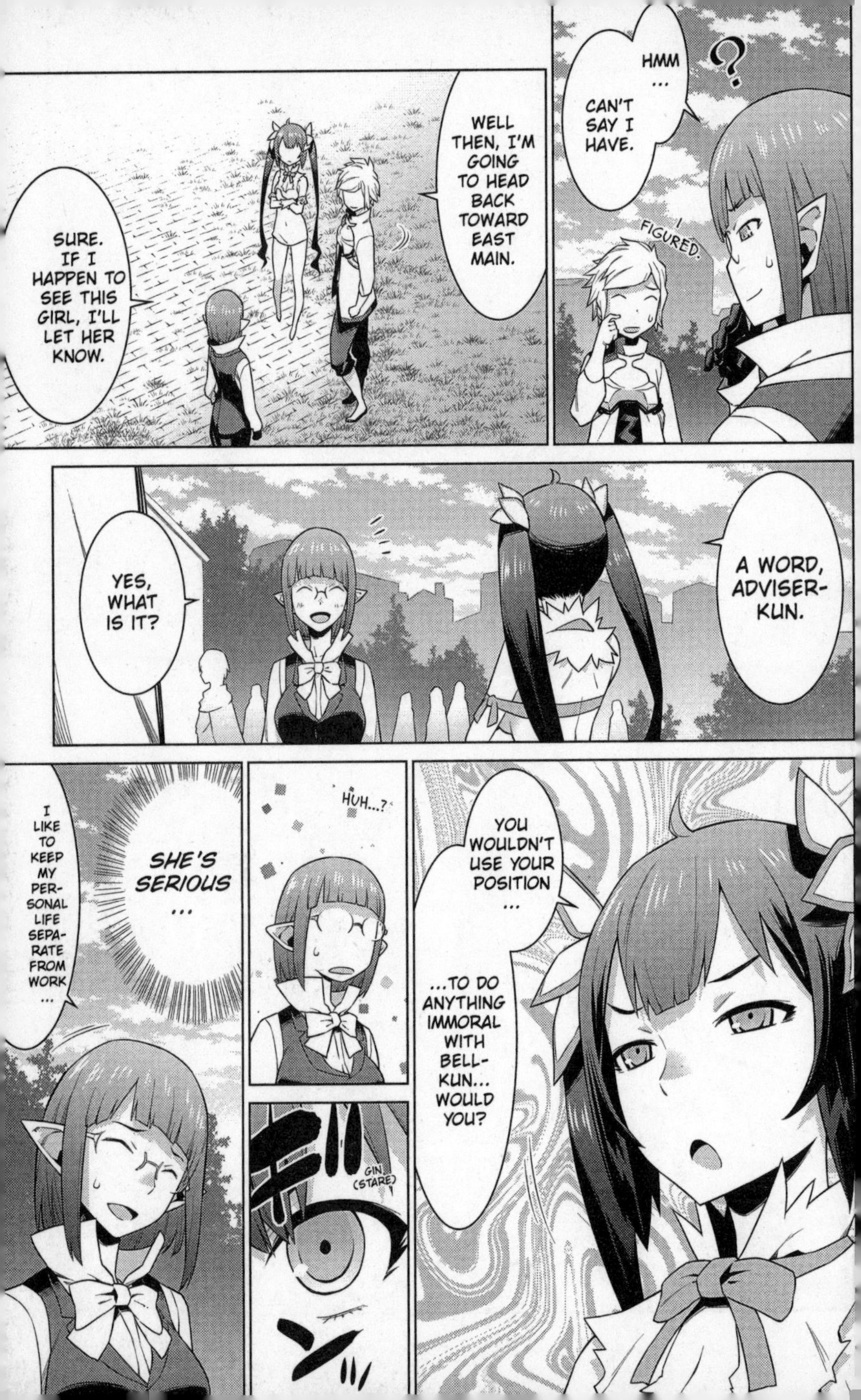
HMM... CAN'T SAY I HAVE.
I FIGURED.
WELL THEN, I'M GOING TO HEAD BACK TOWARD EAST MAIN.
SURE. IF I HAPPEN TO SEE THIS GIRL, I'LL LET HER KNOW.
A WORD, ADVISER-KUN.
YES, WHAT IS IT?
YOU WOULDN'T USE YOUR POSITION...
...TO DO ANYTHING IMMORAL WITH BELL-KUN... WOULD YOU?
HUH...?
GIN (STARE)
SHE'S SERIOUS...
I LIKE TO KEEP MY PERSONAL LIFE SEPARATE FROM WORK...

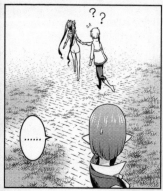

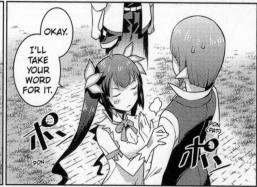

OKAY. I'LL TAKE YOUR WORD FOR IT.
PON (PAT)
ポン
ポン
PON
......
WAIT A SECOND...
WAS THAT A WARNING...?
BACK TO WORK...
THE HELL ARE THEY DOIN' OVER THERE?
CUT THE CHATTER AND GET MOVING!
GACHA
ガチャ
......?
GACHA (CHIK)
ガチャ

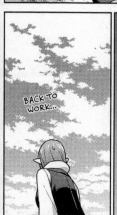

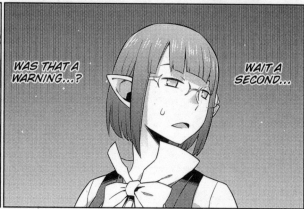

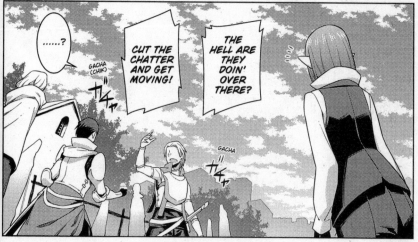

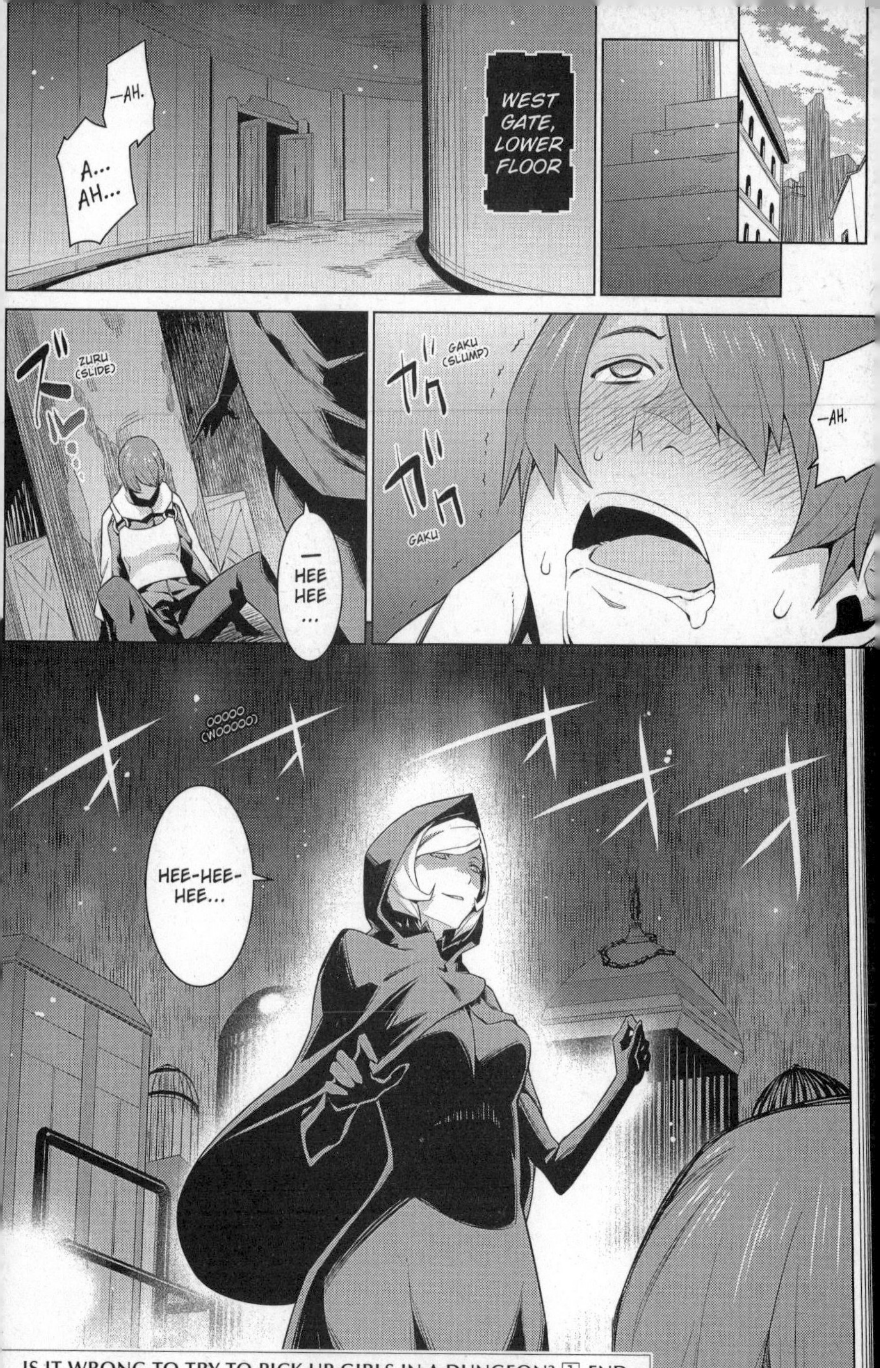
WEST GATE, LOWER FLOOR
—AH.
A... AH...
—AH.
GAKU (SLUMP)
GAKU
ZURU (SLIDE)
—HEE HEE...
OOOOO (WOOOOO)
HEE-HEE-HEE...

IS IT WRONG TO TRY TO PICK UP GIRLS IN A DUNGEON? 1 END

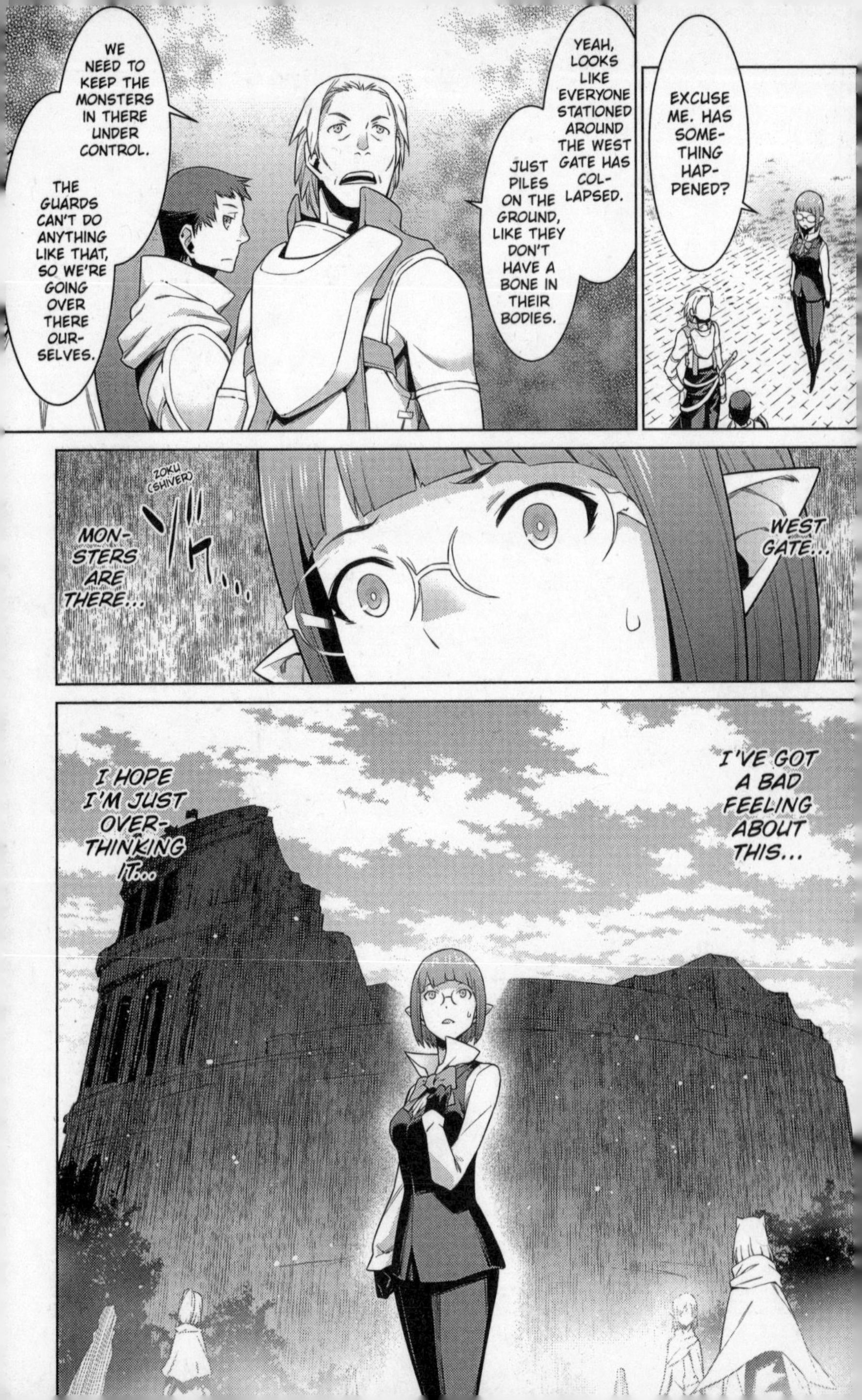
EXCUSE ME. HAS SOME-THING HAP-PENED?
YEAH, LOOKS LIKE EVERYONE STATIONED AROUND THE WEST GATE HAS COL-LAPSED.
JUST PILES ON THE GROUND, LIKE THEY DON'T HAVE A BONE IN THEIR BODIES.
WE NEED TO KEEP THE MONSTERS IN THERE UNDER CONTROL.
THE GUARDS CAN'T DO ANYTHING LIKE THAT, SO WE'RE GOING OVER THERE OUR-SELVES.
WEST GATE...
ZOKU (SHIVER)
MON-STERS ARE THERE...
I'VE GOT A BAD FEELING ABOUT THIS...
I HOPE I'M JUST OVER-THINKING IT...

ADVEN-
TURER'S
GUIDE
6

DUNGEON

➤ *The only one like it in the world, it sits beneath Orario and extends for miles around.*

➤ *Not much is known about it, only that nothing else compares.*

➤ *Forty or more layers deep. Monsters are born from its walls. It's the source of all monsters.*

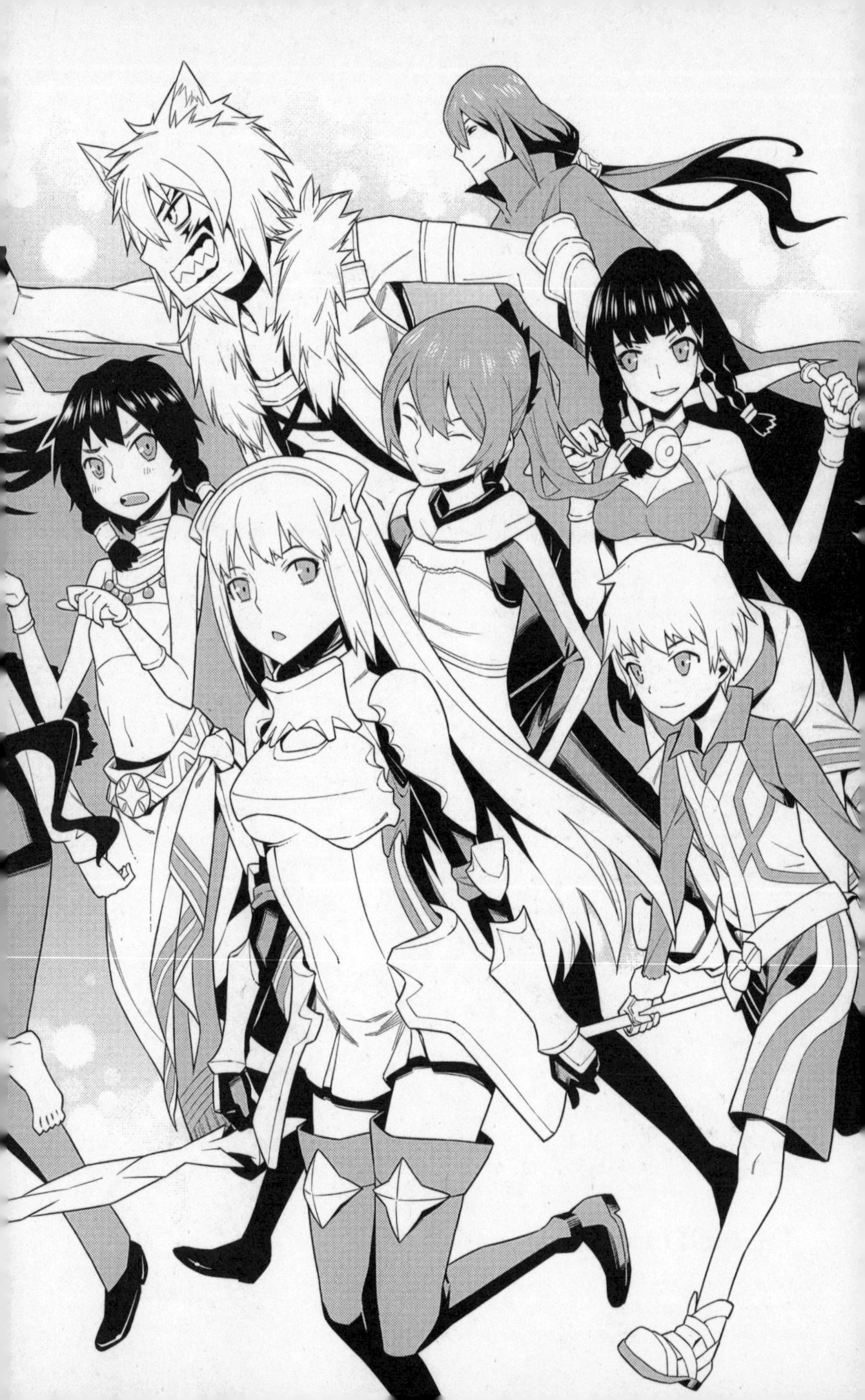

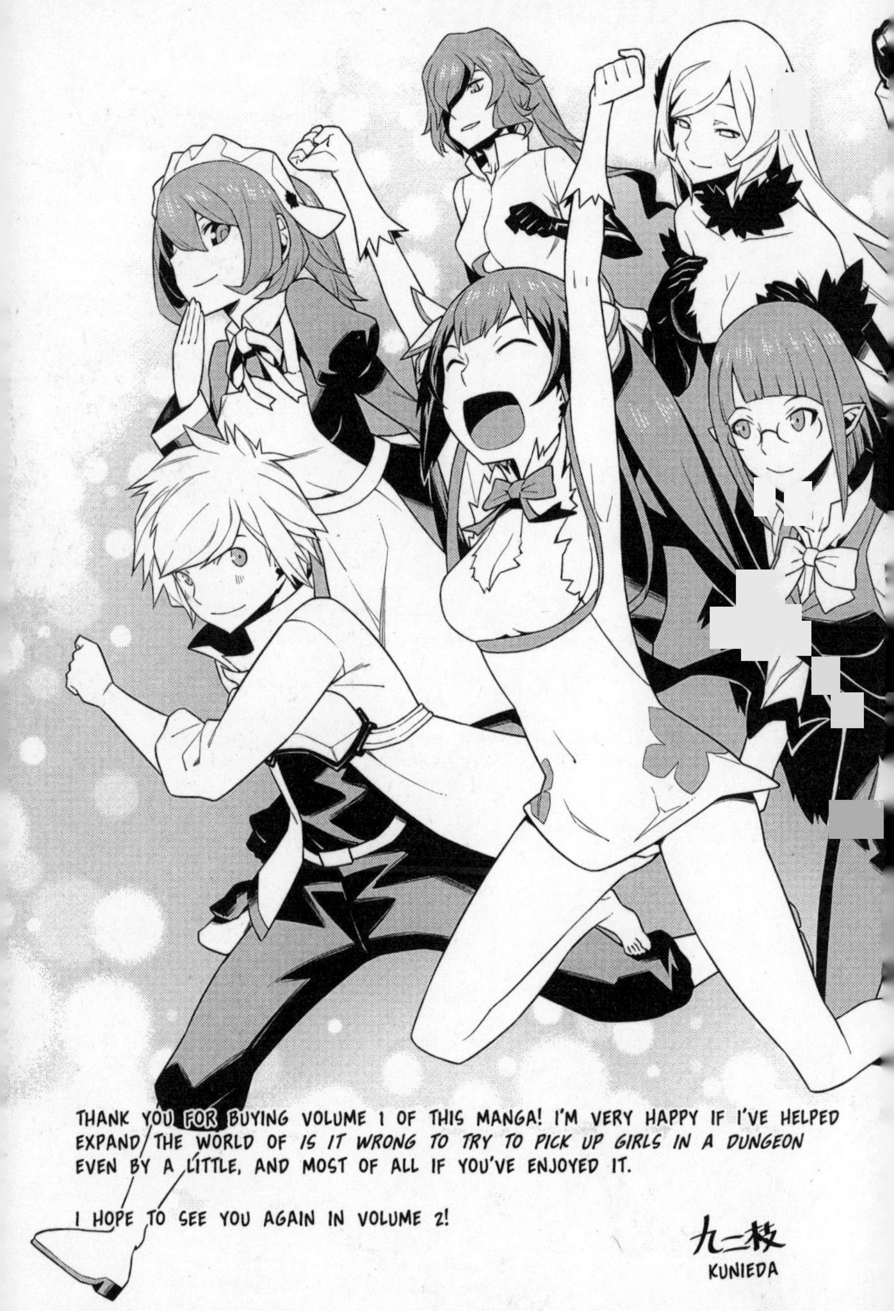

THANK YOU FOR BUYING VOLUME 1 OF THIS MANGA! I'M VERY HAPPY IF I'VE HELPED EXPAND THE WORLD OF *IS IT WRONG TO TRY TO PICK UP GIRLS IN A DUNGEON* EVEN BY A LITTLE, AND MOST OF ALL IF YOU'VE ENJOYED IT.

I HOPE TO SEE YOU AGAIN IN VOLUME 2!

九二枝

KUNIEDA

TRANSLATION NOTES

Common Honorifics
no honorific: Indicates familiarity or closeness; if used without permission or reason, addressing someone in this manner would constitute an insult.
-san: The Japanese equivalent of Mr./Mrs./Miss. If a situation calls for politeness, this is the failsafe honorific.
-shi: Not unlike -san; the equivalent of Mr./Mrs./Miss but conveying a more official or bureaucratic mood
-sama: Conveys great respect; may also indicate that the social status of the speaker is lower than that of the addressee.
-kun: Used most often when referring to boys, this indicates affection or familiarity. Occasionally used by older men among their peers, but it may also be used by anyone referring to a person of lower standing.
-chan: An affectionate honorific indicating familiarity used mostly in reference to girls; also used in reference to cute persons or animals of either gender.

PAGE 14
Kenki: "Sword princess." The nickname Aiz Wallenstein's feats have earned her.

PAGE 15
Senki: "Battle princess." The nickname Aiz would prefer, one earned through feats of bravery rather than skill with a blade.

PAGE 32
Gekai: Literally "The lower world," this refers to the Earth, including the city of Orario and the Dungeon.

PAGE 135
Dogeza: The deepest bow possible in Japanese culture, performing dogeza involves kneeling down and touching one's forehead to the ground.

PAGE 139
Tenkai: Literally "the heavenly world," this refers to the heavens—the realm from which the gods descended.

IS IT WRONG TO TRY TO PICK UP GIRLS IN A DUNGEON? ➊

FUJINO OMORI
KUNIEDA
SUZUHITO YASUDA

Translation: Andrew Gaippe • Lettering: Brndn Blakeslee, Lys Blakeslee

DUNGEON NI DEAI WO MOTOMERU NO WA MACHIGATTEIRUDAROUKA vol. 1
© 2013 Fujino Omori / SB Creative Corp.
© 2013 Kunieda / SQUARE ENIX CO., LTD.
First published in Japan in 2013 by SQUARE ENIX CO., LTD.
English Translation rights arranged with SQUARE ENIX CO., LTD.
and Hachette Book Group through Tuttle Mori Agency, Inc.

Translation © 2015 by SQUARE ENIX CO., LTD.

Yen Press
Hachette Book Group
1290 Avenue of the Americas, New York, NY 10104

www.HachetteBookGroup.com
www.YenPress.com

Yen Press is an imprint of Hachette Book Group, Inc. The Yen Press name and logo are trademarks of Hachette Book Group, Inc.

The publisher is not responsible for websites (or their content) that are not owned by the publisher.

First Yen Press Edition: May 2015

ISBN: 978-0-316-30217-3

10 9 8 7 6 5 4 3 2

BVG

Printed in the United States of America